A SHORT HISTORY OF THE DOCTRINE OF THE ATONEMENT

BY

L. W. GRENSTED, M.A., B.D.

Principal of Egerton Hall, Manchester
Lecturer in the History of Doctrine in the University of Manchester

Τὰ μὲν δὴ Χριστοῦ τοιαῦτα, καὶ τὰ πλείω σιγῇ σεβέσθω

Wipf and Stock Publishers
EUGENE, OREGON

Wipf and Stock Publishers
199 West 8th Avenue, Suite 3
Eugene, Oregon 97401

A Short History of the Doctrine of the Atonement
By Grensted, L. W.
ISBN: 1-57910-559-9
Publication date: January, 2001
Previously published by Longmans, Green and Co., 1920.

TO

MY FATHER

PREFACE

This brief history of the doctrine of the Atonement is an attempt to fill a gap in a literature already voluminous. It is the outcome of a series of lectures given to theological students, in the course of which I found the difficulty of referring my pupils to any book which made the sources accessible in a systematic manner. I have tried to meet this need by using quotation as far as possible, and by giving the *ipsissima verba* of the original Greek or Latin in footnotes throughout. The quotations are usually taken from current translations, but I have sometimes made my own version. There is no pretence at completeness, which would demand a far larger treatise, but it is hoped that no considerable development has been ignored, and that sufficient comment has been introduced to make the history both readable and consecutive.

The footnotes will indicate my very many obligations to various books. I have made especial use of Oxenham's *The Catholic Doctrine of Atonement*, Scott Lidgett's *The Spiritual Principle of Atonement*, and G. B. Stevens' *The Christian Doctrine of Salvation*. My greatest debt, though in another way, is to Moberly's *Atonement and Personality*, from which my own thinking upon the whole subject derives most of its impetus. That I have written from a fairly definite standpoint will be obvious to the reader, and, indeed, history can be written in no other way. But I trust that my own opinions have not prevented me altogether from appreciating and presenting those of others.

L. W. GRENSTED.

1st December 1919.

CONTENTS

CHAPTER I

THE BIBLICAL DOCTRINE OF THE ATONEMENT

CHRISTIAN doctrine is the attempt to state the meaning of Jesus Christ for the world. Its history is therefore moulded by two great forces, the force of the original Fact, and the force of present Experience, the force of that which was, and the force of that which is. For Christianity is no mere developing system of ideals with its origin shrouded in the mists of the past. It is of the essence of Christianity that it rests upon a Fact, the Fact of Christ, and to remove that Fact is to remove the very corner-stone of Christian doctrine. But the Fact of Christ is neither its own witness nor its own explanation. "Ye shall be my witnesses," said the Master, and so it has been. It is to living Christian Experience, individual and corporate, that we must turn if we would understand the Fact. Slowly and painfully its meaning has been wrought out in the life of the Church. Definitions have been made, tested, and cast aside, and the few brief phrases of the Creeds, tried in the fire of years, have been approved by Experience among many rivals to bear witness to a Fact that does not change. Doctrine is the attempt to state the Fact. Experience is the test wherein we know the worth of the attempt.

And the Experience and the Fact are not two but one, since the Life of the Church is Christ Himself.

In the case of any doctrine the basis of all reconstruction must be the Bible, and in particular the New

Testament, since practically the whole of our available historical knowledge of the original Fact is contained therein. In the case of certain doctrines, however, as, for example, the doctrines of the Trinity and of the Incarnation, we have the additional guidance of definite statements, approved by the experience and voice of the Church as embodying, however vaguely, that which must yet be true. In the case of the doctrine of the Atonement we have no such assistance. The Church, convinced of the great reality of the fact of Atonement, has never found it necessary or desirable to set her seal to any special theory for the explanation of that fact. The Creeds, while they lay stress upon "the remission of sins," hardly do more than hint at its connection with the life and death of Christ in the phrases, "Who for us men and for our salvation came down from heaven,"[1] "And was crucified also for us,"[2] "Who suffered for our salvation."[3] Here is the assertion of a fact, but no theory, and those who would frame for themselves a theory of the Atonement have indeed the guidance of many doctors of the Church, but have no one clear ruling attested by Experience as true up to the limits of human truth.

Since this is so, the doctrine of the Atonement is dependent upon the Bible to a peculiar extent. It is directly from the Bible that all theories must begin. There is not, and has never been, any possibility of an appeal to authoritative statements which might serve to limit the field of inquiry. Speculation has been wholly free, unchecked, save in rare cases, such as that of Abelard, by the pressure of any traditional orthodoxy. Theorists have been responsible to the Fact alone, and Experience has not as yet given her casting vote.

And thus any history of the doctrine of the Atonement, however cursory in character, must begin at the

[1] *Τὸν δι' ἡμᾶς τοὺς ἀνθρώπους καὶ διὰ τὴν ἡμετέραν σωτηρίαν κατέλθοντα ἐκ τῶν οὐρανῶν.*

[2] *Σταυρωθέντα τε ὑπὲρ ἡμῶν.* [3] Qui passus est pro salute nostra.

Bible, the source and the inspiration of all the diverse theories which men have framed. Here, however, we must content ourselves with a very brief sketch, such as may suffice to show the organic connection between the Biblical statements and the later developments of the doctrine.

The Bible supplies the necessary starting-point for all doctrines of the Atonement in two ways:

(*a*) It contains such data as are now available as to the actual facts of the life and death of Jesus Christ. The exact ascertaining of those facts is the task of the student of the Bible, with such aids as the science of Biblical criticism, lower and higher, has put within his reach. In their broad outline, however, those facts are and have always been obvious to any reader of the New Testament narratives. All that concerns us here is to emphasise the controlling force that the historical data must have upon any theory of the Atonement. That which does not conform to the facts is not true.

(*b*) It contains the views based on those data by the first generation of Christians, suggested, in part at least, by the recorded words of Christ Himself. These views, the views of men very near to the event itself and endowed in no ordinary measure with the Spirit of Christ, have rightly formed the basis of all subsequent theorising. It is very significant to note the diversity and richness of the thought of the New Testament as compared with that of the next few centuries, or indeed of any subsequent age.

That Christians should endeavour to give some explanation of the life and death of Christ was inevitable. For His life there were ready to hand the prophecies which spoke of a Divine Messiah, and these were readily augmented by more or less vague Incarnation doctrines. But that this Divine Messiah should be a sufferer, rejected of men, an outcast among His people, and, above all, that He should perish by a death which lay under the curse of God's own Law, was more difficult to explain. And yet, under all the diversities of expression, the whole New Testament bears witness to one central belief of Christians, and a belief based upon a central experience, that in the death and the rising again of Jesus Christ is really solved the world-problem of sin. That the fact of the Atonement and the fact of the Cross are one is, as Dr. Dale has so impressively shown,[1] the triumphant theme of every New Testament writer.

At first, however, while the event was still young in men's minds, the need for theory did not obtrude itself. It is a striking testimony to the primitive and historical character of St. Peter's speeches in the early chapters of Acts, that they simply connect the death of Christ with the fulfilment of the prophecies which acclaimed Him the Messiah (Acts 2 23, 3 18; cf. St. Luke 24 25, 26). And the reason is not that the idea of the remission of sins had not as yet arisen. It is mentioned more than once in these speeches, but is always connected with the Risen Christ (Acts 2 38, 3 19, 20, 26, 5 31). The Church had had no time for reflection upon the meaning of the Cross.

This simple, unreflective, explanation of the death of Christ reappears, naturally enough, in the writings of the Apostolic Fathers, whose work was done before the days of theology, and at a time when there was still a very real need of confuting the Jewish opponent of Christianity from the pages of his own sacred writings. Even as late as the end of the second century, in the writings of Tertullian, this appeal to prophecy as an explanation of the Cross is still a dominant note.

Very soon, however, the conviction grew that the Cross was the central fact of all, that to which the whole life of Christ led up. In the Cross was the key to the problem of sin, and the various New Testament writers almost exhaust language in their attempts to express

[1] *The Atonement*, being the Congregational Union Lecture for 1875, Lectures I.-VII.

this fact. But widely different as their accounts are, the difference is not due to any difference in their apprehension of the fact itself, but to the difficulty of finding any adequate metaphor to describe all that is involved in any solution of this all-important problem.

Two sayings of Jesus Himself, recorded in the Synoptic tradition,[1] supply the starting-point for these attempts at expression :

(*a*) St. Matt. 20 28 = St. Mark 10 45, perhaps quoted in 1 Tim. 2 6.

> The Son of Man came not to be ministered unto, but to minister, and to give his life a ransom for many.[2]

This saying naturally suggested a transaction into which God enters with the enemy who holds man in prison or in the bondage of slavery. In St. Paul this transactional idea is carried out with a great wealth of metaphor. It is contained in the term "redemption,"[3] a favourite Pauline word (Rom. 3 8, etc. ; cf. St. Luke 21 28 ; Heb. 9 15, 11 35). Similar language occurs in the other writers (see especially Heb. 9 12, 1 Peter 1 18). The conception is worked out by St. Paul in especial connection with metaphors drawn from the manumission of a slave upon the payment of a specified price, in accordance with the terms of Roman Law. This is one of the leading notes of the Epistle to the Galatians (*e.g.* 1 10, 2 4, 3 29, 4 5, 5 1, 24) and occurs again and again throughout St. Paul's writings. He himself has summarized the metaphor in 1 Cor. 7 23 (cf. 6 20) :

> Ye were bought with a price.[4]

This conception of a legal transaction or bargain

[1] For a very clear discussion of the evidence of the Synoptic Gospels, especially with regard to the two sayings here emphasized, see J. K. Mozley, *The Doctrine of the Atonement* (1915), ch. ii. Numerous references to modern opinion are there given.

[2] Ὁ υἱὸς τοῦ ἀνθρώπου οὐκ ἦλθεν διακονηθῆναι ἀλλὰ διακονῆσαι καὶ δοῦναι τὴν ψυχὴν αὐτοῦ λύτρον ἀντὶ πολλῶν.

[3] Ἀπολύτρωσις.

[4] Τιμῆς ἠγοράσθητε.

between God and the devil became characteristic of the theologians of the Greek Church down to the eighth century, from Irenaeus to John of Damascus. In its crudest form it seems to ignore altogether the part that man himself must take in the transaction, but, as in the New Testament, the Greek fathers never allowed this metaphor to stand alone, and thus its essential inadequacy was long obscured. In a modified form it survived in the Western Church down to the time of Anselm.

(*b*) The words of Christ at the Last Supper, variously preserved in our four accounts but agreeing in essential idea:

> This is my blood of the covenant, which is shed for many for the remission of sins (St. Matt. 26 28).[1]
>
> This is my blood of the covenant which is shed for many (St. Mark 14 24).[2]
>
> This cup is the new covenant in my blood which is shed for you (St. Luke 22 20).[3]
>
> This cup is the new covenant in my blood (1 Cor. 11 25).[4]

The divergence between these forms is of no importance for our purpose. They clearly agree in general meaning, and even the added phrase in the First Gospel, which is often suspected as not authentic, is quite in keeping with the older Pauline tradition, since the reference to Jer. 31 34 quite clearly connects the " new covenant " with " the remission of sins." The suggestion of this saying was worked out along three different lines by the New Testament writers.

1. The phrase "New Covenant" naturally had sacrificial associations both in its context in Jer. 31 and upon the lips of Christ. It pointed to a contrast

[1] *Τοῦτο γάρ ἐστιν τὸ αἷμά μου τῆς διαθήκης τὸ περὶ πολλῶν ἐκχυννόμενον εἰς ἄφεσιν ἁμαρτιῶν.*

[2] *Τοῦτό ἐστιν τὸ αἷμά μου τῆς διαθήκης τὸ ἐκχυννόμενον ὑπὲρ πόλλων.*

[3] *Τοῦτο τὸ ποτήριον ἡ καινὴ διαθήκη ἐν τῷ αἵματί μου τὸ ὑπὲρ ὑμῶν ἐκχυννόμενον.*

[4] *Τοῦτο τὸ ποτήριον ἡ καινὴ διαθήκη ἐστὶν ἐν τῷ ἐμῷ αἵματι.*

between the old covenant-sacrifice, sealed by "the blood of the covenant" (Exodus 24 8), and a new covenant-sacrifice, also sealed with blood, whereby was established the fellowship of the Church of Christ. This conception of the death of Christ as a supreme Sacrifice, made once for all and for ever complete, fulfilling through Christ's High-Priestly intercession all that the temporal sacrifices had tried in vain to do, is the theme of the Epistle to the Hebrews (cf. 9 11-28, 10 8-18). The same idea lies behind much of the Johannine symbolism (cf. St. John 1 29; Rev. 5 12, 13 8) and St. Paul has a notable saying dependent upon the same idea in 1 Cor. 5 7 (cf. Eph. 5 2). Thus, as Dr. Moberly has said: "The whole meaning of Priesthood and Sacrifice becomes a part of the meaning of the sacrificial Death of Christ; not in the sense that Sacrifice, in Him, can be simply measured by what Sacrifice meant in the old Covenant, or before even that: but rather that all the lines of true tendency which are discernible as underlying, or implied in, the older sacrifices, must find their ultimate fulness of meaning in Him."[1] It is in this atmosphere that the metaphor of "propitiation" must be placed.[2]

In language of this kind it is the Godward aspect of Atonement that is mainly prominent, and the true inheritor of the thought of the Epistle to the Hebrews is Anselm, with his view of the death of Christ as an offering made to satisfy God's outraged honour. At the same time exponents of the sacrificial aspect of Christ's death have never been wanting in the Church, though their language has seldom been developed into a definite theory, and it is interesting to notice how often the Anselmic satisfaction theory has itself tended to revert to sacrificial phrases and ideas.

2. St. Paul's treatment of the conception of the New Covenant, though it has sacrificial elements, is profoundly

[1] *Atonement and Personality* (1909 ed.), p. 333.

[2] Ἱλάσκομαι (St. Luke 18 13, Heb. 2 17), *ἱλασμός* (1 John 2 2, 4 10).

affected by the legal bias of his mind. Just as the "ransom" of St. Mark 10 45 suggested to him the ceremony of setting free a slave, so the word διαθήκη, which means not only a covenant but also a testament, suggested to him the legal process whereby a will might be made in favour of an adopted son (cf. Gal. 3 15 ff., 4 5-7; 1 Cor. 11 25; 2 Cor. 3 6; Rom. 8 17). But he passes on from this to a much broader use of legal language, with especial emphasis upon the wrath of God as the wrath of a Judge before whose bar man stands guilty, an idea in the development of which the Old Testament prophecies of the Day of Judgement played a great part. And so arises the whole group of metaphors which gathers round the term "justification," or "acquittal."[1] Through this legal act we who are guilty become "not guilty" in Christ (cf. Rom. 3 24, 8 1, 33; 1 Cor. 1 8; 2 Cor. 5 21; Gal. 2 17; Col. 1 22). This acquittal can be pronounced because now justice is duly satisfied by the penalty exacted in Christ, whom God "made to be sin for us,"[2] and who "became a curse for us."[3] This emphasis upon God's wrath and upon the claims of justice is especially prominent in the Epistle to the Romans.

This Pauline language has had a great influence upon the history of the doctrine of the Atonement. It lay at the very basis of the theology of the Reformation with its strangely harsh but exceedingly virile theories of Atonement through the vicarious penal suffering of Christ, who endures the sentence of the Judge in place of the prisoners at the bar. It is also connected with the thought of Augustine and the earlier Latin fathers, who were, indeed, advancing from the idea of God's justice in the direction of the later penal theory when this natural line of development was interrupted by the genius of Anselm.

3. The creative insight of the prophet Jeremiah had

[1] Δικαίωσις, but more commonly the verb, δικαιόω.

[2] Ὑπὲρ ἡμῶν ἁμαρτίαν ἐποίησεν. [3] Γενόμενος ὑπὲρ ἡμῶν κατάρα.

given mystical associations to the New Covenant : " In their heart I will write it," " all shall know me " (Jer. 31 33, 34). So, too, St. Paul's interpretation of the words of Christ rests upon a basis of mystical experience which profoundly modifies its character. His interest is not in theories or metaphors descriptive of the Atonement, but in his strong and clear personal experience, not only in occasional vision, but throughout his life, of the presence of the Risen Christ. Nothing is more typical of his writings than the often repeated " in Christ." In everything the believer and Christ are one, and by that unity the death of Christ and His rising again directly involve the believer too.

> I am crucified with Christ : nevertheless I live : yet not I, but Christ liveth in me.[1]
>
> Our old man is crucified with Him.[2]

Such sayings modify the harshness of the penal language which St. Paul sometimes uses. It is not his whole meaning that Christ bears the penalty instead of us. In that mystical union with Him which faith achieves we become actual sharers both of His sufferings and of the triumph of His conquest of sin and death. He is now our " righteousness " (1 Cor. 1 30), our " life " (Rom. 8 2). His Spirit has become our Spirit, since He dwells in us (Rom. 8 9, 10). In this is accomplished our " reconciliation " to God,[3] a metaphor in which the sacrificial and mystical conceptions come together (Rom. 5 10, 11, 11 15 ; 2 Cor. 5 18, 19 ; Eph. 2 16 ; Col. 1 20).

The mystical aspect of St. Paul is strikingly developed by St. John, who sees in the Cross the supreme revelation of Divine love (St. John 3 16 ; 1 John 4 9, 10 ; cf. Rom. 5 8), which love is the guarantee that the problem

[1] Χριστῷ συνεσταύρωμαι· ζῶ δὲ οὐκέτι ἐγώ, ζῇ δὲ ἐν ἐμοὶ Χριστός (Gal. 2 20).

[2] Ὁ παλαιὸς ἡμῶν ἄνθρωπος συνεσταυρώθη (Rom. 6 6).

[3] Καταλλάσσειν, ἀποκαταλλάσσειν. It is never said that God is reconciled to man.

of sin can be solved in the mystical union of Christ with the believer (*e.g.* St. John 6, 15 4, etc.). This union is the same thing as eternal life (St. John 3 16), which is also equated with faith (St. John 5 24, 6 47), and, still more significantly, with knowledge (St. John 17 3). The conception of illumination by knowledge is fully in keeping with his view of revelation as the purpose of the life and death of Christ, the light shining amid the darkness, which threatened to overwhelm it, but " overcame it not " (St. John 1 5).

And this leads to a further point of importance in the Johannine theology. The Cross is now regarded from the standpoint of the whole Incarnate life, wherein this saving love is manifested. It is not that St. John does not recognize the central significance of the death of Christ (St. John 3 14, 6 51, 12 32). The very arrangement of his Gospel is sufficient to disprove such a charge. But he is still more strongly conscious of the great eternal fact of the Incarnation itself, as the process whereby " life " and " light " entered the darkness of this world and became available for mankind, and the Cross takes its place for him as an incident in this process, of central importance, it is true, but still not to be understood except as part of a larger whole.

This explanation of the Cross as the revelation of divine love, making its appeal direct to the heart of man, is characteristic of the so-called " Moral " or " Ethical " theories of the Atonement. These have never been wholly lacking in the Church, but have seldom been regarded as adequate in themselves, being usually held in conjunction with some other type of thought. They have, however, attained a considerable vogue during the past century, and constitute a powerful factor in the thought of the present day. It may be said broadly that it is only when they rest upon a basis of mysticism, as in St. John himself, that such theories are at all successful.

CHAPTER II

THE FIRST TWO CENTURIES

DURING the first two centuries after Christ little or no attempt was made to advance beyond or to interpret the statements of the New Testament. It was not in theory but in life that the Living Fact approved itself to men, and so it is natural that the earliest days of the Church should be marked by emphasis upon the Atonement as a fact. Of theory there is none. The subject is treated in the main devotionally, and the language of the New Testament is used freely and without comment. Such terms as "sacrifice," "propitiation," "redemption," recur again and again, but no conscious effort is ever made to work out what is implied in them. They were felt to suffice as they stood to express the Christian experience of the Cross. The age of doubts and questionings had not yet begun.

It is possible, however, to trace definite tendencies of thought during this period. The language of devotion is often very significant, and it can at least be seen that the various aspects of New Testament thought appealed to the early Church in very different degrees. The clearest statements that have been preserved are in the main upon the lines of the Fourth Gospel, with its emphasis upon the revelation of God's love and its occasional sacrificial language. It would not be a very distant generalization to characterize the whole period, and especially its earlier years, as Johannine, though few of the writers even approach the spirit and insight of St. John himself. The Pauline theology, especially on its penal and legal side, remains quite undeveloped, though his more mystical language finds frequent echoes. In general it may be said that the thought of this period is of two main types.

(I.) There are a number of statements along the lines of the Moral theory. In several writers there is a very marked emphasis upon the love of God, as revealed more especially in the Cross, the effect of which is to bring about in our hearts a changed spirit, the "grace of penitence."

This attitude of mind is well illustrated in Clement of Rome. In the First Epistle love is taken as the key to the character and purpose of God, the basis of redemption:

> Love joineth us unto God . . . In love were all the elect of God made perfect; without love nothing is well-pleasing to God: in love the Master took us unto Himself; for the love which He had towards us, Jesus Christ our Lord hath given His blood for us by the will of God, and His flesh for our flesh, and His life for our lives.[1]

Here it is quite clear that Clement regards the Cross as central in the work of Atonement, and as resting upon God's love as its motive cause. And the result of this display of love is to turn us into the way of truth and righteousness, making us sons of God.

> Let us see what is good and what is pleasant and what is acceptable in the sight of Him that made us. Let us fix our eyes on the blood of Christ and understand how precious it is

---

[1] Ἀγάπη κολλᾷ ἡμᾶς τῷ Θεῷ . . . ἐν τῇ ἀγάπῃ ἐτελειώθησαν πάντες οἱ ἐκλεκτοὶ τοῦ Θεοῦ· δίχα ἀγάπης οὐδὲν εὐάρεστόν ἐστιν τῷ Θεῷ· ἐν ἀγάπῃ προσελάβετο ἡμᾶς ὁ δεσπότης· διὰ τὴν ἀγάπην ἣν ἔσχεν πρὸς ἡμᾶς, τὸ αἷμα αὐτοῦ ἔδωκεν ὑπὲρ ἡμῶν Ἰησοῦς Χριστὸς ὁ Κύριος ἡμῶν ἐν θελήματι Θεοῦ, καὶ τὴν σάρκα ὑπὲρ τῆς σαρκὸς ἡμῶν καὶ τὴν ψυχὴν ὑπὲρ τῶν ψυχῶν ἡμῶν (Clem. *Ep.* i. 49. The text and translation of the passages from the Apostolic Fathers are from Bishop Lightfoot's edition).

unto His Father, because being shed for our salvation it won for the whole world the grace of repentance.[1]

How this transformation is brought about Clement does not explain, contenting himself with emphasising the outpouring of the blood of Christ as the means adopted to that end by God's love. No stress can be laid upon the curious distinction made between the offering of Christ's flesh and the offering of His Life, though it is strikingly suggestive of the later theory which supposed the resurrection body to be built up by the partaking of the body of Christ in the Eucharist.[2]

The most eloquent statement of this appeal of God's love is contained in the well-known passage from the Epistle to Diognetus.

> The very Artificer and Creator of the Universe Himself . . . Him He sent unto them. Was He sent think you, as any man might suppose, to establish a sovereignty, to inspire fear and terror? Not so. But in gentleness [and] meekness has He sent Him, as a king might send his son who is a king, He sent Him as sending God, He sent Him as [a man] unto men; He sent Him as Saviour, as using persuasion, not force; for force is no attribute of God. He sent Him as summoning, not as persecuting; He sent Him as loving, not as judging. . . . For what man at all had any knowledge what God was before He came? . . . For God, the Master and Creator of the Universe, Who made all things and arranged them in order, was found to be not only friendly to men, but also long-suffering. And such indeed He always was, and is, and will be, kindly and good and dispassionate and true, and He alone is good. . . . And when our iniquity had been fully accomplished, and it had been made perfectly manifest that punishment and death were

---

[1] Ἴδωμεν τί καλὸν καὶ τί τερπνὸν καὶ τί προσδεκτὸν ἐνώπιον τοῦ ποιήσαντος ἡμᾶς. ἀτενίσωμεν εἰς τὸ αἷμα τοῦ Χριστοῦ καὶ γνῶμεν ὡς ἔστιν τίμιον τῷ πατρὶ αὐτοῦ, ὅτι διὰ τὴν ἡμετέραν σωτηρίαν ἐκχυθὲν παντὶ τῷ κόσμῳ μετανοίας χάριν ὑπήνεγκεν (*ib.* ch. 7).

[2] This view is characteristic of the writers at the end of the second century, though they express themselves with much confusion. Cf. esp. Tert. *De Resurr. Carnis* 8, Iren. *Adv. Haer.* v. 2. 2. J. F. Bethune-Baker gives an excellent summary in *Introd. to Early History of Christian Doctrine*, pp. 397 ff. Cf. Harnack, *History of Dogma* (E.V.). ii. pp. 145 f.

expected as its recompense, and the season came which God had ordained, when henceforth He should manifest His goodness and power (O the exceeding great kindness and love of God), He hated us not, neither rejected us, nor bore us malice, but was long-suffering and patient, and in pity for us took upon Himself our sins, and Himself parted with His own Son as a ransom for us, the holy for the lawless, the guileless for the evil, the just for the unjust, the incorruptible for the corruptible, the immortal for the mortal. For what else but His righteousness would have covered our sins ? In whom was it possible for us lawless and ungodly men to have been justified, save only in the Son of God ? O the sweet exchange, O the inscrutable creation, O the unexpected benefits ; that the iniquity of many should be concealed in One Righteous Man, and the righteousness of One should justify many that are iniquitous ! [1]

We should have to turn to St. Paul himself for a finer statement of the wonder of the Cross. Yet even here is little in the way of theory. More than half a century has passed since the days of Clement of Rome, and some of the writer's phrases show that a consciousness of the problems of later years is just beginning to dawn, but

[1] *Αὐτὸν τὸν τεχνίτην καὶ δημιουργὸν τῶν ὅλων . . . τοῦτον πρὸς αὐτοὺς ἀπέστειλεν. ἆρά γε, ὡς ἀνθρώπων ἄν τις λογίσαιτο, ἐπὶ τυραννίδι καὶ φόβῳ καὶ καταπλήξει; οὐμενοῦν· ἀλλ' ἐν ἐπιεικείᾳ [καὶ] πραΰτητι ὡς βασιλεὺς πέμπων υἱὸν βασιλέα ἔπεμψεν, ὡς Θεὸν ἔπεμψεν, ὡς [ἄνθρωπον] πρὸς ἀνθρώπους ἔπεμψεν, ὡς σώζων ἔπεμψεν, ὡς πείθων, οὐ βιαζόμενος· βία γὰρ οὐ πρόσεστι τῷ Θεῷ. ἔπεμψεν ὡς καλῶν, οὐ διώκων· ἔπεμψεν ὡς ἀγαπῶν, οὐ κρίνων. . . . τίς γὰρ ὅλως ἀνθρώπων ἠπίστατο τί ποτ' ἐστὶ Θεός, πρὶν αὐτὸν ἐλθεῖν; . . . ὁ γὰρ δεσπότης καὶ δημιουργὸς τῶν ὅλων Θεός, ὁ ποιήσας τὰ πάντα καὶ κατὰ τάξιν διακρίνας, οὐ μόνον φιλάνθρωπος ἐγένετο ἀλλὰ καὶ μακρόθυμος. ἀλλ' οὗτος ἦν μὲν ἀεὶ τοιοῦτος, καὶ ἔστι, καὶ ἔσται· χρηστὸς καὶ ἀγαθὸς καὶ ἀόργητος καὶ ἀληθής, καὶ μόνος ἀγαθός ἐστιν· . . . ἐπεὶ δὲ πεπλήρωτο μὲν ἡ ἡμετέρα ἀδικία, καὶ τελείως πεφανέρωτο ὅτι ὁ μισθὸς αὐτῆς κόλασις καὶ θάνατος προσεδοκᾶτο, ἦλθε δὲ ὁ καιρὸς ὃν Θεὸς προέθετο λοιπὸν φανερῶσαι τὴν ἑαυτοῦ χρηστότητα καὶ δύναμιν (ὢ τῆς ὑπερβαλλούσης φιλανθρωπίας καὶ ἀγάπης τοῦ Θεοῦ), οὐκ ἐμίσησεν ἡμᾶς οὐδὲ ἀπώσατο οὐδὲ ἐμνησικάκησεν, ἀλλὰ ἐμακροθύμησεν, ἠνέσχετο, ἐλεῶν αὐτὸς τὰς ἡμετέρας ἁμαρτίας ἀνεδέξατο, αὐτὸς τὸν ἴδιον υἱὸν ἀπέδοτο λύτρον ὑπὲρ ἡμῶν, τὸν ἅγιον ὑπὲρ ἀνόμων, τὸν ἄκακον ὑπὲρ τῶν κακῶν, τὸν δίκαιον ὑπὲρ τῶν ἀδίκων, τὸν ἄφθαρτον ὑπὲρ τῶν φθαρτῶν, τὸν ἀθάνατον ὑπὲρ τῶν θνητῶν. τί γὰρ ἄλλο τὰς ἁμαρτίας ἡμῶν ἠδυνήθη καλύψαι ἢ ἐκείνου δικαιοσύνη; ἐν τίνι δικαιωθῆναι δυνατὸν τοὺς ἀνόμους ἡμᾶς καὶ ἀσεβεῖς ἢ ἐν μόνῳ τῷ υἱῷ τοῦ Θεοῦ; ὢ τῆς γλυκείας ἀνταλλαγῆς, ὢ τῆς ἀνεξιχνιάστου δημιουργίας, ὢ τῶν ἀπροσδοκήτων εὐεργεσιῶν· ἵνα ἀνομία μὲν πολλῶν ἐν δικαίῳ ἑνὶ κρυβῇ, δικαιοσύνη δὲ ἑνὸς πολλοὺς ἀνόμους δικαιώσῃ* (*Ep. ad Diog.* chh. 7-9).

the thought of God's love is still sufficient to satisfy his mind. If we analyse the passage, a thing that the writer himself was very far from doing, the following conceptions appear:

1. Not justice but love is the secret of Atonement, for love and not force is the essential attribute of God. And in this love the Father and the Son agree. There is no question of an imposition of God's will upon the Son, for the Father's will is His also.

2. It is by man's sin that Atonement is rendered necessary, sin that might reasonably have incurred the wrath of God, that might reasonably have expected punishment and death. And there seemed to be no hope of any release from sin. Man is utterly incapable of that holiness which he needs. But this state calls forth not judgement upon him, but the pity of God.

3. God's pity is shown in the sending of His Son to be "a ransom for us." The phrase is unexplained, though the writer quite plainly felt both the appeal to the hearts of men ("as using persuasion not force") and the conviction that the place of sinful man has been taken by Another. It is clear, however, that that which makes the ransom effective is the righteousness rather than the suffering of Christ.

4. In that righteousness we are justified. The Pauline term is used, but the meaning has become much less forensic. The thought is not that of an externally imputed righteousness, but of a real change in the sinful heart of man, and the writer seems to feel that the righteousness of Christ becomes actually ours.

In the main this is the Moral theory of the Atonement, a theory which indeed is directly suggested by the reference to "persuasion." As a theory, however, it is quite unconscious, and, indeed, incomplete. It lacks the clear-sighted mysticism of St. Paul and St. John, and falls back instead upon phrases which were to expand later into transaction theories ("ransom"), satisfaction theories ("what else but His righteousness would have covered our sins "), substitution theories (" O the sweet exchange ").

The Moral theory is also prominent, in a much less lofty form, in the one passage of the Shepherd of Hermas which alludes to the doctrine of Atonement, though here too it does not stand alone. It occurs in the explanation of the story of the vineyard, of which God, as the owner, has placed the Son in charge to work as a slave.

> And the Son Himself cleansed their sins, by labouring much and enduring many toils; for no one can dig without toil or labour. Having Himself then cleansed the sins of His people, He shewed them the paths of life, giving them the law which he received from His Father.[1]

There is here no very direct allusion to the death of Christ. It is rather to all the sufferings of His Incarnate life that the " cleansing " of sin is attributed. This emphasis upon the life rather than the death of Christ shows the influence of the Johannine tendency, but the writer has totally failed to grasp the Johannine thought which he reproduces. He has missed the meaning of the great saying, " the Life was the Light of men,"[2] and evidently has not approached the conception of any real transference of the righteousness of Christ to sinful humanity, that transference which meant so much to the author of the letter to Diognetus. And as a consequence we have in this passage a curious anticipation of the not very successful doctrine of active and passive obedience, a doctrine typical of the rigid and unsympathetic theology of scholastic Protestantism. The work of Christ is divided into two parts, the endurance of suffering in the fulfilment of the Father's will, and the revelation of that will to men, that they too

[1] *Καὶ αὐτὸς τὰς ἁμαρτίας αὐτῶν ἐκαθάρισε πολλὰ κοπιάσας καὶ πολλοὺς κόπους ἠντληκώς· οὐδεὶς γὰρ δύναται σκαφεῦσαι ἄτερ κόπου ἢ μόχθου. αὐτὸς οὖν καθαρίσας τὰς ἁμαρτίας τοῦ λαοῦ ἔδειξεν αὐτοῖς τὰς τρίβους τῆς ζωῆς, δοὺς αὐτοῖς τὸν νόμον ὃν ἔλαβε παρὰ τοῦ πατρὸς αὐτοῦ* (*Sim.* 5, 6).

[2] (St. John 1 4.)

may obey. How that suffering atones for sin, and how men may be moved to obey that will which Christ reveals, are questions to which the writer does not attempt an answer.

Closest of all the early Christian writers to St. John is the mystic Ignatius, whose letters to the Churches through which he passed on his way to martyrdom show how deeply the experience of the passion of Christ had entered into his soul. This experience is for him the very centre of the faith. His purpose in writing is to oppose those who were attacking the historical reality of the manhood of Christ, and he dwells with the utmost emphasis upon the fact of His Cross:

> Who . . . was truly persecuted under Pontius Pilate, was truly crucified and died in the sight of those in heaven and those on earth and those under the earth: Who moreover was truly raised from the dead . . .[1]

By the power of this fact man was delivered from the demons,[2] and

> Even the heavenly beings and the glory of the angels and the rulers, visible and invisible, if they believe not in the blood of Christ [who is God], judgement awaiteth them also.[3]

It is by faith and love that man is able to grasp this great fact. But faith and love are not things supplied from the side of man. They are themselves dependent upon the Cross, and are mediated to us by the Eucharist, through which we are brought into mystical union with the passion of Christ.

> Recover yourselves in faith which is the flesh of the Lord, and in love which is the blood of Jesus Christ.[4]

---

[1] Ὃς . . . ἀληθῶς ἐδιώχθη ἐπὶ Ποντίου Πιλάτου, ἀληθῶς ἐσταυρώθη καὶ ἀπέθανεν, βλεπόντων [τῶν] ἐπουρανίων καὶ ἐπιγείων καὶ ὑποχθονίων· ὃς καὶ ἀληθῶς ἠγέρθη ἀπὸ νεκρῶν (*Trall.* 9, cf. *Smyrn.* 1).

[2] *Eph.* 19.

[3] Καὶ τὰ ἐπουράνια καὶ ἡ δόξα τῶν ἀγγέλων καὶ οἱ ἄρχοντες ὁρατοί τε καὶ ἀόρατοι, ἐὰν μὴ πιστεύσωσιν εἰς τὸ αἷμα Χριστοῦ [τοῦ Θεοῦ], κἀκείνοις κρίσις ἐστίν (*Smyrn.* 6).

[4] Ἀνακτήσασθε ἑαυτοὺς ἐν πίστει, ὅ ἐστιν σὰρξ τοῦ Κυρίου, καὶ ἐν ἀγάπῃ, ὅ ἐστιν αἷμα Ἰησοῦ Χριστοῦ (*Trall.* 8).

I desire the bread of God, which is the flesh of Christ who was of the seed of David; and for a draught I desire His blood, which is love incorruptible.[1]

Thus the passion of Christ is not only a past fact, but something wrought in the very heart of the believer himself through union with God.

. . . the Cross whereby He through His passion inviteth us being His members. Now it cannot be that a head should be found without members, seeing that God promiseth union, and this union is Himself.[2]

Unless of our own free choice we accept to die unto His passion, His life is not in us.[3]

This is upon the lines of the Moral theory of the Atonement. Ignatius feels the appeal of God's love to the heart, "inviting" us. But this is not all. The answer to that appeal is also the work of the Cross. In the passion Christians are "united and elect."[4] In the passion they find their peace.[5] And the love in which they make the passion their own, is, as the passages quoted above show, one with the love of God himself. For Ignatius himself the love of Christ involved the passionate desire to suffer with Him:

Permit me to be an imitator of the passion of my God. If any man hath Him within himself, let him understand what I desire, and let him have fellow-feeling with me, for he knoweth the things which straiten me.[6]

There is no theory here. We are in the presence of a

[1] *Ἄρτον Θεοῦ θέλω, ὅ ἐστιν σὰρξ τοῦ Χριστοῦ τοῦ ἐκ σπέρματος Δαυείδ, καὶ πόμα θέλω τὸ αἷμα αὐτοῦ, ὅ ἐστιν ἀγάπη ἄφθαρτος* (*Rom.* 7).

[2] . . . *τοῦ σταυροῦ . . . δι' οὗ ἐν τῷ πάθει αὐτοῦ προσκαλεῖται ὑμᾶς, ὄντας μέλη αὐτοῦ. οὐ δύναται οὖν κεφαλὴ χωρὶς γεννηθῆναι ἄνευ μελῶν, τοῦ Θεοῦ ἕνωσιν ἐπαγγελλομένου, ὅς ἐστιν αὐτός* (*Trall.* 11). Lightfoot's translation of the last clause seems doubtful.

[3] *Ἐὰν μὴ αὐθαιρέτως ἔχωμεν τὸ ἀποθανεῖν εἰς τὸ αὐτοῦ πάθος, τὸ ζῆν αὐτοῦ οὐκ ἔστιν ἐν ἡμῖν* (*Magn.* 5).

[4] *Eph.* inscr.

[5] *Trall.* inscr.

[6] *Ἐπιτρέψατέ μοι μιμητὴν εἶναι τοῦ πάθους τοῦ Θεοῦ μου. εἴ τις αὐτὸν ἐν ἑαυτῷ ἔχει, νοησάτω ὃ θέλω καὶ συμπαθείτω μοι εἰδὼς τὰ συνέχοντά με* (*Rom.* 6).

great experience, and no theory can ever set forth the mystery of Atonement as vividly as it is revealed in life.

(II.) Side by side with this more ethical and emotional treatment of the fact of the Cross, we may set a number of statements treating redemption rather as a matter of knowledge, revealed in the life of the Incarnate Word. Here again the treatment of the Atonement is very Johannine, the influence of the opening verses both of the Gospel and of the First Epistle of St. John being very marked. This emphasis on salvation through a divinely revealed "knowledge"[1] is perhaps the most typical attitude of mind in the second century. The age of heresy is now beginning, but the belief that redemption is to be attained through knowledge, and that this knowledge is in Christ Jesus, is common ground to thinkers of every type.

This belief is the central conviction of Gnosticism, so far as that strange medley of ideas can be called Christian at all. From it, indeed, Gnosticism takes its name, since the claim of the Gnostic initiates[2] was that they alone possessed the knowledge, or Gnosis, which saves. And for this reason Gnosticism found little room for the Cross.[3] It did not regard redemption as wrought upon Calvary, but as brought down into the material world by the coming of the aeon-life, the light of knowledge, in the person of Jesus. By this light of knowledge the initiate is saved automatically, and the Demiurge or World-Creator, who is less than God, whether regarded as evil or merely as deluded and ignorant, is powerless to prevent it. He could, it is true, put the material body of the Christ to death, but that was not a thing of any importance, since it is not in the material sphere that redemption is wrought. Often indeed Christ's body

[1] Γνῶσις. [2] Τέλειοι.

[3] In Valentinianism, however, σταυρός is found among the aeons, coming to restore order amid the disorder into which the inquisitiveness of σοφία had cast the universe.

was regarded as a mere phantom and the Crucifixion as unreal.[1]

The Apologists held a view not very far removed from this central belief of their Gnostic opponents, though their adherence to the Christian tradition led them to lay more stress upon the Cross. Justin Martyr, for example, thinks of Christianity mainly as the true philosophy, whereby men are reclaimed from the false opinions which demons have invented and imposed upon the world in order that the light of the truth might be obscured.

> Becoming man according to His will, He taught us these things for the conversion and restoration of the human race.[2]

> His strong Word persuaded many to leave the demons whom they served, and through Him to believe in God Almighty.[3]

> We ever pray God, through Jesus Christ, to keep us from the demons who oppose the worship of God and whom of old we worshipped, that we may turn to God through Him and so may be blameless.[4]

It is noteworthy here that the intellectualism of the Gnostics has undergone a change. It is the truth that saves, but it saves because it brings about a real moral change in the heart of the believer.

This is also the leading thought in the reply of Clement of Alexandria to Gnosticism. His treatise entitled "The Paedagogue"[5] might indeed be described as a

[1] Marcion, as so often, stands apart not only from the other Gnostics but from all other thinkers of his age. His distinction between the God of justice and the God of mercy, suggests in a crude form that antithesis between the attributes of God which perplexed many of the early fathers, and which forms the basis of the Protestant doctrine of vicarious penal suffering.

[2] Καὶ τῇ βουλῇ αὐτοῦ γενόμενος ἄνθρωπος ταῦτα ἡμᾶς ἐδίδαξεν ἐπ' ἀλλαγῇ καὶ ἐπαναγωγῇ τοῦ ἀνθρωπείου γένους (*Ap.* i. 23).

[3] Καὶ ἰσχυρὸς ὁ λόγος αὐτοῦ πέπεικε πολλοὺς καταλιπεῖν δαιμόνια οἷς ἐδούλευον, καὶ ἐπὶ τὸν παντοκράτορα Θεὸν δι' αὐτοῦ πιστεύειν (*Dial.* 83).

[4] Ἀπὸ γὰρ τῶν δαιμονίων, ἅ ἐστιν ἀλλότρια τῆς θεοσεβείας τοῦ Θεοῦ, οἷς πάλαι προσεκυνοῦμεν, τὸν Θεὸν ἀεὶ διὰ Ἰησοῦ Χριστοῦ συντηρηθῆναι παρακαλοῦμεν, ἵνα μετὰ τὸ ἐπιστρέψαι πρὸς Θεὸν δι' αὐτοῦ ἄμωμοι ὦμεν (*Dial.* 30).

[5] Ὁ παιδαγωγός, *i.e.* the Tutor.

series of variations upon this theme. In his opening chapter he writes as follows:

> Our Tutor, being practical, first exhorts us to attain a good disposition and character, and after persuades us energetically to perform our duties, laying upon us pure commandments. . . . Hence follows the healing of our passions . . . the Tutor strengthening our souls, and by His kind commands, as by gentle medicines, guiding the sick to the perfect knowledge of the truth.[1]

So again in the Exhortation to the Heathen:

> I would shew fully what these your gods are like, so that now at last you may abandon your delusion, and speed your flight back to heaven. . . . For the Word lives, and having been buried with Christ, is exalted with God. But those who still disbelieve are described as children of wrath, raised up for wrath. We, who have been freed from error, and restored to the truth, are no more wrath's nurslings.[2]

For Clement the idea of Gnosticism is true, but the only real Gnostic is the Christian, in whom Christ, Wisdom Incarnate, calls out the hidden wisdom of man's true nature.

> Not without the Saviour, who by the divine Word removes from the eye of the soul the darkness of ignorance which springs from evil training.[3]

This ethical transformation of the Gnostic idea of salvation through the illuminating power of knowledge

[1] Πρακτικὸς δὲ ὢν ὁ Παιδαγωγός, πρότερον μὲν εἰς διάθεσιν ἠθοποιίας προυτρέψατο, ἤδη δὲ καὶ εἰς τὴν τῶν δεόντων ἐνέργειαν παρακαλεῖ, τὰς ὑποθήκας τὰς ἀκηράτους παρεγγυῶν . . . ἴασις οὖν τῶν παθῶν ἐνθένδε ἕπεται . . . ἐπιρρωννύντος τοῦ Παιδαγωγοῦ τὰς ψυχάς, καθάπερ ἠπίοις φαρμάκοις, ὑποθήκαις φιλανθρώποις εἰς τὴν παντελῆ τῆς ἀληθείας γνῶσιν τοὺς κάμνοντας διαιτωμένου (*Paed.* 1).

[2] Ἐθέλω δὲ ὑμῖν ἐν χρῷ τοὺς Θεοὺς αὐτοὺς ἐπιδεῖξαι, ὁποῖοι καὶ τίνες εἰσίν, ἵν' ἤδη ποτὲ τῆς πλάνης λήξητε, αὖθις δὲ παλινδρομήσητε εἰς οὐρανόν· . . . ζῶν γὰρ ὁ Λόγος, καὶ συνταφεὶς Χριστῷ, συνυψοῦται Θεῷ. οἱ δὲ ἔτι ἄπιστοι τέκνα ὀργῆς ὀνομάζονται, τρεφόμενα ὀργῇ· ἡμεῖς δὲ οὐκ ὀργῆς θρέμματα ἔτι, οἱ τῆς πλάνης ἀπεσπασμένοι, ἀΐσσοντες δὲ ἐπὶ τὴν ἀλήθειαν (*Protrept.* 2 128 ff.).

[3] Οὐκ ἄνευ τοῦ Σωτῆρος, τοῦ καταγαγόντος ἡμῶν τῷ θειῷ Λογῷ τοῦ ὁρατικοῦ τῆς ψυχῆς τὴν ἐπιχυθεῖσαν ἐκ φαύλης ἀναστροφῆς ἄγνοιαν ἀχλυώδη (*Strom.* i. 28).

constitutes the characteristic reply of the Apologists to Gnosticism, besides affording a powerful answer to the pagan traducers of Christianity.

The stress upon the saving power of knowledge had, however, a serious difficulty from the point of view of Christian tradition. In the tradition of the Church the Cross held an undisputed and central place. From this position it had been displaced by Gnosticism, and the thought of the Apologists is in general so far akin to that of Gnosticism that they too found themselves without any explanation ready to their hand to account for the fact of the passion of Christ. There was no obvious reason why the Cross should be necessary to the revelation of Divine knowledge, and it is no small testimony to the common feeling of primitive Christianity that such stress should be laid upon it by these writers.

The most frequent suggestion which they offer is that the Cross is the final and complete confirmation of the appeal to prophecy. By the fulfilment of prophecy the claim of Jesus Christ to be the Incarnate Word, revealing the very truth of God, is placed beyond dispute. And all prophecy culminates in the great prophecies of a suffering Christ, "by whose stripes we are healed." As is natural, this argument is most fully developed in writings directed against Jewish controversialists, of which examples survive in the so-called Epistle of Barnabas, and in Justin's Dialogue with Trypho.

The whole idea of the Epistle of Barnabas [1] is that the Old Testament belongs no longer to the Jews, but to the Christians alone,[2] seeing that its types and its prophecies are all fulfilled in Christ.

> Forasmuch then as He was about to be manifested in the flesh and to suffer, His suffering was manifested beforehand.[3]

---

[1] The idea of redemption by knowledge is not prominent here, but appears in ch. 14.

[2] *Ep. Barn.* 4.

[3] *Ἐν σαρκὶ οὖν αὐτοῦ μέλλοντος φανεροῦσθαι καὶ πάσχειν, προεφανερώθη τὸ πάθος* (ch. 6; cf. ch. 4).

Accordingly phrase after phrase from the Old Testament is taken and applied, by the methods of Alexandrian allegorical exegesis, to the life and death of Christ. And thus, as is natural, such phrases as seem to imply any theory of the Cross are upon the lines of the Old Testament idea of sacrifice.

> For to this end the Lord endured to deliver His flesh unto corruption, that by the remission of sins we might be cleansed, which cleansing is through the blood of His sprinkling.[1]

In another passage the writer draws out at some length the type of the brazen serpent as being

> a type of Jesus, how that He must suffer, and that He Himself whom they shall think to have destroyed shall make alive. . . .[2]

This emphasis on new life is clearly a dominant thought with the writer, though he attempts no explanation of the way in which this life is made available for man.

> He Himself endured that He might destroy death and shew forth the resurrection of the dead.[3]
>
> If then the Son of God, being Lord and future Judge of quick and dead, suffered that His wound might give us life, let us believe that the Son of God could not suffer except for our sakes.[4]

In one passage the writer suggests that the death of Christ was necessary in order that the tale of wickedness of the Jews might be complete :

> Therefore the Son of God came in the flesh to this end, that

---

[1] Εἰς τοῦτο γὰρ ὑπέμεινεν ὁ Κύριος παραδοῦναι τὴν σάρκα εἰς καταφθοράν, ἵνα τῇ ἀφέσει τῶν ἁμαρτιῶν ἁγνισθῶμεν, ὅ ἐστιν ἐν τῷ αἵματι τοῦ ῥαντίσματος αὐτοῦ (ch. 5).

[2] Τύπον τοῦ Ἰησοῦ, ὅτι δεῖ αὐτὸν παθεῖν καὶ αὐτὸς ζωοποιήσει ὃν δόξουσιν ἀπολωλεκέναι (ch. 12).

[3] Αὐτὸς δὲ ἵνα καταργήσῃ τὸν θάνατον καὶ τὴν ἐκ νεκρῶν ἀνάστασιν δείξῃ . . . ὑπέμεινεν (ch. 5).

[4] Εἰ οὖν ὁ υἱὸς τοῦ Θεοῦ, ὢν Κύριος καὶ μέλλων κρίνειν ζῶντας καὶ νεκρούς, ἔπαθεν ἵνα ἡ πληγὴ αὐτοῦ ζωοποιήσῃ ἡμᾶς, πιστεύσωμεν ὅτι ὁ υἱὸς τοῦ Θεοῦ οὐκ ἠδύνατο παθεῖν εἰ μὴ δι' ἡμᾶς (ch. 7).

He might sum up the complete tale of their sins against those who persecuted and slew His prophets.[1]

Justin Martyr takes up exactly this same general position with regard to the fulfilment of Old Testament prophecy in the Cross of Christ. Large parts of his Dialogue with Trypho, a work intended especially for Jewish readers, are devoted to a detailed exposition of this idea,[2] much on the lines of the Epistle of Barnabas.[3]

> Will not all who have understood the writings of the prophets, if they do but hear that He has been crucified, say that this is He and no other?[4]

But Justin has more to say about the Cross than this, and though his language does not suggest that he has reached any definite theory, various thoughts are present to his mind.

1. Christ shares our sufferings that He may thereby heal the disease of sin.

> For our sake He became man that by becoming a partaker of our sufferings He might effect a cure.[5]

2. The Cross was due to the demons, urging on the Jews. There is a hint here of the idea of the conquest of Satan by Christ.

> But now by the will of God having become man for the sake of the human race, He endured all the sufferings which the demons brought upon Him by the hands of the senseless Jews.[6]

---

[1] Οὐκοῦν ὁ υἱὸς τοῦ Θεοῦ εἰς τοῦτο ἐν σαρκὶ ἦλθεν, ἵνα τὸ τέλειον τῶν ἁμαρτιῶν ἀνακεφαλαιώσῃ τοῖς διώξασιν ἐν θανάτῳ τοὺς προφήτας αὐτοῦ (ch. 5).

[2] E.g. *Dial.* 40-43, 90-99.

[3] Compare, *e.g.*, *Dial.* 90, 91 with *Barn.* 12.

[4] Καὶ ὅσοι νενοήκασι τὰ τῶν προφητῶν τοῦτον φήσουσιν οὐκ ἄλλον εἰ μόνον ἀκούσειαν ὅτι οὗτος ἐσταυρωμένος; (*Dial.* 89).

[5] Δι' ἡμᾶς ἄνθρωπος γέγονεν ὅπως καὶ τῶν παθῶν τῶν ἡμετέρων συμμέτοχος γενόμενος καὶ ἴασιν ποιήσηται (*Ap.* ii. 13).

[6] Νῦν δὲ διὰ θελήματος Θεοῦ ὑπὲρ τοῦ ἀνθρωπείου γένους ἄνθρωπος γενόμενος ὑπέμεινε καὶ παθεῖν ὅσα αὐτὸν ἐνήργησαν οἱ δαίμονες διατεθῆναι ὑπὲρ τῶν ἀνοήτων Ἰουδαίων (*Ap.* i. 63).

3. A fuller treatment of the subject occurs in the Dialogue with Trypho, in connection with Gal. 3 13.

> In the same way that God bade the sign to be made in the brazen serpent, and is Himself guiltless, so in the Law does the curse lie upon men that are crucified. Yet no curse lies upon the Christ of God, by whom He saves all who have wrought things worthy of a curse. For all mankind will be found to be under a curse. . . . If then the Father of all wished His Christ on behalf of all mankind to take upon Himself the curses due to all, knowing that after His crucifixion and death He would raise Him up again, why do you reason about Him, who endured this suffering in accordance with the Father's will, as though He were accursed, and do not rather bewail yourselves? For although His Father, and He Himself too, brought it about that He should suffer these things for mankind, yet it was not in obedience to the will of God that you did it. . . . And as for what is said in the Law, that cursed is every one that is hanged upon a tree, it is not as though God cursed this crucified One. . . .[1]

This passage has sometimes been urged as showing that Justin held the later Penal theory of Atonement. As a matter of fact it proves the exact opposite. Justin is most careful to show that the curse which lies upon Christ is in no sense the curse of God. It is from the Jews and not from God that the curse comes, and not only God but also Christ Himself were willing that He should undergo this curse, the curses due to all, that all those to whom the curse was due might by belief

[1] *Ὅνπερ οὖν τρόπον τὸ σημεῖον διὰ τοῦ χαλκοῦ ὄφεως γενέσθαι ὁ Θεὸς ἐκέλευσε, καὶ ἀναίτιός ἐστιν, οὕτω δὴ καὶ ἐν τῷ νόμῳ κατάρα κεῖται κατὰ τῶν σταυρουμένων ἀνθρώπων· οὐκ ἔτι δὴ κατὰ τοῦ Χριστοῦ τοῦ Θεοῦ κατάρα κεῖται, δι' οὗ σώζει πάντας τοὺς κατάρας ἄξια πράξαντας. καὶ γὰρ πᾶν γένος ἀνθρώπων εὑρεθήσεται ὑπὸ κατάραν ὄν. . . . εἰ οὖν καὶ τὸν ἑαυτοῦ Χριστὸν ὑπὲρ τῶν ἐκ παντὸς γένους ἀνθρώπων ὁ Πατὴρ τῶν ὅλων τὰς πάντων κατάρας ἀναδέξασθαι ἐβουλήθη, εἰδὼς ὅτι ἀναστήσει αὐτὸν σταυρωθέντα καὶ ἀποθανόντα, διὰ τί ὡς κεκατηραμένου τοῦ ὑπομείναντος κατὰ τὴν τοῦ Πατρὸς βουλὴν ταῦτα παθεῖν τὸν λόγον ποιεῖτε, καὶ οὐχὶ μᾶλλον ἑαυτοὺς θρηνεῖτε; εἰ γὰρ καὶ ὁ Πατὴρ αὐτοῦ καὶ αὐτὸς παθεῖν ταῦτα αὐτὸν ὑπὲρ τοῦ ἀνθρωπείου γένους ἐνήργησεν, ὑμεῖς οὐχ ὡς γνώμῃ Θεοῦ ὑπηρετοῦντες τοῦτο ἐπράξατε. . . . καὶ γὰρ τὸ εἰρημένον ἐν τῷ νόμῳ, ὅτι ἐπικατάρατος πᾶς ὁ κρεμάμενος ἐπὶ ξύλου, οὐχ ὡς τοῦ Θεοῦ καταρωμένου τούτου τοῦ ἐσταυρωμένου . . .* (*Dial.* 94-96; cf. also 111).

be saved. There is some confusion of thought in the passage between the curse assigned by the Law, and the "curse" involved in the treatment of Christians by the Jews.

4. Justin emphasizes the Resurrection as a real conquest of death.

> For the salvation of them that believe in Him He endured to be set at nought and to suffer, that by dying and rising again He might conquer death.[1]

Like the other writers of his age Justin offers no explanation of the way in which this conquest takes effect for the believer, though his language shows that it is to be made available for man by faith.

Clement of Alexandria is mainly interested in matters of ethics and he makes little allusion to the special meaning of the Cross. He uses Old Testament prophecies and types comparatively little, as is natural in works addressed to Gentile readers, and usually in phrases derived directly from the New Testament, *e.g.*

> We were ransomed by the precious blood of Christ, as of a lamb blameless and undefiled.[2]

"Lamb of God" is the only sacrificial title which he applies to Christ.[3] More often he views the Cross, in connection with his general outlook, as the supreme martyrdom, making a moral appeal to the hearts of men and inspiring Christ's followers to suffer as He suffered. In one noteworthy passage this is combined apparently with the idea of an expiatory sacrifice, exercising a magical cleansing effect quite apart from any question of the deserts of the recipients of the benefit. Such sacrifices were well known in Egypt.

[1] *Ὑπὲρ σωτηρίας τῶν πιστευόντων αὐτῷ καὶ ἐξουθενηθῆναι καὶ παθεῖν ὑπέμεινεν, ἵνα ἀποθανὼν καὶ ἀναστὰς νικήσῃ τὸν θάνατον* (*Ap.* i. 63).

[2] *Ἐλυτρώθημεν . . . τιμίῳ αἵματι ὡς ἀμνοῦ ἀμώμου καὶ ἀσπίλου Χριστοῦ* (*Paed.* iii. 12; cf. 1 Pet. I 19).

[3] Cf. Bigg, *Christian Platonists of Alexandria* (1913 ed.), p. 105.

> Alone, therefore, the Lord, for the purification of those who conspired against Him and disbelieved Him, "drank the cup"; in imitation of whom the apostles suffered for the churches which they had founded, that they might be really Gnostics and perfect.[1]

This passage by itself would suggest that Christ's death simply resembled that of the later martyrs in its purifying effect and had no unique force, but that this is not Clement's meaning is shown by the one or two allusions which he makes to reconciliation and propitiation, phrases which he takes over from the New Testament without comment.

> And He is the propitiation for our sins, as John says, who heals both our body and our soul.[2]

This healing is wrought by the implanting of new life through the Cross.

> Unto life He crucified death and dragging man away from destruction, uplifted him to the skies.[3]

Clement is quite sure that Christ's suffering is not due to the Father's will—

> Neither did the Lord suffer by the will of the Father[4]—

and here his thought is less clear than that of Justin, who recognised the will of God as underlying the passion, even though the curse upon Christ was not the curse of God.

The conception of a conquest of Satan occurs in the

[1] *Μόνος τοίνυν ὁ Κύριος διὰ τὴν τῶν ἐπιβουλευόντων αὐτῷ ἀνθρώπων καὶ τὴν τῶν ἀπίστων ἀποκάθαρσιν ἔπιε τὸ ποτήριον· ὃν μιμούμενοι οἱ ἀπόστολοι, ὡς ἂν τῷ ὄντι γνωστικοὶ καὶ τέλειοι, ὑπὲρ τῶν ἐκκλησιῶν ἃς ἔπηξαν ἔπαθον* (*Strom.* iv. 9).

[2] *Καὶ αὐτὸς ἱλασμός ἐστι περὶ τῶν ἁμαρτιῶν ἡμῶν, ὥς φησιν ὁ Ἰωάννης, ὁ ἰώμενος ἡμῶν καὶ σῶμα καὶ ψυχήν* (*Paed.* iii. 12; cf. 1 John 2 2). For "reconciliation" cf. *Protrept.* 1.

[3] *Τὸν θάνατον εἰς ζωὴν ἀνεσταύρωσεν· ἐξαρπάσας δὲ τῆς ἀπωλείας τὸν ἄνθρωπον προσεκρέμασεν αἰθέρι* (*Protrept.* 11).

[4] *Οὔτε γὰρ ὁ Κύριος θελήματι ἔπαθε τοῦ Πατρός* (*Strom.* iv. 12, where great emphasis is laid on Christ's sinlessness).

following rhetorical passage, which well illustrates Clement's best thought:

> Man, who had been free for his simplicity, was found enchained by sins. The Lord then wished to free him from his chains, and clothing Himself in flesh—O mystery Divine—overcame the serpent and enslaved the tyrant death; and, most wonderful of all, man that had been deceived by pleasure, and bound fast to corruption, had his hands unloosed and was set free. O mysterious wonder! The Lord was laid low, and man uprose, and he who fell from Paradise gains as reward something greater, even heaven itself.[1]

These words, as Oxenham points out,[2] appear to be the first hint of the belief that man gained by the Incarnation and Atonement more than he had lost by the Fall.

Tertullian, in so many ways one of the creative forces in the theology of the West, makes no contribution to the development of the doctrine of atonement. His interests, like those of Clement of Alexandria, are severely ethical, and it is only in the reply to Marcion and in the short treatise "Against the Jews," amid all his voluminous works, that there is any very definite reference to the passion of Christ. The most important passage is a comment on Gal. 3 13, as compared with Deut. 21 22, 23, in the treatise "Against the Jews":

> Therefore He did not maledictively adjudge Christ to this passion, but drew a distinction, that whoever, in any sin, had incurred the judgement of death, and died suspended on a tree, he should be "cursed by God," because his own sins were the cause of his suspension on the tree. On the other hand, Christ, who spake not guile from His mouth, and who

---

[1] 'Ο δι' ἁπλότητα λελυμένος ἄνθρωπος ἁμαρτίαις εὑρέθη δεδεμένος. τῶν δεσμῶν λῦσαι τοῦτον ὁ Κύριος αὖθις ἠθέλησεν· καὶ σαρκὶ ἐνδεθείς, μυστήριον θεῖον, τούτῳ τὸν ὄφιν ἐχειρώσατο, καὶ τὸν τύραννον ἐδουλώσατο, τὸν θάνατον· καὶ τὸ παραδοξότατον, ἐκεῖνον τὸν ἄνθρωπον, τὸν ἡδονῇ πεπλανημένον, τὸν τῇ φθορᾷ δεδεμένον χερσὶν ἡπλωμέναις ἔδειξε λελυμένον. ὢ θαύματος μυστικοῦ. κέκλιται μὲν ὁ Κύριος, ἀνέστη δὲ ἄνθρωπος· καὶ ὁ ἐκ τοῦ παραδείσου πεσών, μεῖζον ὑπακοῆς ἆθλον, οὐρανοὺς ἀπολαμβάνει (*Protrept.* 11.)

[2] Oxenham, *The Catholic Doctrine of the Atonement* (1881 ed.), p. 123.

exhibited all righteousness and humility, not only (as we have above recorded it predicted of Him) was not exposed to that kind of death for His own deserts, but [was so exposed] in order that what was predicted by the prophets as destined to come upon Him through your means might be fulfilled.[1]

Here the thought of Justin is repeated without any advance. The appeal to prophecy is held sufficient to account for the Cross, and Tertullian only feels it necessary to guard, as his predecessor had done, against the idea that the curse which rested upon Christ was the curse of the Father. The types of Christ in the Old Testament are also worked out in the reply to Marcion, and here Tertullian makes it clear that he assigns a unique value to the Cross for the putting away of sin. Thus in expounding the brazen serpent he says:

Did he not here also intend to shew the power of our Lord's cross, whereby that old serpent the devil was vanquished,—whereby also to every man who was bitten by spiritual serpents, but who yet turned with an eye of faith to it, was proclaimed a cure from the bite of sin, and health for evermore ?[2]

Most significant of all in this direction is his argument, in opposition to Marcion's docetic teaching, that if Christ's body was merely a phantom He could not really have died and the whole meaning and object of Christianity would be destroyed.[3]

But Tertullian's main importance for the history of

[1] Igitur non in hanc passionem Christum maledixit; sed distinctionem fecit, ut qui in aliquo delicto judicium mortis habuisset et moreretur suspensus in ligno, hic maledictus a Deo esset, quia propter merita delictorum suorum suspenderetur in ligno. Alioquin Christus, qui dolum de ore suo locutus non est, quique omnem justitiam et humilitatem exhibuit, et, ut supra de eo praedictum memoravimus, non pro meritis suis in id genus mortis expositus est, sed ut ea quae praedicta sunt a prophetis per vos ei obventura implerentur (*Adv. Jud.* 10; the translations from Tertullian are taken from the *Ante-Nicene Christian Library*). See also *De Fuga*, xii.

[2] Et hic Dominicae crucis vis intentabat, qua serpens diabolus publicabatur, et laeso cuique a spiritualibus colubris, intuenti tamen et credenti in eam sanitas morsuum peccatorum, et salus exinde praedicabatur (*Adv. Marc.* iii. 18).

[3] *Adv. Marc.* iii. 8.

the doctrine lies in his use of the word "satisfaction." Not that he ever uses it in any connection with the Atonement made by Christ. There is no trace in him of any theory of a vicarious satisfaction offered to God. He believes, inconsistent though it may be with any conception of the unique value of the death of Christ, that the sinner can himself offer a certain satisfaction to God in penitence and in good works.[1]

> He who through repentance for sins had begun to make satisfaction to the Lord, will through another repentance of his repentance, make satisfaction to the devil.[2]

> We confess our sins to the Lord, not indeed as if He were ignorant of them, but inasmuch as by confession satisfaction is settled; of confession repentance is born; by repentance God is appeased.[3]

This idea of satisfaction remained unfruitful for many centuries. It was taken up by Cyprian,[4] but only in language which echoes that of Tertullian, assigning to the penitence of the sinner the power to make satisfaction to God. It was not possible to apply the conception to the doctrine of Atonement until the Godward aspect of that doctrine came to be worked out, and up to the time of Anselm only desultory and fragmentary attempts were made at such a treatment of the subject. For the present theological interest was concerned with theories either of a conquest of the devil by God, or of a transaction with the devil entered into by God. The conception of satisfaction was turned to other uses, and formed the basis of the doctrine of Merits, a doctrine

[1] This thought leads up to that of Jonathan Edwards and McLeod Campbell, who saw that a perfect penitence, if it could be offered, would make satisfaction for sin. The two writers, of course, draw widely different conclusions from this premiss.

[2] Ita qui per delictorum poenitentiam instituerat Domino satisfacere, diabolo per aliam poenitentiae poenitentiam satisfaciet (*De Poen.* 5).

[3] Delictum Domino nostrum confitemur: non quidem ut ignaro, sed quatenus satisfactio confessione disponitur, confessione poenitentia nascitur, poenitentia Deus mitigatur (*De Poen.* 9; cf. chh. 7, 8, 10; *De Pat.* 13; *De Pud.* 9; *De Cult. Fem.* i. 1).

[4] *De Lapsis*, 17: Dominus nostra satisfactione placandus est.

which is certainly very closely allied to the thought of Tertullian himself, and which comes into clear view in the writings of Cyprian.[1]

[1] See Wirth, *Der 'Verdienst'-Begriff* (Leipzig, 1892 and 1901), and note in Bethune-Baker, *op. cit.* p. 353. Also R. S. Franks, *A History of the Doctrine of the Work of Christ* (1918) i. pp. 103 ff.

CHAPTER III

THE DOCTRINE OF A RANSOM OR BARGAIN

THE treatment of the doctrine of the Atonement in the first two centuries was followed in the main by the fathers of the Greek Church and by those Latin fathers who came under their influence down to the time of Anselm. Both in the New Testament and in the immediately subsequent literature great stress had been laid upon the fact of the Atonement as solving for man the problem of sin. At the very centre of the Christian tradition stood the Cross, "to the Jews a snare, and to the Greeks folly; but to the elect, both Jews and Greeks, Christ, the power of God and the wisdom of God."[1] Men did not assign meanings to the Cross, but it was to the Cross that they turned in every need. There is no better commentary on St. Paul's words, and no better witness to the place of the Cross in the thoughts and worship of the early Church, than the rude scratching, found on the Palatine Hill, of a crucified figure with an ass's head, and with the mocking inscription, "Alexamenos worships his God."[2] The mocker had made no mistake as to the central fact of the faith which he despised.

But emphasis upon the fact of the Atonement had not as yet led to theory. Great wealth of metaphor was employed to express the fact, but the meaning of the metaphors so used was never stressed. Interest was in the result of the fact upon the status of sinful

[1] 1 Cor. I 23, 24.

[2] Ἀλεξάμενος Θεὸν σέβεται.

man, rather than in discussions as to the intrinsic nature of the fact itself.

This balance of interest, which it has been the work of the last century to restore, was characteristic of the Greek Church. Throughout its early history there is found the same wealth of metaphor, based on the New Testament, used in the endeavour to describe the fact of the Atonement. Speculative interest was slight in this department. The philosophers of the Church were occupied with the great problems of the nature of the Godhead and of the Person of Christ, endeavouring to utilize the canons of Greek thought for the clearer statement of that which was implied in the Christian tradition. Redemption remained throughout a fact rather than a doctrine. It was, indeed, by the fact of Redemption that rival doctrines of the Trinity or of the Incarnation were tested.[1] Hence it came about that writers when driven to speculate upon the subject, which happened but seldom, were content with a theory of the crudest description, based upon the idea of a transaction between God and the devil, who was regarded as in some way the possessor of certain rights against man.

That such a theory could stand for nine hundred years as the ordinary exposition of the fact of the Atonement is in itself a sufficient proof that the need for serious discussion of the doctrine had not as yet been felt. It was, indeed, the very crudity of this theory which, at the revival of theological learning, drove the Western Church to speculate on the doctrine, a process which has at times threatened to obscure the fact.

[1] This is the key to the history of the great heresies of the fourth and fifth centuries. The appeal to redemptive value as the necessary condition to be satisfied by any doctrinal theory is well shown, for example, in the writings of Athanasius against Arianism. This does not, however, mean, as Harnack would seem to suggest, that the Chalcedonian doctrine is a Hellenistic distortion of primitive Christianity, but rather that the fact of redemption was so essential a part of the Christian experience that no doctrine incompatible with that fact could possibly survive. Christianity was always a soteriology.

It would thus not be true to say that the Ransom or Bargain Theory of the Atonement represents the whole thought of the early Church upon the subject, or that it was in any sense official and authoritative. As the speculation of isolated thinkers, more curious than their fellows in solving the deeper problems of the faith, it recurs again and again. Yet so great a scholar as Athanasius can write as though he had never heard of the theory as it is stated by Origen, and Gregory of Nazianzum expressly attacks it, despite the fact that his friend, Gregory of Nyssa, is one of its chief exponents.

It is desirable, therefore, for the sake of clearness, to divide the history of the doctrine in the writers of the early Church into two parts, dealing in the first place with Ransom or Bargain theories properly so called, and then going on to consider some of the less definite but very suggestive utterances which serve to indicate the real mind of the various writers. This is the method which, at the risk of occasional repetition, is followed below.

We proceed, then, to consider the development of the theory of a transaction between God and the devil, often known as the Ransom or Bargain theory.[1]

It is very probable that we should seek the sources of the later Ransom theories, as of so much else, amongst those tendencies of thought and practice which came to be grouped together under the name of Gnosticism. The Gnostics regarded man as lying, in virtue of his material nature, in the power of a Demiurge, the Maker and Lord of the material world. In some men, however, there is also a spark of aeon-nature, the true spiritual light, and the problem of redemption is the problem of freeing this aeon-nature through knowledge from its defiling bondage in matter. It

[1] For an admirably full catena of passages on this theory, ranging from Barnabas to Wessel, see the Appendix to *The Death of Christ*, by N. Dimock, a book of great learning, which does not seem to have been adequately recognized. See also his attempt to find the Penal Theory in the majority of the early fathers, pp. 88-110.

was to this end that the revelation in Christ was sent from the aeon-world. But even the aeons could not ignore the position and power of the demiurge, the lord of matter, and thus man could only be redeemed by a conforming of the aeon-nature, at least in appearance, to material conditions.[1] By this conforming the demiurge is deceived as to the true character of the Christ. In some forms of Gnosticism, as, for example, in Valentinianism and in the system of Marcion, the Cross is regarded as being the supreme moment of this deception, the crucified Christ being a mere appearance, while the true aeon-Christ ascends to the spiritual realms, thereby opening a way for those in whom the spark of spiritual knowledge has been kindled into flame.

Bizarre as this conception is, it is not very far removed from the thought of some of the Greek fathers. Here the devil takes the place of the Gnostic demiurge, and a theory is worked out upon the basis of the idea of a ransom paid to him, as suggested by St. Mark 10 45. The devil, like the demiurge, is found in possession of man, and his rights as possessor cannot be ignored, however he came by them. Therefore God consents to pay a price, the death of His Own Son, for the release of man. But in accepting this price the devil is deceived.[2] He loses his power over man, and he is not competent to hold in his power the holy Son of God.

[1] This Gnostic tendency of thought appears very early. It underlies the Docetism attacked by Ignatius and is not obscurely hinted at in the First Epistle of St. John (4 2, cf. 2 22, 4 15, 5 1). The mythological form of the thought is a later development.

[2] This conception of a deception of the devil is contained, in a form closely akin to the thought of Gnosticism, in Ignatius, *Ep. ad Eph.* 19, where the "prince of this world" is said to have been deceived by the three mysteries wrought in silence. The thought here rests on that of 1 Cor. 2 8 (*ἣν οὐδεὶς τῶν ἀρχόντων τοῦ αἰῶνος τούτου ἔγνωκεν· εἰ γὰρ ἔγνωσαν οὐκ ἂν τὸν* Κύριον *τῆς δόξης ἐσταύρωσαν*). The recent study of Pauline angelology has made it practically certain that the reference here is to supernatural world-powers. (Cf. M. Dibelius, *Die Geisterwelt im Glauben des Paulus*, and a good summary in A. S. Peake's Introduction to Colossians, in *Expos. Gk. Test.*)

The first suggestion of this theory appears in a well-known passage of the treatise of Irenaeus against Heresies.

And since the apostasy (*i.e.* the kingdom of Satan) held unjust sway over us, and, though naturally we belonged to God Almighty, had estranged us from Him unnaturally, making us his own disciples, the all-powerful Word of God, who lacks not in His own righteousness, justly turned against that same apostasy, redeeming from it His own not by force, after the manner in which the devil had held sway over us at the first, greedily seizing what was not his own, but by persuasion, even as it befitted God to take what He wished by persuading and not by imposing force, so that there should neither be any infringement of justice, nor should God's ancient creation perish utterly.[1]

It is hardly possible that this passage can be altogether independent of the passage quoted above from the Epistle to Diognetus, which is closely parallel in idea. But here the influence of a new thought is making itself felt. We have not now merely the language of devotion, dealing by means of hardly analysed metaphor with the mysteries of the faith as they make their appeal to the hearts of men. The mind of the theologian is now at work, and an effort, however slight, is being made to correlate the fact of Atonement with the other great facts of the kingdom of Satan and the justice of God. And so Irenaeus is led to suggest that it was by an unjust act of forcible aggression that the devil had established his power over man. Nevertheless his rights as possessor could not be arbitrarily set aside. A certain justice forbade God to employ the methods characteristic of the devil, though indeed it is probably rather in justice to His own character of love than from any recognition of the devil's claims that Irenaeus conceives God as

[1] Et quoniam injuste dominabatur nobis apostasia, et cum natura essemus Dei omnipotentis alienavit nos contra naturam, suos proprios faciens discipulos; potens in omnibus Dei Verbum, et non deficiens in sua justitia, juste etiam adversus ipsam conversus est apostasiam, ea quae sunt sua redimens ab ea non cum vi, quemadmodum illa initio dominabatur nostri, ea quae non erant sua insatiabiliter rapiens, sed secundum suadelam, quemadmodum decebat Deum suadentem, et non vim inferentem, accipere quae vellet, ut neque quod est justum confringeretur neque antiqua plasmatio Dei deperiret (*Adv. Haer.* v. I. I).

acting. And so God uses persuasion and not force, appealing to men to leave the service of that lord whose rule is based upon aggression and not upon love.

The older historians of Christian doctrine, *e.g.* Baur, Neander, Oxenham, saw in this reference to "persuasion" the first hint of the theory of a transaction between God and the devil, as though God had bartered with the devil for the souls of men. Such a view was soon to appear, but it is not possible to read it into this passage, with the parallel passage from the Epistle to Diognetus lying in the background. More modern writers for the most part agree that Irenaeus is thinking of an appeal made not to the devil but to the hearts of men, and that he is contrasting the gentle methods used by God with the aggressive violence of the devil.[1]

But whatever doubts may be left by the language of Irenaeus, none remains when we come to Origen. Here among passages of a very different character, there are some which speak quite explicitly of the transaction by which the soul of man was reclaimed:

> If then we were "bought with a price," as also Paul asserts, we were doubtless bought from one whose servants we were, who also named what price he would for releasing those whom he held from his power. Now it was the devil that held us, to whose side we had been drawn away by our sins. He asked, therefore, as our price the blood of Christ. But until the blood of Jesus, which was so precious that alone it sufficed for the redemption of all, was given, it was necessary that those who were established in the Law should give each for himself his blood (*i.e.* in circumcision) as it were in imitation of the redemption that was to be.[2]

---

[1] So *e.g.* Dorner, Gieseler, Moberly, etc.

[2] Si ergo pretio emti sumus, ut etiam Paulus adstipulatur, ab aliquo sine dubio emti sumus, cujus eramus servi, qui et pretium poposcit quod voluit, ut de potestate dimitteret quos tenebat. Tenebat autem nos diabolus, cui distracti fueramus peccatis nostris. Poposcit ergo pretium nostrum sanguinem Christi. Verum donec Jesu sanguis daretur, qui tam pretiosus fuit, ut solus pro omnium redemtione sufficeret, necessarium fuit eos, qui instituebantur in lege, unumquemque pro se, velut ad imitationem quandam futurae redemtionis, sanguinem suum dare (*In Rom.* ii. 13).

> To whom gave He His life "a ransom for many"? It cannot have been to God. Was it not then to the evil one? For he held us until the ransom for us, even the soul of Jesus, was paid to him, being deceived into thinking that he could be its lord, and not seeing that he could not bear the torment of holding it.[1]

Elsewhere Origen speaks of an equivalent[2] for man's soul as due to Satan. From man's point of view, though not necessarily from the point of view of God, the devil was in just possession. He had a right to name his price for the release of man. The price demanded was the blood of Christ, and this price was paid. But yet the devil was at war with all good, and in accepting this payment, named by himself and paid by God, he found himself deceived, though it is not clear whether Origen regards this deception as due to God or to the Devil himself. The devil did not perceive that mankind, partially freed by Christ's teaching and miracles, would be completely delivered by His death.[3] He released man, only to discover that he has no power over the soul of Jesus which he had accepted in exchange.

That such an action is unworthy of God does not seem to occur to Origen. As a commentator he expands his thought with reference to particular passages, and is at little pains to reconcile or to justify his various statements. It is not probable that he had in his mind any very definite view of the nature of the deception of the devil, though the language which he uses would certainly imply that God was responsible.[4]

What is left uncertain by Origen becomes quite clear

[1] Τίνι δὲ ἔδωκε τὴν ψυχὴν αὐτοῦ λύτρον ἀντὶ πολλῶν; οὐ γὰρ δὴ τῷ θεῷ· μή τι οὖν τῷ πονηρῷ; οὗτος γὰρ ἐκράτει ἡμῶν ἕως δοθῇ τὸ ὑπὲρ ἡμῶν αὐτῷ λύτρον, ἡ τοῦ Ἰησοῦ ψυχή, ἀπατηθέντι ὡς δυναμένῳ αὐτῆς κυριεῦσαι καὶ οὐκ ὁρῶντι ὅτι οὐ φέρει τὴν ἐπὶ τῷ κατέχειν αὐτὴν βάσανον (*In Matt.* xvi. 8). On this idea see the note in Bigg, *Christian Platonists of Alexandria*, p. 255: "Origen only means that Satan gained nothing by the tortures he was permitted to inflict upon our Lord."

[2] Ἀντάλλαγμα (*In Matt.* xiii. 28).

[3] Tom. xxxv. 75 (cited by Oxenham, *op. cit.*).

[4] So especially *In Matt.* xiii. 8, 9.

in the classical expression given to this theory a century later by Gregory of Nyssa. Gregory, like Irenaeus, starts from the idea of the justice of God, and dwells on the fact that it was by a voluntary act that man had placed himself in the devil's power. The devil must have no ground for a just complaint.

> For as they who have bartered away their freedom for money are the slaves of those who have purchased them . . ., on the same principle, now that we had voluntarily bartered away our freedom, it was requisite that no arbitrary method of recovery, but the one consonant with justice should be devised by Him who in His goodness had undertaken our rescue. Now this method is in a manner this: to make over to the master of the slave whatever ransom he may agree to accept for the person in his possession.[1]

The devil, urged on by "his own special passion of pride," was very ready to accept a price more valuable than the souls which he held in bondage, and such a price was offered to him in Christ, the Deity being veiled in flesh so that the devil might feel no fear in approaching Him.

> To have devised that the Divine power should have been containable in the envelopment of a body, to the end that the dispensation on our behalf might not be thwarted through any fear inspired by the Deity actually appearing, affords a demonstration of all these qualities at once—goodness, wisdom, justice. His choosing to save man is a testimony of His goodness; His making the redemption of the captive a matter of exchange exhibits His justice, while the invention whereby He enabled the enemy to apprehend that of which he was before incapable, is a manifestation of supreme wisdom.[2]

---

[1] Καθάπερ γὰρ οἱ χρημάτων τὴν ἑαυτῶν ἐλευθερίαν ἀποδόμενοι δοῦλοι τῶν ὠνησαμένων εἰσίν, . . . κατὰ τὸν αὐτὸν τρόπον ἑκουσίως ἡμῶν ἑαυτοὺς ἀπεμπολησάντων ἔδει παρὰ τοῦ δι' ἀγαθότητα πάλιν ἡμᾶς εἰς ἐλευθερίαν ἐξαιρουμένου μὴ τὸν τυραννικὸν ἀλλὰ τὸν δίκαιον τρόπον ἐπινοηθῆναι τῆς ἀνακλήσεως. οὗτος δέ ἐστί τις τὸ ἐπὶ τῷ κρατοῦντι ποιήσασθαι πᾶν ὅπερ ἂν ἐθέλοι λύτρον ἀντὶ τοῦ κατεχομένου λαβεῖν (*Or. Cat.* 22).

[2] Τὸ γὰρ διὰ τῆς τοῦ σώματος περιβολῆς χωρητὴν τὴν θείαν δύναμιν ἐπινοῆσαι γενέσθαι, ὡς ἂν ἡ ὑπὲρ ἡμῶν οἰκονομία μὴ παραποδισθείη τῷ φόβῳ τῆς θεικῆς ἐπιφανείας, πάντων κατὰ ταὐτὸν τὴν ἀπόδειξιν ἔχει, τοῦ ἀγαθοῦ, τοῦ σοφοῦ, τοῦ δικαίου. τὸ μὲν γὰρ ἐλέσθαι σῶσαι τῆς ἀγαθότητός ἐστι μαρτυρία· τὸ δὲ συναλλαγματικὴν ποιήσασθαι τὴν τοῦ κρατουμένου λύτρωσιν τὸ δίκαιον δείκνυσι· τὸ δὲ χωρητὸν δι' ἐπινοίας ποιῆσαι τῷ ἐχθρῷ τὸ ἀχώρητον τῆς ἀνωτάτω σοφίας τὴν ἀπόδειξιν ἔχει (*Or. Cat.* 23).

The result of this deception is stated by Gregory in a strange form:

> In order to secure that the ransom in our behalf might be easily accepted by him who required it, the Deity was hidden under the veil of our nature, that so, as with ravenous fish, the hook of the Deity might be gulped down along with the bait of flesh.[1]

Gregory is quite aware that some may feel that such an act of deception is wholly unworthy of God, and devotes a chapter to its justification. He argues that two things are involved in justice and wisdom, first, that all should have their due; and second, that, while justice is done, kindness should not swerve from the aim of the love of man.[2] In the redemption wrought by God both conditions are fulfilled.

> So in this instance, by the reasonable rule of justice, he who practised deception receives in return that very treatment the seeds of which he had himself sown of his own free will. He who first deceived man by the bait of sensual pleasure is himself deceived by the presentation of the human form. But as regards the aim and purpose of what took place, a change in the direction of the nobler is involved; for whereas he, the enemy, effected his deception for the ruin of our nature, He who is at once the just, and good, and wise one, used His device, in which there was deception, for the salvation of him who had perished, and thus not only conferred benefit on the lost one, but on him too who had wrought our ruin.[3]

---

[1] Ὡς ἂν εὔληπτον γένοιτο τῷ ἐπιζητοῦντι ὑπὲρ ἡμῶν τὸ ἀντάλλαγμα, τῷ προκαλύμματι τῆς φύσεως ἡμῶν ἐνεκρύφθη τὸ θεῖον, ἵνα κατὰ τοὺς λίχνους τῶν ἰχθύων τῷ δελέατι τῆς σαρκὸς συγκατασπασθῇ τὸ ἄγκιστρον τῆς θεότητος (*Or. Cat.* 24).

[2] Τῇ μὲν δικαιοσύνῃ τὸ κατ' ἀξίαν ἀντιδιδόντα, τῇ δὲ ἀγαθότητι τοῦ σκοποῦ τῆς φιλανθρωπίας οὐκ ἐξιστάμενον (*Or. Cat.* 26).

[3] Οὕτω καὶ ἐνταῦθα τῷ μὲν κατὰ τὸ δίκαιον λόγῳ ἐκεῖνα ὁ ἀπατεὼν ἀντιλαμβάνει, ὧν τὰ σπέρματα διὰ τῆς ἰδίας προαιρέσεως κατεβάλετο· ἀπατᾶται γὰρ καὶ αὐτὸς τῷ τοῦ ἀνθρώπου προβλήματι ὁ προαπατήσας τὸν ἄνθρωπον τῷ τῆς ἡδονῆς δελεάσματι· ὁ δὲ σκοπὸς τῶν γιγνομένων ἐπὶ τὸ κρεῖττον τὴν παραλλαγὴν ἔχει. ὁ μὲν γὰρ ἐπὶ διαφθορᾷ τῆς φύσεως τὴν ἀπάτην ἐνήργησεν, ὁ δὲ δίκαιος ἅμα καὶ ἀγαθὸς καὶ σοφὸς ἐπὶ σωτηρίᾳ τοῦ καταφθαρέντος τῇ ἐπινοίᾳ τῆς ἀπάτης ἐχρήσατο, οὐ μόνον τὸν ἀπολωλότα διὰ τούτων εὐεργετῶν, ἀλλὰ καὶ αὐτὸν τὸν τὴν ἀπώλειαν καθ' ἡμῶν ἐνεργήσαντα (*Or. Cat.* 26).

There is no question here about the character of the deception. It is God who deceives the devil, and that this should be so is entirely just, entirely merciful, and, indeed, a mark of the most supreme wisdom.

This strange theory exercised a quite extraordinary fascination over the minds of later writers. In Gregory of Nyssa himself its essential crudity is to a great extent covered by the hint that even the devil himself is deceived for his own good, as the physician might deceive a patient. But this thought "smacked of Origen's heresy," as a glossator wrote in the margin of a manuscript of Gregory's works,[1] and later writers would have none of it. Nevertheless they fall back again upon Gregory's theory, taking up and even embellishing his strange similes with obvious relish, and seldom pausing even to consider his presuppositions. His last serious critic down to the time of Anselm was his contemporary and friend, Gregory of Nazianzum.

As a typical statement of the theory in the writers following Gregory of Nyssa we may take the explanation of the Cross given by Rufinus in his Commentary on the Apostles' Creed.[2]

In the first place he sets out to explain why the Cross was chosen for the Saviour's death. It was, he says, a token of victory over "things in heaven and things on earth, and things under the earth" (Phil. 2 10). By being lifted up in the air He displayed His victory over the supernatural and celestial powers. By stretching forth His hands He made protestation to unbelievers and invited believers. By the part of the Cross sunk in the earth He signified the subjecting to Himself of the kingdoms of the nether world. Rufinus then goes more into detail.

When God made the world in the beginning, He set over it and appointed certain powers of celestial virtues, by whom the

[1] Published by Krabinger, and quoted in *N. and P. N. Fathers.*

[2] Chh. 14-16 (Translations from *N. and P. N. Fathers*).

race of mortal men might be governed and directed. . . . But some of these, as he who is called the Prince of this world, did not exercise the power which God had committed to them according to the laws by which they had received it, nor did they teach mankind to obey God's commandments, but taught them rather to follow their own perverse guidance. Thus we were brought under the bonds of sin. . . . Under that bond then every man was held by those most wicked rulers.[1]

Over these rulers the Cross of Christ is a triumph, while to mankind it is an example of obedience.

The Cross of Christ, then, brought those who had wrongfully abused the authority which they had received into subjection to those who had before been in subjection to them. But to us, that is mankind, it teaches first of all to resist sin even unto death, and willingly to die for the sake of religion.[2]

The actual triumph over the Prince of this world is stated thus, in language obviously based upon that of Gregory of Nyssa:

For the object of that mystery of the Incarnation which we expounded just now was that the divine virtue of the Son of God—as though it were a hook concealed beneath the form and fashion of human flesh—might lure on the Prince of this world to a conflict, to whom offering His flesh as a bait, His divinity underneath might catch him and hold him fast with its hook, through the shedding of His immaculate blood. For He alone who knows no stain of sin hath destroyed the sins of all, of those, at least, who have marked the door-posts of their faith with His blood. As, therefore, if a fish seizes a baited hook, it not only

---

[1] Ab initio Deus cum fecisset mundum, praefecit ei et proposuit quasdam virtutum coelestium potestates, quibus regeretur et dispensaretur mortalium genus. . . . Sed et horum nonnulli, sicut et ipse qui princeps appellatus est mundi, datam sibi a Deo potestatem non his quibus acceperant legibus temperarunt, nec humanum genus divinis obedire praeceptis, sed suis parere praevaricationibus docuerant. Et hinc adversus nos peccatorum chirographa scripta sunt. . . . Per istud ergo unusquisque chirographum illis rectoribus pessimis tenebatur. (*Comm. in Symb. Ap.* 15.) On the *chirographum* see p. 45.

[2] Illos itaque qui accepta potestate male abusi sunt subjectis quondam suis subjecit crux Christi. Nos vero, hoc est humanum genus, edocet primo omnium usque ad mortem resistere adversus peccatum, et libenter interitum pro pietate suscipere (*Comm. in Symb. Ap.* 15).

does not take the bait off the hook, but is drawn out of the water to be itself food for others, so he who had the power of death seized the body of Jesus in death, not being aware of the hook of divinity inclosed within it, but having swallowed it he was caught forthwith, and the bars of hell being burst asunder, he was drawn forth as it were from the abyss to become food for others.[1]

It is not necessary to pursue this strange metaphor through its later forms. As it stands in Gregory of Nyssa and Rufinus it is perhaps suggested by Job 41 1, "Canst thou draw out leviathan with a hook?" which is actually quoted by Rufinus as a prophecy of the snaring of the devil by the Cross. The metaphor occurs again in connection with the same passage in Gregory the Great:

He immediately announces the coming of the Lord's Incarnation, saying, In his eyes He will take him as with a hook. Who can be ignorant that on a hook the bait is shown, the point is concealed? For the bait tempts that the point may wound. Our Lord, therefore, when coming for the redemption of mankind, made as it were a kind of hook of Himself for the death of the devil.[2]

Sometimes the metaphor takes curious forms. It

[1] Nam sacramentum illud susceptae carnis, quod supra exposuimus, hanc habet causam, ut divina filii Dei virtus, velut hamus quidam habitu humanae carnis obtectus . . . principem mundi invitare possit ad agonem: cui ipse carnem suam velut escam tradens, hamo eum divinitas intrinsecus teneret insertum ex profusione immaculati sanguinis. Solus enim qui peccati maculam nescit omnium peccata delevit, eorum duntaxat qui sanguine ejus postes fidei suae signassent. Sicut ergo hamum esca contectum si piscis rapiat, non modo escam ab hamo non removet, sed et ipse de profundo, esca aliis futurus, educitur, ita et is qui habebat mortis imperium rapuit quidem in morte corpus Jesu, non sentiens in eo hamum divinitatis inclusum; sed ubi devoravit, haesit ipse continuo, et, diruptis inferni claustris, velut de profundo extractus trahitur ut esca caeteris fiat (*Comm. in Symb. Ap.* 16).

[2] Ipsum illico dominicae incarnationis adventum annuntiat, dicens: In oculis ejus quasi hamo capiet eum. Quis nesciat quod in hamo esca ostenditur, aculeus occultatur? Esca enim provocat ut aculeus pungat. Dominus itaque noster ad humani generis redemptionem veniens, velut quemdam de se in necem diaboli hamum fecit (*Moral.* xxxiii. 7).

will suffice here to quote two. Gregory the Great compares the Cross to a net for catching birds.

> The Lord deceived him like a bird when in the Passion He displayed before him His only-begotten Son as bait, but hid the noose.[1]

And the strangest variation of all occurs in one of the sermons of St. Augustine, who compares the Cross to a mouse-trap, baited with Christ's blood.

> As our price He held out His Cross to him like a mouse-trap, and as bait set upon it His own blood.[2]

It is clear that these later statements of what originated as a Ransom theory cannot have been in any degree adequate to the real thought of the writers who made them. The metaphor is now little more than a metaphor, and is only of service in so far as it throws into clear relief the utter hostility of God to the powers of evil. There is also, perhaps, as Hagenbach suggests,[3] the secondary thought that the devil is after all a fool. Despite all his apparent cunning he is at last outwitted by God's wisdom and appears in comparison stupid. But in the earlier forms of the doctrine there had been another thought, combined, however illogically, with that of the outwitting and conquest of the devil, the thought of a certain justice to be satisfied. In such writers as Rufinus this idea seems to have passed out of sight altogether, but in others the emphasis laid upon it by Irenaeus, Origen, and Gregory of Nyssa is retained. God cannot be supposed to act unjustly, even towards

[1] Quasi avi quippe Dominus illusit dum ei in passione unigeniti Filii sui ostendit escam sed laqueum abscondit (*Moral.* xxxiii. 15, on Job 40 24). The simile is borrowed from Gregory by Isidore Hispalensis, *Sententiarum* lib. i. 14.

[2] Ad pretium nostrum tetendit muscipulam crucem suam; posuit ibi quasi escam sanguinem suam (*Serm.* cxxx. 2, cf. cxxxiv. 6; cclxiii. 1). I owe the reference to Rivière, *Le Dogme de Rédemption*, p. 422, a passage to which the Rev. Harold Smith has called my attention. The metaphor has usually been quoted from Peter Lombard (*Sent.* iii. 19), who is, however, citing Augustine verbally, as is his wont.

[3] *History of Doctrines* (E.V.) ii. 54.

the devil. However the devil came by his rights they cannot be set arbitrarily aside. It is this thought that gives the theory its transactional form, the Atonement being regarded as in some sense a bargain in which the devil receives his due, as it were, by agreement with God.

A curious suggestion, for which parallels occur in other writers of the same period,[1] occurs in Chrysostom's comment on Col. 2 14, to account for the rights held by the devil over man. After offering two interpretations of the "bond" mentioned in that passage, he gives as a third the following:

> . . . or otherwise, that the devil held that bond that God made with Adam, saying, On the day that thou eatest of the tree thou shalt die. This bond, then, the devil held.[2]

This suggestion turns upon the idea that the devil had the right and the power, assigned to him by God, or at least not restricted by God, of punishing man with death when once man had by sin laid himself open to that punishment. It became a regular part of the stock-in-trade of later writers. Leo the Great, for example, refers to it more than once,[3] and Anselm considered it of sufficient importance to criticise it in his *Cur Deus Homo?*,[4] a fact which suggests that it was well known.[5]

This emphasis upon the rights of the devil led to a considerable modification of the theory in the legally minded Latin writers, profoundly influenced as they were by the majestic system of Roman Law, the very embodiment of the great ideal of justice. We see in Augustine the attempt to carry through the idea of

[1] Rufinus, *Comm. in Symb. Ap.* 15 (see p. 42) mentions the "chirographum," but not with the same definite reference to the Genesis narrative. Cf. also Aug. *De Trin.* iv. 13, Ambrose, *De Virgin.* 19. 126.

[2] *Ἢ εἰ μὴ τοῦτο ὅτι κατεῖχεν αὐτὸ ὁ διάβολος τὸ χειρόγραφον ὃ ἐποίησε πρὸς τὸν Ἀδὰμ ὁ Θεός, εἰπών Ἧι ἂν ἡμέρᾳ φάγῃς ἀπὸ τοῦ ξύλου, ἀποθανῇ. κατεῖχεν οὖν τὸ χειρόγραφον τοῦτο ὁ διάβολος* (*Hom. in Col.* vi.).

[3] *Ep.* 104-7; *Serm.* xxii. 4.

[4] *Cur Deus Homo?* i. 7.

[5] It appears also in Peter Lombard, *Sent.* iii. 19.

justice more thoroughly and consistently than the Greek fathers had done. It was absolutely just that man should be in the devil's power, yet the treatment of the devil was also just. And the latter justice is in some sense regarded as superior to the former.

By the justice of God in some sense the human race was delivered into the power of the devil. . . . But the way in which man was thus delivered into the power of the devil ought not to be so understood as if God did this, or commanded it to be done; but that He only permitted it, yet that justly.[1]

It was by man's own consent that he had been placed in this predicament, the devil thus ruling over him "as by an absolute right."[2] But in Christ there came to redeem man One over whom the devil had no authority. He had never sinned, and death was not His due. And so the devil was justly overcome. For, in the pride of his power over weak humanity:

The devil thought himself superior to the Lord Himself, inasmuch as the Lord in His sufferings yielded to him . . . so that He, being Himself put to death, although innocent, by the unjust one acting against us as it were by just right, might by a most just right overcome him, and so might lead captive the captivity wrought through sin, and free us from a captivity that was just on account of sin.[3]

And how was he conquered? Because when he found in Him nothing worthy of death, yet he slew Him. And certainly it is just, that we whom he held as debtors should be dismissed free by believing in Him whom he slew without any debt.[4]

---

[1] Quadam justitia Dei in potestatem diaboli traditum est genus humanum. . . . Modus autem iste quo traditus est homo in diaboli potestatem non ita debet intelligi tanquam hoc Deus fecerit aut fieri jusserit, sed quod tantum permiserit, juste tamen (*De Trin.* xiii. 12).

[2] Tanquam jure integro (*De Trin.* iv. 13).

[3] Quocirca etiam ipso Domino se credebat diabolus superiorem in quantum ille Dominus in passionibus cessit . . . ut ab iniquo velut aequo jure adversum nos agente, ipse occisus innocens eum jure aequissimo superaret, atque ita captivitatem propter peccatum factam captivaret, nosque liberaret a captivitate propter peccatum justa (*De Trin.* iv. 13).

[4] Et quomodo victus est? Quia cum in eo nihil morte dignum inveniret, occidit eum tamen. Et utique justum est ut debitores quos tenebat liberi dimittantur, in eum credentes quem sine ullo debito occidit (*De Trin.* xiii. 14).

And thence He proceeds to His passion, that He might pay for us debtors that which He did not owe.[1]

Thus it is now no longer by God that the devil is deceived but by his own inordinate pride. Augustine clearly does not regard the Incarnation as a veiling of the Godhead in flesh in order to trick the devil, but simply as the taking of a body liable to suffering and to death in order that the debt which was due to the devil might be paid. The blood of Christ was a price paid for us, but by accepting that price the devil was not enriched but bound,[2] since he claimed payment from One who was under no obligation to him.

So the devil was conquered, not by might, but by justice and righteousness.[3] Augustine, like Irenaeus, is quite clear that this is the method that befits God. The might of God was shown, it is true, in the resurrection of Christ from the dead, but this final triumph was withheld until the victory had already been won justly and righteously "through the weakness which He took upon Him in mortal flesh."

Would then the devil be conquered by this most just right, if Christ had willed to deal with him by might, not by righteousness? But He held back what was possible to Him, in order that He might first do what was fitting.[4]

---

[1] Et pergit inde ad passionem ut pro debitoribus nobis quod ipse non debebat exsolveret (*De Trin.* xiii. 14).

[2] *De Trin.* xiii. 15.

[3] Both these ideas are included under the one Latin word *justitia* which represents not only the justice under which the judge gives judgement, but also the legal condition of one upon whom the judge pronounces the verdict of acquittal. This double meaning of the word, in its objective and subjective aspects, has been fruitful of confusion in Western theories of the Atonement. Again and again it is impossible to translate a passage because *justus* and *justitia* slip across from one meaning to the other. The righteousness of Christ and God's just dealing with men and the devil through Him were constantly confused. The difficulty occurs already in the Latin version of Irenaeus, as is illustrated in the passage quoted above (*Adv. Haer.* v. I. I).

[4] Numquid isto jure aequissimo diabolus vinceretur, si potentia Christus cum illo agere non justitia voluisset? Sed postposuit quod potuit ut prius ageret quod oportuit (*De Trin.* xiii. 14).

And therefore He conquered the devil first by righteousness and afterwards by might: by righteousness, because He had no sin, and was slain by him most unjustly; and then by might, because having been dead He lived again, never afterwards to die.[1]

Scott Lidgett well brings out the dual aspect of this theory:[2] "It will be seen that in this account of the transaction with the devil there is a commingling of the sublimer view that God was dealing with a certain just right according to the eternal principles of His righteousness, with the somewhat grotesque view that the devil overreached himself owing to his excessive pride, and lost the human race by taking unjust advantage of its Head." The conception of a direct conquest of the devil has, as we have seen, fallen into the background, and from this time remains, in the Latin fathers in general, subordinate to the central thought of the operation of the justice of God.

On this subject of the conquest of the devil it is not necessary to dwell further, save to notice that in some of the later fathers, as, for example, in Leo the Great and in Gregory the Great, the conquest takes the form of an ethical victory over the devil, who was unable, for all his temptations, to seduce Christ to the committal of any sin.[3] This thought of the unswerving obedience of Christ forms a connecting link with the theories of the next period, when the Godward aspect of Atonement came to be worked out by Anselm and his successors.

[1] Et justitia ergo prius et potentia postea diabolum vicit: justitia scilicet quia nullum peccatum habuit, et ab illo injustissime est occisus; potentia vero quia revixit mortuus, nunquam postea moriturus (*De Trin.* xiii. 14).

[2] *The Spiritual Principle of the Atonement*, p. 438.

[3] A view also occurring, according to Hagenbach, in Hilary and, in the East, in Theodoret. In Gregory the Great this idea is expressed thus: Hunc ergo cum post baptisma vidit antiquus hostis mox tentationibus impetiit, et, per diversos aditus ad interiora ejus molitus irrepere, victus est, atque ipsa inexpugnabilis mentis ejus integritate prostratus (*Moral.* xvii. 30).

The Augustinian theory of the Atonement is repeated in very much the same terms in the writers of the Western Church during the next seven hundred years. As a typical statement we may take that given by Leo the Great. Here we find exactly the same feeling that it befits God to act by justice, and not by might, coupled with the same idea that the devil by claiming too much lost even that which was originally his due:

> For though the true mercy of God had infinitely many schemes to hand for the restoration of mankind, it chose that particular design which put in force for destroying the devil's work, not the efficacy of might, but the dictates of justice. For the pride of the ancient foe not undeservedly made good its despotic rights over all men, and with no unwarrantable supremacy tyrannised over those who had been of their accord lured away from God's commands to be the slaves of his will. . . . When, therefore, the merciful and almighty Saviour so arranged the commencement of His human course as to hide the power of His Godhead which was inseparable from His manhood under the veil of our weakness, the crafty foe was taken off his guard. . . . The unscrupulous thief and greedy robber persisted in assaulting Him who had nothing of His own, and in carrying out the general sentence on original sin went beyond the bond on which he rested, and required the punishment of iniquity from Him in whom he found no fault. And thus the malevolent terms of the deadly compact are annulled, and through the injustice of an overcharge the whole debt is cancelled.[1]

---

[1] Verax namque misericordia Dei, cum ad reparandum humanum genus ineffabiliter ei multa suppeterent, hanc potissimum consulendi viam elegit, qua ad destruendum opus diaboli non virtute uteretur potentiae sed ratione justitiae. Nam superbia hostis antiqui non immerito sibi in omnes homines jus tyrannicum vindicabat, nec indebito dominatu premebat quos a mandato Dei spontaneos in obsequium suae voluntatis illexerat. . . . Cum igitur misericors omnipotensque Salvator ita susceptionis humanae moderaretur exordia, ut virtutem inseparabilis a suo homine deitatis per velamen nostrae infirmitatis absconderet, illusa est securi hostis astutia. . . . Perstitit ergo improbus praedo et avarus exactor in eum qui nihil ipsius habebat insurgere, et dum vitiatae originis praejudicium generale persequitur, chirographum quo nitebatur excedit, ab illo iniquitatis exigens poenam, in quo nullam reperit culpam. Solvitur itaque lethiferae pactionis male suasa conscriptio, et per injustitiam plus petendi totius debiti summa vacuatur (*Serm.* xxii. 3, 4).

It is noteworthy that Leo is not so careful as Augustine had been to avoid asserting that the deception of the devil is directly due to God. He reverts to language very like that of Gregory of Nyssa when he speaks of the Incarnation as the putting on of a kind of veil whereby the devil was led to believe that

> . . . the Child who was born for the salvation of mankind was as much subject to him as all others are at their birth.[1]

But the remainder is exactly upon the lines laid down by Augustine. The devil claims from Christ that to which he has no right, and by this act of injustice his claim is put out of court, and the whole debt is dissolved.

One further quotation will suffice to illustrate this form of the transactional theory; Bernard of Clairvaux, one of its last exponents, writes, in language that might almost be a quotation from Augustine's writings:

> The prince of this world came, and in the Saviour found nothing, and since notwithstanding he laid his hands on the innocent One, he most justly lost those whom he was holding in his possession; since He who owed nothing to death, having accepted the injury of death, rightly loosed him who was liable to them both from the debt of death and from the dominion of the devil.[2]

Bernard, however, is a traditionalist, the fiery opponent of doctrinal innovators. Yet even he is standing at the turn of the road, and while his theological idiom is drawn from the past, it is no longer adequate to the thought which was affecting him, as it affected the other writers of his day.

Before turning from the Ransom theories proper to

[1] Nativitatem pueri in salutem generis humani procreati non aliter sibi quam omnium nascentium putavit obnoxiam (*Serm.* xxii. 4). The Augustinian idea, however, that the humanity was taken in order that Christ might suffer, appears in the context.

[2] Venit princeps hujus mundi, et in Salvatore non invenit quidquam: et cum nihilominus innocenti manus injecit, justissime quos tenebat amisit: quando is qui morti nihil debebat, accepta mortis injuria, jure illum qui obnoxius erat et mortis debito et diaboli solvit dominio (*Ep.* 190. 6).

the wider and fuller conceptions of the patristic age, we may pause to notice one or two special points in connection with those theories.

The common later view that the death of Christ was superabundant payment for man's sin, appears in a number of writers, and at an early date. Thus Cyril of Jerusalem says:

> Our sin was not as great as the righteous deed of Him who laid down His life for us.[1]

And Chrysostom has the same thought in a more rhetorical form:

> Christ paid far more than we owed, as much more in comparison as is the boundless ocean to a tiny drop.[2]

The thought, however, has hardly yet become a matter of doctrine. It is still the property rather of the preacher than of the theologian.

It is a more important matter to note how far doubts arose within this period as to the propriety of assigning any rights at all to the devil. Throughout the patristic writers we can feel the conflict of two ideas, the idea of the devil as the eternal enemy of God, ever at war with Him, and at the last conquered in fair fight, and the idea of the devil as in some sense God's servant, punishing man by God's permission, and, though he had very far overstepped the bounds assigned him, still possessing a certain just status which could not be ignored. It is clear that little progress was possible until this confusion of thought was dispelled. Yet strangely few of the early fathers were sufficiently clear-sighted in this respect to reject altogether, as unworthy of a good God, the recognition in any form of the devil's claims. The two noteworthy examples are Gregory of Nazianzum, who rejected the whole

[1] Οὐ τοσοῦτον ἡμάρτομεν ὅσον ἐδικαιοπράγησεν ὁ τὴν ψυχὴν ὑπὲρ ἡμῶν τεθεικώς (*Cat.* xiii. 33).

[2] Πολλῷ γὰρ πλείονα ὧν ὀφείλομεν κατέβαλεν ὁ Χριστός, καὶ τοσούτῳ πλείονα ὅσῳ πρὸς ῥανίδα μικρὰν πέλαγος ἄπειρον (*Hom. in Rom.* x. 17).

theory, and Athanasius, who writes, in his treatise on the Incarnation, as though he were not aware of its existence.[1] To these two great thinkers, both many centuries in advance of their time, we shall return. We may, however, notice here a writer noteworthy for his position as the last of the great Greek theologians of the early period, and important for our subject as marking in some degree the transition from devilward to Godward theories of Atonement.

John of Damascus is essentially a writer of his own age. In idea and in language he is almost wholly dependent upon his predecessors. He adopts without question the methods of thought honoured by three centuries of tradition since the days of Gregory of Nyssa. But he has felt the doubt to which Gregory of Nazianzum had given expression, and he endeavours to meet this by avoiding any mention of the devil as receiving the blood of Christ. Like Gregory of Nazianzum he holds that such a thought would be profane indeed. Yet he has no other theory to fall back upon, and he goes on to use all the language of the crudest form of the Ransom theory, simply avoiding the difficulty of which he is conscious by writing "death" instead of "the devil."

Since the enemy snares man by the hope of Godhead, he himself is snared in turn by the screen of flesh, and so are shown at once the goodness and wisdom, the justice and might of God.[2]

For He who was omnipotent did not in His omnipotent

---

[1] Harnack, *History of Dogma*, ii. 291, quotes an interesting passage from a writer of the third century whose works have been preserved among those of Origen (*De Recta in Deum Fide*, ed. Wetstein, i. pp. 38 f.), where the theory of a price offered to the devil is mercilessly criticized: *εἰ κακὸς ὢν ὁ διάβολος τῷ ἀγαθῷ πέπρακεν, οὐκ ἔστι κακὸς ἀλλὰ ἀγαθός.* The whole passage is worth consulting as a precursor of Gregory of Nazianzum and a protest against the theory which was becoming dominant.

[2] *Καὶ ἐπειδὴ θεότητος ἐλπίδι ὁ ἐχθρὸς δελεάζει τὸν ἄνθρωπον, σαρκὸς προβλήματι δελεάζεται, καὶ δείκνυται ἅμα τὸ ἀγαθὸν καὶ τὸ σοφόν, τὸ δίκαιόν τε καὶ τὸ δυνατὸν τοῦ Θεοῦ* (*De Fid. Orth.* iii. 1).

authority and might lack the power to rescue man out of the hands of the tyrant. But the tyrant would have had a ground of complaint if, after he had overcome man, God should have used force against him. Wherefore God in His pity and love for man wished to reveal man himself as conqueror, and became man to restore like with like.[1]

Since our Lord Jesus Christ was without sin . . . He was not subject to death, since death came into the world through sin. He dies, therefore, because He took on Himself death on our behalf, and He makes Himself an offering to the Father for our sakes. For we had sinned against Him, and it was meet that He should receive the ransom for us, and that we should thus be delivered from the condemnation. God forbid that the blood of the Lord should have been offered to the tyrant. Wherefore death approaches, and swallowing up the body as a bait is transfixed on the hook of divinity, and after tasting of a sinless and life-giving body, perishes, and brings up again all whom of old he swallowed up. For just as darkness disappears on the introduction of light, so is death repulsed before the assault of life, and brings life to all, but death to the destroyer.[2]

This latter passage is a good example of the dawning of the Godward consciousness in theology. The thought that sin is sin against God, and that therefore it is within the Godhead that redemption must be wrought, was to bear much fruit when the Dark Ages passed and theological interest revived with Anselm and the Schoolmen.

[1] Οὐκ ἀδύνατος γὰρ ἦν ὁ τὰ πάντα δυνάμενος, καὶ τῇ παντοδυνάμῳ αὐτοῦ ἐξουσίᾳ καὶ δυνάμει ἐξελέσθαι τοῦ τυραννοῦντος τὸν ἄνθρωπον· ἀλλ' ἦν ἐγκλήματος τῷ τυραννοῦντι ὑπόθεσις, ἄνθρωπον νικήσαντι καὶ ὑπὸ θεοῦ βιασθέντι. αὐτὸν οὖν τὸν πεσόντα νικητὴν ἀναδεῖξαι βουληθεὶς ὁ συμπαθὴς Θεὸς καὶ φιλάνθρωπος ἄνθρωπος γίνεται τῷ ὁμοίῳ τὸ ὅμοιον ἀνακαλούμενος (*De Fid. Orth.* iii. 18).

[2] Ἀναμάρτητος ὢν ὁ κύριος ἡμῶν Ἰησοῦς Χριστὸς . . . οὐκ ὑπέκειτο θανάτῳ, εἴπερ διὰ τῆς ἁμαρτίας εἰς τὸν κόσμον εἰσῆλθεν ὁ θάνατος. θνήσκει τοίνυν, τὸν ὑπὲρ ἡμῶν θάνατον ἀναδεχόμενος, καὶ ἑαυτὸν τῷ Πατρὶ προσφέρει θυσίαν ὑπὲρ ἡμῶν. αὐτῷ γὰρ πλημμελήκαμεν, καὶ αὐτὸν ἔδει τὸ ὑπερ ἡμῶν λύτρον δέξασθαι, καὶ οὕτως ἡμᾶς λυθῆναι τῆς κατακρίσεως· μὴ γὰρ γένοιτο τῷ τυράννῳ τὸ τοῦ δεσπότου προσενεχθῆναι αἷμα. πρόσεισι τοιγαροῦν ὁ θάνατος, καὶ καταπιὼν τὸ σώματος δέλεαρ, τῷ τῆς θεότητος ἀγκίστρῳ περιπείρεται, καὶ ἀναμαρτήτου καὶ ζωοποιοῦ γευσάμενος σώματος, διαφθείρεται, καὶ πάντας ἀνάγει, οὓς πάλαι κατέπιεν. ὥσπερ γὰρ τὸ σκότος τῇ τοῦ φωτὸς ἐπεισαγωγῇ ἐξαφανίζεται, οὕτως ἡ φθορὰ τῇ τῆς ζωῆς προσβολῇ ἀπελαύνεται, καὶ γίνεται πᾶσι ζωή, φθορὰ δὲ τῷ φθείραντι (*De Fid. Orth.* iii. 27).

But though most of the early writers are prepared to recognize that the devil is in possession of certain rights, there was a very widespread sense of the difficulty of regarding these rights as binding upon God in any absolute sense. They are due to our sin, and are conditioned by that sin. Both Origen[1] and Gregory of Nyssa,[2] for example, are quite clear that man is to blame. The punishment of death rests upon an agreement made by God with man, which agreement man of his own free will has broken.[3] But this fact does not impose any obligation upon God. Practically all the fathers agree that God might have saved man in any way that He pleased, even by a bare word, or by the mere exercise of His will, and that the reasons for the choice of this particular method of redemption are only very partially revealed. Gregory of Nyssa asks the question:

> Why does He not effect His purpose by the mere exercise of His will?[4]

and replies that

> . . . to this with all candid persons it were sufficient to reply that the sick do not dictate to their physicians the measures for their recovery.[5]

Athanasius suggests that though God might have saved man by a mere word He yet chose that method most profitable for him.[6] Gregory of Nazianzum says that as He made all by a word, He might have saved man by His will.[7] Augustine puts it very forcibly:

> They are fools who say The wisdom of God could not otherwise free men than by taking human nature, and being born of a woman, and suffering all that He did at the hands of sinners.[8]

---

[1] *Comm. in Rom.* ii. 13. [2] *Cat. Or.* 22, see p. 39.

[3] So Chrysostom, *Hom. in Col.* vi., see p. 45. With this thought cf. Athan. *De Inc.* c. 6; Cyril of Jerm. *Cat.* xiii. 33.

[4] Τί οὐχὶ θελήματι μόνῳ τὸ κατὰ γνώμην ποιεῖ; (*Cat. Or.* 17).

[5] Πρὸς δὲ τὸν τοιοῦτον λόγον ἱκανὸν μὲν ἦν πρὸς τοὺς συγγνώμονας τοσοῦτον εἰπεῖν, ὅτι καὶ τοῖς ἰατροῖς οὐ νομοθετοῦσι τὸν τρόπον τῆς ἐπιμελείας οἱ κάμνοντες (*Cat. Or.* 17).

[6] *Or. con. Ar.* ii. 68. [7] *Or.* c. 9.

[8] Sunt autem stulti qui dicunt, Non poterat aliter sapientia Dei

But Augustine also says that the method chosen by God was good and suitable to His dignity[1] and to our restoration:

> . . . we must show also, not indeed that no other mode was possible to God, to whose power all things are equally subject, but that there neither was nor need have been any other mode more appropriate for curing our misery.[2]

Similar ideas occur in the later Latin fathers.[3]

With one noteworthy exception the question of the extent of the Atonement does not come much under discussion in this period. The theory of universal restoration preached by Origen was rejected as a heresy, though Gregory of Nyssa does not seem to have been attacked for hinting that the devil might ultimately be saved and all creation restored to harmony.[4] The one great attempt to limit the scope of the Atonement was that of Augustine, whose general theory of sin and of predestination led him to assert that though all were in need of redemption the Atonement only availed for the elect. In this he was not followed by the later Latin fathers. Leo the Great says that the Atonement was a price sufficient to pay for a universe of captives,[5] while Gregory the Great extends its efficacy even to heavenly beings.[6]

---

homines liberare nisi susciperet hominem, et nasceretur ex femina, et a peccatoribus omnia illa pateretur (*De Agone Christi*, c. xi. not c. x. as quoted by Hagenbach and Oxenham).

[1] *De Trin.* xiii. 10.

[2] Verum etiam ut ostendamus non alium modum possibilem Deo defuisse, cujus potestati cuncta aequaliter subjacent; sed sanandae nostrae miseriae convenientiorem modum alium non fuisse nec esse oportuisse (*De Trin.* xiii. 10).

[3] *E.g.* Gregory the Great, *Moral.* xx. 36.

[4] See above, p. 40, and *Or. Cat.* 25.

[5] *Ep.* 134. 14.

[6] *Moral.* xxxi. 49.

CHAPTER IV

THE MIND OF THE EARLY FATHERS: THE EAST

THE theory of a transaction with the devil remained the customary and orthodox statement of the doctrine of the Atonement for nearly a thousand years, yet it would not be far from the truth to say that it never represents the real thought of those who used it. It was a convenient explanation, suitable to the conceptions of the day, and well adapted to homiletic purposes. But it was little more. In almost every writer we find its deficiencies made good by the introduction of ideas of a widely different character, though not as yet crystallized into definite theory, until at last in Bernard, and again in Peter Lombard, we find the old transactional language adopted and defended simply because it is the language of tradition, hallowed by its association with the fathers of the Church, and not lightly to be thrown aside, even though now inadequate to carry the thought of those who use it. And thus the interest of the period lies very largely outside the transactional theories proper, in those floating ideas which were never clearly worked out, but in which was contained the germ of almost every type of later speculation.

It is necessary, therefore, to make some attempt to estimate the real mind of the more important of the early fathers upon the whole question of redemption. To pursue the subject through the works of any large number of the writers of the period would be more confusing than profitable. It will suffice for our purpose to consider a few of the more typical writers, and, in particular, of those who have been already quoted as exponents of the Ransom theory. We begin, then, with Irenaeus.[1]

The real thought of Irenaeus about redemption may be said to be a combination of the Moral and Mystical views. Even the central passage, quoted above, which speaks of a transaction with the devil entered into by God as just seems to regard the efficacy of Atonement as lying rather in a persuasive force appealing to men. And the words which follow point to that union between man and God which alone can make such an appeal effective.

> Since the Lord thus has redeemed us through His own blood, giving His soul for our souls, and His flesh for our flesh, and has also poured out the Spirit of the Father for the union and communion of God and man, imparting God to men by means of the Spirit, and, on the other hand, attaching man to God by His own incarnation, and bestowing upon us at His coming immortality durably and truly, by means of communion with God.[2]

This passage suggests a thought which may be taken as characteristic of the Greek fathers, viz. that it is by the whole incarnate life of Christ that we are saved, the death being but its climax. And this may account for the attempt to find a special function for that death on lines so much akin to the thought of Gnosticism, by introducing the conception of the defeat of the devil. In another passage the unity of man with God is brought into direct connexion with this defeat. Since it was man that originally suffered defeat at the devil's hands, it is by man that that defeat must be reversed.

[1] For a useful summary of the position of Irenaeus in relation to his general theology see Franks, *op. cit.* i. p. 35.

[2] Suo igitur sanguine redimente nos Domino, et dante animam suam pro nostra anima et carnem suam pro nostris carnibus, et effundente Spiritum Patris in adunitionem et communionem Dei et hominis, ad homines quidem deponente Deum per Spiritum, ad Deum rursus imponente hominem per suam incarnationem, et firme et vere in adventu suo donante nobis incorruptelam per communionem quae est ad eum . . . (*Adv. Haer.* v. 1. 1).

He made man one with God. For if man had not overcome man's adversary, the enemy would not have been justly conquered.[1]

It is not merely that God defeats the devil, but that man defeats him in God. This conception of mystical union lies at the centre of the thought of Irenaeus about the Atonement. Man does not stand outside the action of God through Christ. There is no bargain made over his head. He is himself intimately and directly concerned. It is to him that Christ makes His appeal, and it is through mystical union with God through Christ that he is able to respond to the appeal. Irenaeus here shows himself a true heir to the thought of St. Paul.

The mystical union depends for Irenaeus upon his characteristic doctrine of "recapitulation."[2] He has the clearest possible apprehension of the great truth of the "solidarity" of mankind, bound together in Christ's victory as in Adam's sin. "Following up the meaning of the title 'Son of man,' which St. Paul had been the first to expand, he points to Christ as the great representative of the race, in whom are summed up all its ripe experiences as they are contained in germ in Adam. What Christ achieves the whole race achieves. Just as mankind in Adam lost its birthright, so in Christ mankind recovers its original condition. The effect of Adam's acts extended to the whole company of his descendants, and the effect of Christ's acts is equally co-extensive with the race. In each case it is really the whole race that acts in its representative."[3]

By the Incarnation this unity of Christ with humanity was accomplished.

For in what way could we be partakers of the adoption of sons, unless we had received from Him through the Son that fellow-

---

[1] *Ἥνωσεν τὸν ἄνθρωπον τῷ θεῷ. εἰ γὰρ μὴ ἄνθρωπος ἐνίκησε τὸν ἀντίπαλον τοῦ ἀνθρώπου οὐκ ἂν δικαίως ἐνικήθη ὁ ἐχθρός* (*Adv. Haer.* iii. 18. 7).

[2] *Recapitulatio*, in Greek *ἀνακεφαλαίωσις*.

[3] J. F. Bethune-Baker, *op. cit.* p. 334.

ship which reters to Himself, unless His Word having been made flesh had entered into communion with us? Wherefore also He passed through every stage of life restoring to all communion with God.[1]

When he became incarnate and was made man, He recapitulated in Himself the long roll of humanity, furnishing us all with a summary salvation.[2]

Irenaeus does not merely mean by this that Christ had a complete human experience, though that is included. Our experience has a real place in Him. Not only does Christ's obedience overcome the devil, a point upon which Irenaeus lays great stress in connexion with the temptations:

Thus, vanquishing him for the third time, He drove him from Him for the future as having been lawfully conquered, and the infringement of the command which had taken place in Adam was done away, by means of the command of the law which the Son of man observed, not transgressing the commandment of God.[3]

But this obedience, even unto death, becomes man's obedience too.

In the second Adam we were reconciled, becoming obedient unto death.[4]

All this is pure Pauline mysticism of the highest order. We are very far indeed from any conception of

[1] Qua enim ratione filiorum adoptionis ejus participes esse possemus, nisi per Filium eam quae est ad ipsum recepissemus ab eo communionem; nisi Verbum ejus communicasset nobis caro factum, omnibus restituens eam quae est ad Deum communionem (*Adv. Haer.* iii. 18. 7).

[2] Quando incarnatus est et homo factus longam hominum expositionem in se ipso recapitulavit, in compendio nobis salutem praestans (*Adv. Haer.* iii. 18. 1). For this idea cf. esp. *Adv. Haer.* ii. 22. 4.

[3] Et tertio itaque vincens eum de reliquo repulit a semetipso quasi legitime victum; et soluta est ea quae fuit in Adam praecepti Dei praevaricatio, per praeceptum legis quod servavit Filius hominis non transgrediens praeceptum Dei (*Adv. Haer.* v. 21. 2). It is impossible here to press either the legal sense of *praevaricatio*, or the metaphor involved in *soluta est*. The thought of Irenaeus is greater than his metaphors. For *praevaricatio* cf. Rufinus, *Comm. in Symb. Ap.* 15 (see p. 42).

[4] Ἐν τῷ δευτέρῳ Ἀδὰμ ἀποκαταλλάγημεν ὑπήκοοι μέχρι θανάτου γενόμενοι (*Adv. Haer.* v. 16. 3).

God coming to terms with the powers of evil. There is no thought of a price paid for us in the payment of which we have no part at all. It is in the hearts of men that redemption is wrought. A payment is made by Christ, it is true, but it is a payment made in virtue of His union with us.

> He would not truly have had flesh and blood, through which He paid for us, if He had not summed up in Himself the ancient creation of the line of Adam.[1]

What Christ pays, we pay. What Christ achieves, we achieve. And so the life to which Christ was raised up becomes our life too.[2]

The mystical conception of a union of the human and the divine is frequently found in writers of the third and fourth centuries, in the form that man attains salvation in Christ by "becoming God." This thought is common to such diverse thinkers as Origen and Athanasius. We may quote an example from Hippolytus.

> For Christ is the universal God, who determined to wash men clean from sin, making the old man new . . . whose holy

---

[1] *Οὐδὲ γὰρ ἦν ἀληθῶς σάρκα καὶ αἷμα ἐσχηκώς, δι' ὧν ἡμᾶς ἐξηγοράσατο, εἰ μὴ τὴν ἀρχαίαν πλάσιν τοῦ Ἀδὰμ εἰς ἑαυτὸν ἀνακεφαλαιώσατο* (*Adv. Haer.* v. 1. 2).

[2] *Adv. Haer.* v. 21. 1. In his *Εἰς ἐπίδειξιν τοῦ ἀποστολικοῦ κηρύγματος*, recently discovered in the Armenian and published, with a German version, by Dr. Karapet Ter-Mekerttschian and Dr. Ervand Ter-Minassiantz (Leipzig, 1907), Irenaeus does not add any new thoughts. See esp. §§ 31, 34, 37-39; also § 69. The Ransom-theory does not appear at all, except for such phrases as "Death lorded it over the body, and it was fitting that by bringing that body to nought He should free man from death's oppression," "He has broken the fetters in which we sat captive." But the strong sense of mystical union with God finds clear expression: "Now has He made man one with God." And this union is directly associated with the Incarnation: "The Word has now been made flesh, that through that same body through which sin had established itself and lorded it over us, sin might be brought to nought, and be no more in us." Christ's obedience is also emphasized, as also the truth that this obedience is to be ours too, together with the eternal life to which it leads, since He, in life and death and resurrection, is "Head and Leader of the godly life."

commands if thou obey, becoming a good imitator of the good, thou shalt be honoured by Him as His like. For God is not poor, even God who makest thee God for His own glory.[1]

Beyond this mystical suggestion, with its hint of the Moral theory, Hippolytus has little to say about the Atonement, and the more definite ideas of Irenaeus find no place in his works.

The comparative paucity of ideas as to the Atonement in earlier writers is more than made good when we come to Origen, the greatest and most many-sided theologian of the first three centuries. We have already seen that it was Origen who first gave form to the explanation of the Atonement along the lines of the Ransom theory, as a transaction in which the devil was outwitted. But this account, despite the great influence which it exercised over later writers, is by no means Origen's only point of view. His work as a commentator led him to consider various aspects of New Testament thought, and to develop the ideas which he found there in more directions than one. His suggestions anticipate most of the more modern theories.

The transactional, devilward, aspect of Atonement occupies, indeed, a comparatively small place in his real thought. His statement of it has obvious deficiencies, when regarded by itself. But a much truer grasp of the essentials of any adequate statement of the doctrine becomes apparent when it is realised how clearly he saw in Atonement both a Godward and a manward aspect.

And first of the Godward aspect. Origen dwells with recurring emphasis upon the idea of sacrifice, drawing out at length the Old Testament analogies. This, as might be expected, is especially illustrated in his homilies on the Pentateuch.

[1] Χριστὸς γάρ ἐστιν ὁ κατὰ πάντων Θεός, ὃς τὴν ἁμαρτίαν ἐξ ἀνθρώπων ἀποπλύνειν προέταξε, νέον τὸν παλαιὸν ἄνθρωπον ἀποτελῶν . . . οὗ προστάγμασιν ὑπακούσας σεμνοῖς, καὶ ἀγαθοῦ ἀγαθὸς γενόμενος μιμητής, ἔσῃ ὅμοιος ὑπ' αὐτοῦ τιμηθείς. οὐ γὰρ πτωχεύει Θεὸς καὶ σὲ Θεὸν ποιήσας εἰς δόξαν αὐτοῦ (*Philos.* x. 34).

But since sin entered into this world, and the necessity of sin demands a propitiation, and since propitiation cannot be made except through a victim, it was necessary that a victim for sin should be provided. . . . But amongst all these there is one Lamb who could take away the sin of all the world, and therefore the other victims have ceased, because this one Victim was such that alone He sufficed for the salvation of all the world. For the rest put away sins by entreaty, He alone by power . . . through whom let the world hold spiritual feast-days, not to the satiety of the flesh, but to the profit of the soul, the mind being purified through the offering of spiritual sacrifices.[1]

This conception of the spiritual sacrifice is one of the loftiest thoughts of the patristic period. It is hardly compatible with the current transactional theory, but the incompatibility was not felt, and until the transactional theory fell before Anselm's criticism the two forms of statement commonly stand side by side without any attempt at reconciliation. It is obvious, of course, that there is in all sacrificial language a danger that the thought implied may be rather that of the Old Testament than of the New, and this is abundantly illustrated not only in the writings of the early fathers but in those of every period. Origen himself is no exception. Yet he is on sure ground when he dwells upon Christ's eternal priesthood, and speaks in mystical language of the spiritual sacrifice offered upon the heavenly altar.

Unless perhaps he means that the blood of Jesus was not only shed in Jerusalem, where the altar stood . . . but that that same blood sprinkled the altar which is in heaven above, where is the congregation of the men of old.[2]

---

[1] Verum quoniam introiit peccatum in hunc mundum, peccati autem necessitas propitiationem requirit, et propitiatio non fit nisi per hostiam, necessarium fuit provideri hostiam pro peccato. . . . Sed et in his omnibus unus est agnus qui totius mundi potuit auferre peccatum, et ideo cessaverunt ceterae hostiae: quia talis haec fuit hostia ut una sola sufficeret pro totius mundi salutem. Ceteri enim precibus peccata, hic solus potestate dimisit . . . per quem festivitates agat spirituales non ad satietatem carnis sed ad profectum spiritus sacrificiis spiritualibus purificatione mentis oblatis (*Hom. in Num.* xxiv. 1).

[2] Nisi quia forte hoc intellegi voluit quod sanguis Jesu non solum in Jerusalem effusus est, ubi erat altare . . . sed et quod supernum altare quod est in coelis, ubi et ecclesia primitivorum est, idem ipse sanguis adsperserit (*Hom. in Lev.* i. 3).

Here indeed for men He poured out the bodily material of His blood, but amongst whatever ministering priests there be in the heavenly realms He offered the vital virtue of His body, as it were a kind of spiritual sacrifice.[1]

Origen clearly does not mean that there was any repetition of the sacrifice of Christ in heaven. It was One Sacrifice, offered once for all, having an eternal aspect as well as a temporal, whereby were reconciled things in heaven as well as things in earth. And so shall all creation, including even the angels who have sinned, ultimately be restored.

Sometimes, however, the mysticism fails, and language of a different type is used. Thus Origen speaks of Christ as suffering all the infamies of the passion for us, who had deserved to suffer them.[2] This might easily be interpreted as involving a theory of vicarious punishment, and in some unguarded passages Origen seems to suggest not that the passion is a revelation of God's eternal attitude to sinful man, but that in some way the passion exerted an influence upon that attitude.

Now Paul adds something more sublime, saying, God set Him forth to be a propitiation, that is, that by offering the victim of His body He might make God propitious to men.[3]

So again he calls Christ

The true priest, who with His own blood made God propitious to thee and reconciled thee to the Father.[4]

In connexion with these phrases it is interesting to notice that Origen makes use in one passage of the

[1] Et hic quidem pro hominibus ipsam corporalem materiam sanguinis sui fudit, in coelestibus vero ministrantibus, si qui illi inibi sunt, sacerdotibus vitalem corporis sui virtutem, velut spirituale quoddam sacrificium immolavit (*Hom. in Lev.* i. 3). The meaning of this is by no means clear.

[2] *In Matt. Comm.* Series 113, vol. iii. p. 912 (ap. Moberly, *op. cit.*).

[3] Nunc addit aliquid sublimius et dicit, proposuit eum Deus propitiationem, quo scilicet per hostiam sui corporis propitium hominibus faceret Deum (*Comm. in Rom.* iii. 8).

[4] Pontificem verum, qui sanguine suo Deum tibi propitium fecit et reconciliavit te Patri (*Hom. in Lev.* ix. 10).

suggestion made by his predecessor, Clement of Alexandria, that the death of Christ, like those of martyrs for their country, may be regarded as having a purifying force.

> He that was crucified willingly accepted this death on behalf of mankind, like those who die for their countries to put an end to pestilences, or to bad harvests, or to stormy weather.[1]

The thought here is purely pagan, of a sacrifice piacular only in the magical sense.

But such language as this, un-Pauline in character, and occurring only in a few chance phrases, must not be stressed. Origen is quite clear that the redemption wrought by Christ is not, as it might suggest, wrought externally to the will of God. Behind the passion lies not only the will of Christ Himself but the will of the Father too. The act itself, indeed, was the act of Satan, and his human agents. Hence Origen can say:

> It was not God that delivered Him up into the hands of men.[2]

But it was only by divine permission that Satan was able so to act, and the act was to his own undoing.

> The Son gave Himself to death for us, so that He was delivered up not only by the Father, but also by Himself. . . . It was from love to men that the Father delivered Him up for us all, but the hostile powers which delivered the Saviour up into the hands of men did not mean to deliver Him up for the salvation of any one, but, so far as in them lay, since none of them knew the wisdom of God hidden in a mystery, they delivered Him up to die, that His enemy death might overcome Him.[3]

---

[1] Ὁ σταυρωθεὶς ἑκὼν τοῦτον τὸν θάνατον ὑπὲρ τοῦ τῶν ἀνθρώπων γένους ἀνεδέξατο, ἀνάλογον τοῖς ἀποθανοῦσι ὑπὲρ πατρίδων ἐπὶ τῷ σβέσαι λοιμικὰ κρατήσαντα καταστήματα ἢ ἀφορίας ἢ δυσπλοΐας (*Con. Cels.* i. 1).

[2] Οὐχ ὁ θεὸς εἰς χεῖρας ἀνθρώπων παρέδωκεν αὐτόν (*Comm. in Matt.* xiii. 9).

[3] Ἔδωκε δὲ καὶ ὁ υἱὸς ὑπὲρ ἡμῶν ἑαυτὸν εἰς θάνατον, ὥστε οὐ μόνον ὑπὸ τοῦ πατρὸς ἀλλὰ ὑφ' ἑαυτοῦ παρεδόθη . . . ὁ μὲν πατὴρ ὑπὲρ ὑμῶν πάντων παρέδωκεν αὐτὸν ἀπὸ φιλανθρωπίας· αἱ δὲ ἀντικείμεναι δυνάμεις παραδοῦσαι τὸν σωτῆρα εἰς χεῖρας ἀνθρώπων οὐκ ἐσκοποῦν τὸ ὑπέρ τινων σωτηρίας παραδιδόναι αὐτόν, ἀλλὰ τὸ ὅσον ἐπ' αὐταῖς, ἐπεὶ οὐδεὶς αὐτῶν ἐγίνωσκε τὴν τοῦ θεοῦ σοφίαν τὴν ἐν μυστηρίῳ ἀποκεκρυμμένην, παρεδίδουν αὐτὸν ἀποθανούμενον ἵνα ὁ ἐχθρὸς αὐτοῦ θάνατος ὑποχείριον αὐτὸν λάβῃ (*Comm. in Matt.* xiii. 8).

The Atonement does not bring about love in God, since it is from God's love that it proceeds. And it is no injustice to Christ, since the Father's will is His will too.

But these Godward statements of Origen's thought need expansion upon the manward side. It remains to be explained how this sacrifice, offered to God, this transaction with the devil, whereby we are released, takes effect in our lives. This manward aspect of Atonement is repeatedly emphasized by Origen. It is within the souls of men that the defeat of the devil takes place.

> That by His power He might destroy our death and dispel the darkness that is upon our soul. . . . And this light which was made in the Word, being also life, appears in the darkness of our souls, and has come to dwell where were the world-rulers of this darkness.[1]

It is by the mystical union with Christ that this is brought about. Origen is just as clear as Irenaeus upon this point, though he does not borrow the characteristic "recapitulation" theory.

> That those who took Him and delivered Him into the hands of men might be laughed to scorn by Him that dwells in the heavens and might be mocked by the Lord, since, to the destruction of their kingdom and rule, contrary to their expectation, they received from the Father the Son, who rose the third day, bringing to nought His enemy death, and making us fellows not only of His death, but also of His resurrection.[2]

---

[1] *Ἵνα τῇ δυνάμει αὐτοῦ καταργήσῃ ἡμῶν τὸν θάνατον καὶ ἐξαφανίσῃ τὸ ἐν τῇ ψυχῇ ἡμῶν σκότος . . . τοῦτο δὲ τὸ φῶς ὃ γέγονεν ἐν τῷ λόγῳ, τύγχανον καὶ ζωή, φαίνει ἐν τῇ σκοτίᾳ τῶν ψυχῶν ἡμῶν καὶ ἐπιδεδήμηκεν ὅπου οἱ κοσμοκράτορες τοῦ σκότους τούτου* (*Comm. in Joann.* ii. 21).

[2] *Ἵν' οἱ παραλάβοντες αὐτόν, καὶ παράδοντες αὐτὸν εἰς χεῖρας ἀνθρώπων, ὑπὸ τοῦ κατοικήσαντος ἐν τοῖς οὐρανοῖς ἐγγελασθῶσι, καὶ ὑπὸ τοῦ κυρίου ἐκμυκτηρισθῶσιν, εἰς κατάλυσιν τῆς ἰδίας βασιλείας καὶ ἀρχῆς παρὰ προσδοκίαν παραλάβοντες ἀπὸ τοῦ πατρὸς τὸν υἱόν, ὅστις τῇ τρίτῃ ἡμέρᾳ ἠγέρθη, τῷ τὸν ἐχθρὸν αὐτοῦ θάνατον κατηργηκέναι καὶ ἡμᾶς πεποιηκέναι συμμόρφους, οὐ μόνον τοῦ θανάτου αὐτοῦ ἀλλὰ καὶ τῆς ἀναστάσεως* (*Comm. in Matt.* xiii. 9). The last clause is based on Phil. 3 10: *συμμορφιζόμενοι τῷ θανάτῳ.*

The thought receives a fuller expression, free from the fetters of the Ransom theory, elsewhere.

They see that, starting with Him, the divine and human natures began to be woven together, so that by fellowship with that which is more divine the human may become divine, not only in Jesus, but also in all those who come to believe and so receive the life which Jesus taught, leading up to friendship with God and to fellowship with Christ Himself every man who lives in accordance with the commands of Jesus.[1]

Here Origen realizes something of St. Paul's mystical sense of the solidarity of mankind in Christ. And thus when he speaks of what Christ suffered for us, we are not to understand that suffering in any rigidly vicarious sense. We, too, have our place in that suffering of Christ, and it is for that reason that Origen can describe it not as mere vengeance but as discipline.[2]

He did not die for us that we may not die, but that we may not die for ourselves; and He was buffeted for us, and spat upon, not that we, who deserved all these things, should not suffer them for our sins, but that suffering them for the sake of justice we may accept them gladly.[3]

We are not so much released from suffering as enabled to suffer in the true way. And so Origen gives a new exegesis of Isaiah 53:

And he took our sins and was bruised for our iniquities, and the chastisement that was owing to us that we might be instructed and receive peace fell upon Him.[4]

---

[1] Ὁρῶσιν ὅτι ἀπ' ἐκείνου ἤρξατο θεία καὶ ἀνθρωπίνη συνυφαίνεσθαι φύσις· ἵν' ἡ ἀνθρωπίνη τῇ πρὸς τὸ θειότερον κοινωνίᾳ γένηται θεία οὐκ ἐν μόνῳ τῷ Ἰησοῦ ἀλλὰ καὶ πᾶσι τοῖς μετὰ τοῦ πιστεύειν ἀναλαμβάνουσι βίον, ὃν Ἰησοῦς ἐδίδαξεν, ἀνάγοντα ἐπὶ τὴν πρὸς τὸν θεὸν φιλίαν καὶ τὴν πρὸς ἐκεῖνον κοινωνίαν πάντα τὸν κατὰ τὰς Ἰησοῦ ὑποθήκας ζῶντα (*Con. Cels.* iii. 28). On this passage see Franks, *op. cit.* i. pp. 60 f.

[2] Not mere ποινή but κόλασις.

[3] Non enim mortuus est pro nobis ut nos non moriamur sed ut pro nobis non moriamur; et alapis caesus est pro nobis, et exputus est, ut ne nos, qui digni fueramus omnibus his, propter nostra peccata patiamur ea, sed ut pro justitia patientes ea gratanter excipiamus (*In Matt. Comm.* series 113, vol. xii. p. 912, ap. Moberly, *op. cit.*).

[4] Καὶ οὗτός γε τὰς ἁμαρτίας ἡμῶν ἔλαβε, καὶ μεμαλάκισται διὰ τὰς ἀνομίας ἡμῶν, καὶ ἡ ὀφειλομένη ἡμῖν εἰς τὸ παιδευθῆναι καὶ εἰρήνην ἀναλαβεῖν κόλασις ἐπ' αὐτὸν γεγένηται (*Comm. in Joann.* xxviii. 14).

The suffering of Christ, in which we too have mystical fellowship, is the awakening of new life in us. It is not merely a penalty, but a true chastisement. And so it is that Origen, with the piacular aspect of Atonement in his mind, can call it a purging or cleansing[1] of our sin. The chastening of God works a real change upon our hearts, and by Christ's example we are enabled to see that this chastisement is sent by God's love, and not by His wrath, and to accept it thankfully.

> Death, which is imposed as a penalty for sin, is the purging of that very sin for which it is ordered that it should be imposed. Sin therefore is done away through the penalty of death, and there remains nothing upon this charge for the day of judgement and the penalty of eternal fire to find. . . . Wherefore now if any one of us should chance to find in himself the memory of any sin upon his conscience, if any knows himself to be liable to punishment, let him flee to penitence, and accept a willing doing to death of the flesh, that, cleansed from sin during this present life, our spirit may find its way clean and pure to Christ.[2]

Such language as this quite outweighs the objectionable features of the Ransom theory as stated by Origen, while at the same time avoiding the danger of overstatement along the lines of vicarious punishment.

We may notice, finally, that Origen sometimes uses phrases which suggest the Moral theory:

> Even apart from the value for all of His death on behalf of men, He showed men how they ought to die for righteousness' sake,[3]

with the triumphant result that

---

[1] *Κάθαρσις* (*Con. Cels.* vi. 44).

[2] Mors, quae poenae causa infertur pro peccato, purgatio est peccati ipsius pro quo jubetur inferri. Absolvitur ergo peccatum per poenam mortis, nec superest aliquid quod pro hoc crimine judicii dies et poena aeterni ignis inveniat. . . . Unde et nunc si quis forte nostrum recordatur in semet ipso alicujus peccati conscientiam, si quis se obnoxium vita, spiritus noster mundus et purus pergat ad Christum Dominum nostrum (*Hom. in Lev.* xiv. 4).

[3] *Ὑποδεδειχέναι ὡς δεῖ ὑπὲρ εὐσεβείας ἀποθνήσκειν, χωρὶς τοῦ χρήσιμόν τι τῷ παντὶ γεγονέναι τὸ ὑπὲρ ἀνθρώπων αὐτὸν ἀποθανεῖν* (*Con. Cels.* ii. 16).

> . . . many even in our day, though they knew that if they confessed Christianity they would die, while if they denied Him they would be set free and would receive their property back again, yet scorned death and gladly chose to die for the sake of righteousness.[1]

So, too, Christ's death is said to have given weight to His teaching and to have assisted in spreading it abroad.[2] But such thoughts as these do not stand by themselves. They must be taken in conjunction with Origen's thought as a whole, and there fall naturally, as Origen himself sees,[3] into their true position.

This general attitude of Origen towards the Atonement may be taken as characteristic of the Eastern Church during the first seven centuries. Though there is a certain variation in detail, the main outlines of his thought are followed by nearly all the subsequent writers who have anything definite to say about the doctrine. As with him the transactional theory is rather introduced to explain a difficult point in connexion with God's justice than intended as a complete account of the method of redemption. The Godward and manward aspects were never forgotten, even though they seldom received formal statement. In particular the description of Christ's death as a sacrifice, fulfilling the intention of the Old Testament sacrifices, and thereby abrogating them, is in constant evidence.

It is especially noteworthy that the very Johannine emphasis upon the Incarnation which we have seen in both Irenaeus and Origen continues throughout this whole period. The Passion was always to the Greek mind an episode crowning and consummating the work of the whole incarnate life of Christ. It is the completion of that which was begun when " the Word became

[1] *Πολλοὶ δὲ καὶ τῶν καθ' ἡμᾶς, ἐπιστάμενοι ὡς ὁμολογήσαντες μὲν Χριστιανισμὸν ἀποθανοῦνται, ἀρνησάμενοι δὲ ἀπολυθήσονται καὶ τὰ ὑπάρχοντα ἀπολήψονται, κατεφρόνησαν μὲν τοῦ βίου, ἑκουσίως δὲ τὸν ὑπὲρ εὐσεβείας θάνατον εἵλοντο* (*Con. Cels.* ii. 17).

[2] *Hom. in Jer.* x. 2

[3] See *Con. Cels.* ii. 16, cited above.

flesh." It is true that the language of the fathers upon this subject varies considerably, from the strong mysticism of Irenaeus and Origen to the crude idea of Gregory of Nyssa that the flesh was a veil adopted for the purpose of deceiving Satan. But on the whole it may be said that the mystical apprehension prevails, and that there is a real sense throughout the period of a real relation to man into which Christ has entered, so that we may be one with Him in dying to sin and in rising again to newness of life.

This width of outlook among the Greek fathers may be illustrated from Eusebius the historian, who, as bishop of Caesarea in the early fourth century, was heir to the tradition of Origen. Eusebius is content to enumerate six reasons for the death of Christ, leaving the connexion between them quite unexplained:[1] Christ died to prove His lordship over both living and dead, to redeem from sin, to make atonement, to destroy Satan's power, to show by His resurrection the reality of the future life, and to do away with the sacrifices of the old covenant. Such a thinker as this, however vague his views may be, is clearly not at the mercy of any hide-bound transactional theory.

Even in Gregory of Nyssa, the writer who beyond all others gave the transactional theory its characteristic form, we may find hints of a higher point of view. His conception of the purpose of creation is a very grand one. God, in His superabundant love, made man free that he might share in the divine perfection. Man was therefore free, and ought for ever to have progressed towards the good. Through the fall, however, the direction of this progression was changed.[2] Evil prospered instead of good, and the whole universe was out of harmony. It was to restore this harmony that the Incarnation was necessary, since so alone could the power of the evil one be broken.

[1] *Demonstr. Evang.* iv. 12. [2] *Or. Cat.* 8.

When there has been a restoration of those now lying in sin to their primal state, a harmony of thanksgiving will arise from all creation, as well from those who in the process of the purgation have suffered chastisement, as from those who needed not any purgation at all. These and the like benefits the great mystery of the divine Incarnation bestows.[1]

The thought is much wider than that of a mere deception of the devil. Christ's death achieves a true cleansing of the soul of man, and even, it is hinted, of the devil himself.

. . . both freeing man from evil and healing even him who introduced the evil. For the chastisement of moral disease, however painful it may be, is a healing of its infirmity.[2]

There is something living and vital in this view of Atonement as the purging of a corruption. In this respect Gregory comes closer to Athanasius than to any other early writer, though the suggestion was not unknown to Origen.[3] And it is clearly untrue to Gregory's thought to regard the Atonement as something wrought outside man, having, as it were, only a secondary effect upon man's heart. It is by repentance that man must be brought back, and his diseased nature restored to its original beauty.[4] And though Gregory regards the Incarnation as necessary in the first place to the outwitting of the devil, he has grasped also its mystical effect, whereby the life of Christ becomes our life too.

Now He who holds nature together in existence is transfused in us; while at that other time He was transfused throughout our nature, in order that our nature might by this transfusion

---

[1] Ἐπειδὰν ἡ εἰς τὸ ἀρχαῖον ἀποκατάστασις τῶν νῦν ἐν κακίᾳ κειμένων γένηται, ὁμόφωνος ἡ εὐχαριστία παρὰ πάσης ἔσται τῆς κτίσεως, καὶ τῶν ἐν τῇ καθάρσει κεκολασμένων καὶ τῶν μηδὲ τὴν ἀρχὴν ἐπιδεηθέντων καθάρσεως. ταῦτα καὶ τὰ τοιαῦτα παραδίδωσι τὸ μέγα μυστήριον τῆς θείας ἐνανθρωπήσεως (*Or. Cat.* 26).

[2] Τόν τε ἄνθρωπον τῆς κακίας ἐλευθερῶν καὶ αὐτὸν τὸν τῆς κακίας εὑρετὴν ἰώμενος. ἴασις γάρ ἐστιν ἀρρωστίας ἡ τοῦ νοσήματος κάθαρσις, κἂν ἐπίπονος ᾖ (*Or. Cat.* 26).

[3] See p. 67.

[4] *Or. Cat.* 8.

of the divine become itself divine, rescued as it was from death, and put beyond the reach of the caprice of the antagonist. For His return from death becomes to our mortal race the commencement of our return to the immortal life.[1]

There is nothing here unworthy or untrue. Even though sin stands in the way, God works out His purpose for the soul of man. Despite the emphasis which Gregory has unfortunately laid upon the transaction with the devil, that is after all a mere episode in the grand plan of salvation, which is wrought out through the transformation of man's nature, made one with the divine through the power of the Incarnation.

What has been said will perhaps suffice as an attempt to illustrate the characteristic methods of thought of the early Greek Church. We may turn to the two great and independent thinkers in whose works the ideas which were to mould the future were beginning to make themselves felt.

Athanasius,[2] the great champion of the Nicene faith against Arius, in the closest touch with all the men and movements of his day, yet stands curiously apart in the history of the doctrine of the Atonement. He has been claimed as the father, not only of the later satisfaction theories,[3] but even of the penal theories of the Reformation divines.[4] For the former position there is certainly something to be said, since it is upon the Godward aspect of the Atonement that Athanasius, like Anselm, lays especial stress, though the feudal idea of the dignity of God, which lies at the foundation

[1] Νῦν μὲν οὖν ἐγκέκραται ἡμῖν ὡς συνέχων ἐν τῷ εἶναι τὴν φύσιν· τότε δὲ κατεμίχθη πρὸς τὸ ἡμέτερον, ἵνα τὸ ἡμέτερον τῇ πρὸς τὸ θεῖον ἐπιμιξίᾳ γένηται θεῖον, ἐξαιρεθὲν τοῦ θανάτου καὶ τῆς τοῦ ἀντικειμένου τυραννίδος ἔξω γενόμενον· ἡ γὰρ ἐκείνου ἀπὸ τοῦ θανάτου ἐπάνοδος ἀρχὴ τῷ θνητῷ γένει τῆς εἰς τὴν ἀθάνατον ζωὴν ἐπανόδου γίγνεται (*Or. Cat.* 25).

[2] For a full and sympathetic treatment of Athanasius, and his point of view, see Moberly, *op. cit.* pp. 349 ff. With this should be contrasted Denney's discussion in *The Christian Doctrine of Reconciliation* (pp. 36 ff.), and Melville Scott, *Athanasius on the Atonement*.

[3] So *e.g.* Gieseler, Scott Lidgett.

[4] So *e.g.* Hagenbach.

of Anselm's thought, had no parallel in the political or theological theory of the days of Athanasius.

There is, indeed, a fundamental difference between the two thinkers in their conception of sin and its effects. Here Athanasius resembles the other writers of his day far less than does Anselm himself. The ordinary view of sin was that it was disobedience to the command of God, beginning at the disobedience of Adam, and bringing all mankind under the power of the devil, God's opponent. Anselm merely transmuted this by regarding the disobedience as a dishonour to the dignity of God, demanding the fullest reparation.[1] Athanasius has a far stronger and deeper conception. For him, too, sin begins with disobedience, but he sees that disobedience not merely in its effects upon the relations of man with the devil or with God, but in its terrible influence upon the soul of the sinner. It enters into the very essence of his being like a destroying force. It is no longer regarded as an act or acts, calling for punishment, but as a corruption bringing forth death and in sore need of the healing touch of the physician. And such healing can only be brought by the Logos, the creative Word, the source of all life, who alone can give men new life, overcoming the death due to the corruption of sin.

Athanasius has given his thought clear and full expression in his Treatise on the Incarnation,[2] a work which perhaps owes its unsurpassed freshness and vigour to the fact that it was written while its author was still

[1] *Cur Deus Homo?* i. 11. 21.

[2] J. K. Mozley (*op. cit.* p. 105) protests against "the tendency to expound Athanasius by an almost exclusive reference to this work." It remains, however, his one full treatment of the subject, and the references in his later writings are in the main in keeping with it, except that the Logos doctrine recedes into the background, and more emphasis is laid on the Sonship of Christ. Melville Scott (*op. cit.*) argues at length that his works show a development of thought in which more and more justice is done to the efficacy of the human experience of Christ, culminating in the Cross, and the metaphysical Incarnation is not so much stressed.

quite a young man, before the stress of the long struggle with Arianism. The argument, so far as it concerns our subject, is as follows.

Athanasius begins with the origin of the universe. It was by the Word of God that the world, including man, was made out of nothing. But to mankind He gave a further special privilege.

He did not barely create man, as He did all the irrational creatures on the earth, but made them after His own image, giving them a portion even of the power of His own Word; so that having as it were a kind of reflexion of the Word, and being made rational, they might be able to abide ever in blessedness.[1]

But knowing that man's will was free to fall He placed man in His own garden and gave them a law

. . . that if they transgressed and turned back, and became evil, they might know that they were incurring that corruption of death which was theirs by nature: no longer to live in paradise, but cast out of it from that time forth to die and to abide in death and in corruption. . . . By "dying ye shall die," what else could be meant than not dying merely, but also abiding ever in the corruption of death.[2]

Athanasius is quite clear upon this distinction between physical and spiritual death, which is one of his most important contributions to the development of the doctrine. It is not so much that sin causes death as that it allows nature to take its normal finite course.

For man is by nature mortal, inasmuch as he is made out of what is not; but by reason of his likeness to Him that is . . . he would stay his natural corruption, and remain incorrupt.[3]

---

[1] Οὐχ ἁπλῶς, ὥσπερ πάντα τὰ ἐπὶ γῆς ἄλογα ζῶα, ἔκτισε τοὺς ἀνθρώπους· ἀλλὰ κατὰ τὴν ἑαυτοῦ εἰκόνα ἐποίησεν αὐτούς, μεταδοὺς αὐτοῖς καὶ τῆς τοῦ ἰδίου Λόγου δυνάμεως, ἵνα ὥσπερ σκιάς τινας ἔχοντες τοῦ Λόγου, καὶ γενόμενοι λογικοί, διαμένειν ἐν μακαριότητι δυνηθῶσι (*De Inc.* 3; the translations are from the version by A. Robertson).

[2] Εἰ δὲ παραβαῖεν καὶ στραφέντες γένοιντο φαῦλοι, γινώσκοιεν ἑαυτοὺς τὴν ἐν θανάτῳ κατὰ φύσιν φθορὰν ὑπομένειν, καὶ μηκέτι μὲν ἐν παραδείσῳ ζῆν, ἔξω δὲ τούτου λοιπὸν ἀποθνήσκοντας μένειν ἐν τῷ θανάτῳ καὶ ἐν τῇ φθορᾷ . . . τὸ δὲ θανάτῳ ἀποθανεῖσθε, τί ἂν ἄλλο εἴη ἢ τὸ μὴ μόνον ἀποθνήσκειν, ἀλλὰ καὶ ἐν τῇ τοῦ θανάτου φθορᾷ διαμένειν; (*De Inc.* 3).

[3] Ἔστι μὲν γὰρ κατὰ φύσιν ἄνθρωπος θνητός, ἅτε δὴ ἐξ οὐκ ὄντων γεγονώς. διὰ δὲ τὴν πρὸς τὸν ὄντα ὁμοιότητα . . . ἤμβλυνεν ἂν τὴν κατὰ φύσιν φθοράν, καὶ ἔμεινεν ἄφθαρτος (*De Inc.* 4).

> But men, having despised and rejected the contemplation of God, and devised and contrived evil for themselves . . . received the condemnation of death with which they had been threatened. . . . For transgression of the commandment was turning them back to their natural state, so that just as they have had their being out of nothing, so also, as might be expected, they might look for corruption into nothing in the course of time.[1]

So in sin God's work in creation is undone. It is noteworthy that Athanasius hardly mentions the devil at all in this account, and that even then the responsibility is expressly laid upon man.

> Men, having rejected things eternal, and, by counsel of the devil, turned to the things of corruption, became the cause of their own corruption.[2]

Yet to some extent "death" takes the place of the devil. It has a certain legal hold, and the law that gives it that hold cannot be evaded, because it was laid down by God. And so arose the great problem. Was God's word to be broken, or was His creation, threatened by the corruption of death, to fail?

> For death, as I said above, gained from that time forth a legal hold over us: and it was impossible to evade the law, since it had been laid down by God because of the transgression, and the result was in truth at once monstrous and unseemly. For it were monstrous, firstly, that God, having spoken, should prove false. . . . For God would not be true, if, when He had said that we should die, man died not. Again, it were unseemly that creatures once made rational, and having partaken of the Word, should go to ruin, and turn again toward non-existence by the way of corruption. For it were not worthy of God's goodness that the things he had made should waste away because of the deceit practised on men by the devil.[3]

---

[1] Ἄνθρωποι δὲ κατολιγωρήσαντες καὶ ἀποστραφέντες τὴν πρὸς τὸν θεὸν κατανόησιν, λογισάμενοι δὲ καὶ ἐπινοήσαντες ἑαυτοῖς τὴν κακίαν, . . . ἔσχον τὴν προαπειληθεῖσαν τοῦ θανάτου κατάκρισιν. . . . ἡ γὰρ παράβασις τῆς ἐντολῆς εἰς τὸ κατὰ φύσιν αὐτοὺς ἐπέστρεφεν, ἵνα ὥσπερ οὐκ ὄντες γεγόνασιν, οὕτως καὶ τὴν εἰς τὸ ⟨μὴ⟩ εἶναι φθορὰν ὑπομείνωσι τῷ χρόνῳ εἰκότως (*De Inc.* 4).

[2] Οἱ δὲ ἄνθρωποι ἀποστραφέντες τὰ αἰώνια, καὶ συμβουλίᾳ τοῦ διαβόλου εἰς τὰ τῆς φθορᾶς ἐπιστραφέντες, ἑαυτοῖς αἴτιοι τῆς ἐν τῷ θανάτῳ φθορᾶς γεγόνασιν (*De Inc.* 5).

[3] Καὶ γὰρ καὶ ὁ θάνατος, ὡς προεῖπον, νόμῳ λοιπὸν ἴσχυε καθ' ἡμῶν· καὶ οὐχ οἷόν τε ἦν τὸν νόμον ἐκφυγεῖν, διὰ τὸ ὑπὸ θεοῦ τεθεῖσθαι τοῦτον

Justice must be considered, but, as Athanasius is careful to point out,[1] this justice is in some part at least a justice towards God Himself.

What then was God to do? Would it suffice that He should demand penitence?

> But repentance would, firstly, fail to guard the just claim of God. For He would still be none the more true if men did not remain in the grasp of death; nor, secondly, does repentance call men back from what is their nature—it merely stays them from acts of sin.[2]

No writer of the early Church has grasped so clearly the twofold condition, the necessity for the satisfaction of justice, and the necessity for a new nature in the sinner. This twofold condition could not be satisfied except by the Word as Creator. By coming in the flesh He could fulfil the law of death. And as the author of life He could give new life to perishing man.

> And thus taking from our bodies one of like nature, because all were under penalty of the corruption of death He gave it over to death in the stead of all, and offered it to the Father—doing this, moreover, of His loving-kindness, to the end that, firstly, all being held to have died in Him, the law involving

---

τῆς παραβάσεως χάριν· καὶ ἦν ἄτοπον ὁμοῦ καὶ ἀπρεπὲς τὸ γινόμενον ἀληθῶς. ἄτοπον μὲν γὰρ ἦν εἰπόντα τὸν θεὸν ψεύσασθαι, . . . οὐκ ἀληθὴς γὰρ ἦν ὁ θεὸς εἰ εἰπόντος αὐτοῦ ἀποθνήσκειν ἡμᾶς μὴ ἀπέθνησκεν ὁ ἄνθρωπος. ἀπρεπὲς δὲ ἦν πάλιν τὰ ἅπαξ γενόμενα λογικὰ καὶ τοῦ Λόγου αὐτοῦ μετασχόντα παραπόλλυσθαι, καὶ πάλιν εἰς τὸ μὴ εἶναι διὰ τῆς φθορᾶς ἐπιστρέφειν. οὐκ ἄξιον γὰρ ἦν τῆς ἀγαθότητος τοῦ θεοῦ τὰ ὑπ' αὐτοῦ γενόμενα διαφθείρεσθαι διὰ τὴν παρὰ τοῦ διαβόλου γενομένην τοῖς ἀνθρώποις ἀπάτην (*De Inc.* 6). Cf. Cyril of Jerm. *Cat.* xiii. 33: ἔδει οὖν ἓν ἐκ τῶν δύο γενέσθαι, ἢ ἀληθεύοντα θεὸν πάντας ἀνελεῖν ἢ φιλανθρωπευόμενον παραλῦσαι τὴν ἀπόφασιν.

[1] *De Inc.* 7.

[2] Ἀλλ' ἡ μετάνοια οὔτε τὸ εὔλογον τὸ πρὸς τὸν θεὸν ἐφύλαττεν. ἔμενε γὰρ πάλιν οὐκ ἀληθής, μὴ κρατουμένων ἐν τῷ θανάτῳ τῶν ἀνθρώπων· οὔτε δὲ ἡ μετάνοια ἀπὸ τῶν κατὰ φύσιν ἀνακαλεῖται, ἀλλὰ μόνον παύει τῶν ἁμαρτημάτων (*De Inc.* 7). This thought is more fully expanded in *Con. Ar.* ii. 68, where Athanasius draws out the necessity that God should do more than merely put away the curse by a word. Some security is needed that man may not fall again from grace, "for ever falling short of the law because of the weakness of their flesh."

the ruin of men might be undone (inasmuch as its power was fully spent in the Lord's body, and had no longer holding ground against men, His peers), and, secondly, whereas men had turned towards corruption, He might turn them again toward incorruption.[1]

In virtue of the oneness of the Word with us we in Him satisfy the demand of death. But further He is incorruptible, and therefore the body which he takes is incorruptible too, and so we in Him attain incorruption.

. . . that henceforth corruption might be stayed from all by the grace of the resurrection. Whence, by offering unto death the body He Himself had taken, as an offering and sacrifice free from any stain, straightway He put away death from all His peers by the offering of an equivalent. For, being over all, the Word of God naturally by offering His own temple and corporeal instrument for the life of all satisfied the debt by His death. And thus He, the incorruptible Son of God, being conjoined with all by a like nature, naturally clothed all with incorruption, by the promise of the resurrection. For the actual corruption in death has no longer holding-ground against men, by reason of the Word, which by His one body has come to dwell among them.[2]

It is as when the king takes up his abode in the city.

[1] Καὶ οὕτως ἀπὸ τῶν ἡμετέρων τὸ ὅμοιον λαβών, διὰ τὸ πάντας ὑπευθύνους εἶναι τῇ τοῦ θανάτου φθορᾷ, ἀντὶ πάντων αὐτὸ θανάτῳ παραδιδούς, προσῆγε τῷ Πατρί, καὶ τοῦτο φιλανθρώπως ποιῶν, ἵνα ὡς μὲν πάντων ἀποθανόντων ἐν αὐτῷ λυθῇ ὁ κατὰ τῆς φθορᾶς τῶν ἀνθρώπων νόμος (ἅτε δὴ πληρωθείσης τῆς ἐξουσίας ἐν τῷ κυριακῷ σώματι, καὶ μηκέτι χώραν ἔχοντος κατὰ τῶν ὁμοίων ἀνθρώπων)· ὡς δὲ εἰς φθορὰν ἀναστρέψαντας τοὺς ἀνθρώπους πάλιν εἰς τὴν ἀφθαρσίαν ἐπιστρέψῃ (*De Inc.* 8). Very similar language is used in *Con. Ar.* ii. 69.

[2] Ἵνα . . . λοιπὸν ἀπὸ πάντων ἡ φθορὰ παύσηται τῇ τῆς ἀναστάσεως χάριτι. ὅθεν ὡς ἱερεῖον καὶ θῦμα παντὸς ἐλεύθερον σπίλου, ὃ αὐτὸς ἑαυτῷ ἔλαβε σῶμα προσάγων εἰς θάνατον, ἀπὸ πάντων εὐθὺς τῶν ὁμοίων ἠφάνιζε τὸν θάνατον τῇ προσφορᾷ τοῦ καταλλήλου. ὑπὲρ πάντας γὰρ ὢν ὁ Λόγος τοῦ θεοῦ, εἰκότως τὸν ἑαυτοῦ ναὸν καὶ τὸ σωματικὸν ὄργανον προσάγων ἀντίψυχον ὑπὲρ πάντων, ἐπλήρου τὸ ὀφειλόμενον ἐν τῷ θανάτῳ· καὶ οὕτως συνὼν διὰ τοῦ ὁμοίου τοῖς πᾶσιν ὁ ἄφθαρτος τοῦ θεοῦ υἱὸς εἰκότως τοὺς πάντας ἐνέδυσεν ἀφθαρσίαν ἐν τῇ περὶ τῆς ἀναστάσεως ἐπαγγελίᾳ. καὶ αὐτὴ γὰρ ἡ ἐν τῷ θανάτῳ φθορὰ κατὰ τῶν ἀνθρώπων οὐκέτι χώραν ἔχει διὰ τὸν ἐνοικήσαντα Λόγον ἐν τούτοις διὰ τοῦ ἑνὸς σώματος (*De Inc.* 9). The last words are important as connecting the indwelling of the Word in man directly with the Incarnation.

No hostile force dare any longer make any attack upon it. So now

> The whole conspiracy of evil against mankind is checked.[1]

In this well-known passage there is a combination of two quite distinct ideas as to the reason for the efficacy of Christ's death. In the first place it is mystically the death of all, so that the sentence of the law against all is actually carried out. And, secondly, His body, as the abode of the Word, is infinitely precious, and is thus a real "equivalent" for sin. It is this thought that connects Athanasius with the satisfaction theories. But he clearly does not regard this offering of an equivalent as in itself supplying a complete account of redemption. The progress of corruption in man must be stayed too. And this is accomplished by the continuing presence of the Word among men in the power not only of the Incarnation but of the Resurrection also, completing what the Cross began.[2]

It was thus to Christ's death and following resurrection that the Incarnation looked. In the next few chapters Athanasius goes on to show that Christ's coming was fitting for other reasons also, and especially that the ignorance into which man's sin had brought him might be enlightened by His teaching, by the presence among men of incarnate Wisdom, revealing the invisible through the things of sense.[3]

A summary of the theory is then given:

> It was in the power of none other to turn the corruptible to incorruption except the Saviour Himself that had at the beginning also made all things out of nought: and that none could create anew the likeness of God's image for men, save the

---

[1] *Πᾶσα ἡ κατὰ τῶν ἀνθρώπων παρὰ τῶν ἐχθρῶν ἐπιβουλὴ πέπαυται* (*De Inc.* 9).

[2] For the immanence of Christ in man, so that man actually shares His life and death, cf. *Con. Ar.* i. 41, iii. 33, iv. 67. This is connected in particular with the work of the Holy Spirit (*Con. Ar.* i. 43), and not merely after Pentecost, since when the Spirit descended upon Jesus at His baptism, He came upon us too (*Con. Ar.* i. 47).

[3] *De Inc.* 15.

Image of the Father: and that none other could render the mortal immortal save our Lord Jesus Christ, who is the very life: and that none other could teach men of the Father, and destroy the worship of idols, save the Word that orders all things and is alone the true only-begotten Son of the Father. But since it was necessary also that the debt owing from all should be paid again: for, as I have already said, it was owing that all should die, for which especial cause indeed He came among us: to this intent, after the proofs of His Godhead from His works, He next offered up His sacrifice also on behalf of all, yielding His temple to death in the stead of all, in order firstly to make men quit and free of their old trespass, and further to show Himself more powerful even than death, displaying His own body incorruptible, as first-fruits of the resurrection of all. . . . The body, then, as sharing the same nature with all, for it was a human body, though by an unparalleled miracle it was formed of a virgin only, yet, being mortal, was to die also, conformably to its peers. But by virtue of the union of the Word with it, it was no longer subject to corruption according to its own nature, but by reason of the Word that was come to dwell in it it was placed out of the reach of corruption. And so it was that two marvels came to pass at once, that the death of all was accomplished in the Lord's body, and that death and corruption were wholly done away by reason of the Word that was united with it. For there was need of death, and death must needs be suffered on behalf of all, that the debt owing from all might be paid. Whence, as I said before, the Word, since it was not possible for Him to die, as He was immortal, took to Himself a body such as could die, that He might offer it as His own in the stead of all, and, as suffering, through His union with it, on behalf of all, "Bring to nought him that had the power of death, that is the devil; and might deliver them who through fear of death were all their lifetime subject to bondage."[1]

---

[1] Οὐκ ἄλλου ἦν τὸ φθαρτὸν εἰς ἀφθαρσίαν μεταβαλεῖν, εἰ μὴ αὐτοῦ τοῦ Σωτῆρος, τοῦ καὶ τὴν ἀρχὴν ἐξ οὐκ ὄντων πεποιηκότος τὰ ὅλα· καὶ οὐκ ἄλλου ἦν τὸ κατ' εἰκόνα πάλιν ἀνακτίσαι τοῖς ἀνθρώποις, εἰ μὴ τῆς εἰκόνος τοῦ Πατρός· καὶ οὐκ ἄλλου ἦν τὸ θνητὸν ἀθάνατον παραστῆσαι, εἰ μὴ τῆς αὐτοζωῆς οὔσης τοῦ κυρίου ἡμῶν Ἰησοῦ Χριστοῦ· καὶ οὐκ ἄλλου ἦν περὶ Πατρὸς διδάξαι, καὶ τὴν εἰδώλων καθαιρῆσαι θρησκείαν, εἰ μὴ τοῦ τὰ πάντα διακοσμοῦντος Λόγου, καὶ μόνου τοῦ Πατρὸς ὄντος Υἱοῦ μονογενοῦς ἀληθινοῦ. ἐπειδὴ δὲ καὶ τὸ ὀφειλόμενον παρὰ πάντων ἔδει λοιπὸν ἀποδοθῆναι· ὠφείλετο γὰρ πάντας, ὡς προεῖπον, ἀποθανεῖν, δι' ὃ μάλιστα καὶ ἐπεδήμησεν· τούτου ἕνεκεν μετὰ τὰς περὶ τῆς θεότητος αὐτοῦ ἐκ τῶν ἔργων ἀποδείξεις, ἤδη λοιπὸν καὶ ὑπὲρ πάντων τὴν θυσίαν ἀνέφερεν, ἀντὶ πάντων τὸν ἑαυτοῦ ναὸν εἰς θάνατον παραδιδούς, ἵνα τοὺς μὲν πάντας

Little comment is needed. The theory is that of the earlier chapters, the same combination of Godward and manward ideas being apparent. It is, however, to be noticed that the language has become rather more transactional in character, especially in the twice-used phrase, "the debt owing from all." There is still, however, nothing to suggest the current contemporary theories of this debt as in any sense due to the devil.

The twofold character of the thought of Athanasius is clearly to be seen in the view of death which the above argument implies. Two quite distinct ideas of death are combined, corresponding to spiritual and to physical death respectively.[1] There is, in the first place, the climax of the process of corruption "into nothing," resulting from man's sin. This is spiritual death, in which man abides for ever in corruption.[2] And there is, secondly, death regarded as something due on account of sin. Athanasius does not attempt an analysis of the nature of this debt, further than to say that God's threat of death against man had to be fulfilled. This is physical death, and is a stage in that corruption of which spiritual death is the completion.

ἀνυπευθύνους καὶ ἐλευθέρους τῆς ἀρχαίας παραβάσεως ποιήσῃ· δείξῃ δὲ ἑαυτὸν καὶ θανάτου κρείττονα, ἀπαρχὴν τῆς τῶν ὅλων ἀναστάσεως τὸ ἴδιον σῶμα ἄφθαρτον ἐπιδεικνύμενος . . . τὸ μὲν οὖν σῶμα, ὡς καὶ αὐτὸ κοινὴν ἔχον τοῖς πᾶσι τὴν οὐσίαν· σῶμα γὰρ ἦν ἀνθρώπινον· εἰ καὶ καινοτέρῳ θαύματι συνέστη ἐκ παρθένου μόνης, ὅμως θνητὸν ὂν κατὰ ἀκολουθίαν τῶν ὁμοίων καὶ ἀπέθνησκε· τῇ δὲ τοῦ Λόγου εἰς αὐτὸ ἐπιβάσει, οὐκέτι κατὰ τὴν ἰδίαν φύσιν ἐφθείρετο· ἀλλὰ διὰ τὸν ἐνοικήσαντα τοῦ θεοῦ Λόγον ἐκτὸς ἐγίνετο φθορᾶς. καὶ συνεβαίνεν ἀμφότερα ἐν ταὐτῷ γενέσθαι παραδόξως· ὅτι τε ὁ πάντων θάνατος ἐν τῷ κυριακῷ σώματι ἐπληροῦτο, καὶ ὁ θάνατος καὶ ἡ φθορὰ διὰ τὸν συνόντα Λόγον ἐξηφανίζετο. θανάτου γὰρ ἦν χρεία, καὶ θάνατον ὑπὲρ πάντων ἔδει γενέσθαι, ἵνα τὸ παρὰ πάντων ὀφειλόμενον γένηται. ὅθεν, ὡς προεῖπον, ὁ Λόγος, ἐπεὶ οὐκ οἷόν τε ἦν αὐτὸν ἀποθανεῖν· ἀθάνατος γὰρ ἦν· ἔλαβεν ἑαυτῷ σῶμα τὸ δυνάμενον ἀποθανεῖν, ἵνα ὡς ἴδιον ἀντὶ πάντων αὐτὸ προσενέγκῃ, καὶ ὡς αὐτὸς ὑπὲρ πάντων πάσχων, διὰ τὴν πρὸς αὐτὸ ἐπίβασιν, καταργήσῃ τὸν τὸ κράτος ἔχοντα τοῦ θανάτου, τουτέστι τὸν διάβολον· καὶ ἀπαλλάξῃ τούτους, ὅσοι φόβῳ θανάτου διὰ παντὸς τοῦ ζῆν ἔνοχοι ἦσαν δουλείας (*De Inc.* 20).

[1] Cf. the contrast made by Gregory the Great between external and internal death (*Moral.* ix. 65).

[2] *De Inc.* 3, quoted above.

From what then is man delivered? Not from the death of the body, for that he must still suffer, but from this dissolution "into nothing," the goal of corruption. Death has lost its sting, for it is now but the gate of resurrection.

We may make one or two comments upon the position outlined above.

1. It is not justifiable to claim Athanasius as the precursor of the later Penal theories. There is no sign that he anywhere regards death as penal suffering, and still less that he regards Christ's death as vicarious punishment. He does indeed use the phrases "suffering on behalf of all," "death on behalf of all";[1] but these must be interpreted in accordance with his strong sense of the solidarity of mankind in the incarnate Word, "seeing that all die in Him."

2. The language about "the debt" is much more on the lines of the Satisfaction theory. Though, indeed, Athanasius never explicitly says that it is to God that the debt is due, the Godward trend of his thought is everywhere apparent, and the same metaphor, of that which is owing or due to God, is constantly used by Anselm. There is little real connexion with Origen's conception of a bargain struck with the devil. Anselmic, too, is the emphasis laid by Athanasius upon the great worth of that body which the Word took for Himself.

3. It is peculiar in Athanasius that so much stress is placed upon the work of the Word in creation as bringing about the mystical union of man and God. Sometimes the Incarnation seems to take quite a secondary place, and merely to be due to the necessity that the Word should have a body capable of death wherewith to pay our debt. But at times Athanasius uses expres-

[1] Ὑπὲρ πάντων. Twice at least (*De Inc.* 20, 21) he uses ἀντὶ πάντων, but this cannot possibly be pressed. Harnack, however, sees in it a clear statement of the substitutionary penal theory (*op. cit.* vi. 55). J. K. Mozley (*op. cit.* p. 107) finds "more than a hint of substitution."

sions which show that he too shared the great conviction of the Greek fathers upon this subject :

The Word became flesh that He might make man capable of receiving deity.[1]

He became man that we might be made God.[2]

4. He shows little sense of the Fatherhood of God in relation to the Atonement. It is the Word, creative Wisdom, rather than the Son, that redeems. Hence little is said about the love of God. This is curious in view of the position which he takes up against Arius a few years later.

Athanasius, Greek though he is in all his methods of thought, had written almost as though he did not know the current theory of his day. Gregory of Nazianzum, the one writer to repudiate that theory explicitly, is nevertheless strongly under its influence. We may quote his well-known discussion at length :

To whom was that blood offered that was shed for us, and why was it shed ? . . . We were detained in bondage by the evil one, sold under sin, and receiving pleasure in exchange for wickedness. Now, since a ransom belongs only to him who holds in bondage, I ask To whom was this offered, and for what cause ? If to the evil one, fie upon the outrage ! If the robber receives ransom not only from God, but a ransom which consists of God Himself, and has such an illustrious payment for his tyranny, a payment for whose sake it would have been right for him to have left us alone altogether. But if to the Father, I ask first How ? For it was not by Him that we were held in bondage. And next, On what principle did the blood of His only-begotten Son delight the Father, who would not receive even Isaac, when he was being offered by his father, . . . ? Is it not evident that the Father accepts Him, but neither asked for Him nor demanded Him ; but on account of the providential

---

[1] Ὁ Λόγος σὰρξ ἐγένετο ἵνα τὸν ἄνθρωπον δεκτικὸν θεότητος ποιήσῃ (*Con. Ar.* ii. 59).

[2] Αὐτὸς γὰρ ἐνηνθρώπησεν ἵνα ἡμεῖς θεοποιηθῶμεν (*De Inc.* 54). Scott Lidgett (*op. cit.* p. 66) and Denney still more strongly (*op. cit.* pp. 36 ff.) criticize very severely the effect of the Logos doctrine upon Athanasius' thought. Denney argues that the result is to force the doctrine of the Atonement into a purely speculative and metaphysical mould, the moral aspect receding into the background. See, however, Melville Scott's full discussion (*op. cit.*).

plan, and because humanity must be sanctified by the Humanity of God, that He might deliver us Himself, and overcome the tyrant, and draw us to Himself by the mediation of His Son, who also arranged this to the honour of the Father, whom it is manifest that He obeys in all things? So much we have said of Christ; let what is more be reverenced in silence.[1]

Nothing could be more explicit than this repudiation of the Ransom theory as usually stated. Gregory is clear-sighted enough to see that that theory is invalidated by the conception of God which results from it, and is daring enough to reject it, even though he has no alternative to offer. His premisses are in the main the same as those of Origen and Gregory of Nyssa. It is only from their conclusion that he recoils. This appears, for example, in the view of sin from which he begins, a view essentially transactional in character,[2] and very far below the strong and positive conception of the moral corruption of the soul which had been dominant in the thought of Athanasius. Man is, as by agreement, in the devil's power. A ransom must therefore be paid. Yet that such a ransom as Christ should be paid to the devil is an intolerable thought, to be rejected at once. We can only say, despite all difficulties, that the ransom is paid to the Father.

[1] *Τίνι γὰρ τὸ ὑπὲρ ἡμῶν αἷμα καὶ περὶ τίνος ἐχέθη; . . . κατειχόμεθα μὲν γὰρ ὑπὸ τοῦ πονηροῦ, πεπραμένοι ὑπὸ τὴν ἁμαρτίαν καὶ ἀντιλάβοντες τῆς κακίας τὴν ἡδονήν. εἰ δὲ τὸ λύτρον οὐκ ἄλλου τινὸς ἢ τοῦ κατέχοντος γίνεται, ζητῶ τίνι τοῦτο εἰσηνέχθη, καὶ δι' ἥντινα τὴν αἰτίαν. εἰ μὲν τῷ πονηρῷ, φεῦ τῆς ὕβρεως· εἰ μὴ παρὰ τοῦ θεοῦ μόνον, ἀλλὰ καὶ τὸν Θεὸν αὐτὸν λύτρον ὁ λῃστὴς λαμβάνεται, καὶ μισθὸν οὕτως ὑπερφυῆ τῆς ἑαυτοῦ τυραννίδος, δι' ὃν καὶ ἡμῶν φείδεσθαι δίκαιον ἦν. εἰ δὲ τῷ πατρί, πρῶτον μὲν πῶς; οὐκ ὑπ' ἐκείνου γὰρ ἐκρατούμεθα. δεύτερον δὲ τίς ὁ λόγος μονογενοῦς αἷμα τέρπειν πατέρα, ὃς οὐδὲ τὸν Ἰσαὰκ ἐδέξατο παρὰ τοῦ πατρὸς προσφερόμενον . . .; ἢ δῆλον ὅτι λαμβάνει μὲν ὁ πατὴρ οὐκ αἰτήσας οὐδὲ δεηθείς· ἀλλὰ διὰ τὴν οἰκονομίαν, καὶ τὸ χρῆναι ἁγιασθῆναι τῷ ἀνθρωπίνῳ τοῦ Θεοῦ τὸν ἀνθρώπον. ἵν' αὐτὸς ἡμᾶς ἐξέληται, τοῦ τυράννου βίᾳ κρατήσας καὶ πρὸς αὐτὸν ἐπαναγάγῃ διὰ τοῦ υἱοῦ μεσιτεύσαντος, καὶ εἰς τιμὴν τοῦ πατρὸς τοῦτο οἰκονομήσαντος, ᾧ τὰ πάντα παραχωρῶν φαίνεται. τὰ μὲν δὴ Χριστοῦ τοιαῦτα, καὶ τὰ πλείω σιγῇ σεβέσθω* (*Or.* xlv. 22).

[2] Cf. the fine statement of this position in *Or.* xix.: *καὶ λύπην κατεκρίθην ἄπαυστον ἀντὶ τῆς μικρᾶς ἡδονῆς* (*i.e.* the tasting of the tree) *καὶ πόλεμον πρὸς τὸν φιλωθέντα κακῶς.*

Gregory is quite aware of the difficulties, and states them clearly enough. The first objection, that it is not by the Father that man is held in bondage, Gregory makes no effort to meet. Indeed he could not meet it without revising his whole conception of sin. Nevertheless, he concludes that it is the Father that receives the payment. The second objection which he feels is that the Father could not possibly take pleasure in the blood of His Son. To meet this he is able to offer a certain number of suggestions. These are of considerable interest as showing the strength and vigour of his thought. He avoids interpretations unworthy of God by pointing out that it was not by the Father that the price was demanded, and falls back upon the divine "economy," the mystery of God's government of the world.[1] This has suggested to some the later Rectoral theory, but the phrase is left quite undeveloped, and Gregory passes to a loftier thought still. Humanity is to be saved through the Humanity in God. The Incarnation is the key to redemption, and not only the Incarnation as an earthly fact, but the Incarnation regarded as an eternal fact in the Divine being. This is not merely the participation of man in the creative Word, of which Athanasius had spoken. It is that thought of the Incarnation which we have seen to be characteristic of the Greek fathers as a whole, but now conceived upon a higher plane. There is, perhaps, some connexion with Origen's theory of the union of the Divine Word with the souls of men, and especially with the soul of Jesus, before this mundane stage of existence. The thought probably underlay the heresy of Gregory's contemporary, Apollinarius. But the nearest parallel comes a thousand years later, in the Scotist belief that the Incarnation had its place in the purpose of God quite apart from the Fall. Gregory has

[1] This is apparently the sense of οἰκονομία here. The word is sometimes used to mean the Trinitarian aspect of the Godhead: Tertullian, writing against Praxeas, tells us that the Monarchians objected to the "Economy" in this sense.

elsewhere a view of the Incarnation more upon the lines of his contemporaries, emphasizing Christ's experiences, His sufferings, His tears, His obedience, as representative. He "plays the part"[1] of mankind, that we may make His experience ours.

Other passages may be quoted to illustrate this mystical side of Gregory's thought:

> God became man and died that we might live: we have died with Him to be purified; we are raised from the dead with Him since we have died with Him; we are glorified with Him because we have risen with Him from the grave.[2]

> He has ascended the Cross and taken me with Him, to nail my sin on it.[3]

And the same mysticism comes out in the sentences which follow the main passage under discussion, where Gregory rejects the use of the brazen serpent as a type of Christ, a use which goes back to the earliest days of Christianity, on the ground that the serpent represents sin as dead, whereas Christ is a principle not of death but of life.

But this does not exhaust Gregory's suggestions. He goes on to make it clear that God's attitude to the devil is one of war, a conception recurring throughout this period, but seldom thrown into clear contrast with the thought of the devil as in some way the possessor of rights.[4] And, finally, he suggests that the Son, who mediates our return to God, does so with the Father's honour in view. Here we have, quite unexpectedly, the germ of Anselm's thought, though many years were to pass before this bore fruit in the Satisfaction theory.

[1] *Δραματουργεῖται.* See *Or.* xxx. 5, 6, cited by Bethune-Baker, *op. cit.* p. 344.

[2] *Ἐδεήθημεν θεοῦ σαρκουμένου καὶ νεκρουμένου, ἵνα ζήσωμεν· συνενεκρώθημεν ἵνα καθαρῶμεν· συνανέστημεν ἐπειδὴ συνενεκρώθημεν· συνεδοξάσθημεν ἐπειδὴ συνανέστημεν* (*Or.* xlv. 28).

[3] *Ἐπὶ τὸν σταυρὸν ἀνελθόντος, κἀμὲ συναγόντος, ἵνα προσηλώσῃ τὴν ἐμὴν ἁμαρτίαν* (*Or.* xxiv. 4).

[4] It is curious that elsewhere (*Or.* xxxix. 13) Gregory admits that the adoption of the human form was an artifice, which led the devil to believe that he had only to deal with a being like ourselves, the Godhead being hidden beneath it.

It is indeed with the Satisfaction theory that Gregory's whole conception has most affinity. The real significance of his criticism is the effort which it makes to pass from a devilward to a Godward view of Atonement. To describe him as a precursor of Abelard and of modern writers of the type of Bushnell is quite misleading. It is true that statements may be quoted which seem to assign a purely ethical significance to Christ's death.

> When He became man for our sake, and took the fashion of a slave, and was led to death for our sins, the Saviour did these things although, as God, He could have saved by His will alone, since He created all things by a word of command, But He offered us a thing greater and more fitted to strike us with shame, even fellowship in suffering and in degree.[1]

But such passages as this occur throughout the early fathers, and must not be taken as especially characteristic of Gregory's thought. It would be more true to describe him as a mystic, since the highest elements of his thinking are mystical in type. But this again would be true of the majority of the Greek fathers, even of those who give their adherence most explicitly to transactional theories. It may be granted that Gregory stands apart from his age, but we must not therefore attempt to classify him in any age but his own. His conception of the Atonement was full and living, but the time had not come for its expression in definite doctrinal form.

It is of no importance to pursue the history of the doctrine of Atonement further through the various writers of the Greek Church. The thought of the East remains practically unchanged in its general outlines down to the time of John of Damascus, and with Augustine the centre of interest is transferred to the West.

[1] Ἐπεὶ καὶ ἄνθρωπος ἐγένετο δι' ἡμᾶς καὶ δούλου μορφὴν ἀνεδέξατο, καὶ ὑπὲρ τῶν ἀνομιῶν ἡμῶν ἤχθη εἰς θάνατον, ταῦτα μὲν ὁ σωτήρ, καὶ τῷ θελήματι μόνον ὡς Θεὸς σῶσαι δυνάμενος, ἐπεὶ καὶ τὰ πάντα προστάγματι συνεστήσατο, μεῖζον δὲ καὶ δυσωπητικώτερον εἰσήνεγκεν ἡμῖν, τὴν συμπάθειαν καὶ τὸ ὁμότιμον (*Or.* xix.).

We may pause to gather up the lines of speculation in the East as follows:

1. Throughout the period, from the time of Origen, the Ransom theory is prominent wherever writers are consciously attempting to give an explanation of the significance of the Cross. One or two writers challenge its conclusions, but Athanasius alone is in any degree free from its spell. Yet, despite its influence, this theory was never held alone, and its harshness is very largely covered by the less definite ideas with which it is associated.

2. Sacrificial language, based in the main directly upon the Bible, constantly recurs. It was thus that the Godward aspect of Atonement found expression, but no attempt was made to reconcile this language with the metaphors of the Ransom theory. As in Origen, so in practically all his successors, the two groups of ideas stand side by side, apparently unrelated.

3. The Moral conception of Atonement exercised a wide influence. Passages expressing this type of thought have been quoted from Irenaeus, Origen, and Gregory of Nazianzum, and the examples might easily have been multiplied. Many writers of the period emphasize the influence of the Death of Christ as an example inspiring the believer. But here again there is no consciousness of theory.

4. Least conscious of all, and most suggestive, is the mystical language which writer after writer employs. The unity of the Christian believer with Christ, as the pre-existent Word (Justin, Athanasius), as Incarnate (Irenaeus, Gregory of Nyssa, and Gregory of Nazianzum), as dying (Irenaeus, Origen, Athanasius, Gregory of Nazianzum), as risen from the dead (Origen, Athanasius, Gregory of Nazianzum), had evidently entered very deeply into the thought of the Eastern Church.

It would hardly be untrue, in spite of the continued appearance of the Ransom theory, to say that the real mind of the early Greek fathers held to a combination of

Godward and manward conceptions of Atonement, expressed in sacrificial and ethical language respectively, and that these two aspects were framed as a single picture by the aid of the strong mysticism characteristic of Eastern Christianity. And in this respect these writers show themselves true successors not only of the Apostolic fathers, but of St. Paul himself.

CHAPTER V

THE MIND OF THE EARLY FATHERS—THE WEST

THE Western Church has on the whole been practical rather than speculative, and many of the doctrines of the Church have not been developed appreciably since they were laid down by the Greek fathers of the fourth and fifth centuries. In the case of the doctrine of the Atonement, however, we are dealing with a doctrine the developments of which have been almost exclusively Western. And though these more special developments really begin in the eleventh century, with the work of Anselm, it is of great interest to study the treatment of the subject in the earlier Western writers, and especially in Augustine, who marks the transition from East to West.

It is not necessary to dwell further on the Ransom theory itself than has been done above. This remained the common property of all writers for many years to come. But it is only natural that we should find changes in the mode of presentation. The Western mind was very different from the Eastern in type. It was almost wholly lacking in that strong speculative mysticism which was so marked a feature in the East. Its interests were very largely ethical, and the great Roman system of jurisprudence has left its mark upon it in the legalistic bias which is everywhere visible. The idea of abstract justice meant far more to Rome than it had ever done to Greece, and it is thus natural to find that this is the thought which is emphasized in the West in connexion with the Atonement.

The Ransom theory had been more or less loosely connected in the East with two rather divergent positions.

There was in the first place the conception of God as at war with the devil, who was ultimately defeated by the Cross. This underlies the thought of Origen, and goes far to explain two such divergent positions as those of the two Gregories. To Gregory of Nyssa it seemed a mark of God's wisdom that He should defeat His enemy so cleverly. To his friend Gregory of Nazianzum it seemed unworthy of God that He should make any concession to one with whom He was at war. In the West the same general attitude towards the conflict with the devil appears, for example, in Ambrose. But by degrees the Western mind gave a more ethical character to the conception. The struggle was not one of strength but of will, and it was the failure of the devil to make Jesus commit the least sin that constituted his defeat. The main importance of this view, which, as we have seen, occurs in Leo the Great and Gregory the Great, is in the stress which it lays upon the sinlessness, the absolute obedience, of Christ, a point which becomes central in Anselm.

In the second place there had been the conception of a certain justice which only the death of Christ could satisfy. It was from a Western theologian, Irenaeus, that the thought had originally come, but it had been taken up, and to a certain extent developed, in the East. Usually the conception was not clearly thought out. The devil was regarded as having some vague right, however he came to possess it. There was also, however, the more definite suggestion that God's sentence had been uttered against sin, and that that sentence might not fail. And in Athanasius there is side by side with this the further thought of the eternal law by which the corruption of sin naturally and inevitably ends in death.

This conception of Justice, never, except in Athanasius, very prominent in the East, appealed strongly to the legal mind of the West. Quite a new stress is laid upon it by Augustine and subsequent Latin writers.[1] It is true that the theory of a transaction with the devil is retained, but all the emphasis is now laid upon the complete justice of that transaction. All that God does is just. The devil is not deceived by God, but by his own great pride, which makes him think himself strong enough to claim the life of the holy Son of God.[2]

But Augustine's real thought about the Atonement really lies far deeper than the transactional statement. The devil, great as is the part which he plays in Augustine's writings, now begins to take a subordinate place. It is only by permission that he is a penal agent. His very existence, like that of all created things, depends directly upon God.

> God did not indeed desert His own creature so as not to manifest Himself as a God creating and making alive, and, in the midst of penal evils, even affording many good gifts to evil men. For He did not restrain His compassions in His anger. Nor did He lose man from the law of His own power when He permitted him to be in the power of the devil, for the devil himself is a stranger neither to the power of the Omnipotent, nor to His goodness.[3]

It is by God's just anger that man, for his sins, is subjected to the power of the devil. It is by God's compassion that wrath is laid aside, and that the redemption

[1] It was by Augustine that this change of emphasis was brought about. Ambrose, writing just before Augustine, has the theory in its ordinary Eastern form. He speaks of the Incarnation as a deception practised upon the devil (*Opp.* iii. 10. 1, cited by Hagenbach). He emphasizes, too, the fulfilment of the sentence pronounced by God against sin: "suscepit mortem ut impleretur sententia" (*De Fug. Saec.* 7). But he does not press the thought further than Athanasius and Cyril of Jerusalem had done. It is interesting to find Ambrose using the idea of Satisfaction. Christ died, he says, "ut satisfieret judicato" (*ib.*). His emphasis on the conception of Sacrifice is also noteworthy.

[2] See pp. 46 f.

[3] Nec ita sane Deus deseruit creaturam suam ut non se illi exhiberet Deum creantem et vivificantem, et inter poenalia mala etiam bona malis multa praestantem. Non enim continuit in ira sua miserationes suas. Nec hominem a lege suae potestatis amisit, quando in diaboli potestate esse permisit: quia nec ipse diabolus a potestate omnipotentis alienus est, sicut neque a bonitate (*De Trin.* xiii. 12).

wrought by Christ is set on foot. The mystery of the Atonement lies in the very nature of God Himself. The Death of Christ is only an expression of something lying further back. And thus the whole problem as to the meaning of the Fact of Atonement is carried up to a higher plane, to a region where the old transactional metaphors are of little service.

Augustine himself seems to be hardly aware of the great questions that are thus raised. He never asks what it is that works this change from wrath to compassion in God's attitude towards man. Even where, as in the passage just quoted, Augustine reminds himself that God's goodness had never failed completely, despite man's sin, wrath and compassion remain contrasted states, and no reconciliation of them within the nature of Godhead is attempted. All his theological interest lies in the means by which God, through Christ, overthrows that dominion of the devil which He Himself has allowed, and he does not deal with the more fundamental problem which he has suggested.

Yet this transference of the problem to the nature of the Godhead is really Augustine's greatest contribution to the history of thought upon the subject of Atonement. The position of the devil has now become insignificant, and so the way is prepared for the Godward theories of Anselm and his successors, who saw the death of Christ as meeting, not the questionable rights of the devil, but the just demands of God's eternal honour.

Augustine himself, however, does not go beyond the asking of the question :

> What is the meaning of being "reconciled through the death of His Son"? Does it mean that while God the Father was angry with us He saw the death of His Son on our behalf and was placated towards us? Can it be the fact that His Son was so far placated towards us as even to deign to die for us, but that the Father was so angry with us that, had not the Son died for us, He would not have been placated?[1]

[1] Quid est, reconciliati per mortem Filii ejus? Itane vero, cum irasceretur nobis Deus Pater, vidit mortem Filii sui pro nobis, et

For such a question the thought of the day was not prepared, and Augustine is as little ready with an answer as Gregory of Nazianzum had been. Usually he falls back upon the language of a transaction with the devil. This has been quoted above,[1] and we need not dwell upon it further. Sometimes, however, like so many of his Eastern predecessors, he comes practically to the Moral argument. God might, he says, have saved us in many ways, but that which was actually chosen was the most fitting to reveal God's love, and to provide us with an example.

For what was so necessary for the building up of our hope, and for the freeing of the minds of mortals cast down by the condition of mortality itself from despair of immortality, as that it should be demonstrated to us at how great a price God rated us and how greatly He loved us.[2]

It pleased God that . . . men, imitating Christ, should seek to conquer the devil by righteousness, not by might.[3]

What greater reason could there be for the coming of the Lord than that God might show His love towards us, greatly commending it? . . . So that we too, in our turn, may love, and may lay down our life for our brethren, just as He laid down His life for us.[4]

And so all His life on earth, through that manhood which He deigned to take, was an instruction in character.[5]

---

placatus est nobis? Numquid ergo Filius ejus usque adeo nobis jam placatus erat, ut pro nobis etiam dignaretur mori, Pater vero usque adeo adhuc irascebatur, ut nisi Filius pro nobis moreretur non placaretur? (*De Trin.* xiii. 11).

[1] See p. 46.

[2] Quid enim tam necessarium fuit ad erigendam spem nostram, mentesque mortalium conditione ipsius mortalitatis abjectas ab immortalitatis desperatione liberandas, quam ut demonstraretur nobis quanti nos penderet Deus, quantumque diligeret? (*De Trin.* xiii. 10). The passage goes on to show that Christ did this by sharing our lot ("consortium").

[3] Placuit Deo ut . . . homines, imitantes Christum, justitia quaererent diabolum vincere non potentia (*De Trin.* xiii. 13).

[4] Quae autem major causa est adventus Domini nisi ut ostenderet Deus dilectionem suam in nobis, commendans eam vehementer? . . . ut et nos invicem diligamus et quemadmodum ille pro nobis animam suam posuit, sic et nos pro fratribus animam ponamus (*De Cat. Rud.* 4).

[5] Tota itaque vita ejus in terris, per hominem quem suscipere dignatus est, disciplina morum fuit (*De Vera Relig.* 16).

And sometimes Augustine approaches the conception of an infused righteousness, which shall make this new life possible for man.

> Man, even when most fully justified, is unable to lead a holy life, if he be not divinely assisted by the eternal light of righteousness. God therefore heals us not only that He may blot out the sin which we have committed, but, furthermore, that He may enable us even to avoid sinning.[1]

But this ethical language, while valuable in its emphasis upon the love of God, makes no attempt to relate that love to His wrath. And the suggestions of sacrificial language which occur are little more than metaphors borrowed from the past, and do not carry the thought much further.

> For whereas by His death the one and most real sacrifice was offered up for us, whatever fault there was, whence principalities and powers held us fast as of right to pay its penalty, He cleansed, abolished, extinguished; and by His own resurrection He also called us whom He predestined to a new life.[2]

> For we indeed came to death through sin; He through righteousness: and therefore as our death is the punishment of sin, so His death was made a sacrifice for sin.[3]

In such hints as these, ethical and sacrificial, Augustine does not go beyond the current ideas of his age.

In one respect, however, he makes a real advance towards the solution of the problem, though only indirectly. No writer since St. Paul, with the partial exception of Athanasius, had so clear and full a vision of

[1] Sic et homo etiam perfectissime justificatus, nisi aeterna luce justitiae divinitus adjuvetur, recte non potest vivere. Sanat ergo Deus, non solum ut deleat quod peccavimus, sed ut praestet etiam ne peccemus (*De Nat. et Grat.* 26).

[2] Morte sua quippe uno verissimo sacrificio pro nobis oblato, quidquid culparum erat unde nos principatus et potestates ad luenda supplicia jure detinebant, purgavit, abolevit, exstinxit; et sua resurrectione in novam vitam nos praedestinatos vocavit (*De Trin.* iv. 13).

[3] Nos enim ad mortem per peccatum venimus; ille per justitiam: et ideo cum sit mors nostra poena peccati mors illius facta est hostia pro peccato (*De Trin.* iv. 12).

the stern realities of sin. By this vision all his theology was coloured, even in the days before the controversy with Pelagius. The depths from which the grace of God had raised him were never forgotten. To him, as to Athanasius, sin is no mere disobedience, lightly to be set aside, were it not for God's spoken word. He sees it as some horrible disease, an inherited corruption, deep-seated in the soul of all the race of Adam. And, unlike Athanasius, he lays enormous stress upon the guilt of this inherited sin. For Adam's sin all mankind lies under condemnation, and justice must be done.

Naturally, therefore, Augustine has a very strong sense of the significance of Christ's sinlessness, His freedom from all taint whether of original or of actual sin. It was this that freed Him from all obligation to die. The thought is no new one, but it now begins to receive a new emphasis.

> Herein lies the punishment in the death of the body, that the spirit leaves the body against its will, because it left God willingly . . . The spirit of the Mediator showed how it was through no punishment of sin that He came to the death of the flesh, because it did not leave Him against His will, but because He willed, when He willed, as He willed.[1]

As in previous writers we find the thought that this sinlessness prevented the devil from having any claim against Christ.

> Death found in Him nothing to punish . . . for as (the devil) had most unjustly put Christ to death, though there was no sin in Him to deserve death, it was most just that through Christ he should lose his hold of those who by sin were justly subject to the bondage in which he held them.[2]

---

[1] Eaque sit poena in morte corporis ut spiritus, quia volens deseruit Deum, deserat corpus invitus . . . ; demonstravit spiritus mediatoris, quam nulla poena peccati usque ad mortem carnis accesserit, quia non eum deseruit invitus, sed quia voluit, quando voluit, quomodo voluit (*De Trin.* iv. 13).

[2] Mors nihil quod puniret invenit; ut diabolus . . . quoniam ipsum sine ullo peccati merito iniquissime occiderat, per ipsum justissime amitteret quos peccati merito detinebat (*Enchir.* 49).

But this is not the uppermost thought in Augustine's mind when he contemplates the sinlessness of Christ. The devil is now but an agent under the supreme law of justice, that law of which, apart from Christ, man could neither obey the commands nor pay the penalties. In Christ alone does "justitia," which is both righteousness and justice, find its complete fulfilment.

But the time for the development of this great thought along the lines of a Godward theory of Atonement had not yet come. Augustine's thinking is hampered at every point by his legalistic language. When he says, for example, that the payment of the debt by Christ justly releases the debtors, if they believe in Him,[1] we can only feel that the metaphor has been strained beyond all meaning. Faith has no place in a civil court of justice. The transference to us of the efficacy of the atoning work of Christ remains utterly unexplained. The Greek fathers had been helped at this point by their mysticism, but mysticism was a thing very foreign to the Western mind. Augustine's statements in this direction do not go very far.

> He wills His own to be one, but in Him, since they could not be so in themselves, separated as they are from one another by divers pleasures and desires and uncleannesses of sin; whence they are cleansed through the Mediator, that they may be one in Him, not only through the same nature in which all become from mortal men equal to the angels, but also through the same will most harmoniously conspiring to the same blessedness, and fused in some way by the fire of charity into one spirit.[2]

Such language is very unlike the terse, full phrases of Athanasius or of St. Paul. And even in Augustine's

[1] See, *e.g.*, *De Trin.* xiii. 10.

[2] Vult esse suos unum, sed in ipso; quia in se ipsis non possent, dissociati ab invicem per diversas et cupiditates et immunditias peccatorum: unde mundantur per mediatorem, ut sint in illo unum; non tantum per eamdem naturam qua omnes ex hominibus mortalibus aequales angelis fiunt, sed etiam per eamdem in eamdem beatitudinem conspirantem concordissimam voluntatem, in unum spiritum quodam modo igne charitatis conflatam (*De Trin.* iv. 9). Cf. *De Pecc. Mer.* 26-39, *Serm.* 144. 2, 2, quoted by Franks, *op. cit.*

mysticism, such as it is, the ethical, Western type of mind makes itself apparent. It has in view primarily the restoring of right relations between man and man. Of a mystical union between man and God there is very little trace.

When we pass to the later writers of the Western Church we find the influence of Augustine everywhere. The resemblance is not merely general, due to the legalistic and non-mystical character of the Western mind, but extends even to direct echoes of thought and phrase. Little violence to historical sequence would be done if we were to pass straight from Augustine to Anselm. Throughout this long interval there is practically no advance. The old theory of a transaction with the devil remains, often stated in the very crudest manner. There is even some reversion to the thought of the Incarnation as a deception practised by God upon the devil. This idea had seemed abhorrent to Augustine, but it reappears in Leo the Great, and is not wholly lacking in later writers.[1] As a rule, however, Augustine's view that the devil was deceived by his own pride is adopted. And there is, further, a constant tendency to emphasize Godward and manward aspects of the transaction. Especially prominent is the emphasis upon its complete justice, an emphasis which prepares the way for the Satisfaction theory. Statements in the direction of the Moral theory are also not infrequent. The great exponent of this theory, Abelard, who comes at the close of the period, was by no means as isolated a thinker as is often supposed.

It is unnecessary, therefore, to pause long over the early Latin theologians. What has been already said concerning Leo the Great may perhaps suffice, and, as an example of the general tendencies of the period, we may turn to Gregory the Great, a writer who has also a certain individual interest because of the approximation of some of his language to the later Penal view.

[1] *E.g.* in Luther.

In Gregory we find the old transactional theory stated quite crudely, though with Augustine's modification that it is the devil's pride that causes his deception :

And so our Lord, when He came to redeem mankind, made as it were a sort of hook of Himself for the death of the devil.[1]

Him who for His weakness he despised and thought to be but man, he felt by His power to be more than man.[2]

Savouring of nought but pride, when he saw Him in humility he doubted of His being God.[3]

Through his excessive presumption the ancient foe lost even him whom he possessed by the legal right of wicked persuasion, and when he boldly attacked Him against whom he had no claim, he rightly lost him whom by a sort of justice he held.[4]

We find also the modified ethical conception of the contest with the devil, in which he is defeated not by force but by the unswerving obedience of One over whose will no temptation had any power.

When the ancient foe saw Him after His baptism he presently assailed Him with temptations, and was defeated in his attempts to creep by divers approaches into His inmost soul, and was laid low by the integrity of His unconquerable will.[5]

And as in other early writers this language is combined with sacrificial phrases, no attempt being made to reconcile the two groups of metaphors.

[1] Dominus itaque noster ad humani generis redemptionem veniens velut quemdam de se in necem diaboli hamum fecit (*Moral.* xxxiii. 7).

[2] Sed quem infirmitate despectum hominem credidit, virtute supra hominem sensit (*Moral.* xxx. 25).

[3] Nil quippe nisi superbum sapiens, dum esse hunc humilem conspicit Deum esse dubitavit (*Moral.* ii. 24).

[4] Antiquus hostis per excessum praesumptionis suae eum etiam perdidit quem iniquae persuasionis lege possedit ; et dum audacter eum in quo nihil sibi competebat appetiit, jure illum quem quasi juste tenebat amisit (*Moral.* xvii. 30).

[5] Hunc ergo cum post baptisma vidit antiquus hostis mox tentationibus impetiit, et per diversos aditus ad interiora ejus molitus irrepere, victus est, atque ipsa inexpugnabilis mentis ejus integritate prostratus (*Moral.* xvii. 30).

He wrought a sacrifice for us; He displayed on behalf of sinners His body, a victim without sin, which through its manhood could die, and through its righteousness could cleanse.[1]

Such ideas as these were characteristic of the age in which Gregory lived. But, like Augustine, he was very conscious of their inadequacy. Even in its modified form the idea of a conquest of the devil failed to explain either the apparent change in the attitude of God or the way in which the fruits of that conquest become available for man. Gregory has something to say upon both parts of the problem.

He has, in the first place, a very clear discussion of the justice of God, a discussion which is freed from its most confusing factor by the complete ignoring of the devil and his quasi-rights.

But we must consider how He can be just, and can dispose all things justly, if He condemns Him who ought not to be punished. For our Mediator owed no punishment for Himself, since He wrought nothing that could infect Him with guilt. But if He had not undergone a death that was not His due, He would never have freed us from the death due to us. Therefore, though the Father is just, yet when He punishes the Just He orders all things justly; because through Him He justifies all things, in that on behalf of sinners He condemns Him who is without sin, so that all the elect might rise up to the height of righteousness in Him in whom He who is above all endures the penalties of our unrighteousness. . . . For the rust of vice can only be purged by the fire of torment. And so He came, without fault, freely to submit Himself to the torment, that the punishments due to our iniquity might lose their rightful victims, in that they unjustly held Him who was free from their power.[2]

---

[1] Fecit pro nobis sacrificium, corpus suum exhibuit pro peccatoribus victimam sine peccato, quae et humanitate mori et justitia mundare potuisset (*Moral.* xvii. 30).

[2] Sed pensandum est quomodo justus sit et omnia juste disponat si eum qui non debet puniri condemnat. Mediator etenim noster puniri pro semetipso non debuit, quia nullum culpae contagium perpetravit. Sed si ipse indebitam non susciperet nunquam nos a debita morte liberaret. Pater ergo cum justus sit, justum puniens, omnia juste disponit; quia per hoc cuncta justificat, quod eum qui sine

The passage is a notable one as being the first clear discussion of the apparent contradiction between the justice of God and the injustice of the punishment of One who was innocent. The last sentence is an unfortunate reminiscence of Augustinian language, but the remainder of the discussion has hardly any parallel until the Reformation, with its theories of vicarious penal suffering. Such views were quite foreign to the ordinary thought of the early Church, but they were a natural outcome of any theorising which paid sole attention to the Godward aspect of Atonement. In Gregory we see the beginning of a tendency which might well have produced the full Penal theory in the eighth or ninth century, had not the Dark Ages intervened. When in the eleventh century theology shook off its sleep the whole conception of God's justice had changed, and the development of the Godward theory took a very different course.

In Gregory, indeed, the discussion is not carried very far. He is content with the assertion, unexplained and undefended, that the punishment of the innocent sets free those who are guilty. There is no discussion of the exact equivalence of Christ's punishment with that due to us. Nor does Gregory attempt to make it clear how one injustice can make just a lapse of justice, save to point out that it was by His own choice, and not involuntarily, that Christ underwent suffering and death. And he touches upon a much higher thought when he adds that the result of the Atonement upon the elect is "the height of righteousness," and no mere barren remission of sins.

And this brings us to the second feature of Gregory's thought, his strong grasp of the manward aspect of

---

peccato est pro peccatoribus damnat; ut eo electa omnia ad culmen justitiae surgerent, quo is qui est super omnia damna injustitiae nostrae sustineret. . . . Rubigo quippe vitii purgari non potuit nisi igne tormenti. Venit itaque sine vitio, qui se subjiceret sponte tormento; ut debita nostrae iniquitati supplicia eo reos suos juste amitterent, quo hunc a semetipsis liberum injuste tenuissent (*Moral.* iii. 14).

Atonement. Gregory is careful not to assign the whole responsibility for the sufferings of Christ to Satan, thereby lifting it from the shoulders of man. Pilate, Judas, the chief priests, acted as "Satan's members."

> Who does not know that of that same Satan all they are members who are joined unto him by living frowardly? . . . When therefore the Lord for our redemption delivered Himself into the hands of Satan's members, what else was it than that He allowed Satan's hand to rage against Himself, so that that which laid Him low outwardly, set us free both outwardly and inwardly.[1]

The responsibility is man's, and the redemption is man's too, and in no merely external sense. It is a deliverance which not only sets man free from the punishment of sin but also inspires him to live righteously. In one passage the Penal and Moral theories are explicitly combined:

> For the Redeemer of mankind, who was made the Mediator between God and man through the flesh, because that He alone appeared righteous among men, and yet, even though without sin, was nevertheless brought to the punishment of sin, did both convict man that he might not sin, and withstand God that He might not smite; He gave an example of innocence, and endured the punishment of wrongdoing. Thus by suffering He convinced both the one and the other, in that He both rebuked the sin of man by inspiring righteousness, and moderated the wrath of the Judge by undergoing death. To either task He set His Hand, giving to men examples that they might imitate, and displaying to God in Himself those works whereby He might be reconciled to men.[2]

---

[1] Quis nesciat quod ejusdem Satanae membra sunt omnes qui ei perverse vivendo junguntur? . . . cum ergo se pro nostra redemptione Dominus membrorum Satanae manibus tradidit, quid aliud quam ejusdem Satanae manum in se saevire permisit; ut unde ipse exterius occumberet inde nos exterius interiusque liberaret? (*Moral.* iii. 16).

[2] Redemptor quippe humani generis, mediator Dei et hominis per carnem factus, quia justus in hominibus solus apparuit, et tamen ad poenam culpae etiam sine culpa pervenit, et hominem arguit ne delinqueret, et Deo obstitit ne feriret, exempla innocentiae praebuit, poenam malitiae suscepit. Patiendo ergo utrumque arguit qui et culpam hominis justitiam aspirando corripuit, et iram judicis moriendo temperavit; atque in utrisque manum posuit, quia et exempla hominibus quae imitarentur praebuit, et Deo in se opera, quibus erga homines placaretur, ostendit (*Moral.* ix. 39). This makes a near approach to the later phrase "justitia infusa."

The example which Christ has given us to follow is a great thing, but by itself it is not enough. The grace of God must not merely open the gate by putting away sin, not merely show us the way by giving us an example of godly life, but must also support us as we walk therein. Here and elsewhere[1] Gregory approaches the idea, and almost the language, of the doctrine of "infused righteousness," which was to become a commonplace of later theology. The new life won by Christ in His resurrection must come into our hearts here and now.

> To this end, therefore, the Lord appeared in the flesh, that He might arouse the life of man by His warnings, might inspire it by giving it examples, might redeem it by dying, might restore it by rising again.[2]

This is the Moral Theory, but in a stronger form than that in which it appears in most of the earlier Western theologians. The thought of a new life, a new righteousness, implanted in the hearts of sinful men had lain at the very root of the Pauline theology, and had always been implicit in the mysticism of the East, with its vision of the union of man and God brought about in Christ. It was this mysticism that gave the necessary fulness of meaning to phrases about the example set by Christ for man to follow. But with the decline of mysticism in the West such language threatened to become barren and empty. And thus it was that the conception of "infused righteousness," itself really mystical in character, though often stated in a singularly literal and unmystical way, came to receive formal expression.

With the passing of Gregory Western theology enters the long night of the Dark Ages. Save for the Neo-Platonist and mystic, John Scotus Erigena, the history of theological thought shows no names of outstanding

[1] *E.g. Moral.* xviii. 40, a very suggestive passage, where Gregory speaks of the grace bestowed upon the Penitent Thief.

[2] Ad hoc itaque Dominus apparuit in carne ut humanam vitam admonendo excitaret, exempla praebendo accenderet, moriendo redimeret, resurgendo repararet (*Moral.* xxi. 6).

importance. And though Erigena had his own peculiar theory of the Atonement it exercised little or no influence upon later writers, and need not be dwelt upon here.[1]

The new era of intellectual vigour dawned towards the end of the eleventh century, when the strong speculative mind of Anselm, the greatest of the pioneers of scholasticism, faced the old problems of theology afresh. In no direction did his work produce more lasting results than in connexion with the doctrine of the Atonement. The theory which he framed of a satisfaction offered to God remained dominant until the Reformation, and has underlain much of the thought of even more recent times.

To the Satisfaction theory we must return. Before doing so, however, we must pause to notice the closing phases of the patristic period proper. The influence of Anselm did not immediately dominate his younger con-

[1] For a good sketch of Erigena's position see Oxenham, *op. cit.* pp. 171-4. Erigena was rather a philosopher than a theologian, and his thought is Eastern in type rather than Western. He was largely under the influence of the works ascribed to Dionysius the Areopagite, which he translated, and of Maximus. His general theory is very pantheistic in type, but its Platonism shows several points of contact with Greek Fathers. His view of the Fall resembles that of Origen. "Homo prius in se ipso lapsus est quam a diabolo tentaretur, non enim credibile est eundem hominem et in contemplatione aeternae pacis stetisse, et, suadente femina, serpentis veneno corrupta, corruisse" (*De Div. Nat.* iv. p. 196). Thus man was separated from God, the Creator, in whom are the archetypes of all creation, and the mind of man was divided from that of which it was the image. That the union of the Creator and the created, the idea and the thing, might be restored, the Word took human nature, and, therewith, all created nature. Thus, as in the Greek Fathers, the Incarnation is made the key of reconciliation. For the death of Christ little place is found. Erigena regards the destruction of the body as a boon rather than as suffering. It is the last hold that dissolution has upon man, and therewith he passes back to the realms of the pure contemplation of the ideal, from which he had fallen by his sin. Erigena finds a curious significance in the Resurrection. He ascribes to the Fall the division of ideal humanity into the sexes, each imperfect in itself. The restoration of ideal, undivided, humanity, as it was before the Fall, results from the Resurrection: "Non enim in sexu corporeo sed in homine tantum surrexit ex mortuis, in ipso enim nec masculus nec femina erat" (*ib.* ii. p. 49). This idea of the division of the sexes goes back to Plato (*Symposium*, 190 D ff.).

temporaries, and in the earlier part of the twelfth century there still remained exponents of the traditional view. The greatest of these was Bernard of Clairvaux, who was moved to anger by the outspoken rationalism of Abelard. He writes as the indignant champion of authority, upholding the doctrines which had been taught for so long by the doctors of the Church, and crying out for the condemnation of the audacious critic who had ventured to dispute them. Abelard's doctrine of redemption is one of the points especially singled out for attack.

The controversy between Bernard and Abelard is very significant, and its bearing is often misunderstood. Abelard is commonly regarded as a solitary exponent of the Moral theory, one born out of due time, remote from the thought of his age. But such a conception is very largely erroneous. Abelard stands by no means alone. In some ways he illustrates well the tendencies of his day. Like Gregory of Nazianzum, while he rebels against the prevalent statements of the Atonement, he remains, in his less theological moments, very much under their influence. It is certainly true that he presents the Moral aspect of the Atonement with a fulness and a vigour unparalleled until modern times. But this aspect was no new one. We have found it developed again and again by earlier writers, both Greek and Latin, though, indeed, always in subordination to transactional statements of different kinds. Great stress is laid upon it by several of Abelard's contemporaries, notably by his friend, Robert Pulleyn, and by Peter Lombard, while his great opponent, Bernard, is by no means free from its influence. It is really mainly in emphasis that he differs from these writers, though he laid himself peculiarly open to attack by the vigorous language in which he couched his criticisms and by his readiness to cast aside the venerated traditions of the past. His life, too, was no commendation of his doctrine. He was, in fact, an opponent who played into Bernard's hand. His condemnation was easily secured, but whether it was wholly deserved is open to question.

The views for which Abelard was condemned are to be found in his Commentary on the Epistle to the Romans. His central thesis is the Cross as the manifestation of the love of God, and to the thought of this love he continually returns. The justification of man is the kindling of this divine love in his heart in the presence of the Cross. And to love is to be free from the slavery of sin, to attain to the true liberty of the sons of God. Our justification and reconciliation, he says, consist in the singular grace shown to us in the Incarnation, and in the endurance of Christ in teaching us by word and by example even unto death.

> That fired by so great a benefit of God's grace, true love may not fear to suffer anything on His behalf.[1]

And he continues :

> Thus our redemption is that loftiest love inspired in us by the passion of Christ, which not only frees us from the slavery of sin, but also gives us the true freedom of the sons of God, that we may be wholly filled not with fear, but with love of Him who has displayed such grace to us. . . . He testifies, therefore, that He came to extend among men this true liberty of love.[2]

The thought is repeated elsewhere :

> It is to be noted that the apostle here clearly expresses the mode of our redemption through the death of Christ, viz. when he says that He died for us to no other end than that true liberty of love might be propagated in us, through that loftiest love which He displayed to us.[3]

---

[1] Ut tanto divinae gratiae accensi beneficio, nil jam tolerare propter ipsum vera reformidet caritas (on *Rom.* iii. 26).

[2] Redemptio itaque nostra est illa summa in nobis per passionem Christi dilectio, quae non solum a servitute peccati liberat sed veram nobis filiorum Dei libertatem acquirit; ut amore ejus potius quam timore cuncta impleamus, qui nobis tantam exhibuit gratiam. . . . Ad hanc itaque veram caritatis libertatem in hominibus propagandam se venisse testatur (*ibid.*).

[3] Notandum vero est apostolum hoc loco modum nostrae redemptionis per mortem Christi patenter exprimere cum videlicet eum pro nobis non ob aliud mortuum dicit, nisi per veram illam caritatis libertatem in nobis propagandam, per hanc videlicet qua nobis exhibuit summam dilectionem (on *Rom.* v. 5).

And he goes on to explain that this exhibition of love was made:

By dying for us while we were yet sinners.[1]

These two passages are noteworthy as being an attempt to set the ethical, manward, aspect of Atonement in a primary and not in a secondary place. The thought that the display of God's love inspires love in man is no new one. Many writers had said that the example of Christ fired men to imitate His endurance in suffering. But, in these passages at least, Abelard seems to regard this as a complete account of Redemption. As Moberly[2] says: "It is a matter for sincere regret that he seems to lay so much causal stress upon the 'exhibition' of the love of the Cross, as though he conceived it as working its effect mainly as an appeal, or incitement, to feeling."

That this is no mere casual language is shown by the very definite attempt which Abelard makes to expound this theory in relation to the putting away of sin. The Law, he says, had commanded that love of God and of our neighbour which is justification, but had failed to enforce its command. In Christ the appeal of love succeeds where the Law had failed.

The true love of Christ as God and of our neighbour is compelled by that greatest of benefits which he displayed to us; and this is the condemnation of sin in us, that is the destruction of all offence and guilt through the love inspired by this greatest of benefits.[3]

He goes on to explain that this is what is intended when Christ is called a victim for sin. Remission of sins and reconciliation are wrought in His blood, but the power is love, love in God working as love in us. Such teaching

[1] Pro nobis scilicet adhuc peccatoribus moriendo (*ibid.*).

[2] *Op. cit.* p. 375. The above paragraphs are much indebted to Moberly's admirable and sympathetic sketch.

[3] Ipsum quippe Christum tanquam Deum, ipsum proximum vere diligere, summum illud beneficium, quod nobis exhibuit, compellit; quod est in nobis peccatum damnare, id est, reatum omnem et culpam destruere per caritatem ex hoc summo beneficio (on *Rom.* viii. 3).

as this was clearly quite incompatible with the old transactional theories, and Abelard made no attempt to veil the inconsistency. He drew attention to it, indeed, by his explicit interpretations of sacrificial and transactional language in terms of his own theory. It was not without reason that Bernard took alarm. In the letter which he wrote accusing Abelard to Pope Innocent II. he fastens upon these more extreme statements, and exposes their weaknesses with great rhetorical vigour.

He holds and argues that it must be reduced just to this, that by His life and teaching He handed down to men a pattern of life, that by His suffering and death He set up a standard of love. Did He then teach righteousness and not bestow it; reveal love and not infuse it; and so return to His own place?[1]

The Father did not demand the blood of the Son, but yet He accepted it when offered; thirsting not for blood but for salvation, for salvation was in the blood—salvation, of course, and not, as that fellow thinks and writes, the mere display of love. For he sums up the string of invectives which, impiously and unguardedly, he has vomited out against God by saying that the whole reason for the appearance of God in the flesh was our education, or, as he says lower down, our instruction, by His word and example; the whole reason for His suffering and death was the display or commendation of His love towards us.[2]

But what profit is it that He has instructed us if He has not restored us? . . . If Christ's benefit consisted only in the display of good works, it remains but to say that Adam only harmed us by the display of sin.[3]

---

[1] Ad id solum putat et disputat redigendum, ut traderet hominibus formam vitae vivendo et docendo; patiendo autem et moriendo caritatis metam praefigeret. Ergo docuit justitiam et non dedit; ostendit caritatem sed non infudit; et sic rediit in sua? (*Tractatus ad Innocentium II. Pontificem contra quaedam capitula errorum Abaelardi; Ep.* 190. 7).

[2] Non requisivit Deus Pater sanguinem Filii, sed tamen acceptavit oblatum; non sanguinem sitiens, sed salutem, quia salus erat in sanguine. Salus, plane, et non sicut iste sapit et scribit sola caritatis ostensio. Sic enim concludit tot calumnias et invectiones suas quas in Deum tam impie quam imperite evomuit, ut dicat: Totum esse quod Deus in carne apparuit, nostram de verbo et exemplo ipsius institutionem, sive ut postmodum dicit, instructionem; totum quod passus et mortuus est, suae erga nos caritatis ostensionem vel commendationem (*ib.* 8).

[3] Ceterum quid prodest quod nos instituit si non restituit? . . . si omne quod profuit Christus in sola fuit ostensione virtutum, restat ut dicatur quod Adam quoque ex sola peccati ostensione nocuerit (*ib.* 9).

On this presentation and refutation of his case Abelard was condemned unheard. His extremest statements were taken as representative of his whole position and were even exaggerated by Bernard's rhetoric. His very real concessions to traditional language were ignored. And yet, whatever may be thought of the justice of the whole procedure, there is no doubt that Bernard saw the true bearing of Abelard's thought, and that his criticism exposed a real weakness. It was the Pelagian danger over again, as the last of the above passages points out,[1] and if pressed to its logical conclusion could only tend to belittle both the sin of man and the grace of God. The whole standpoint is that of an individualist who does not appreciate adequately either the solidarity of mankind in sin, or the solidarity of the redeemed in Christ. Abelard is no mystic, and has failed to appreciate the great truth, so clearly set forth by the writers of the early Church, of the summing up of humanity in Christ, so that the experiences and sufferings of Christ are ours too. And he has failed equally to grasp the equivalent truth which was replacing the Greek mysticism in the West, the doctrine of infused righteousness. And so the Cross remains for him a mere incentive to love, making its appeal to emotion and to feeling, but not entering in the power of the Holy Spirit into the very heart of man.

To this extent, then, Bernard is justified. He saw a real weakness and he exposed it effectively and relentlessly. Yet he did no justice to the real devotional value which this Moral aspect of Atonement could possess. Moberly cites an admirable example of this devotion from Abelard's letters to Heloissa. A sentence or two may be quoted:

Gaze upon Him as He goes out to be crucified for thee, laden with His own cross. Be thou of the people and of the women

[1] In the context Bernard refers explicitly to the Pelagian character of Abelard's thought.

who were bewailing and lamenting Him. . . . Suffer thou with Him who suffered willingly for thy redemption, and be thou pierced with Him who was crucified for thee. . . . So, with love's utter devotion be thou pierced to the heart.[1]

It may be true that the theory does not really account for the devotion, that it ignores the dreadful reality of sin as a condition of the soul, that it fails to apprehend the fulness of the working of the grace of God. Yet the devotion is there, deep and unquestionable, and in the language of that devotion Abelard more than once goes back to language such as Bernard himself might have used.

He has bought thee, not with what is His but with Himself. With His own blood He bought thee and redeemed thee. See what right He has over thee, and consider of how high a price thou art. . . . Thou art greater than heaven, greater than the world, for thy price is the very Creator of the world.[2]

Bernard may be excused for not knowing this letter, but he must have known, and should in fairness have quoted the similar language which appears, side by side with the passages given above, in the Commentary on Romans.

It is written in the Epistle of Peter that we have been redeemed by the precious blood of the Only-begotten, bought without doubt from one whose slaves we were and who named the price he desired for the release of his property. Now we were held by the devil, to whose side we had been drawn by our sins. And so he named as our price the blood of Christ.[3]

---

[1] Intuere hunc exeuntem ad crucifigendum pro te et bajulantem tibi crucem. Esto de populo et de mulieribus quae plangebant et lamentabantur eum. . . . Patienti sponte pro redemptione tua compatere, et super crucifixo pro te compungere. . . . Super his toto devotionis affectu compungere (*Ep.* 5).

[2] Emit te iste non suis sed seipso. Proprio sanguine emit te, et redemit. Quantum jus in te habeat vide, et quam preciosa sis intuere. . . . Major es coelo, major es mundo; cujus pretium ipse conditor mundi factus est (*ibid.*).

[3] Scriptum est in epistola Petri quia redempti sumus precioso sanguine unigeniti, ab aliquo sine dubio empti cujus eramus servi, qui et pretium proposuit quod voluit ut dimitteret quod tenebat. Tenebat autem nos diabolus, cu idistricti eramus peccatis nostris. Poposcit ergo pretium nostrum sanguinem Christi (on *Rom.* iv. 11).

This passage is, of course, not Abelard's own, being a verbatim quotation from Origen,[1] whose Commentary on Romans was clearly before him, in the Latin version. But it is at least significant that he should have made the quotation. And the same thoughts reappear at intervals.

That He might justly deliver us from the dominion of sin or the devil.[2]

God caused His co-eternal Wisdom to assume passible and mortal humanity, that while He subjected Himself to the punishment of sin, He might appear to have a personal share in the flesh of sin, *i.e.* the flesh that is conceived in sin.[3]

And on Rom. iv. 25, he supplies that which Bernard accused him of denying.

In two ways He is said to have died for our faults: first, because the faults for which He died were ours, and we committed the sins of which He bore the penalty; secondly, that by dying He might remove our sins, *i.e.* might take away the penalty of our sins, introducing us into Paradise at the price of His own death, and might, by the display of such grace, draw our minds away from the will to sin, and incline them to the fullest love of Himself.[4]

It is true that Abelard's heart is in this last thought, the Moral aspect of Atonement, and Bernard was justified in singling it out for criticism. But it was not fair to argue that he ignored the change in our hearts from sin to righteousness, however unsatisfactory it may be to

[1] *In Rom.* ii. 13, quoted above, p. 37.

[2] Ut nos juste a dominio peccati sive diaboli possit eruere (on *Rom.* vii. *ad fin.*). Abelard also states this thought explicitly in his *Apologia.*

[3] Coaeternam sibi sapientiam fecit humiliari usque ad assumptionem passibilis et mortalis hominis, ita ut per poenam peccati cui subjacebat, ipse etiam carnem peccati, id est in peccato conceptam, habere videretur (on *Rom.* viii. 3).

[4] Duobus modis propter delicta nostra mortuus dicitur, tum quia nos deliquimus propter quod ille moreretur, et peccatum commisimus cujus ille poenam sustinuit, tum etiam ut peccata nostra moriendo tolleret, i.e. poenam peccatorum introducens nos in Paradisum pretio suae mortis auferret, et, per exhibitionem tantae gratiae, . . . animos nostros a voluntate peccandi retraheret, et in summam suam dilectionem intenderet (on *Rom.* iv. 25).

regard this simply as due to the exhibition or display of God's love. Abelard's instinctive feeling of the power of love as a triumphant force was a true one, even though he failed to give that feeling coherent expression. To this extent he was undoubtedly in advance of his age. But where his own thought was lacking he was just as ready as his contemporaries to fall back upon the language of tradition. And even though he fails utterly to reconcile the two modes of thought, and seems to be wholly without that reserve of mysticism which had been the strength of so much of the earlier theology, it is yet quite unjust to him to leave unnoticed the passages in which he conforms to the ordinary thought of his day. Despite Bernard's accusations it was on the basis of tradition that Abelard was able to be original. It was perhaps partly because of the influence of tradition that he did not carry his thought far enough for it to be a complete and self-consistent whole.

Orthodoxy is seldom as interesting as heterodoxy, and Bernard's own view of the Atonement seems almost timid beside the daring speculations of his opponent. Yet, defender of traditional authority though he be, he is no mere traditionalist. He has his own contribution to make and sometimes strains the thought of his predecessors almost to breaking-point. His position is outlined in his letter against Abelard. Largely for the sake of traditional authority he restates the transactional theory, very much on the lines, and even in the language, of Augustine.

> Since none the less he laid his hands on the innocent one, he most justly lost those whom he held, since He who owed nothing to death by accepting the injury of death rightly loosed both from the debt of death and from the power of the devil him who was liable to them.[1]

---

[1] Cum nihilominus innocenti manus injecit, justissime quos tenebat amisit: quando is qui morti nil debebat, accepta mortis injuria, jure illum qui obnoxius erat, et mortis debito, et diaboli solverit dominio (*Ep.* 190. 6).

But like Augustine Bernard emphasizes the justice of this in such a manner that the devil passes almost out of sight altogether.

> But although we call the devil's power just, we do not so term his will also. . . . For it is not in accordance with power but in accordance with will that any one is called just or unjust. The devil then had this right, such as it was, over man, justly permitted, though not justly acquired, but wickedly usurped. Thus, then, man was justly held captive; but in such a manner that the justice was not in man, nor in the devil, but in God.[1]

This thought, if worked out to its conclusion, clearly demands a Godward theory of Atonement, whether on the penal lines suggested by Gregory the Great, or of the type of Anselm's Satisfaction theory. And the influence of Anselm's language is clearly shown in the context.

> That the satisfaction of One may be imputed to all, even as One bare the sins of all; nor was it one who sinned, and another who made satisfaction, for the Head and the body is one Christ. The Head therefore made satisfaction for the members.[2]

But though we have here an echo of Anselm's language, Bernard has not understood, or adopted, the Satisfaction theory. His thought is indeed one that is even more profound, for he has grasped, what so few of the Latin theologians ever grasped, the great truth of the solidarity of mankind in Christ, the Head who suffered for his members, and in whom His members suffer. Bernard was, indeed, one of the greatest of the mystics, and here his mysticism reveals itself, giving life to the dry bones of traditional theology. He framed no new theory,

[1] Caeterum etsi justam dicimus diaboli postestatem, non tamen et voluntatem. . . . Non enim a potestate, sed a voluntate, justus injustusve quis dicitur. Hoc ergo diaboli quoddam in hominem jus, etsi non jure acquisitum, sed nequiter usurpatum, juste tamen permissum. Sic itaque homo juste captivus tenebatur; ut tamen nec in homine nec in diabolo illa esset justitia, sed in Deo (*ib.* 5).

[2] Ut videlicet satisfactio unius omnibus imputetur, sicut omnium peccata unus ille portavit: nec alter jam inveniatur qui forefecit, alter qui satisfecit; quia caput et corpus unus est Christus. Satisfecit ergo caput pro membris (*ib.* 6).

for he needed none. The living Fact was too clear to him to need explanations other than those which the saints of old had given.

As might be expected in a mystic, Bernard, here again following Augustine, finds the source of redemption in God's love, God "thirsting not for blood but for salvation."[1]

> It was not the death, but the good will of Him who died that pleased Him, of Him that by that abolished death and wrought salvation.[2]

But in thus emphasizing God's love Bernard is really, despite his indignation, drawing closer to Abelard than he knows. The strict traditional view had no explanation to offer for the apparent change in God from wrath to love, while Abelard sees the love of God, and only the love of God, throughout the whole work of salvation. And Bernard comes still closer, though here again he is only following the lines of the Augustinian tradition, when, in discussing the reason why God chose this out of many ways of redemption, he says:

> Perchance that method is the best whereby in a land of forgetfulness and sloth we might be the more strongly and vividly reminded of our fall, through the many and great sufferings of Him who made it good.[3]

In this, however, Bernard does not go beyond the limits laid down for him by the writers of the past, and, like Gregory the Great he saw the need of some manward influence of Atonement which is more in its effects than the mere stimulus of a great example. This is the very key to his criticisms of Abelard quoted above. Not merely an example, but also an infusion, of righteousness is necessary if man is to be made righteous. This thought

[1] *Ib.* 8; quoted above, p. 106.

[2] Non mors sed voluntas placuit sponte morientis, et illa morte expungentis mortem, operantis salutem (*ib.* 8).

[3] Fortasse is praestat, per quem in terra oblivionis, gravedinis, lapsus nostri tot et tantis gravaminibus Reparatoris fortius et vivacius admoneremur (*ib.* 8).

is expanded by Bernard elsewhere, especially in his treatise On Grace and Freewill, in which he draws out the three works of grace upon man—creation, reformation, consummation.[1] The whole Christian life is for him a work of the Divine grace.

If, then, God works in us good thought, will, act, He does the first without us, the second with us, the third through us.[2]

The same thought is put quite plainly, if more shortly, in this Epistle.

I might call myself righteous, but with His righteousness.[3]

If from Adam I am tainted with original lust, I am also infused with spiritual grace of Christ.[4]

But Bernard gives this conception a new turn through his mysticism. The summary at the close of the Epistle is characteristic.

And indeed I discern three things especially in this work of our salvation: the form of humility, in which God emptied Himself; the measure of love, which reached even to death, and that the death of the Cross; the sacrament of redemption, in which He undertook that death which He endured. Of these the two first, without the last, are as though you should paint on empty air. Great indeed, and very necessary is the example of humility, great and worthy of all acceptation that of love: but they have no foundation, and therewith no position, if redemption be lacking. With all effort would I follow the lowly Jesus; I desire to embrace in the arms of vicarious love Him who loved me and gave Himself for me: but I must also eat the Paschal Lamb. For, unless, I eat His flesh and drink His blood, I shall have no life in me. It is one thing to follow Jesus, one thing to embrace Him, another to eat Him.[5]

---

[1] *De Gratia et Libero Arbitrio*, xiv.

[2] Si ergo Deus bonum cogitare, velle, perficere operatur in nobis, primum profecto sine nobis, secundum nobiscum, tertium per nos facit (*ib.* 14). This side of Bernard's thought is fully illustrated by Ritschl, *Hist. of the Christian Doctrine of Justification and Reconciliation*, pp. 95 ff.

[3] Justum me dixerim sed illius justitia (*Ep.* 190. 6).

[4] Si infectus ex illo originali concupiscentia, etiam Christi gratia spirituali perfusus sum (*ib.* 6).

[5] Et quidem tria quaedam praecipua in hoc opere nostrae salutis intueor: formam humilitatis, in qua Deus semetipsum exinanivit; charitatis mensuram, quam usque ad mortem, et mortem crucis extendit;

It is striking indeed that in this summary Abelard's theory finds a place, though only a secondary one, while the traditional view seems almost to have vanished in the far higher mystical conception of the Sacrament with which it is involved. In this view of the sacramental means of grace as bringing about that unity with Christ which is so essential to any real appropriation of the power of the Atonement Bernard goes far beyond any earlier Western writer, beyond even Anselm himself. The doctrine of infused righteousness becomes a great and living reality, and no mere scholastic formula. Abelard's thought is indeed pale and thin beside such a faith as this, but Bernard failed to see that his own position could be reached at least as easily from the point of view of Abelard as from that which he himself maintained out of a conservative respect for traditional authority.

Peter Lombard, though he writes rather after the middle of the twelfth century, may be considered here, as being the last writer who explicitly supports the old traditional view. His discussion on this, as on other subjects, has an importance beyond its own intrinsic value, since his Sentences formed the theological textbook of the Middle Ages, and later scholars spent much of their time in commenting upon his work. He himself, however, had the mind rather of a collector than of an original thinker, and in the passage where he discusses the Atonement[1] we find a medley of thoughts, no very clear attempt at co-ordination being made. It is

---

redemptionis sacramentum, quo ipsam mortem, quam pertulit, sustulit. Horum duo priora sine ultimo sic sunt ac si super inane pingas. Magnum profecto et valde necessarium humilitatis, magnum et omni acceptatione dignum charitatis exemplum: sed non habent fundamentum, ac proinde nec statum, si desit redemptio. Volo totis nisibus humilem sequi Jesum; cupio eum qui dilexit me et tradidit semetipsum pro me quibusdam brachiis vicariae dilectionis amplecti: sed oportet me et Agnum manducare paschalem. Nisi enim manducavero carnem ejus, et bibero ejus sanguinem, non habebo vitam in memetipso. Aliud sequi Jesum, aliud tenere, aliud manducare (*ib.* 9).

[1] *Sent.* iii. 19; from this passage the following quotations are taken.

interesting, however, to find that of his two great predecessors, Anselm and Abelard, it is Abelard who has made the greatest impression upon him. He is singularly lacking in any appreciation of the Godward aspect of Atonement, and, as a result, we have the curious and practically unique phenomenon of a theologian who tried to hold both a manward and a devilward reference of Christ's passion without attaching any great importance to its Godward side.

The strange language borrowed from Augustine, in which Peter Lombard compares the Cross to a mouse-trap set for the devil has been given above,[1] and we need not dwell upon it further. He quotes at considerable length from his predecessors, and, though his concessions to tradition are in reality little greater than those which Abelard had made, the obviously orthodox intention of the writer sufficed for most of the critics of his day, and his further suggestions, though they were to some extent suspect, did not provoke any violent antagonism, as those of Abelard had done.

The only hint of a Godward explanation of Atonement is more upon the lines of the Penal aspect suggested by Gregory the Great than of Anselm's Satisfaction theory. It occurs in connexion with the idea of penance, and serves to illustrate the ease with which the doctrine of merits might have been developed into the full Penal theory had not the genius of Anselm intervened.

> That punishment by which the Church binds the penitent would not suffice, did not the punishment of Christ, who pays for us, work with it.[2]

Here, however, the thought of a substitution made, a vicarious punishment, is hardly suggested. Man at least bears his part of the punishment, and the logical conclusion that the remainder is simply lifted from our

[1] See p. 44.

[2] Non enim sufficeret illa poena qua poenitentes ligat ecclesia, nisi poena Christi cooperaretur qui pro nobis solvit.

shoulders by being laid upon Christ is not clearly before the writer's mind at all. And Peter Lombard, here following the Augustinian tradition, definitely rejects any suggestion that the attitude of God with regard to the sinner can have been modified by the death of Christ.

> We are reconciled to God, as the apostle says, by the death of Christ. This is not to be understood as though Christ had reconciled us to Him in such wise that He began to love those whom He had hated, as enemy is reconciled to enemy, so that those who before hated one another, afterwards become friends; but we are now reconciled to a loving God. For He did not begin to love us when we were reconciled by the blood of His Son, but before the world, before we were anything.[1]

This reference of the motive power of Atonement to the love of God is derived from Augustine, whom Peter Lombard quotes freely, a great part of his discussion being made up of passages from Augustine's writings. He quotes at length Augustine's discussion of the goodness of God in its relation to the authority which He has allowed the devil to exercise over man.[2] But this thought leads him not to a Godward but to a manward conception of Atonement. The love of God is the one eternal truth. It is the heart of man that changes and is changed.

Thus, at the beginning of Peter Lombard's discussion, we find the Moral theory stated almost as Abelard might have stated it.

> But how were we freed from sins by His death? Because by His death, as says the apostle, God commendeth His love towards us, *i.e.* the wonderful and laudable love of God towards us appears

---

[1] Reconciliati sumus Deo, ut ait apostolus, per mortem Christi, quod non sic intelligendum est quasi nos ei sic reconciliaverit Christus ut inciperet amare quos oderat, sicut reconciliatur inimicus inimico, ut deinde sint amici, qui ante se oderant, sed jam nos diligenti Deo reconciliati sumus. Non enim, ex quo ei reconciliati sumus per sanguinem filii nos coepit diligere, sed ante mundum, priusquam nos aliquid essemus.

[2] iii. 20, cf. Aug. *De Trin.* xiii. 12. Part of this passage has been quoted above. See p. 90.

in this, that He gave His son to death for us sinners. Now in that the pledge of such love has been displayed we are both stirred and kindled to love God, who has wrought such great things for us, and through this we are justified, *i.e.* are loosed from sins and are made righteous.[1]

Here we have again the emphasis upon the display of God's love which was so noticeable in Abelard, and again it would seem that the function of the Cross consists simply in an appeal to human feeling and emotion. Peter Lombard clearly felt the difficulty of reconciling this with the old language about a transaction with the devil and makes a conscious effort to harmonize the two points of view. It is through this stirring of love, he says, that the devil is defeated, for the chain by which we are held is the chain of our own sin, and love destroys our sin.

In that we are justified, *i.e.* are released from sin, we are freed from the devil, for he held us by the chains of sin.[2]

Then we are freed from bondage.

Thus the Son of God took passible humanity, in which also He tasted death, by which He opened heaven to us, and redeemed us from the slavery of the devil, *i.e.* from sin (for the slavery of the devil is sin), and from punishment.[3]

But this attempt to reconcile the traditional with the moral view really annihilates the former. The devil

[1] Sed quomodo a peccatis per ejus mortem soluti sumus? Quia per ejus mortem, ut ait apostolus, commendatur nobis charitas Dei, id est, apparet eximia et commendabilis charitas Dei erga nos in hoc quod filium suum tradidit in mortem pro nobis peccatoribus. Exhibita autem tantae erga nos dilectionis arrha, et nos movemur accendimurque ad diligendum Deum, qui pro nobis tanta fecit; et per hoc justificamur, id est soluti a peccatis justi efficimur. This passage provides an excellent example of the mediaeval use of "justification," which henceforth, except among Protestant theologians, includes "sanctification."

[2] In eo quod sumus justificati, id est a peccato soluti, a diabolo sumus liberati qui nos vinculis peccatorum tenebat.

[3] Ideo Dei Filius hominem passibilem sumpsit, in quo et mortem gustavit, quo caelum nobis aperuit, et a servitute diaboli, id est, a peccato (servitus enim diaboli peccatum est) et a poena redemit.

has become little more than a name. The responsibility is man's responsibility, and the sin is the sin of man, and the power of the devil over man's heart is broken so soon as man responds to the appeal of the Cross. The whole transaction is wrought out in the heart of man and not with the lord of evil. And thus it is with the heretic Abelard, and not with Bernard, that the Master of the Sentences joins hands.

Peter Lombard, standing at the dawn of the new era of thought, marks the end of the old. Henceforward in the West the Fact of the Atonement was to be enshrined in doctrine. Instead of brief allusions, hard to interpret justly, we now come to long and elaborately argued discussions, in which every detail is subjected to minute scrutiny by the theologians of warring schools of thought. In a sense the history of the doctrine begins at this point, and it may be felt that too much space has been given to the hints and chance phrases of earlier days. Yet it is with regret that we pass on to the days of scholasticism, mediaeval and Protestant. There is a life and a reality in the many-sided thought of the old fathers which is often sadly lacking in the full disquisitions of later theology. The cry of recent years has been that we need to get back from the theology to the Fact, and the theologians have given the Church good cause for weariness of soul. It is good for us to go back to those early days when, in connexion with the doctrine of the Atonement at least, souls were not wearied with the subtleties of theological distinction, when a theory utterly unworthy of the Fact sufficed, just because the ever-present fact needed the support of no theory, when the language of every type of theory is constantly present, inconsistent and unashamed, just because no type of theory was adequate to the Experience of the Church.

It was wonderful that these young days could last so long. But the inevitable end came at last. With Anselm, Bernard, and Abelard, Experience became self-conscious, and at once the era of definition and controversy dawned. It was inevitable, and the age of definition has not been without fruit. We are learning its lessons to-day. But the fathers have a lesson for us too, a lesson, it may be, that comes nearer to life and to reality than all the theories that the wit of man has framed.

CHAPTER VI

THE SATISFACTION THEORY OF ANSELM

BOLD as were the speculations of Abelard, in reality the most revolutionary thinker of his day was Anselm, saint and loyal upholder of the authority of the Church. This fact was obscured for his contemporaries by his life of devoted suffering for the Papal cause, by his unquestioned sanctity, and by the supreme dialectical skill of his writings. Yet it has seldom been given to any writer to work such a change in the history of thought as that wrought by Anselm's short treatise, *Cur Deus Homo?*

The effect of this treatise, written, as Anselm tells us, partly in England and partly during his exile, was to transfer the interest of theological speculation to the Godward aspect of Atonement, and finally to put an end to all attempts to state the doctrine of Redemption in terms of a transaction with the devil. In itself this did not constitute anything more than an advance upon lines suggested by earlier writers. As we have seen, language of this Godward type had often been used, though except perhaps in the case of Athanasius, it seldom received any great emphasis. In the Latin theologians the Godward aspect of Atonement appears in the stress laid upon the complete justice of the transaction with the devil. Augustine and Gregory the Great had gone even further, and had suggested that it was some absolute justice, something lying in the very essence of God's own nature, that demanded the Atonement. But neither writer had developed this thought. They had regarded God very much as a Judge administering a law like the law of Rome. Augustine's main interest is to defend the Judge from the charge of injustice towards the devil, and though he realises also the fact of God's eternal love, he fails to co-ordinate the conceptions of love and of justice. Gregory is more concerned to show that the Judge does not take a light view of man's sin. The question of the justice of God's action with regard to Christ finds a ready solution throughout the Latin writers in the fact of His willingness to die.

Anselm tries to penetrate further into the problem of the meaning of the Atonement for God Himself. He dismisses at once, as unthinkable, all attempts to regard the devil as being in any sense the possessor of rights. And the mere conception of God as just does not cover the facts of the case. Where is the justice of releasing the guilty and of punishing the innocent, however willing the latter may be to suffer? Some further thought than that of mere unanalysed justice is necessary, if we are to regard God as Judge at all. It is Anselm's great contribution to the history of doctrine that he both saw this difficulty and supplied a solution.

Among the principles of Roman Law[1] current in

[1] Harnack's assertion that the conception of satisfaction was derived from Roman law (see *Hist. of Dogma*, vi. 56-58) has been strongly contested by Cremer (*Stud. und Krit.*, 1893, pp. 316 ff.), who argues for a Germanic origin. Harnack admits that a correspondence with Germanic ideas may easily be proved, but points out that the conception existed in Roman law quite apart from any Germanic influence. It is true that in the case of Roman public law the "poena" was identical with the "satisfactio." But, as Tertullian's language shows, even Roman law must have recognized the principle, common, apparently, to all civilizations, "that private injuries are cancelled by indemnifications which restore to the injured party his honour." This is the idea which underlies the penitential system of the Church, which was developed before there is any probability of Germanic influence, going back to Cyprian and Tertullian (see Wirth, *Die Verdienstbegriff bei Tertullian*, and Bethune-Baker, *op. cit.* pp. 353 ff.).

the thought of the age was that of satisfaction as an alternative to punishment in the case of private offences. Such an offence must be punished unless satisfaction is made. Thus Sulpitius Severus says:

> Fornication is liable to punishment unless it is purged by satisfaction.[1]

We have already quoted passages from Tertullian, whose legal training adds to their significance, in which a similar conception is present. And the whole penitential system of the Church had long rested upon the idea that penance, as a satisfaction offered to God in this life, might, through the mediation of the Church, be accepted as an alternative to eternal death, the proper punishment of sin in the world to come. It was through this principle of satisfaction that Anselm sought his solution of the problem of Atonement.

With this application of the principle of satisfaction went another change, less conscious, but at least equally far-reaching in its results. The political outlook had changed greatly since the days of Augustine and Gregory. The Roman Empire stood no longer as the visible embodiment of the idea of justice, and had been replaced by the more concrete personal dignity of the great feudal overlords. Justice and law had now become a personal matter, and any breach of the law was a direct offence against a person. And thus the whole conception of satisfaction was bound up closely with

---

And it was probably by the penitential system of the Church that Anselm's theory was primarily suggested. Harnack admits, however, that such Germanic conceptions as that of Weregild may very probably have strengthened and coloured the theory of penance already developed in the Church, and also that " the peculiar expression Anselm gives to the notion 'honour' of God is *perhaps* due to Germanic influence, although one must look very closely to discover a shade of difference on this point between Anselm's God and the injured and wrathful God of Tertullian."

[1] Fornicatio deputatur ad poenam, nisi satisfactione purgatur (*Dial.* ii. 10).

the feudal ideal.[1] As always the doctrine of Redemption was affected by current politics. And thus we find Anselm regarding God no longer as a Judge, but rather as a feudal Overlord, bound above all things to safeguard His honour and to demand an adequate satisfaction for any infringement of it. The idea of such satisfaction was deep-seated in the thought of the day. Could it be applied, where the idea of justice seemed to have failed, to explain the problem of the Cross of Christ?

To this question the *Cur Deus Homo?* attempted an answer.

The key to the whole book is to be found in the Preface. Anselm proposes to argue from pure principles of logic, making no assumptions as to the truth of the claims of Christianity. He undertakes to show (1) that salvation apart from Christ is impossible, (2) that humanity must needs be saved, and therefore (3) that all that we believe of Christ must be true.

> The first book contains the objections of unbelievers who reject the Christian faith, thinking it opposed to reason, and the reply of the believer; and then it proves by necessary reasoning, Christ being set aside, as though nothing had ever been known of Him, that it is impossible for any man to be saved without Him. In the second book in the same way, as though nothing were known of Christ, it is shown by equally clear and true reasoning, that human nature has been constituted to this end that at some time the whole man, *i.e.* both in body and in soul, should enjoy a blessed immortality; and that it is necessary that this end, for which man was made, should be effected in his case, but only by means of a God-man; and that, therefore, all that we believe of Christ ought of necessity to have occurred.[2]

The book is thus primarily a defence of the doctrine

---

[1] Here lies the fundamental truth of Cremer's position. The feudal idea had in fact enormously increased the scope of the idea of satisfaction, since now the personal dignity of the ruler became the basis of all law, public and private alike. The true Roman conception of abstract justice reappears in Reformation times, when it led, as it had nearly done in the days of Gregory the Great, to the Penal Theory.

[2] Prior quidem infidelium respuentium Christianam fidem, quia rationi putant illam repugnare, continet objectiones, et fidelium responsiones; ac tandem remoto Christo, quasi nunquam aliquid fuerit de illo, probat rationibus necessariis esse impossibile ullum

of the Incarnation, and the question of the Atonement is only discussed with the wider problem in view. This served to some extent to cover the real novelty of Anselm's theories, which were thus able to pose as a fresh line of defence for an accepted doctrine. It also enabled Anselm to state indirectly his objections to the crude statements of his predecessors.

It is noticeable that Anselm does not doubt his ability to show the logical necessity of the Incarnation, and therewith of his own view of the Atonement. He is not content that it should be regarded as merely suitable or convenient that God should so save man. His whole argument is that God must have saved man, and must of necessity have saved him in this particular way. From this presupposition that a logically complete argument is possible spring most of Anselm's difficulties. Yet it was a real truth that he had grasped when he thus asserted the inherent power of human reason to probe the deep things of God. Religion and reason cannot be divorced without irreparable injury to both. And if Anselm and the schoolmen trusted too heroically to reason and its powers, there have been periods which would have been all the richer for a portion of the same great faith.

In the opening chapters of the *Cur Deus Homo?* Anselm lays down the presuppositions upon which the whole is to depend. He depicts the critic of Christianity as asking

> by what rational necessity a God-man was made, and, as we believe and confess, restored life to the world by His death.[1]

---

hominem salvari sine illo. In secundo autem libro similiter, quasi nihil sciatur de Christo, monstratur non minus aperta ratione et veritate, naturam humanam ad hoc institutam esse, ut aliquando immortalitate beata totus homo, id est in corpore et in animo, frueretur; ac necesse esse ut hoc fiat de homine propter quod factus est, sed non nisi per hominem Deum, atque ex necessitate omnia quae de Christo credimus fieri oportere (*Cur Deus Homo?* Praef.).

[1] Qua scilicet ratione vel necessitate Deus homo factus sit, et morte sua, sicut nos credimus et confitemur, mundo vitam reddiderit (i. 1).

This is the question which he proposes to answer. He pays a delicate compliment to his predecessors, remarking that what they have said ought really to be sufficient. Nevertheless he thinks that he has a real contribution to offer, though he is careful to add, in a spirit very unlike that of Abelard, that what he says is only to be regarded as a private opinion, subject to ratification by superior authority.[1]

Anselm then proceeds to clear the ground by a series of preliminary discussions, couched in the form of objections raised by unbelievers and brought forward for discussion by Anselm's interrogator, Boso.

1. The objection that the story of the Incarnation is unworthy of God, who could not fittingly endure weariness, hunger, thirst, and a cruel death, is met by the old argument that it was the most fitting way to man's salvation. But this is made to lead up to a more important point. Boso points out that mere poetical parallels between the method of the fall and the method of salvation have little weight with unbelievers, who demand something more firmly based in logical necessity.

> Wherefore, when we present to unbelievers these congruities of which you speak . . . they consider us to be, as it were, painting upon a cloud. We must, therefore, show first a rational basis for the truth, *i.e.* a necessity which may prove that God should or could stoop to the indignities which we proclaim.[2]

Thus Anselm sets aside a whole series of "congruities" much in vogue among his predecessors. He will have reason, and reason only.

2. Boso then asks why some other man or angel should not have made the Atonement. This Anselm dismisses for the present with the rather sophistical argument that man would not thus be restored to his

[1] *Ib.* 2.

[2] Quapropter cum has convenientias, quas dicis, infidelibus . . . obtendimus . . . quasi super nubem pingere nos existimant. Monstranda est ergo prius veritatis rationabilis soliditas, id est necessitas, quae probet Deum ad ea quae praedicamus debuisse aut potuisse humiliari (i. 4).

original position as the servant of God, since he would become the servant of his redeemer.[1]

3. Boso next passes to the old theories of the Atonement, and frames an indictment as unanswerable as it is scathing. It was a stroke of genius on Anselm's part to disarm ecclesiastical criticism by making the unbeliever responsible for his very outspoken comments. He deals first with the theory of a ransom paid to the devil, as stated by the Greek fathers. The unbeliever, Boso says, wonders especially why we speak of a "redemption."

For in what captivity, they say, or in what prison, or in whose power were you held from which God could not free you unless He redeemed you by such toil, and, at the last, by His own blood? And when we say, "He redeemed us from sins, and from His own wrath, and from hell, and from the devil's power, whom He Himself came to conquer because we could not do so ourselves, and bought back for us the Kingdom of heaven; and by thus doing all this He showed how greatly He loved us," they reply: "If you say that God could not do all these things by a bare command, while you assert that He created all things by commanding them, you contradict yourselves, representing Him as not almighty. Or if you confess that He was able, but was unwilling, to do these things otherwise, how can you prove Him wise, when you assert that without any reason He was willing to suffer such indignities. For all these things which you allege that He did depend upon His own will; for the wrath of God is nothing else than the will to punish. If, therefore, He does not will to punish the sins of man, man is free from sins, and from God's wrath, and from hell, and from the power of the devil, and he receives those things which he forfeited on account of sins. For in whose power is hell or the devil? Or whose is the kingdom of heaven, save His who made all things? [2]

---

[1] i. 5.

[2] In qua namque, aiunt nobis, captione, aut in quo carcere, aut in cujus potestate tenebamini, unde vos Deus non potuit liberare, nisi vos tot laboribus et ad ultimum suo sanguine redimeret? Quibus cum dicimus: Redemit nos a peccatis, et ab ira sua, et de inferno, et de potestate diaboli, quem, quia nos non poteramus, ipse pro nobis venit expugnare, et redemit nobis regnum coelorum; et quia haec omnia hoc modo fecit, ostendit quantum nos diligeret; respondent: Si dicitis quia Deus haec omnia facere non potuit solo jussu, quem cuncta jubendo creasse dicitis, repugnatis vobismetipsis, quia

To reply, as Augustine had done, that this way was a fitting one for the revelation of God's love, is to deny God's power of showing love to us as and when He pleases. And to say simply that Christ came to defeat the devil will not serve.

> Does not the omnipotence of God reign everywhere ? What then did God lack, that He should descend from heaven to defeat the devil ? [1]

The form which the argument had taken in the Latin fathers is then reviewed, and Boso practically quotes Augustine and Leo :

> But there is also the following account which we are wont to give, viz. that God was bound to act against the devil for man's release by judicial means before He did so by force, so that when the devil slew Him in whom was no cause of death, and who was God, he might justly lose the power which he had over sinners ; otherwise God would have done him unjust violence, since he held just possession of man, whom he had not drawn to him by violence, but who had himself freely surrendered to him. I do not see what force this account has. For if the devil or man were his own, or belonged to another than God, or were under any other power than that of God, perhaps such a statement might rightly be made. But since, neither the devil nor man belonged to any other than God, and neither exists apart from His power, what reason bound God to deal with His own, concerning His own, in His own, otherwise than to punish His servant who had persuaded his fellow-servant to leave their common Lord, and to join him, and as a traitor had received the fugitive, as a thief the fellow-thief laden with his Master's property. . . . Or, if God, the Judge of all, should rescue man

---

impotentem illum facitis. Aut si fatemini quia potuit, sed non voluit nisi hoc modo, quomodo sapientem illum ostendere potestis, quem sine ulla ratione tam indecentia velle pati asseritis ? Omnia enim haec, quae obtenditis, in ejus voluntate consistunt ; ira namque Dei non est aliud quam voluntas puniendi. Si ergo non vult punire peccata hominum, liber est homo a peccatis et ab ira Dei et ab inferno et a potestate diaboli, quae omnia propter peccata patitur, et recipit ea quibus propter eadem peccata privatur. Nam in cujus potestate est infernus aut diabolus ? aut cujus est regnum coelorum nisi ejus qui fecit omnia ? (i. 6).

[1] Nonne Dei omnipotentia regnat ubique ? Quomodo ergo indigebat Deus ut ad vincendum diabolum de coelo descenderet ? (i. 6).

thus held from the power of him who so unjustly held him, either to punish him otherwise than through the devil, or to spare him, how is this an injustice. For even though man were justly tormented by the devil, yet it was unjustly that the devil tormented him.[1]

Boso develops this point at length and it is a contribution of the first importance to the development of the doctrine. The agent of God's just punishment is not himself necessarily just. It was no merit in the devil but rather malice that made him torment man, his fellow-sinner. The old theory had been based upon a confusion of thought, a failure to perceive that that which is justly suffered may yet be unjustly wrought. Neither the devil nor man has any status at all in God's court of justice.

In this sense, then, the devil is said justly to torment man, that God justly permits it, and man justly suffers it.[2]

And the position is not changed by the introduction of metaphors about a "bond," as though the devil had rights under some agreement.[3] The decree which man broke was not the devil's decree, but God's.

[1] Sed et illud quod dicere solemus, Deum scilicet debuisse prius per justitiam contra diabolum agere ut liberaret hominem, quam per fortitudinem, ut cum diabolus eum in quo nulla mortis erat causa, et qui Deus erat, occideret, juste potestatem, quam super peccatores habebat, amitteret, alioquin injustam violentiam fecisset illi, quoniam juste possidebat hominem, quem non ipse violenter attraxerat, sed idem homo se sponte ad illum contulerat: non video quam vim habeat. Nam si diabolus aut homo suus esset aut alterius quam Dei, aut in alia quam in Dei potestate maneret, forsitan hoc recte diceretur. Cum autem diabolus aut homo non sit nisi Dei, et extra potestatem Dei neuter consistat: quam causam debuit Deus agere cum suo, de suo, in suo, nisi ut servum suum puniret, qui suo conservo communem dominum deserere et ad se persuasisset transire, ac traditor fugitivum, fur furem cum furto sui suscepisset? . . . . Aut si judex omnium Deus hominem sic possessum de potestate tam injuste possidentis, vel ad puniendum illum aliter quam per diabolum, vel ad parcendum illi, eriperet, quae haec injustitia esset? Quamvis enim homo juste a diabolo torqueretur, ipse tamen illum injuste torquebat (i. 7).

[2] Hoc itaque modo diabolus dicitur juste vexare hominem, quia Deus hoc juste permittit, et homo hoc juste patitur (i. 7).

[3] See p. 45.

There was, therefore, as regards the devil, no reason why God might not use His strength against him to deliver man.[1]

The cogency of the argument is complete. Despite his earlier deference to his predecessors Anselm does not even pretend to make out a case against Boso on their behalf. Nor indeed has any writer ever attempted to do so. Within a very few years the theory of a transaction with the devil had passed altogether out of the field of serious theology.

4. Boso finally raises difficulties as to the Penal aspect of the Atonement, and the theologians of the Reformation would have done well to take this chapter of the *Cur Deus Homo?* to heart:

> What justice is it to deliver the most just man of all to death in the sinner's stead? What man would not be adjudged culpable if he condemned the innocent that he might free the guilty? . . . If God cannot save sinners otherwise than by condemning the just, where is His omnipotence? But if He could, but would not, how are we to defend both His wisdom and His justice?[2]

Anselm answers on traditional lines. The death of Christ was not inflicted upon an unwilling victim. No compulsion whatever was involved. Christ Himself freely accepted a death which was not His due. That His death was voluntary is shown by the fact of His sinlessness, for God could not rightly have required death from one who was sinless. He died because He willed to save the world, and the world could be saved in no other way.[3] Anselm is not very happy with this solution, and offers some alternative suggestions. He points out that the good will wherewith the Son was

[1] Nihil igitur erat in diabolo cur Deus contra illum ad liberandum hominem sua uti fortitudine non deberet (i. 7).

[2] Quae autem justitia est hominem omnium justissimum morti tradere pro peccatore? Quis homo, si innocentem damnaret ut nocentem liberaret, damnandus non judicaretur? . . . Si aliter peccatores non potuit salvare quam justum damnando, ubi est ejus omnipotentia? Si vero potuit, sed noluit, quomodo defendemus sapientiam ejus atque justitiam? (i. 8).

[3] i. 9.

obedient unto death was derived from the Father, so that no violence of constraint was involved. Further, it was not of the death of Christ that the Father approved, but of the good will which led to the death. At the end Boso is still dissatisfied.

> Only this fact, that God permits Him thus to be treated, though willingly, does not seem to befit such a Father in dealing with such a Son. . . . It not only seems unbefitting for God to save man in this way, but it is not obvious how that death avails to save man. For it is strange if God so likes or needs the blood of the innocent that unless he is slain He will not or cannot spare the guilty.[1]

The question recurs later on, and for the present Anselm leaves it.

At this point the main argument begins, with two postulates, first

> . . . that we should not allow even the least thing unbecoming on the part of God, and that no argument, even the slightest, should be set aside unless a stronger is opposed to it; [2]

and secondly,

> . . . the remission of sins is therefore necessary to man that he may attain to blessedness.[3]

Apart from any record of an Incarnation, what is needed that this may be accomplished?

Anselm starts by defining sin.

> Sin is nothing else than not to render God His due.[4]

---

[1] Hoc solum, quia permittit Deus illum sic tractari, quamvis volentem, non videtur tali Patri de tali Filio convenire. . . . Nam et inconveniens videtur esse Deo hominem hoc modo salvasse; nec apparet quid mors illa valeat ad salvandum hominem. Mirum enim est si Deus sic delectatur aut eget sanguine innocentis ut non, nisi interfecto eo, parcere velit aut possit nocenti (i. 10).

[2] Ut nullum vel minimum inconveniens in Deo a nobis accipiatur, et nulla vel minima ratio, si major non repugnat, rejiciatur (i. 10).

[3] Necessaria est igitur homini peccatorum remissio ut ad beatitudinem perveniat (i. 10).

[4] Non est itaque aliud peccare quam Deo non reddere debitum (i. 11).

And God's due is the subjection of every will to His supreme will. Only thus can we pay Him the honour which we owe, by preserving righteousness, or a good will.

The man who does not render God this honour, which is His due, takes away from God what is His own, and dishonours God, and this is to sin.[1]

And it does not suffice only to restore what was taken away. A further restitution must be made for the dishonour done to God.

It does not suffice only to restore what has been taken away, but for the injury inflicted he ought to restore more than he took away. For just as when one injures another's health it does not suffice to restore his health without some additional compensation for the suffering caused, so when one wrongs another's honour, it does not suffice to restore his honour, unless he repay to him whom he has dishonoured something pleasing to him, in proportion to the injury due to his dishonour. . . . This is the satisfaction which every sinner should make to God.[2]

To the objection that God might in His mercy remit sins without any reference to His injured honour, Anselm replies that this would be an offence against all order.

To remit sin thus is simply not to punish it, and, since sin cannot be rightly ordered without satisfaction, apart from punishment, if it is not punished it remains not rightly ordered.[3]

But this, Anselm feels, is quite impossible. Sin cannot be given this position of special privilege as the one thing in God's universe not subject to law. It is not

[1] Hunc honorem debitum qui Deo non reddit aufert Deo quod suum est, et Deum exhonorat; et hoc est peccare (i. 11).

[2] Nec sufficit solummodo reddere quod ablatum est, sed pro contumelia plus debet reddere quam abstulit. Sicut enim, qui laedit salutem alterius, non sufficit si salutem restituit, nisi pro illata doloris injuria recompenset; ita qui honorem alicujus violat, non sufficit honorem reddere, si non secundum exhonorationis factam molestiam aliquid, quod placeat illi quem exhonoravit, restituat. . . . Haec est satisfactio quam omnis peccator debet Deo facere (i. 11).

[3] Sic dimittere peccatum non est aliud quam non punire; et quoniam recte ordinare peccatum sine satisfactione non est nisi punire, si non punitur, inordinatum dimittitur (i. 12).

fitting that God should do anything unjust or disorderly, and so it is no part of His liberty or goodness to leave unpunished the sinner who does not make satisfaction.[1] He concludes :

> Nothing is less tolerable in the order of things, than that the creature should take away the honour due to the Creator, and should not repay what he takes away. . . . It is necessary, then, that either the honour taken away be repaid, or punishment follow ; otherwise God will either be unjust to Himself or be powerless to secure either alternative—which it is impious even to imagine.[2]

This is Anselm's central thesis. He distinguishes satisfaction and punishment, upon the analogy of civil offences at law. Either satisfaction or punishment would vindicate God's outraged dignity, and God cannot suffer His personal honour to be violated without vindication. But which is it to be ? [3]

The next few chapters appear at first sight to be a digression. Anselm wishes to show that some men must needs be saved, and that therefore satisfaction and not punishment must be the solution of the problem of sin. Otherwise God might have been content with the punishment of mankind. He proves his point by adopting Augustine's argument [4] that the number of the fallen angels must needs be restored from among men. But if this is so the punishment due for sin must, in some cases at least, be set aside. It was necessary, therefore, that God should proceed by the way of satisfaction.[5]

The ground being thus cleared Anselm can pass on to define more closely the satisfaction that is required.

[1] i. 12.

[2] Nihil minus tolerandum est in rerum ordine, quam ut creatura Creatori debitum honorem auferat, et non solvat quod aufert. . . . Necesse est ergo, ut aut ablatus honor solvatur, aut poena sequatur ; alioquin aut sibiipsi Deus justus non erit, aut ad utrumque impotens erit ; quod nefas est vel cogitare (i. 13).

[3] i. 14, 15.

[4] Cf. Aug. *Enchiridion* 29.

[5] i. 16-19.

Man himself cannot possibly make it, for he can do nothing more than is already due from him.[1] And even if this were not so, the satisfaction for the very slightest sin, one glance taken contrary to the will of God, is a matter of infinite magnitude, greater than the preservation of an infinite number of worlds, with all the life therein.[2] Further, man has done God a special dishonour in permitting himself to be defeated by God's adversary, the devil. Therefore the satisfaction to be made must include a special reparation for this indignity. Man, weakened by his defeat, must yet conquer the very adversary to whom he yielded so easily in the days of his original strength and glory.[3] This thought, a very unnecessary piece of legalism, is Anselm's most definite point of contact with the older theory.

Thus the first book ends with the conclusion that man, destined for blessedness, yet cannot make the reparation that must be made if that blessedness is to be attained. Unless there is salvation in Christ, no way of salvation can be seen at all. Anselm challenges the unbeliever, through Boso:

> You should now demand of those for whom you speak, who do not believe that Christ is necessary for the salvation of man, to tell us in what way man can be saved without Christ. If they cannot in any way do this, let them cease to deride us, and come over and join us, who do not doubt that man can be saved by Christ; or else let them despair of salvation being possible at all. If they shrink from this, let them believe in Christ with us, that they may be saved.[4]

In the closing chapter Boso goes on to demand a clear explanation of the way in which the Atonement is made by Christ. Anselm is careful to point out that

[1] i. 20. [2] i. 21. [3] i. 22, 23.

[4] Hoc debes nunc ab illis exigere qui Christum non esse credunt necessarium ad illam salutem hominis, quorum vice loqueris, ut dicant qualiter homo salvari sine Christo possit. Quod si non possunt ullo modo, desinant nos irridere, et accedant et jungant se nobis, qui non dubitamus hominem salvari posse per Christum; aut desperent hoc ullo modo posse fieri. Quod si horrent, credant nobiscum in Christum ut possint salvari (i. 24).

the fact of satisfaction is not impaired by any imperfection of theory. Boso, however, demands a theory, and a theory based on necessary reasoning, and to this task Anselm now proceeds.[1]

The second book opens with a recapitulation. Rational beings were made righteous that they might choose and enjoy the highest good for its own sake, and that highest good is God.[2] Death was due directly to man's sin.[3] Yet despite that sin, and the death which it entailed,

> . . . God must accomplish for human nature that which He has begun, or else have made in vain so sublime a nature designed for so great a good.[4]

The difficulty at once arises that this makes it appear that God is controlled by some necessity higher than Himself. Boso asks:

> But if this is so it seems as though God were compelled to procure man's salvation, by the necessity of avoiding what is unbecoming to Himself. How then can it be denied that He does this more for His own sake than for ours? And if this is so, what thanks do we owe Him for that which He does for His own sake? And how are we to impute our salvation to His grace, if He saves us of necessity?[5]

The question is very natural. It is, in fact, the inevitable consequence of the presuppositions with which Anselm set out. He is seeking for a logical necessity of an absolute kind, for a proof that God could not have acted otherwise. He has arrived at the conclusion that God of necessity must save us, for the sake of His honour. Does it not follow then that God is bound and

[1] i. 25. [2] ii. 1. [3] ii. 2.

[4] Aut hoc de humana natura perficiet Deus quod incepit, aut in vanum fecit tam sublimem naturam ad tantum bonum (ii. 4).

[5] Sed si ita est, videtur quasi cogi Deus, necessitate vitandi indecentiam, ut salutem procuret humanam. Quomodo ergo negari poterit, plus hoc propter se facere quam propter nos? At si ita est, quam gratiam illi debemus pro eo quod facit propter se? Quomodo etiam nostram imputabimus salutem ejus gratiae, si nos salvat necessitate? (ii. 5).

not free? Anselm answers that the only necessity which binds God is of God Himself, being nothing else than His own free grace, whereby He freely undertakes His changeless purpose.

> And when we say that God does anything as it were from the necessity of avoiding dishonour, . . ., we should rather understand that He does this from the necessity of preserving His honour, which necessity is obviously nothing else than the immutability of His honour, which He has from Himself and not from another, and which is therefore improperly called necessity.[1]

For the moment this somewhat vague explanation satisfies Boso.

But how is satisfaction to be made? It must be greater in value than all which is not God. Therefore only God can make it. Yet it must be made by man. Necessarily, therefore, it must be the work of a God-man,[2] perfect God and perfect man.[3] He must be of Adam's race and not of some new race,

> . . . for he who makes satisfaction must be identical with the sinner, or of the same race.[4]

It is fitting that He should be born of a virgin.[5] To prove this Anselm resorts to a mere juggling with words, which becomes still more marked in the following section, where he argues that it was necessarily the function of the Second Person of the Trinity to become incarnate.[6]

[1] Et cum dicimus Deum aliquid facere quasi necessitate vitandi inhonestatem . . . potius intelligendum est quia hoc facit necessitate servandae honestatis, quae scilicet necessitas non est aliud quam immutabilitas honestatis ejus, quam a se ipso et non ab alio habet, et idcirco improprie dicitur necessitas (ii. 5).

[2] ii. 6.

[3] ii. 7.

[4] Necesse est ut satisfaciens idem sit qui peccator, aut ejusdem generis (ii. 8). It should be noted that no reason whatever is given for this alternative. The pressing of the identity would have given a different, and a far higher view of the Atonement, upon mystical lines.

[5] ii. 8.

[6] ii. 9—a typical sample of the worst side of mediaeval scholasticism.

The God-man will not deserve death, being sinless.[1] His pure humanity, indeed, will not be liable to death at all, since death has no place in incorrupt human nature. But as God He has power to lay down His life and to take it again. Therefore He will be able to die.

> But there is nothing more severe and arduous that a man can suffer for the honour of God, freely, and not as a matter of debt, than death; and there is no way in which a man can more entirely give himself up to God than when he delivers himself up to death for His honour. . . . It is needful, therefore, that he who would make satisfaction for man's sin should be one who can die, if he wills to do so.[2]

The death of such a man will be of infinite value, for the least hurt to His body would be a more grievous thing than the punishment of all sin (this is the only passage where Anselm actually speaks of sin as infinite).[3] And so that death would avail for all sinners, including not only those who slew Christ,[4] but also Adam and Eve, and all who died before Him.[5]

A discussion of original sin and the Immaculate Conception is here introduced and is made to lead up once more to the question of necessity, which now receives its final treatment. Boso asks:

> How then can it be that He did not die of necessity, since He could not have been unless He had been going to die? For if He had not been going to die the virgin from whom He was taken would not have been pure, since this could only be by belief in His actual death, and He could not otherwise have been taken from her.[6]

---

[1] ii. 10.

[2] Nihil autem asperius aut difficilius potest homo ad honorem Dei sponte et non ex debito pati quam mortem; et nullatenus seipsum potest homo magis dare Deo quam cum se morti tradit ad honorem illius. . . . Talem ergo oportet eum esse, qui pro peccato hominis satisfacere volet, ut mori possit, si velit (ii. 11).

[3] ii. 14. [4] ii. 15. [5] ii. 16.

[6] Quomodo ergo non necessitate mortuus est qui non nisi quia moriturus erat potuit esse? Nam si moriturus non esset, virgo de qua assumtus est munda non fuisset, quoniam hoc nequaquam valuit esse, nisi veram ejus mortem credendo, nec ille de illa potuit aliter assumi (ii. 17).

To this rather involved question Anselm returns his former answer, that the necessity binding Christ to die was the necessity of His own free will, which was the will of God.

> Since then God's will acts under no necessity, but by its own power, and His will was God's will, He died under no necessity, but by His own power alone.[1]

But Boso refuses to be satisfied, arguing that if this is so Christ might have chosen not to die, and thereby not to be Himself.

This drives Anselm back to a detailed discussion of necessity in its relation to the will of God. He shows that necessity is simply identical with that will, which is free and which yet, being supreme, cannot be changed.

> For whenever it is said that God cannot, power is not denied Him, but His invincible strength and force is implied. For nothing else is meant than nothing can make Him do what is said to be impossible for Him.[2]

So Anselm concludes that the death of Christ was under what he calls "sequent necessity," necessity which does not compel the fact to be, but which is itself based upon the occurrence of the fact. The rule of this kind of necessity is:

> Whatever was, must necessarily have been; whatever is must necessarily be, and must necessarily have been about to be; whatever is to be, must necessarily be about to be.[3]

Such necessity does not precede God's will, but depends upon it.

[1] Quoniam ergo voluntas Dei nulla necessitate facit aliquid, sed sua potestate, et voluntas illius fuit voluntas Dei, nulla necessitate mortuus est, sed sola sua potestate.

[2] Quotiens namque dicitur Deus non posse, nulla negatur in eo potestas, sed insuperabilis significatur potentia et fortitudo. Non enim aliud intelligitur nisi quia nulla res potest efficere ut agat ille quod negatur posse (ii. 18*a*).

[3] Quidquid fuit necesse est fuisse. Quidquid est, necesse est esse, et necesse est futurum fuisse. Quidquid futurum est, necesse est futurum esse (ii. 18*a*).

If you would know the true necessity of all that He did and suffered, know that they all necessarily took place, because He willed them. But no necessity preceded His will.[1]

It is difficult to see that any real necessity is left at all. The absolute logical necessity for which Anselm is seeking seems to have passed out of sight altogether.

How then did Christ's death make satisfaction? Because of the obedient righteousness in which it was incurred, whereby it was an example to men, showing them that no trials should ever turn them aside from the righteousness which they owe to God. (This hint of the Moral theory is quite out of keeping with the rest of Anselm's thought. It is a grievous lapse from "logical necessity.") And Christ was under no obligation to die, save the obligation of His own will.[2]

What reward then was He to receive for this great and free gift of His life? Here Anselm's argument is at its very weakest. He assumes that some reward must be given.

I see that it is necessary that the Father should recompense the Son; otherwise He will appear either unjust, if He is unwilling, or impotent, if He cannot; which things are foreign to God's nature.[3]

And yet there is nothing to be given, since Christ, as God, possesses all things already.

To whom then is it more fitting that He should give the fruit and recompense of His death than to those for whose salvation (as true reason has taught us) He made Himself man, and to whom (as we said) He gave by dying an example of dying for the sake of righteousness? For vainly will they be imitators of Him, if they are not partakers of His merit. Or whom can He

---

[1] Si vis omnium quae fecit et quae passus est, veram scire necessitatem, scito omnia ex necessitate fuisse, quia ipse voluit. Voluntatem vero ejus nulla praecessit necessitas (ii. 18*a*).

[2] ii. 18*b*.

[3] Imo necesse esse video ut Pater Filio retribuat; alioquin aut injustus esse videretur, si nollet, aut impotens, si non posset; quae aliena sunt a Deo (ii. 19).

more justly make heirs to that which is His due, and which He Himself does not need, and of the abundance of His fulness, than His parents and brethren, whom He sees laden with debts so numerous and so great, and languishing in profound misery, so that they may be forgiven what they owe for their sins, and may receive what they lack on account of their sins ?[1]

With this very slight and inadequate recognition of the manward aspect of Atonement the argument closes. Anselm repeats, now in his own person, that nothing was due to the devil either from God or from man, and in a short appendix rejects the suggestion of Gregory of Nyssa, that the devil might perhaps be saved.[2] Finally he declares that his view sums up the teaching of the Old and New Testaments, and submits to the judgement of theologians, "if," he adds significantly, "it be given in accordance with reason."[3]

The above sketch of the argument of the *Cur Deus Homo?* will suffice to show how great is the gulf which separates it from the earlier Latin theology. It is an attempt to carry through consistently a single logical principle, and Anselm retains practically nothing of the theories of his predecessors. Such points of contact as remain are only in points of detail. The following are the more noteworthy :

(*a*) Anselm's argument that since man was defeated by the devil the Atonement must include a defeat of the devil by man. The conception of a conquest of the devil had lain at the root of the older theory, from the time when Origen gave it prominence. But in Origen

[1] Quibus convenientius fructum et retributionem suae mortis attribueret, quam illis propter quos salvandos (sicut ratio veritatis nos docuit) hominem se fecit, et quibus (ut diximus) moriendo exemplum moriendi propter justitiam dedit? Frustra quippe imitatores ejus erunt, si meriti ejus participes non erunt. Aut quod justius faciet haeredes debiti, quo ipse non eget, et exundantiae suae plenitudinis, quam parentes suos et fratres, quos aspicit tot et tantis debitis obligatos egestate tabescere in profundo miseriarum, ut eis dimittatur quod pro peccatis debent, et detur, quo propter peccatum carent? (ii. 19).

[2] ii. 21.

[3] ii. 22. Non renuo correctionem, si rationabiliter fit.

and Gregory of Nyssa the conquest intended is wrought by God. The whole point of the conception is now changed. God may fittingly demand, as part of the satisfaction of His honour, that the defeat of man by the devil should be reversed by man. But this is quite secondary to Anselm's main argument, and might, indeed, have been omitted without affecting it.

(*b*) The emphasis on Christ's sinless obedience is retained, but the point is largely changed. In the earlier Latin writers it is used to show that the devil had no rights over Christ and had, by attacking Him, lost all claim to man. Anselm follows Augustine so far as to say that the sinlessness of Christ freed Him from all liability to death, so that His death was purely voluntary. But the reference of the argument now becomes wholly Godward, and the devil passes out of sight. It is the sinlessness of Christ which makes His offering both voluntary and worthy, an adequate satisfaction even for the wounded honour of God.

(*c*) Anselm is most like his predecessors in his greatest inconsistency, viz. in his attempt to explain how the effects of the Atonement are made operative for and in humanity. Here he falls back, like Augustine and Gregory the Great, upon the Moral theory. Abelard might easily have quoted one or two sections of the *Cur Deus Homo?* in support of his case. Christ's death is an example of obedience for us to follow. How we can ever find strength to follow that example Anselm never explains. Like most of the Latin writers he is very weak on that mystical side which had been so prominent and so vital in the thought of the Greeks. He has no apparent sense of the truth, fundamental alike to St. Paul, Origen, and Athanasius, that all humanity is one with Christ in His death and in His rising again to new life. Augustine had echoed this somewhat faintly. Gregory the Great had at least recognized that an infusion of righteousness was needed. Bernard felt, without expressing it very clearly, the mystical side of the Eucharist as the Sacrament of Redemption. Anselm's only hint of anything of the kind is the passage where he speaks of satisfaction as a "washing,"[1] fitting man for paradise. The thought is not worked out, nor indeed is there any reference to the Christian's life in this world, but only to his preparation for entry into the next.

The main theory of the *Cur Deus Homo?* is stated with the greatest clearness. It applies to the Atonement the highest social principle of which the thought of the day was aware, the principle of honour and satisfaction, and carries it through as completely and consistently as possible. The logical clearness of the book makes it an easy task to criticize it, and rather less easy to appreciate its real greatness. But its enormous influence over the thought of the Western Church shows that it was very largely adequate to the intellectual needs of its age. And the theory which the earlier Reformers developed upon the basis of Anselm's thought was in fact far inferior. He himself had seen the possibility of stating the Godward view of Atonement along Penal lines, and had rejected it decisively. The Governmental theory of Grotius was in many respects a reversion to Anselm's point of view.[2] It has only been within the last two hundred years, with the fuller perception of the meaning of personality, and of all that is implied by speaking of God as personal, that the possibility of a fuller account has been clearly seen.

The general character of the Satisfaction theory is sufficiently indicated in the preceding analysis of the *Cur Deus Homo?* and a further exposition is unnecessary. The following points are, however, of special importance:

1. In justice to Anselm it should be noticed that he does not press his view as final.

[1] *Lavatio* (i. 19).

[2] Compare, *e.g.*, the conception of God in i. 12 with that of Grotius. See p. 292.

It must be remembered that whatever a man can say or know about the subject, the deeper reasons for such a truth still lie concealed.[1]

2. Yet Anselm does claim that by his line of argument it can be seen that the Atonement must not only have been made, but have been made in accordance with the New Testament record. Here he definitely breaks with his predecessors, who had constantly asserted that God might have saved man by a word, or in any way He pleased. Anselm is sure that some necessity must lie behind God's action and that this necessity is not wholly outside the scope of human reason. Except in one or two details, not necessary to the main argument, he thinks that even Jews and pagans would have to accept his reasoning.[2]

But Anselm gets into great difficulties over this necessity. It is hard to avoid the feeling that it is something above God, binding Him to act in a fixed way. Anselm's explanation that it is God's own immutable will does not do much to remove this feeling. The difficulty is obscured, and, for the reader, complicated, by a continual play of thought between what is "necessary" and what is "fitting," and again between what is "fitting" and what is morally "obligatory."[3] But in the end Anselm has to face it, and his explanation really does away with necessity altogether. It is simply God's free will, and, though Anselm does not explicitly say so, God might have acted otherwise, had He so willed.

3. This attempt to make the Atonement logically necessary in terms of honour almost puts God's love out of sight. It is a witness to the real truth of Anselm's thought that his argument again and again needs the

[1] Imo sciendum est, quidquid homo inde dicere vel scire possit, altiores tantae rei adhuc latere rationes (i. 2).

[2] ii. 22.

[3] It is an instructive study to follow the alternation of meaning and usage between *convenientia* and *necessitas*, *debet* and *decet*, throughout the treatise.

equation of necessity and love. But he never makes this equation. The explanation in terms of honour and satisfaction seems complete without, and it is only as an afterthought, of a rhetorical kind, that the love of God is introduced at all.

4. Anselm is weak at every point in his expression of the manward side. His definition of sin, "Not to render God His due," is far below that of Athanasius and Augustine, who at least did justice to the tremendous positive force of evil. Though he emphasizes its enormity he does so on crudely quantitative lines. Satisfaction he regards as a quantitative equivalent for such and such quantities of sin. This view is, of course, closely bound up with the ecclesiastical doctrines of penance and of merits, which played a considerable part in the life of the Church, and could not but affect theological thought. The result of this quantitative view of satisfaction is that Anselm does not feel the need of an Atonement taking effect in the life of mankind. All that is necessary, and all that is effected, is a change of status, and that by the mere accident that there was no other reward that could possibly be given to Christ for His offering. Why a reward should be given at all is by no means obvious.

5. It is important, in view of later developments, that Anselm regards Christ's offering as totally adequate in itself, quite apart from its acceptance by God.

CHAPTER VII

THE LATER MIDDLE AGES

ANSELM'S influence upon his contemporaries was immediate and far-reaching upon its negative side.[1] Within a few years the theory of a transaction with the devil had found its last exponent in Peter Lombard, and though echoes of the old language may still be heard in Bonaventura, in Aquinas, and even in Luther, its phrases have often become mere rhetoric, illustrative of various aspects of the Satisfaction theory, and where more consciously introduced are usually carefully adapted to the Anselmic scheme. One or two writers in the twelfth century still try to find a place for the devil in their system. Hugh of St. Victor, for example, starts from the position that the devil has acquired certain rights against man, though he has none as against God. God alone, therefore, can help man, but He Himself is angry at man's sin and demands an adequate satisfaction for the dishonour done to Himself. The argument thus proceeds quite on Anselmic lines. Man having neither an adequate obedience nor an adequate punishment to offer, God supplies both through the Incarnation and the Cross.

The cure is to be seen in this that the devil laid his hand on Him who was free from sin, in whom he found nothing of his own. And so he rightly lost those whom he seemed to hold by some sort of right, through their faith in Him who by His death

[1] Upon this whole period Franks, *op. cit.*, is full and illuminating. He treats Hugh of St. Victor and Alexander of Hales at considerable length.

became the cause of salvation to all who obey Him. For He suffered not for Himself but for us.[1]

Question: Was our price given to the devil or to God? *Answer*: It was given to God, not the devil; for no injustice was done to the devil who was but a sort of gaoler.[2]

God freely gave to man that which man might pay as due to God. He gave therefore to man that Man whom man might pay for man, who, that a worthy recompense might be made, was not only equal to but greater than the former man. That therefore Man greater than man might be given for man, God was made man for man. Christ, therefore, by His birth paid man's debt to the Father and by His death expiated man's guilt, so that, in that He endured for man a death which He owed not, man might justly through that death escape the death which he owed, and that the devil might find no ground for complaint, since dominion over man was not his due, and man was worthy of his freedom.[3]

This latter passage is entirely Anselmic. The devil has become quite a secondary figure, and the Godward aspect of Atonement, which alone remains important, is characteristically worked out in dual emphasis upon Christ's life of obedience and His death of suffering. Hugh refuses, however, to accept Anselm's difficult argument for the absolute necessity of the Atonement. In this, and, indeed, in all respects, Anselm finds a more

[1] Remedium in hoc consideratur, quia diabolus misit in eum qui immunis erat a peccato, in quo quicquam quod suum erat non invenit. Ideo merito eos, quos quodam jure tenere videbatur, amisit, credentes in eum qui per mortem suam omnibus obtemperantibus sibi factus est causa salutis: non enim pro se sed pro nobis passus est (*Quaest. circa Ep. ad Rom.* 90).

[2] Quaeritur, Cui pretium nostrum sit datum an diabolo an Deo? Solutio, Deo datum non diabolo est; quia nulla injuria facta est diabolo, qui non erat nisi tanquam carcerarius (*ib.* 92).

[3] Dedit Deus gratis homini quod homo ex debito Deo redderet. Dedit igitur homini hominem quem homo pro homine redderet, qui, ut digna recompensatio fieret priori non solum aequalis sed major esset. Ut ergo pro homine redderetur homo major homine, factus est Deus homo pro homine. Christus ergo nascendo debitum hominis patri solvit, et moriendo reatum hominis expiavit, ut, cum ipse pro homine mortem quam non debebat sustineret, juste homo propter ipsam mortem quam debebat evaderet, et jam locum calumniandi diabolus non inveniret, quia et ipse homini dominari non debuit, et homo liberari dignus fuit (*Dial. de Sacramentis*, 4).

direct adherent in Richard of St. Victor, whose *De Incarnatione Verbi* is largely modelled upon the *Cur Deus Homo?* Richard argues that the fullest satisfaction certainly demanded the Cross:

> Without satisfaction man could not fully be restored, but for full satisfaction it was required that there should be as great humility in expiation as there had been presumption in sin.[1]

But, as Oxenham points out, this is not as definite as the position taken up by Anselm. "His language does not imply anything more than that the death of Christ was necessary, if an adequate satisfaction were to be made at all."[2] Other methods of salvation are not excluded from possibility.

Apart from these two writers Anselm's positive influence upon the century is not very marked, and upon the special point of the absolute necessity of the Atonement to God he finds no support. His criticisms took more immediate effect than his suggestions, though hints of these may be seen in almost every writer, from Bernard onwards. And the great weakness of his theory, its utter failure to account for the assignation to man of the fruits of Christ's death, left a clear field for the influence of Abelard. Peter Lombard is not alone in his statement of the Moral theory. Abelard's friend, Robert Pulleyn, though he regards the price of redemption as paid to God, sees also in Christ's Passion an example to man, and even Hugh of St. Victor falls back upon a similar view to account for God's choice of this particular mode of redemption.

> That in Him who suffered men may see what they ought to repay to God, in Him who was glorified they may consider what

---

[1] Sine satisfactione hominem ad plenum reparari non posse, ad plenitudinem autem satisfactionis oportuisse ut tanta esset humiliatio in expiatione quanta fuerat praesumptio in praevaricatione (*De Incarn. Verbi*, 8).

[2] Oxenham, *op. cit.* p. 195.

reward they may expect from Him ; so that in example He may be the Way, in promise the Truth, in reward the Life.[1]

In the following century, however, Anselm came to his own. The thirteenth century is the typical age of scholasticism. Its literature is voluminous and tedious. It consists largely of elaborate commentaries upon the *Sentences* of Peter Lombard, examined in minute detail. Theology is drawn out in long series of propositions and conclusions, based upon the methods of Aristotle's logic, and much time and effort is spent on matters of very small importance. It was natural that Anselm's close reasoning should appeal to such an age, and the influence of the *Cur Deus Homo?* now becomes dominant. Such writers as Alexander of Hales, Albert the Great, and Bonaventura adopt the Satisfaction theory practically as Anselm had stated it, though they elaborate it considerably and not always very consistently. The principal divergence is upon the vexed question of necessity. In spite of the difficulties in which this had involved Anselm his whole argument was based on the idea that God could not leave anything unregulated, out of place, in His universe, and that therefore He was not only bound to save man, but was also bound to use the one way which did not injure either His purpose or His honour. Alexander of Hales[2] accepts this argument, but yet refuses to draw the conclusion that any necessity is laid upon God. In that justice which is God's very Being, he says, God might have elected to save man without satisfaction rendered, though He could not do so in that justice which goes by congruity of merits. Albert the Great[3] argues in favour of the necessity of the Atonement, but on different grounds from those given by Anselm. Original sin, he says,

[1] Ut in eo qui passus est videant quid ei retribuere debeant, in eo autem qui glorificatus est considerent quid ab eo debeant exspectare ; ut et ipse sit via in exemplo et veritas in promisso et vita in praemio (*Dial. de Sacr.* 10).

[2] *Summa*, iii. Q. i. 4-7.

[3] *Comm. in Sent.* iii. 20.

being a corruption of the nature derived from Adam, the natural head of the race, can only be remitted through a supernatural second Head, since a second natural Head is unthinkable. Here we are in touch with a mystical conception of the Incarnation recalling the thought of Bernard and of the early Greek fathers. In such a conception Anselm is sadly lacking.

Bonaventura [1] goes so far as openly to dispute Anselm's contention. Nothing would have been left unregulated, he affirms, even if God had saved man by way of mercy. It was open to God to do so if He would, and such salvation would not even have precluded the due punishment of sin, since sin carries with it its own punishment. And, further, though it is true that the death of Christ was the only proper and complete satisfaction, a point which Bonaventura has previously argued in great detail, God might nevertheless have accepted a less suffering on Christ's part as sufficient.

> As to the liberating of man I firmly believe that he might have been liberated in some other way, but as to redemption I neither deny this nor venture to affirm it, since it is rash, when speaking of the Divine power, to assign to it any limits. For He can do more than we can conceive.[2]

It is difficult to see that such a conclusion, however pious, is really consistent with an argument which is intended to prove by sheer logic that no method is so consistent with both justice and mercy as the method of satisfaction, and that that satisfaction could not possibly be made except by Christ. Bonaventura not only adopts Anselm's argument, but expands it with all manner of fresh reasons and congruities. He adds to it suggestions drawn not only from the Moral argument but even echoes of the old phrases about the ensnaring of

[1] *In Sent.* iii. 20.

[2] De liberatione enim firmiter credo quod alio modo potuit liberari, de redemptione vero nec nego nec audeo affirmare, quia temerarium est, cum de divina potestate agitur, terminum praefigere ei. Amplius enim potest quam nos possumus cogitare (*ib.*).

Leviathan. No other method was so acceptable for the appeasing of God's anger, so fitted to cure the disease of sin, so effectual to attract mankind, so wise to overcome man's enemy. In particular Bonaventura emphasizes the point which was also made by Albert the Great. Man may conceivably, aided by God's grace, make a partial satisfaction for actual sin. But he could not possibly make any satisfaction for original sin. Only the Second Adam could do this, and by thus breaking the power of original sin He wins for man that grace in which man may himself make satisfaction for actual sin.[1] After these accumulated arguments the conclusion that God might nevertheless have chosen some other method seems hardly in place. Yet the instinct that prompted it was a true one, and might well have pointed its possessor to the truth that any Godward theory of Atonement, if carried beyond very modest limits, assumes a knowledge of the Being of God utterly beyond the range of our faculties. But the whole spirit of the age was against such a thought, and Bonaventura has clearly no suspicion of this radical weakness in his position.

After the time of Bonaventura and his contemporaries the current of Western theology divided into the two main streams of the Thomist and Scotist schools, deriving their names and their ideas from Thomas Aquinas and Duns Scotus respectively. On the doctrine of the Atonement, as on most other doctrines, the two schools differed widely. Both Aquinas and Duns Scotus draw their method of thought and much of the detail of their theologies from Anselm, and they agree, as their predecessors had done, in rejecting his view of the absolute necessity of the Atonement. But they reach this position from standpoints which differ fundamentally.

[1] The influence of the ecclesiastical doctrine of penance here makes itself felt. This doctrine was probably of importance in connexion with the origins of the Satisfaction theory (see note, p. 121); it certainly affected its later statements. This is natural, since the whole theory of the efficacy of the merits of Christ rests primarily upon a Godward interpretation of the meaning of His obedience and death.

The divergence between the two schools, due in part to the rivalry between the two great orders, the Dominicans and Franciscans, and in part to the influence of opposed philosophical theories, the Thomists adopting Realism and the Scotists Nominalism, may be traced back in more than one respect to an earlier date than that of the two great writers from whom they took their names. And in particular the very radical difference which appears in connexion with the doctrine of the Atonement begins to show itself in the answers given to a problem formulated by Rupert of Deutz in the twelfth century. Would Christ have become man if man had not sinned? Rupert himself and Alexander of Hales answered that He would, Bonaventura that He would not.

Aquinas [1] followed Bonaventura in his reply to Rupert's question. He admitted that the Incarnation was the crown and consummation of all creation, but nevertheless definitely declared that it was the result of man's sin. Had man not fallen the Incarnation would not have taken place. Thus the Incarnation and the Atonement are very intimately connected in Aquinas' system, and here he is following the tradition of Western thought and, indeed, of much Eastern thought also. It had often been suggested that Christ took flesh in order that He might have wherewith to pay our debt, or, put less commercially, that He might be able to suffer. Anselm had adopted this view in his statement of the Satisfaction theory, and Aquinas follows him closely, in accordance with the current canon.

> Christ suffered not in His Deity but in His manhood.[2]

Yet Aquinas did not draw the obvious conclusion that the Incarnation and the Atonement were therefore

[1] For Aquinas' doctrine of the Atonement see *Summa*, Pars iii. Q. 46-49.

[2] Christus non est passus secundum divinitatem sed secundum carnem (*ib.* Q. 48).

necessary. Like Bonaventura he refuses to be consistent, lest he should presume too far, and takes up the position that neither the Incarnation nor the Atonement was strictly necessary in any sense other than that God so willed to save man.[1] No limit must be set to God's free will. He might without injustice, had He so willed, have forgone satisfaction altogether, simply remitting man's sin.

Why then did God choose this method? Aquinas does not despair of giving an answer to this question. The method of Satisfaction is in many ways the most fitting, bestowing upon us not only freedom from sin but many good gifts besides in connexion with man's salvation. It reveals to us God's great love. It gives us an example of obedience and of other virtues. Above all it inspires us with justifying grace, enabling us to use our new-found freedom.

> Through the fact that man was freed by Christ's passion many things pertaining to man's salvation were bestowed besides freedom from sin. For, firstly, through it man knows how greatly God loves man, and through this is stirred to love Him, in which love the perfecting of man's salvation consists. . . . Secondly, through it He has given us an example of obedience and humility and constancy, of righteousness and of the other virtues displayed in Christ's passion, which are necessary for man's salvation. . . . Thirdly, Christ, by His passion not only freed man from sin, but also won for him justifying grace and the glory of blessedness, as will be said below.[2]

---

[1] This, of course, is the real conclusion of Anselm's own discussion in *Cur Deus Homo?* ii. 18, though Anselm himself failed to give it clear expression. With Aquinas, with whom Scotus here agrees, it becomes an accepted feature of the Western doctrine.

[2] Per hoc autem quod homo per passionem Christi liberatus, multa concurrerunt ad salutem hominis pertinentia praeter liberationem a peccato: Primo enim per hoc homo cognoscit quantum hominem deus diligat, et per hoc provocatur ad eum diligendum, in quo perfectio humanae salutis consistit. . . . Secundo quia per hoc nobis dedit exemplum obedientiae et humilitatis et constantiae, justitiae et ceterarum virtutum in passione Christi ostensarum, quae sunt necessaria ad humanam salutem. . . . Tertio quia Christus per passionem suam non solum hominem a peccato liberavit, sed etiam gratiam justificantem et gloriam beatitudinis ei promeruit, ut infra dicetur (*ib.* Q. 46: the reference *ad fin.* is to Q. 48).

Aquinas goes on to give as fourth and fifth reasons the obligation laid upon man to keep himself from sin, remembering the price paid for his redemption, and the appropriateness of the defeat of the devil by man, thus reversing man's defeat by the devil.

We see here that which was best in the thought of Abelard, and which had been so conspicuously absent in that of Anselm, taken over and given adequate and full expression. The Moral theory is adopted, but without any weakness or sentimentality. It is fully recognized that the power which sanctifies man is not of himself, but is to be identified with the grace of God, which is His love, a thought which, as we shall see, has for Aquinas a mystical significance.

In connexion with this revelation of God's love Aquinas dwells at length on the greatness of Christ's sufferings. And here his view of the Incarnation naturally leads him to emphasize the sufferings of Christ's whole Incarnate life, culminating in the Cross. Throughout His life Christ offered to God the satisfaction of obedience, a satisfaction acceptable to God because He loved Christ's obedience more than He hated our sin. And thus the satisfaction is not only sufficient, but even superabundant.

> By His love and obedience in suffering Christ displayed to God something more than was demanded as a recompense for all the offence of mankind: Firstly, because of the greatness of the love in which He suffered; secondly, through the worth of that life which He offered as a satisfaction, being the life of God and of man; thirdly, because of the universality of the passion and the greatness of the pains which He assumed. . . . And so Christ's passion was not only a sufficient but also a superabundant satisfaction for the sins of mankind.[1]

---

[1] Christus autem ex caritate et obedientia patiendo majus aliquid Deo exhibuit quam exhiberet recompensatio totius offensae humani generis: primo quidem propter magnitudinem caritatis ex qua patiebatur; secundo propter dignitatem vitae suae quam pro satisfactione ponebat, quae erat vita dei et hominis; tertio propter generalitatem passionis et magnitudinem doloris assumpti . . . Et ideo passio Christi non solum sufficiens sed etiam superabundans satisfactio fuit pro peccatis humani generis (Q. 48).

This emphasis upon the superabundant satisfaction made by Christ is the most characteristic contribution made by Aquinas to the Anselmic scheme. In stating the way in which its virtue is made available for us he abandons his own admirable adaptation of the Moral theory and adopts a greatly inferior commercial conception, more after Anselm's own manner.

> Because, then, Christ's passion was a sufficient and superabundant satisfaction for man's sin and liability to punishment, His passion was, as it were, a sort of price freeing us from both our obligations. For that very satisfaction wherewith a man makes satisfaction either for himself or for another, is called a sort of price, by which he redeems himself or another from sin and from punishment.[1]

Sometimes the old sacrificial language, which had never fallen wholly out of use at any period, is adapted to the new system of ideas, a connecting link being found in Christ's obedience.

> By suffering He fulfilled all the precepts of the old Law: He fulfilled its moral precepts, founded in precepts of love, in that He suffered both for love of the Father and for love of His neighbour; and the ceremonial precepts of the Law, which are especially ordained for sacrifices and oblations, Christ fulfilled by His passion, in that all the old sacrifices were figures of that true sacrifice which Christ offered by dying for us. . . . The judicial precepts of the Law, ordained especially for those who suffer injury, Christ fulfilled by His passion, suffering Himself to be nailed to the tree for that apple which man plucked from the tree against God's command.[2]

---

[1] Quia igitur passio Christi fuit sufficiens et superabundans satisfactio pro peccato et reatu poenae generis humani, ejus passio fuit quasi quoddam pretium per quod liberati sumus ab utraque obligatione. Nam ipsa satisfactio qua quis satisfacit, sive pro se sive pro alio, pretium quoddam dicitur, quo seipsum vel alium redimit a peccato et a poena (*ib.* Q. 48).

[2] Patiendo omnia veteris legis praecepta implevit: moralia quidem, quae in praeceptis caritatis fundantur, implevit in quantum passus est et ex dilectione patris et ex dilectione proximi; coeremonialia vero praecepta legis, quae ad sacrificia et oblationes praecipue ordinantur, implevit Christus sua passione, in quantum omnia antiqua sacrificia fuerunt figurae illius veri sacrificii, quod Christus obtulit moriendo pro nobis . . . Praecepta vero judicialia legis, quae praecipue ordinantur ad satisfaciendam injuriam passis, implevit Christus sua passione, permittens se ligno affigi pro pomo quod de ligno homo rapuerat contra Dei mandatum (*ib.* Q. 48).

> And this very work, the voluntary endurance of the Passion, was especially acceptable to God, as springing especially from love; whence it is clear that Christ's Passion was a true sacrifice.[1]

Aquinas has just defined sacrifice as

> . . . anything done as an honour properly due to God, for the purpose of placating Him.[2]

He also quotes Augustine's famous definition:

> A true sacrifice is any work which is done that we may cleave to God in holy fellowship, in relation to that good end in which we may be truly blessed.[3]

To such sacrificial language, as we shall see, the Satisfaction theory has tended more and more to revert, Christ's offering of Himself, the sinless Victim, coming to be equated with the supreme act of homage demanded by God's honour, even while retaining much of its expiatory significance.

Sometimes the language of the Satisfaction theory takes a Penal turn:

> In this is shown the severity of God, who wills not to remit sin without punishment.[4]

But such language is not developed by Aquinas upon Penal lines. "Punishment" for him covers not only the "eternal death" due to sin, but the "satisfying penalty" whereby sin is put away. The penalties inflicted in penance by the Church are before his mind, and, not very consistently with his view of the Satisfaction of Christ as superabundant, he argues that

[1] Et hoc ipsum opus, quod voluntarie passionem sustinuit, Deo maxime acceptum fuit, utpote ex caritate maxime proveniens: unde manifestum est quod passio Christi fuerit verum sacrificium (*ibid.*).

[2] Aliquid factum in honorem proprie Deo debitum ad eum placandum (*ibid.*).

[3] Verum sacrificium est omne opus quod agitur ut sancta societate inhaereamus Deo, relatum scilicet ad illum finem boni quo veraciter beati esse possimus (Aug. *De Civ. Dei*, x. 6).

[4] In quo ostenditur et Dei severitas, qui peccatum sine poena dimittere noluit (*Summa*, iii. Q. 47).

these penalties, in their own little degree, have satisfying force.[1]

But whatever form the language of his theory takes, Aquinas is quite free from any thought of a change wrought in the attitude of God towards sinners, though he expresses himself with some caution.

> It must not be said that the passion of Christ reconciled us to God in such a manner that He began to love us anew, but because through Christ's passion the cause of hatred is removed, both by the removal of sin and by the repayment of a more acceptable benefit.[2]

And even when he is using sacrificial language, adopting the principle that the proper function of sacrifice is to please God, it is to the nature of man and not to that of God that he assigns the change.

> The voluntary suffering of Christ was so great a good that for this good found in human nature God was appeased in regard to all the offence of mankind, as far as concerns those who are joined to Christ in His suffering.[3]

In this passage the mystical tendency of Aquinas reveals itself, a tendency which shapes much of his exposition of the doctrine of Atonement, and which enables him to give a far more living account than his predecessors of the way in which Atonement takes effect in the heart of man. Aquinas is quite at home in the mystical language of St. Paul, and in his mystical view of the Sacraments.

[1] *Ib.* Q. 49. There is really some confusion of thought as to the idea of punishment. *Poena satisfactoria* is not strictly punishment at all, but an equivalent, which, conjoined with Christ's merits, is offered to God as a substitute for sin's proper punishment.

[2] Non dicendum quod passio Christi dicitur quantum ad hoc Deo nos reconciliasse, quod de novo nos amare inciperet, sed quia per passionem Christi sublata est odii causa, tum per ablationem peccati tum per recompensationem acceptabilioris beneficii (*ib.* Q. 49).

[3] Tantum bonum fuit quod Christus voluntarie passus est, quod propter hoc bonum in natura humana inventum Deus placatus est super omni offensa generis humani, quantum ad eos qui Christo passo conjunguntur (*ib.* Q. 49).

That we may gain the effects of Christ's passion we must be conformed to Him. Now we are conformed to Him sacramentally in baptism, according to Rom. 6 4: We are buried with Him in baptism unto death.[1]

In particular Aquinas works out Bernard's thought of the union of Christ, as Head of the Church, with His members, forming together with them one mystical Person.

Grace is given to Christ not only as to a single person, but that it may extend also to His members, in that He is the Head of the Church.[2]

Thus he is able to avoid the difficulty that the effects of the Passion are something utterly external to man, and that it is only by an arbitrary transference that they can become available for him. The sufferings of Christ and their results become in a real sense the atoning sufferings of His members, and

Suffering is not meritorious in so far as it has its source from without; but according as any man endures it voluntarily it has its source from within and so is meritorious.[3]

The Head and the members are as it were one mystical Person, and so Christ's satisfaction pertains to all the faithful, as to His own members.[4]

And the way in which man may make this union effective for himself is faith, yet not the mere intellectual belief of the understanding, but faith that is set on fire by love.

[1] Ad hoc quod consequemur effectum passionis Christi, oportet nos ei configurari. Configuramur autem ei in baptismo sacramentaliter, secundum Rom. 6 4: Consepulti sumus ei per baptismum in mortem (*ib.* Q. 49).

[2] Christo data est gratia non solum sicut singulari personae sed in quantum est caput ecclesiae ut scil. ab ipso redundaret ad membra (*ib.* Q. 48, cf. Q. 49. 1, also Q. 8).

[3] Passio non est meritoria in quantum habet principium ab exteriori; sed secundum quod eam aliquis voluntarie sustinet, sic habet principium ab interiori, et hoc modo est meritoria (*ib.* Q. 48).

[4] Caput et membra sunt quasi una persona mystica, et ideo satisfactio Christi ad omnes fideles pertinet sicut ad sua membra (*ib.* Q. 48).

The faith by which we are cleansed from sin is not unformed faith, which may co-exist even with sin, but faith formed by love, that so Christ's passion may be applied to us not merely theoretically but also effectually.[1]

And thus we come back almost to Abelard and the Moral theory. It is the love of God working as love in man that explains the power of the Atonement. "In love the perfecting of man's salvation consists."[2] But the thought which was lacking in Abelard is now supplied. It is in its power of union that love finds its efficacy. Love can create such a unity that the satisfaction wrought by Christ is wrought by man in Him. And so in Aquinas the thought of Anselm meets that of Abelard, each finding its fulness in that mystical union of which faith is the form and love the force.

Harnack is hardly doing justice to Aquinas when he says that we find in him *multa, non multum.* But his criticism of the exposition given in the *Summa* as exhibiting some confusion of thought cannot be questioned. "The wavering between the hypothetical and the necessary modes of view, between objective and subjective redemption, further, between the different points of view of redemption, and, finally, between a *satisfactio superabundans* and the assertion that for the sins after baptism we have to supplement the work of Christ, prevents any distinct impression arising."[3] It was only by his mysticism that Aquinas overcame these inconsistencies, and they offered a fair field of attack to less mystically minded scholars interested in the subtleties of theological dialectic. It was especially by Duns Scotus and his followers that the attack was developed.

[1] Fides autem per quam a peccato mundamur non est fides informis, quae potest esse etiam cum peccato, sed est fides formata per caritatem, ut sic passio Christi nobis applicetur, non solum quantum ad intellectum sed etiam quantum ad effectum (*ib.* Q. 49).

[2] See the passage quoted on p. 151.

[3] *Hist. of Dogma*, vi. p. 196.

Duns Scotus[1] contested the position of Aquinas at almost every point, also using the Anselmic method, though he definitely rejects Anselm's conclusions. His theory is sometimes known as the theory of Acceptilation, or Acceptation, from its leading thought, the logical outcome of the Satisfaction theory, that all satisfaction derives its value from the arbitrary choice of God.

The divergence between the two systems begins at their view of the Incarnation. Scotus argues against any connexion of the Incarnation with the fall of man. The ancient view of the Latin fathers, that Christ took humanity in order that He might pay man's debt, here gives place to a view much more like that of some of the early Greeks, and notably of Athanasius, though Scotus is not sufficiently mystical to have made his own the Greek conception of the eternal unity of the Word with His creation. Yet for him, too, the Incarnation is an eternal truth. In any case Christ would have come to be the Second Head of the race. His human nature, predestined from all eternity, was, in a sense, prior to the Fall. It was, indeed, in the likeness of that Divine humanity that Adam was formed.[2] The Anselmic argument as to the necessity of the Incarnation is thus deprived of its basis. Its sole cause is the free and arbitrary will of God, self-determined before the creation of the world.

The Fall, and the Atonement which reversed the Fall, are naturally relegated to a lower position in a system which takes such a view of the Incarnation. Here, too, Scotus applies the central principle of his thought, that values are not absolute but relative to God's acceptance of them. Neither human sin nor the satisfaction of Christ is in itself infinite, but only becomes so through God's free choice. No necessity is laid upon God. The conclusion is similar to that reached by

[1] *In Sent.* iii. 19, from which passage the following quotations are taken.

[2] On this particular point see *Summa*, iii. 1. 3.

Aquinas, but obtains a wholly new significance from the premisses upon which it is based. And here, indeed, Scotus is far the more consistent thinker of the two. The rejection of the Anselmic argument for the necessity of the Atonement had been rather a scruple than a reasoned conviction in Aquinas and earlier writers. In Scotus, for the first time, it takes its place in the general scheme.

The result of the Fall upon the Divine humanity was, according to Scotus, that that humanity became thereby liable to suffering. Thus he finds a point of agreement with Aquinas in the canon

> Christ gained merit not as God but as man.[1]

But though the language is the same, the agreement is in fact only verbal, as is shown by the conclusion which Scotus draws. He argues that because Christ only suffered as man, His sufferings had only the value of human sufferings and were therefore finite in every way.

> As regards sufficiency of merit, that merit was certainly finite, because it had a finite cause, viz. the will of that nature which was assumed and the great glory conferred upon it.[2]

---

[1] Non enim Christus quatenus Deus meruit sed in quantum homo.

[2] Quantum vero attinet ad meriti sufficientiam fuit profecto illud finitum, quia causa ejus finita fuit, videlicet voluntas naturae assumptae et summa gloria illi collata.

This is the logical conclusion from the current canon that Christ only suffered in His humanity, an unfortunate heritage from the days of the Patripassian controversies. If pressed it can only result in a Nestorian division of the Person of Christ. The difficulty is naturally overcome by such writers as Aquinas, who are enabled by their mystical sense to apprehend a real *unio mystica* not only of the Person of Christ in Himself, but also of that Person and all suffering humanity. But this did not provide a theological vindication of the canon. Such a vindication was sought in the doctrine of *communicatio idiomatum*, the interchange of the human and Divine attributes in Christ. So far as this interchange was contemplated as real, the Nestorian conclusion was avoided. But in such writers as Scotus and his Nominalist followers the *communicatio idiomatum* is only understood as a verbal escape from the difficulties of the unity of Christ's Person, and the natural result is Nestorianism, bringing Pelagianism in its train.

How then did these finite merits suffice to make satisfaction for the sin of man? Just because God chose so to accept them.

> If you ask how far Christ's merit had sufficing worth, it had worth without doubt so far as it was accepted by God, since the Divine acceptance is the chief cause and reason of all acceptance. For all things other than God are good because they are loved by God, and not *vice versa*. . . . Christ's merit therefore had sufficing worth so far as the Trinity could and would accept it.[1]

> As all things other than God are good because desired by God, and not conversely, so that merit was good so far as it was accepted; and thus it was a merit because it was accepted, and was not, conversely, accepted because it was a merit and good.[2]

There is no trace here of the superabundant satisfaction dwelt upon by Aquinas, and the inconsistency between that conception and the ecclesiastical doctrine of penance has vanished too. Scotus indeed works out the old congruities which made it fitting that Christ should die, and that God should accept this satisfaction. But these thoughts have no true place in his system, and, indeed, he limits the effects of Christ's satisfaction to the bestowal of that initial grace which enables the elect to turn from the life of sin.[3] After receiving the first impulse man must win his own salvation:

---

[1] Si exquiras quantum valuerit Christi meritum secundum sufficientiam, valuit procul dubio quantum fuit a deo acceptatum, si quidem divina acceptatio est potissima causa et ratio omnis meriti. Omne enim aliud a Deo ideo est bonum quia a Deo dilectum, et non e contrario. . . . Tantum ergo valuit Christi meritum sufficienter quantum potuit et voluit ipsum Trinitas acceptare.

[2] Sicut omne aliud a Deo ideo est bonum, quia a Deo volitum, et non e converso, sic meritum illud tantum bonum erat pro quanto acceptabatur, et ideo meritum quia acceptatum, non autem e converso quia meritum est et bonum ideo acceptatum.

[3] Thus Scotus is found in agreement with the extreme Augustinian and Calvinistic positions, to which nothing could be more opposed than his general system, in his denial of the universality of Atonement. Election is for him quite as arbitrary as for any Puritan divine.

What did Christ merit? He merited initial grace for all who receive it, grace which is conferred without any merit of ours.[1]

Christ's passion efficaciously merited for the elect only that initial grace which disposes towards the completed glory.[2]

But this attitude towards grace is at least in part Pelagian, and it is not surprising to find it combined with a very Pelagian belittling of man's sin. Scotus quite abandons the Augustinian and Anselmic tradition of sin as of infinite importance in God's sight. Since man is finite his sin is finite too and demands neither infinite satisfaction nor infinite punishment. An angel, or even a man, if only he were free from original sin, might have made the Atonement, had God willed so to accept it. This conclusion is inevitable upon the presuppositions from which Scotus sets out. If everything is referred to the *acceptatio* of God, there is clearly no limit to that which God may choose to accept. Even the proviso that the man who should make Atonement must be free from original sin, though rendered necessary to Scotus by his doctrine of initial grace, is really inconsistent with his main position. No necessity dominates the Divine will. God is free.

In comparing the systems of Aquinas and Scotus, systems which became characteristic of the two great schools into which later Western thought was divided, we see at once that Aquinas has done little more than fill out the outlines due to Anselm. Even on the fundamental question of necessity the difference of language is more real than that of thought. Scotus, while using the language of the Satisfaction theory, differs from Anselm fundamentally on almost every point. The emphasis is no longer upon an infinite satisfaction wrought to make good an infinite dishonour done to God, but on the goodness of God, who freely

[1] Quid meruit Christus? Meruit sane primam gratiam omnibus qui eam recipiunt, quae et absque nostro merito confertur.

[2] Christi passio electis solum primam gratiam disponentem ad gloriam consummatam efficaciter meruit.

accepts a finite offering for finite human sin. Each of the two systems has its own peculiar strength and its own peculiar weakness. That of Aquinas is strong in its intense realization of the importance and value of the Atonement. It draws out with great power of thought and vigour of illustration the fitness of such a method of saving man. But Aquinas does not really succeed in avoiding the difficulty which Anselm himself felt as to the inconsistency left between God's love and the form of Atonement necessary that His honour might be satisfied. He dwells, it is true, upon the love of God, and upon His free will to save man. But it is hard to reconcile this with a view of the Incarnation as necessitated by human sin. It cannot consistently be argued that the Cross is clearly the one fitting way of salvation, while at the same time it is urged that God might conceivably have chosen some other way.

Duns Scotus is free from this difficulty. His view of the Incarnation as predestined independently of man's sin enables him to dwell upon the love of God without inconsistency. And his view that it is God's acceptance alone that makes Christ's offering worthy throws all the emphasis upon the goodness of God, a goodness which, despite man's sin, yet fulfils the loving purpose which He had before all worlds. But this position fails completely to account for the Cross. There is no apparent reason why God should have chosen this way of salvation rather than any other. The congruities by which Scotus endeavoured to show its appropriateness have no proper place in his theology. When all is said, God might, had He so pleased, have accepted any, or even no, satisfaction. The Cross seems to be a mere accident of God's purpose, to which no clear reason can be assigned. In this respect the instinct of Anselm and Aquinas is the higher. There is no such thing as accident in the purposes of God, and if He has chosen a certain method of working, it is surely within the province of human reason to enquire, by the highest categories at its disposal, into His motives in so doing. It may be that theology in the Middle Ages was not over-modest in its ventures into the unknown. Perhaps in these latter days we are beginning to learn modesty. Yet we are the richer to-day for the work of men who had the faith to trust the reason which God gave them, and to peer, if it might be, into the secrets of His justice and His love.

Before leaving the Middle Ages, and passing on to the Reformation period, we may pause to notice certain writers in whom historians of the doctrine of Atonement have found foreshadowed the ideas which influenced the Reformers.[1] These may be divided into two groups, the mystics, and a few of the later schoolmen in whom certain features of the Satisfaction theory show signs of modification.

It is impossible to give in a short space any serious account of mediaeval mysticism. Itself well-marked in type, it is found in thinkers of many lands and many schools. Sometimes, as in Bernard and Aquinas, it is associated with definite and orthodox theology. More often, as in the great German mystics, Eckhart and Tauler and their followers, the Neo-Platonic tradition, derived ultimately from Dionysius the Areopagite, reveals itself, as it had done in Erigena, in approaches to a theology almost Pantheistic in character. Frequently it is associated rather with practical piety than with theology, and, indeed, its development is very largely associated with the great mendicant orders, of which many of the great mystics were members, and which found their inspiration in the practical example of Francis of Assisi. In no case is there any conscious breach with the orthodox ecclesiastical thought of

[1] On this subject the classical compilation is Ullmann's *Reformatoren vor der Reformation.* Ritschl has a good summary, *op. cit.* pp. 103 ff., in which he reduces the force of many of Ullmann's citations. On the mystics in general see Inge, *Christian Mysticism,* and, on the German school in particular, Dorner, *Person of Christ,* Div. ii. vol. ii. Introd.

the day, and no attempt whatever is made to reduce mysticism to a doctrinal system, though, as we have seen, such writers as Bernard and Aquinas find in it a means of overcoming some of the difficulties of their theology. It is therefore rather in an attitude of mind than in any definite theological statements that anticipations of the Reformation theology may be expected.

We need not, in this connexion, dwell upon the doctrinal aspects of the practical piety of Francis of Assisi, further than to notice that his humility and his full sense of the meaning of self-renunciation in Christ led him to lay aside all pretension to any personal merit.

> To-day in thy wisdom thou hast honoured me rightly, giving to God the praise and honour that are His; thou hast separated the costly from the base, allotting to God the wisdom and the virtue, and to me the ignorance and the baseness.[1]

This truly religious estimate of self, the estimate of Augustine's *Confessions*, and of many of Bernard's sermons, is not strictly compatible with the orthodox theology of penance, which assigned to the merits of man some place in the work of satisfaction. It is true that this view of penance was not in real agreement with the Anselmic theology, but the inconsistency did not come into view until the Reformation, and the language and habit of mind of Francis had little influence even in the order which he founded. The life of humble poverty tended to be regarded as of some intrinsic worth in the eyes of God, "in other cases what is most insisted on is constant resort to the sacraments of penance and the Eucharist; in other cases still, mystical

[1] Tu hodie pro tua sapientia vere me honorasti, Deo, quae sua sunt, laudem et gloriam tribuens; pretiosum a vili separasti, Deo sapientiam et virtutem, mihi inscitiam et vilitatem, appropriasti (*Colloquium* 4; *ap.* Ritschl, *op. cit.* p. 104). Ritschl gives other examples of such language from the Franciscan, Antony of Padua, and from the Dominican mystic, Tauler.

elevation out of and above the sphere of created life into the infinity of the Divine Being."[1]

This association of mysticism with the practical piety of the mendicant orders had an especially characteristic development in Germany, and here there is more ground for asserting a direct connexion with the thought of the Reformers, since it is to a product of the school of Eckhart and Tauler, the anonymous *Deutsche Theologie*, that Luther declares himself to be most indebted, after the Bible and Augustine. As Ritschl shows, this statement must not be overpressed. The *Deutsche Theologie* does not differ materially from the other writings of its school, and it would be impossible to argue seriously that Luther's theology has any close connexion with, for example, that of Eckhart. The abandonment of all personal merit, in order that we may trust solely in the merit of Christ and may be justified by faith alone, is the mainspring of Luther's thought, and this differs widely from the thought of the abandonment of personal individuality in order that we may win to union with God. The mystics, indeed, approach the problem from a point of view very unlike that of the contemporary schoolmen. But it is even more unlike that of the Reformers, and rather resembles the more daring speculations of early Greek theology, with which, indeed, there is a direct connexion through the pseudo-Dionysius.

The characteristic feature of mysticism, whether in Germany or elsewhere, is the devout and often very emotional contemplation of the sufferings of Christ. This in itself suggests the Moral theory, on its weakest side. But the greater mystics went further than this, and saw that the suffering of Christ must be wrought upon the individual also, in order that the deity of Christ may be wrought there too.[2] It is not merely that suffering atones for sin. Sin causes suffering to God, and the more fully a human soul achieves deification,

[1] Ritschl, *loc. cit.*
[2] This immediately suggests the language of Athanasius.

the more keenly will that soul feel the agony of sin. Thus the *Deutsche Theologie* says:

> Though God were to take to Himself all men who exist, and to assume their nature, and be incarnated in them, and make them divine in Him, yet if the same did not take place in me, my fall and apostasy would never be removed.[1]
>
> Although it is not possible for any man to be so pure and perfect in his obedience as Christ, still it is possible for every man to approach so nearly thereto, that he shall be said to be, and shall really be, divine and deified. And the nearer a man draws to this goal of perfect obedience, the more painful and grievous to him is all disobedience, sin, wickedness, and unrighteousness.[2]

There is no hesitation in these writers to attribute suffering directly to God. Tauler, for example, says that it was just because our great God was set at nought and crucified that we should, with suffering humility, see ourselves in His sufferings.[3] In creation God went forth from Himself in man, that man might return to Him. Thus man is, in creation, already in part divine. But man gave himself up to self-seeking, which is sin, and so the divine in him suffers until self is wholly put away and man returns to God.[4] Thus suffering is rather to be embraced than avoided, since in suffering we become partakers of God's own relation to sin. This is the thought which underlies the great efforts made by the mystics to identify themselves with Christ in His sufferings. Some carried the inward contemplation of the Passion, conceived as wrought upon themselves, to such lengths that the Stigmata broke out upon their own persons. Others, as, for example, Suso and the Flagellantes, strove to achieve to unity with Christ by external tortures, intended to overcome the resistance of the self to absorption in the Divine.

It is true that in the greater mystics this conception

[1] C. 3. [2] C. 14.

[3] Quoted by Hagenbach, *Hist. of Doctrines*, ii. 289.

[4] See Dorner, *op. cit.* ii. vol. ii. p. 13.

of the deification of the human soul retains its full religious value, being regarded as entirely due to an action from the side of God, or rather of Christ, the God-man. The true mystic overcomes and abandons his own personality, that he may gain a new personality in Christ. So Ruysbroek says:

> We also must be clothed with the same divinity (as the humanity of Christ), in that we love Him so warmly as to be able to deny ourselves and to surmount our created personality: then shall we be personally united with his personality—that is, with the eternal Truth.[1]

It is easy to see that such language, so long as the emphasis on the Divine action is not lost, might readily be used in conjunction with the orthodox phrases of the Satisfaction theory. And this combination is found in the *Deutsche Theologie*:

> He is at once God and man, and able to make satisfaction for mankind, in that He intervened and freely took our guilt.[2]

> Who by His sincere love redeemed human nature from evil and made satisfaction to the Divine justice for all our guilt.[3]

There was an obvious danger, however, in this idea of deification through suffering. It tended to exalt the personal merit of suffering voluntarily undertaken, as something in itself capable of making satisfaction, and thereby the unique and sole value of the atoning merits of Christ came sometimes to be belittled or even set aside, the extreme in this direction being reached by the heretical Beghards, who taught that Christ died not for mankind, but for Himself.[4] Mysticism seldom wholly escaped this danger. The contemplative self-identifica-

[1] *Spiegel des ewigen Heils*, c. 8 (*ap.* Dorner, *op. cit.* p. 24). On this subject of deification Hagenbach (*op. cit.* pp. 305-308) has some good references.

[2] C. 44.

[3] *Ibid.*

[4] *Ap.* Hagenbach, *op. cit.* ii. 290. Hagenbach also quotes (from Hoffman, *Geschichte des deutschen Kirchenliedes*, s. 94) a fragment of a Flagellant hymn (A.D. 1349): "Through God we shed our blood, which will avail for the expiation of our sins."

tion with Christ's sufferings, like the practical imitation of His poverty, was regarded as of real worth in God's eyes. "Sympathizing with Christ, the Mystic thought, through suffering, to rise to be a co-operator with Christ in the work of redemption. Even at the best, what he looked to learn at the foot of the Cross was love, forgiveness, gentleness towards men; of his own sin, and especially of his own guilt, he was seldom reminded. He preferred rocking himself in the sweet pains of a natural sympathetic love, to seeing in the Cross, on the one hand the condemnation, and on the other hand the atonement of his guilt. This was especially the case with Suso. Tauler, indeed, with his deeper earnestness, speaks of a descent into hell which we have yet to make. And yet he soon again returns to the view of this repentance as itself possessing an atoning virtue, when conjoined with the daily confession of sin to God."[1]

In all this, even at its best, there is little to remind us of the characteristic theology of the Reformation. Rather more tangible is the evidence which has been adduced, especially by Ullmann, from some of the later scholastic writers, in particular from Wyclif, Gerson, Wessel, and Luther's friend and teacher, Staupitz. It is not of any great importance to examine the evidence closely, and, indeed, it does not go very far. Ritschl has shown how little ground exists for asserting a direct connexion between the Reformation theories and the sporadic utterances of earlier thinkers. The most that can be asserted is that the tendencies which were to shape Reformation theology were already exerting an influence at an earlier date. These tendencies reveal themselves in two ways: firstly, in phrases which suggest that the legal and political conceptions underlying the Satisfaction theory were undergoing modification, and, secondly, in an attitude towards the meritorious work of Christ which bears some resemblance to the doctrine of justification by faith.

[1] Dorner, *op. cit.* p. 27.

The legal alternative of satisfaction or punishment had never succeeded in winning its way completely, and throughout the Middle Ages there is some confusion of thought upon the subject, especially in regard to penance, with its conception of *poena satisfactoria*. Thus it is natural to find that the penal language of Gregory the Great has echoes throughout the period, and that occasionally writers tend to state the Satisfaction theory in ways that suggest the penal ideas of the Reformers. This was the more natural as the feudal conception of God's dignity and honour gave way, through political changes, to a more abstract conception of justice, more like that of earlier days. This tendency may be seen in Wyclif,[1] who is interesting as re-asserting, with Anselm, the absolute necessity of the Atonement, as of all God's other acts. His argument is in general Anselmic in character, but it is with the idea of justice that this necessity is connected. God's justice demands that all sin shall be punished, whether in heaven or in hell. Though Wyclif speaks of satisfaction in the customary manner, there is the suggestion of a changed outlook. A similar turn of thought appears in Gerson,[2] who says that the King gave His Own Son to pain and death that justice might agree with mercy.

> God would never permit unpunished evil and therefore laid all our sins and faults upon Jesus Christ.[3]
>
> Sin is very greatly to be hated because it very greatly displeases the Divine justice; for you behold God suffering the penalty due to sin, in order to destroy it.[4]

Here the thought of satisfaction seems quite to have vanished, and yet there is no conscious breach of idea

[1] See esp. *Trialogus*, iii. 25.

[2] *Expositio in Passione Domini* (*Opp.* ed. du Pin, iii. pp. 1157, 1188, from which the quotations are taken).

[3] Nunquam Deus malum impunitum permitteret, eapropter omnia peccata et delicta nostra Jesu Christo supposuit.

[4] Peccatum maximopere habendum est odio quod maxime justitiae divinae displicet: nam ad ipsum destruendam videtis Deum pati poenam peccato debitam.

with the Satisfaction theory. The same contrast between God's justice and His mercy reappears in Gerson's younger contemporary, Wessel. But there is little reason for seeing any direct connexion with the Reformers. These chance phrases are due to a changing political and intellectual atmosphere, and it is to these wider changes that the thought of the Reformers must also be traced.

Even more common than penal language are passages asserting man's absolute dependence upon the Atonement wrought by Christ. Despite the ecclesiastical doctrine of penance, with its tendency to assign some place to human merits, the evangelical estimate of self, as taught by Augustine and Bernard, reappears constantly in later writers, though, as in the case of the mystics, there is no conscious opposition to the orthodoxy of the day, even in Wyclif. In Aquinas himself, as we have seen, there is a real inconsistency between the conception of the superabundant merits of Christ, appropriated through faith "formed by love," and that of the worth of human merit. In several writers this human merit seems almost to pass out of sight. Wyclif, for example, lays such stress upon penitence that he hardly seems to need the Satisfaction theory at all.

> It is right that that man (Adam) should be saved, since he repented so fruitfully, and God cannot deny His pity to such a penitent.[1]
>
> There is no doubt that God cannot refuse to grant the abolition of sin to those who are fruitfully contrite.[2]

Yet here the very repentance might be regarded as meritorious, and though Wyclif's attacks upon ecclesiastical abuses make it tempting to think that he would have repudiated such an idea, he can hardly have broken

[1] Salvari enim oportet illum hominem cum tam fructuose poenituit, et Deus non potest negare suam misericordiam taliter poenitenti (*Trial.* iii. 25).

[2] Nec dubium quin illis fructuose contritis Deus non posset deletionem peccati sui non concedere (*ibid.*).

so completely with the thought of his day. Wessel's language is more explicit.

> He who hears and believes the Gospel . . . whatever he does and suffers to gain Him, praises not his own works or himself as working . . . he attributes nothing to himself, knowing that he has nothing from himself.[1]

But this, the true attitude of the saint of every age, is not associated with any characteristically Lutheran view of faith. Faith, for Wessel, is rather the means whereby the believer is made righteous. He adopts in its fulness the mediaeval view of justification. In order that Christ may take away our sins, he says, He must infuse righteousness.[2] The work is wrought by Christ, and Wessel usually emphazises this, yet he sometimes explicitly states that faith enables us to stand as righteous before God not only through participation in Christ's sacrifice but also by means of our own spiritual sacrifices.[3] And, as in Aquinas, faith tends very much to pass over into the idea of love, a typically mediaeval point of view, due largely to the influence of Abelard. The abolition of sin is for him the possession of "justifying love."[4] This theme is elaborately worked out in his *Exempla Scalae Meditationis*. Thus:

> Dead or bitter is every man who loves nothing. Every life, that it may be life, should be made alive by love. Ugly is an unworthy love. But what is more worthy than that I should seek the love of my God, my Lord, my Lawgiver.[5]

This is not the typical Reformation doctrine of faith, and only differs from that of the Middle Ages in general

[1] Qui evangelium audiens credit . . . quantalibet pro consequendo faciat et patiatur, non sua opera, non se operantem extollit . . . nihil sibi ipsi tribuit, qui scit nihil habere ex se (*De Magnitudine Passionis*, c. 46).

[2] *Ib.* c 7. [3] *Ib.* c. 39, cf. c. 45. [4] *Ib.* c. 7, cf. c. 19.

[5] Mortuus aut amarus omnis homo qui nihil diligit. Omnis autem vita, ut vita sit, a dilectione oportet ut vivificetur. Indigna vero dilectio indecora. Quae autem dignior quam qua Dei mei, Domini mei, Legislatoris mei, dilectionem quaero (*Ex. Scal. Med.* ii. p. 379, cf. iii. p. 388).

in its frequent tendency to depreciate human good works —a tendency as old as St. Paul himself.

Staupitz, as Ritschl shows, adopted a very similar position to that which had been taken up by Wessel.[1] He adopts the usual contemporary view of justification, declaring that it is by regeneration that the sinner is justified. He who is justified may go on to do good works which God rewards, but in so doing God is rewarding His own works, since He is their true cause. Both works and reward are of God's grace. And so Staupitz comes to lay especial stress upon God's love, and here the evangelical turn of his thought is shown in his anger at the foolishness of those who think that they can move God by their good deeds or win Him with devoutness. God's love never varies, though that wrought in us by God may vary, and so we may trust God most when we trust ourselves least, looking only to the Cross.

This again is not Reformation doctrine, but it is essentially the practical religious consciousness which underlay the work of Luther. And, in general, even though we may not see in these writers any very clear anticipations of the new theological era, they are at least of one spirit with those who came after them. Their Experience of the Fact is the same, even though their expression of it differs.

[1] See reff. in Ritschl, *op. cit.* pp. 110 f., from which this paragraph is abridged.

CHAPTER VIII

THE LATER ROMAN VIEW

THE question of the Atonement was not felt to be a primary issue in the Reformation. It was affected radically, but only indirectly, by the protest of the Reformers against the mediaeval doctrine of merits, which seemed to them dangerously inconsistent with the doctrine, insisted upon by Aquinas himself, of the superabundant worth, or, as the Reformers preferred to phrase it, the sole sufficiency, of the satisfaction made by Christ. The nature of justification thus became the centre of discussion, rather than the actual character of the Atonement upon which that justification depends, and it is in connexion with this subject that the statements of the Council of Trent upon the Atonement occur.

The Synod furthermore declares, that in adults the beginning of the said justification is to be derived from the prevenient grace of God, through Jesus Christ, that is to say, from His vocation, whereby, without any merits existing on their parts, they are called; that so they, who by sins were alienated from God, may be disposed, through His quickening and assisting grace, to convert themselves to their own justification, by freely assenting to and co-operating with the said grace: in such sort that, while God touches the heart of man by the illumination of the Holy Ghost, neither is man himself utterly passive while receiving that inspiration, forasmuch as he is also able to reject it; yet is he not able, by his own free will, without the grace of God, to move himself unto justice in His sight.[1]

[1] Declarat praeterea, ipsius justificationis exordium in adultis a Dei per Christum Iesum praeveniente gratia sumendum esse, hoc est, ab ejus vocatione, qua nullis eorum existentibus meritis vocantur, ut,

This disposition or preparation is followed by justification, which is not remission of sins merely, but also the sanctification and renewal of the inward man, through the voluntary reception of the grace and of the gifts whereby man, before unjust, becomes just, before an enemy, becomes a friend, that so he may be an heir according to hope of life everlasting. Of this justification the causes are these: the final cause is the glory of God and of Jesus Christ, and life everlasting; the efficient cause is a merciful God, who washes and sanctifies freely, signing and anointing man with the Holy Spirit of promise, who is the pledge of our inheritance; the meritorious cause is His most beloved only-begotten Son, our Lord Jesus Christ, who, when we were enemies, for the exceeding charity wherewith He loved us, won justification for us by His most holy Passion on the wood of the Cross, and made satisfaction for us unto God the Father; the instrumental cause is the sacrament of Baptism, which is the sacrament of faith, without which no man was ever justified; lastly, the sole formal cause is the justice of God, not that whereby He Himself is just, but that whereby He maketh us just, that, namely, with which we, being endowed by Him, are renewed in the spirit of our mind, and we are not only reputed, but are truly called, and are, just, receiving justice within us, each one according to his own measure, which the Holy Ghost distributes to every one as He wills, and according to each one's proper disposition and co-operation.[1]

---

qui per peccata a Deo aversi erant, per ejus excitantem atque adjuvantem gratiam ad convertendum se ad suam ipsorum justificationem, eidem gratiae libere assentiendo et cooperando, disponantur ita, ut tangente Deo cor hominis per Spiritus sancti illuminationem neque homo ipse nihil omnino agat, inspirationem illam recipiens, quippe qui illam et abjicere potest, neque tamen sine gratia Dei movere se ad justitiam coram illo libera sua voluntate possit (*Sess.* vi. ch. 5).

[1] Hanc dispositionem seu praeparationem justificatio ipsa consequitur, quae non est sola peccatorum remissio, sed et sanctificatio et renovatio interioris hominis per voluntariam susceptionem gratiae et donorum; unde homo ex injusto fit justus, et ex inimico amicus, ut sit heres secundum spem vitae aeternae. Hujus justificationis causae sunt, finalis quidem, gloria Dei et Christi, et vita aeterna; efficiens vero, misericors Deus qui gratuito abluit et sanctificat signans et unguens Spiritu promissionis sancto, qui est pignus hereditatis nostrae; meritoria autem, dilectissimus unigenitus suus, Dominus noster Jesus Christus, qui, quum essemus inimici, propter nimiam caritatem, qua dilexit nos, sua sanctissima passione in ligno crucis nobis justificationem meruit, et pro nobis Deo Patri satisfecit; instrumentalis item, sacramentum baptismi, quod est sacramentum fidei, sine qua nulli unquam contigit justificatio; demum unica formalis causa est justitia Dei, non qua ipse justus est, sed quâ nos

This whole section was composed with direct reference to the doctrine of justification by faith, as stated by the Reformers. In general the Thomist position was adopted, though there is no particular emphasis upon the special features of the Satisfaction theory as stated by Aquinas. In this respect the Tridentine Catechism went further, when it declared the Passion to be a superabundant satisfaction, an acceptable sacrifice, a redemption from our vain conversation, and an example of patience. The language of the Council itself was so worded that Scotists and Thomists alike could accept it. As in Aquinas the harder features of the Satisfaction theory are covered by the references to the pity of God, the prevenient grace of God, the love of God, as the effective cause of the Atonement. No hard necessity of conserving His honour and dignity is laid upon Him. It is of love that He saves. And this conception of God's love is worked out, as in Aquinas, upon the lines suggested, however imperfectly, by Abelard. The love of God becomes love in man, infused in him, together with faith and hope, through the act of God, by the merits of Christ. Man is even said to be able to co-operate in some small degree with God's grace, inasmuch as he can, if he will, accept or refuse it when it is offered, and afterwards, by the aid of that same grace, may himself do good works acceptable to God.

Thus, in direct opposition to the Reformers, the Council defines justification as including sanctification, continuing the mediaeval tradition, which had explained justification as a making righteous, and not merely as a pronouncing righteous. This much disputed question is primarily one of terminology, depending upon the

---

justus facit, qua videlicet ab eo donati renovamur spiritu mentis nostrae, et non modo reputamur, sed vere justi nominamur et sumus, justitiam in nobis recipientes unusquisque suam secundum mensuram, quam Spiritus sanctus partitur singulis prout vult, et secundum propriam cujusque dispositionem et cooperationem (*Sess.* vi. c. 7).

exegesis of St. Paul's Epistles.[1] It is only by the associated theology that the meaning attached to the term becomes of any great importance. But it is important that the Council of Trent, with all its emphasis upon the grace of God in effecting justification, should have regarded man, in however small a degree, as able to co-operate in bringing the change about.

It is noteworthy that love rather than faith takes the central place. Faith, by itself, is declared to be totally inadequate, neither bringing about union with Christ, nor justification, nor life everlasting. Love in man must respond to love in God.

> For although no one can be just but he to whom the merits of the Passion of our Lord Jesus Christ are communicated, yet is this done in the said justification of the impious; when, by the merit of that same most holy Passion, the love of God is poured forth, by the Holy Spirit, in the hearts of those that are justified and dwelleth therein; whence man, through Jesus Christ, in whom he is ingrafted, receives, in the said justification, together with the remission of sins, all infused together, faith, hope, and love. For faith, unless hope and love be added thereto neither unites man perfectly with Christ nor makes him a living member of His body.[2]
>
> Life everlasting, which, without hope and love, faith cannot bestow.[3]

The Council thus set its seal upon the doctrine of "infused righteousness," which represented the attempt

[1] The fact that the Reformers rightly regarded St. Paul's use of δικαιόω, etc., as forensic is not in itself sufficient to justify their whole theology. It is just as possible to make too absolute a breach between justification and sanctification as it is to confuse them.

[2] Quanquam enim nemo possit esse justus, nisi cui merita passionis Domini nostri Jesu Christi communicantur, id tamen in hac impii justificatione fit, dum ejusdem sanctissimae passionis merito per Spiritum sanctum caritas Dei diffunditur in cordibus eorum, qui justificantur, atque ipsis inhaeret, unde in ipsa justificatione cum remissione peccatorum haec omnia simul infusa accipit homo per Jesum Christum, cui inseritur, fidem, spem, et caritatem. Nam fides, nisi ad eam spes accedat et caritas, neque unit perfecte cum Christo, neque corporis ejus vivum membrum efficit (*ibid.*).

[3] Vitam aeternam . . . quam sine spe et caritate praestare fides non potest (*ibid.*).

of the mediaeval Latin Church to do justice to the manward aspect of Atonement. And in this respect its language is richer and fuller than that of the Reformers, in so far as the latter thought only of the Godward side of Atonement, and ignored its direct influence upon the heart of man. There is something very external in the Penal theory, in its ordinary form, which is avoided by the more mystical conception of the Roman theologians. And the treatment of faith as mere assurance,[1] to which the Reformers tended, is obviously far less adequate to the facts of the religious life than the correlation of faith and love.

The objections of the Reformers were, indeed, really directed against the doctrine of infused righteousness not so much for its own sake as for the conclusions drawn from it. The Council of Trent quite definitely adhered to the view that human good works wrought in Christ deserved and would obtain a reward of God in their own right, though they were careful to ascribe the power to do such good works to the grace of God and the merits of Christ Himself.

> If any shall say that the good works of a man justified are the gifts of God in such sense that they are not also the good merits of him that is justified; or that for the good works wrought by him through the grace of God and the merits of Jesus Christ, of whom he is a lively member, he that is justified does not truly deserve increase of grace, life eternal and the continuance of that eternal life, if he depart in grace, and also increase of glory; let him be anathema.[2]

Despite the protests of the Council[3] the Reformers felt that such teaching did away with the whole value

[1] *Sess.* vi. *Can.* 12 condemns this view.

[2] Si quis dixerit, hominis justificati bona opera ita esse dona Dei ut non sint etiam bona ipsius justificati merita; aut ipsum justificatum bonis operibus, quae ab eo per Dei gratiam et Jesu Christi meritum, cujus vivum membrum est, fiunt, non vere mereri augmentum gratiae, vitam aeternam et ipsius vitae aeternae, si tamen in gratia decesserit, consecutionem, atque etiam gloriae augmentum: anathema sit (*Sess.* vi. *Can.* 32, cf. *Can.* 26).

[3] Cf. *Sess.* vi. *Can.* 33.

of the doctrine of the superabundant satisfaction wrought by Christ. It was not really consistent with the evangelical estimate of all human effort as worthless in God's eyes. And though in theory the emphasis upon the grace of God made this Pauline self-estimate quite possible within the Catholic tradition,[1] as in the case of Augustine and Bernard and Francis, in practice the stress upon human merits had become very marked. Upon it rested the whole theory of Indulgences and the Treasury of Merits, with, as its basis, the conception of works of supererogation. And even at the Council itself the satisfaction wrought by Christ was far less emphasized than the satisfaction wrought by man in penance, though, indeed, it is carefully added that such satisfaction

> neither obscures nor in any way diminishes the force of the merit and satisfaction of our Lord Jesus Christ.[2]

So again the satisfaction is said to be wrought "through Christ," and in making it

> . . . we are conformed to Christ Jesus, who made satisfaction for our sins, of whom is all our sufficiency.[3]

Had the emphasis lain, in practice, upon such phrases as these, the protests of the Reformers would have lost much of their point. It may, indeed, be doubted whether the Reformation would have come when and as it did. But in the ordinary life of the Church the exaltation of human merits went on unchecked, and it was only in the consciousness of the few that their true relation to the merits of Christ was felt. And in the end practice and theory had drawn so far apart, and

[1] Ritschl (*op. cit.* pp. 115 f.) shows very aptly that the Roman Canon of the Mass itself bears witness to this devotional estimate of self: Sanctis, intra quorum nos consortium, non aestimator meriti, sed veniae quaesumus largitor, admitte.

[2] (Nec existimarunt) vim meriti et satisfactionis Domini nostri Jesu Christi vel obscurari vel aliqua ex parte imminui (*Sess.* xiv. ch. 8).

[3] Christo Jesu, qui pro peccatis nostris satisfecit, ex quo omnis nostra sufficientia est, conformes efficimur (*ibid.*).

parts at least of the theory had been so far twisted into conformity with practice, that the Reformation, which was, in its essence, a protest against practical abuses, became inevitable, lest the language of humble dependence upon the grace of God and the atoning work of Christ should lose all its meaning.

The decisions of the Council of Trent have remained to so great an extent the norm of all subsequent Roman Catholic doctrine that it is not to be expected that more recent Roman theologians will be found to diverge very far from the lines laid down at the close of the Middle Ages. This holds true of the doctrine of the Atonement, as of other doctrines. It is on the side of Protestantism that speculation upon the subject for the most part develops, and there is little of special historical importance in post-Reformation Roman writers. The doctrine of justification as involving an infusion and not merely an imputation of righteousness remained unaltered. And as to the Atonement itself almost all writers conformed either wholly or partially to the Thomist or Scotist position. In general the language of the Satisfaction theory was used, but the spread of the Scotist view of the Incarnation as independent of man's sin led to an emphasis upon God's love which softened away many of the harder features of the Anselmic doctrine. This tendency, as we have seen, was making itself felt as early as the Council of Trent, and the language of Aquinas himself could be quoted in its support. The conception of satisfaction became broader and more adequate in its application to the work of Christ. It was no longer merely the amends made to a Ruler for His outraged dignity, but rather the reverent homage due to a holy and loving God, to be approached not with the fear of the subject but with the worship and devotion of the believer. And so the idea of satisfaction tended to pass over into the idea of sacrifice, regarded in part as an expiation for sin, but also as an act of homage and worship. We have seen that the application of sacrificial language to the doctrine of Atonement had been a characteristic of every period of doctrinal history, appearing side by side with theories and metaphors of the most diverse character. The mediaeval writers, co-ordinating the views of their predecessors, had given this point of view a definite place in their system, and in more recent Roman writers it has tended more and more to become dominant. Eucharistic doctrine has played no small part in this development. The sacrifice of the altar has been brought into direct relation with the Sacrifice of Calvary, as one with it in all things except manner, and thus the worshipper at the Eucharist feels himself brought into direct contact with the atoning work of Christ.

> And forasmuch as, in this Divine sacrifice which is celebrated in the mass, that same Christ is contained and offered in an unbloody manner, who once offered himself in a bloody manner on the altar of the Cross; the holy synod teaches that this sacrifice is truly propitiatory, and that by means whereof we obtain mercy, and find grace in seasonable aid. . . . For the Lord, appeased by the offering thereof, and granting the grace and gift of repentance, forgives even heinous crimes and sins. [1]

This statement of the Council of Trent may be regarded as typical of subsequent Roman Catholicism. And the emphasis which has been laid upon the doctrine of the Eucharistic sacrifice has naturally tended to bring about a concurrent emphasis upon the sacrificial aspect of the Cross itself. A full discussion of this subject

[1] Et quoniam in divino hoc sacrificio, quod in missa peragitur, idem ille Christus continetur, et incruente immolatur, qui in ara crucis semel se ipsum cruente obtulit, docet sancta synodus, sacrificium istud vere propitiatorium esse, per ipsumque fieri ut . . . misericordiam consequamur et gratiam inveniamus in auxilio opportuno. Hujus quippe oblatione placatus Dominus gratiam et donum poenitentiae concedens, crimina et peccata etiam ingentia dimittit (*Conc. Trid. Sess.* xxii. 2). Compare the statement of the Tridentine Catechism: Unum igitur et idem sacrificium esse fatemur, et haberi debet, quod in missa peragitur et quod in cruce oblatum est; quemadmodum una est et eadem hostia, Christus videlicet Dominus noster, qui seipsum in ara crucis semel tantummodo cruentum immolavit.

would, however, demand a separate treatise on the development of Eucharistic doctrine, from the earliest times, and cannot here be attempted. It must suffice to illustrate the progress of Thomist and Scotist thought in this connexion from a few isolated writers.[1]

We may glance first at the period of the Jansenist controversy, in the seventeenth century, when for a time it seemed possible that the tenets of Calvinism might find a foothold even within the Roman communion. The dispute between Malebranche and the Jansenist leader, Arnauld, extended to matters connected with the doctrine of Atonement. Malebranche[2] adopted the Scotist view of the Incarnation, a view which was naturally congenial to a mind both mystical and philosophical. Though our Lord's human birth occurred in time, He is, before all time, the Beginning of God's ways. In the image of His humanity Adam was formed. He alone, God's Word and Wisdom, was worthy, and so, before all creation, He offered Himself that He might present to God worship and a Victim in His honour. It was to offer such worship in the visible Church that man was created. Thus far Malebranche is upon the direct line of development of Roman theology, and his conception of the eternal Sacrifice shows a close approximation to the idea of satisfaction, regarded as an offering made with direct reference to the honour of God. But when Malebranche comes to speak of the fall and of sin, which gives satisfaction its peculiar character as opposed to sacrifice in general, he seems to become ultra-Calvinistic. The fall, he declares, was necessary, since the elect could in no way win so great merit as by overcoming concupiscence and so reversing the fall through grace, in Jesus Christ. The real thought underlying this is the Thomist thought of the greatness of the merits of Christ, the superabundant value of the

[1] On this subject cf. Oxenham, *op. cit.* ch. vi., to which the following paragraphs are much indebted.

[2] *Traité de la Nature et de la Grâce.*

sacrifice offered by Him, value which even sin only serves to enhance. For all his Scotist view of the Incarnation Malebranche was quite free from any thought of *acceptilatio*, of an offering only adequate through God's acceptance. But his language was wholly unfortunate, and well deserved the reply which it provoked from Arnauld,[1] to the effect that such a theory made God the author of sin. Arnauld himself took the Thomist view that it was because of sin that the Incarnation took place. He even declared that this view had the support of all the fathers. But he went on, following the characteristic Jansenist doctrine of predestination, to deny, as did also the Calvinists of his day, the universality of the Atonement, arguing that the merits of the Passion only applied to the elect. This point of view has, indeed, a real precedent in the thought of Scotus himself, inasmuch as there is a real affinity between the conception of election and the conception of satisfaction, regarded as resting solely upon God's acceptance for its atoning worth.[2] But in this respect Scotus had few followers in the post-Reformation period, and the allied doctrine of the Jansenists was soon and universally rejected.

In the next century the discussion of the subject was continued especially by the great teachers at the Parisian Sorbonne, writing with the Socinian controversy in view. While various opinions were held as to the necessity and purpose of the Incarnation, in general the Thomist theory of satisfaction was adopted. Tournely[3] indeed comes practically to the Anselmic view that the Incarnation was necessary, together with all that is involved, if man was to be saved at all. God might indeed, by some special act, have saved man without adequate satisfaction,[4] but in His justice, which

[1] *Réflexions philosophiques et théologiques.*

[2] See p. 160.

[3] *Praelectiones Theol. de Incarn. Verbi Divini* (1727).

[4] Satisfactio condigna.

is His very Nature, there was no other way than the full satisfaction made by Christ. And in describing this satisfaction Tournely comes very near the Penal theory of the Calvinists with whom he is making common cause against the Socinians, when he argues that Christ not only rendered homage to God but also, as man's substitute, endured the punishment inflicted by God's justice, thus paying man's debt, turning away God's wrath, and expiating sin. A similar position was expressed, more moderately, by Tournely's disciple, Le Grand,[1] who definitely rejects the conclusion that the Incarnation was necessary, arguing that though full satisfaction to God's justice could have been made in no other way, no absolute necessity was laid upon Him. Le Grand's definition of satisfaction much resembles that of Aquinas:

> The voluntary rendering of equivalent honour and reverence out of what is one's own, and not otherwise owed, to compensate an injury done to another.[2]

The similarity between such a conception of satisfaction and that of sacrifice, as held, for example, by Malebranche, is obvious. Both consist primarily in a rendering of honour. It is only in the reference to sin that the two differ, and even in this connexion it is as natural to speak of sacrifice as of satisfaction, and, indeed, there is something to be gained by the use of the wider term. It is impossible not to feel the grandeur of the thought of Malebranche as compared with that of such a writer as Tournely.

The true successors of Malebranche may be found in the more definitely devotional writers of the eighteenth century. Massiot,[3] for example, writing upon the Priesthood and Sacrifice of Christ, treats satisfaction simply as an element in sacrifice. Sacrifice is homage

[1] *Tractatus de Incarn. Verbi Divini* (1750).
[2] Quoted by Oxenham, *op. cit.* p. 277.
[3] *Traité du sacerdoce et du sacrifice de Jésus Christ* (1708).

to God. It is only accidentally, through the coming of sin into the world, that it involves reparation also. This conception of sacrifice is expounded in direct connexion with the sacrifice of the Mass, which is regarded as perpetuating the supreme Sacrifice of the Cross, upon which all mankind was offered in Christ's mystical Body, in an act of worship and reparation. In speaking of satisfaction Massiot adopts the traditional arguments as to the helplessness of man and the completeness of the satisfaction offered by Christ, but it is clear that for him the thought of satisfaction takes but a small place beside that of sacrifice. In Plowden,[1] a later writer of the same school, the transition is complete, since sacrifice is now explicitly declared to be the highest of all acts of satisfaction. The thought is worked out upon the lines much like those followed by Massiot. The purpose of Christ's Sacrifice was threefold—to reconcile man to God, to make mankind one in love, and to bring man into the unity of Christ's mystical Body offered upon the Cross. It is through the Eucharist that the effects of this Sacrifice are communicated to us.

"It will be at once seen that with these writers—and they are but a specimen of many more—the dominant idea . . . is that of Sacrifice, which comprehends more than the notions of satisfaction only, or of the payment of a debt. It includes and exhausts them, but it includes a great deal more. We may further observe that this idea is habitually viewed in connexion with its perpetuation in the Eucharist." [2]

Oxenham's own book, from which the above dictum is quoted, provides an admirable illustration of the modern development of this treatment of the subject of Atonement in the Roman Church. Like the writers mentioned above, he is Scotist in his treatment of the Incarnation and Thomist in his view of Satisfaction:

[1] *Traité du sacrifice de Jésus Christ* (1778).
[2] Oxenham, *op. cit.* p. 283.

So much our hearts will tell us, that in the Lamb slain before the foundation of the world, but offered in time on Calvary, we have the surest pledge and most perfect revelation of a love that cannot fail. From of old He had loved us with an everlasting love, and therefore, when we rebelled against Him, in the compassion of His sufferings He drew us to Himself once more; and He has vouchsafed to reconcile us by so excellent a method of atonement, that it is at once the source of sanctity to the fallen, whose nature He has assumed, and a perfect satisfaction. And further, the voice of tradition combines with the surmises of reason to suggest to us that the mystery of the Atonement is part of a yet deeper mystery in the eternal purpose of God. He had always meant to make His tabernacle among men, but He had not meant to die. Only in so far as we comprehend the charity of the Incarnation, can we hope to comprehend aright its consummation in the shame and self-sacrifice of the Cross.[1]

Let us remember then that He suffered in every part of His Sacred Humanity, in Body and Soul alike, and throughout the entire period of His earthly life. . . . What are sometimes called His "unnecessary sufferings," as not strictly belonging to the actual Atonement, yet belong to that superabundance, that extravagant generosity of self-abandonment, so to call it, characteristic of Him with whom is no bare forgiveness only, but a copious redemption.[2]

The passages may be taken as typical of the ordinary Roman position of to-day, which indeed simply continues the tradition of the later Middle Ages, though the extent of the influence of Aquinas and Scotus still differs in different writers.

The mediaeval account of justification, here implied, is very strongly maintained by all Roman theologians. Thus Oxenham says elsewhere:

Justification is the free gift of Christ, whereby He restores to us our lost inheritance of grace, and in restoring it cleanses every stain whether of actual or original sin, though concupiscence still remains for our trial. But it is more than a simple restoration of our forfeit birthright, for we are raised by justification to a higher state than that from which Adam fell, and made through union with the Redeemer partakers of the Divine nature.[3]

---

[1] *Ib.* pp. 340 f. On the Scotist view of the Incarnation cf. pp. 98-102.
[2] *Ib.* p. 314.
[3] *Ib.* p. 104.

All forensic interpretations are expressly rejected, together with every conception of a substitutionary imputation of righteousness, a doctrine which the Reformers had sometimes stated in a very bald form. Righteousness is "not imputed, but imparted." We may quote in further illustration the definition of justification given in *Catholic Belief*,[1] a popular but authoritative manual which has had a very wide circulation.

> Justification is a divine act which conveys sanctifying grace, and by that grace communicates a supernatural life to the soul, which by sin, whether original or actual, had incurred spiritual death; that is to say, justification is a change in the human soul or translation from the state of sin into the state of grace. . . . The grace of justification produces a change affecting the regenerate by its presence, elevating and perfecting it. By this grace the likeness to God is brought out in them, and they are raised to a state of friendship with Him, and of divine sonship.[2]

However disputable such a definition may be on the grounds of New Testament exegesis, it is at least valuable as bearing witness to the importance of the manward aspect of Atonement. No mere forensic, external, act can satisfy either the sinner's need or the demands of justice. In some way it must be true that the sinner is raised above his sin through the work of Christ, and only so can it be just that a righteous God should treat him as sinless. No bare doctrine of imputation can be complete in itself.

On the question of the superabundant satisfaction, again, Oxenham's language is characteristic of Roman theology in general. A further passage may be quoted:

> The scholastic controversy brought out with peculiar clearness that, while we have no right to assume that an adequate satisfaction was *necessary*, a satisfaction not only sufficient but superabundant has certainly been made, owing to the infinite

---

[1] *Catholic Belief: or A Short and Simple Exposition of Catholic Doctrine*, by the Very Rev. Joseph Faà di Bruno, D.D. (4th ed. 1883).

[2] *Ib.* p. 49.

worth, by virtue of the hypostatic union, of those human acts and sufferings which the Redeemer offered for the sins of His brethren, as the Head and Representative of our race. . . . We cannot, again, say except by a figure of speech, that our sins were imputed to Him, or that He who was sinless endured the wrath of God ; still less, in the blasphemous language of several Lutheran divines, that He suffered the torments of the damned. Yet it is certain that His mental sufferings, which greatly exceeded the bodily pains of the Passion, had an expiatory value, and that they were chiefly, though not exclusively supernatural.[1]

This comes very close indeed to the general position of Aquinas in its estimate both of the value and of the character of Christ's sufferings. And it is noteworthy that, as in so many of the Fathers, the death of Christ is not isolated from His whole Incarnate life.

Every act of that spotless life had a sacrificial power.[2]

The Agony indeed, though wrought out in history, is rather mystical than physical. It is a mystery of "interior martyrdom," in which "Jesus received into His sinless consciousness the burden of our guilt," the contemplation by the Living Source of Sanctity of all the sins of all erring humanity.[3]

But this emphasis upon the supreme value of the work of Christ has not done away with the conception of human merits :

The controversies of the Reformation threw a fresh light on the subjective and moral aspects of the doctrine, and exhibited with peculiar distinctness the error of supposing that the Atonement wrought by Christ was to be understood as superseding our own satisfactions or obedience, instead of sanctifying and transforming them.[4]

It should be noted that there is no attempt to set up human merit as something apart from the merit of Christ. Whatever may be the effect of the doctrine in

[1] Oxenham, *op. cit.* pp. 302 f. [2] *Ibid.*

[3] This should be compared with the language of such writers as Maurice and Moberly. [4] *Ib.* pp. 305 f.

practice—and the abuses which resulted from it at the time of the Reformation are far less in evidence to-day —the Roman theologians are quite clear upon this point. Even such a popular manual as *Catholic Belief* says explicitly:

> All our merits, however, without any exception, are grounded on the merits of Jesus Christ, and on His grace, without which no one can move a step towards heaven. . . . Our merit, therefore, does not take away from Christ's merits, for without Him we can do nothing. We merit through Christ, Christ makes us merit; or still more properly, Christ merits in us, and therefore all the glory is His.[1]

Luther would have objected loudly to such language as illogical, but the underlying devotional attitude is not far removed from Luther's own.

We must notice, finally, the influence of the idea of sacrifice, which, as has been shown, has tended, since the Council of Trent, to displace the language of the Satisfaction theory. The conception of satisfaction has indeed, been very largely restricted in popular usage to the satisfactions offered by man in penance. Thus in *Catholic Belief* the only discussion of satisfaction comes under the head of the Sacrament of Penance, a treatment of the subject for which the Council of Trent provided a precedent. And while, as the passages quoted above show, there is no objection felt to the application of the old Anselmic language to the work of Christ, such language has, in practice, very largely given place to the broader conception of sacrifice, expounded in direct connexion with the Eucharist. How little real change of theory is involved is shown by Oxenham's definition:

> Sacrifice is the spontaneous expression of the homage due from the creature to his Creator. . . . Sin impressed on it, as on all human acts of devotion, an additional character of reparation. But from the beginning it was not so.[2]

---

[1] Pp. 52 f.; cf. Council of Trent, *Sess.* vi. ch. 18.

[2] *Op. cit.* p. 213.

This gives clear expression to the Anselmic idea that the purpose for which man exists is to render to God the honour that is His due, and that it is restoring that honour that Atonement must be made. The definition given in *Catholic Belief*, though obviously framed in the interests of the transubstantiation controversy, has as its basis the same idea.

> Sacrifice is the highest act of religion, because other acts with which we worship God may also be used, though in a limited sense, in honouring the Angels, Saints, Kings, and other high personages, while sacrifice is so exclusively due to God, that it can only be offered to Him; for the natural end of sacrifice is to show, by the destruction of or notable change in the Victim, the sovereign dominion over creation which belongs to God alone.[1]

It is obvious that such an idea of sacrifice is at least as adequate as the idea of satisfaction to express the Christian consciousness of the Fact of Atonement. And it has the great advantage that it is far less liable to inadequate transactional misinterpretations, which depend, as indeed the Satisfaction theory had depended in Anselm's thought, upon a merely quantitative view of sin, akin to that of a civil court of justice. That the sacrificial conception of Atonement should be expounded in relation to the Eucharist is a direct corollary of the Roman view of that service:

> The Incarnation and the Passion are no mere incidents of bygone history, but a presence of abiding power. The Blood that flowed on Calvary flows indeed no more, but the Lamb slain before the worlds were made is offered still, Himself the victim, Priest, and Shrine.[2]

The application of such language to the Sacrament of the Lord's Supper may be questioned, but such questioning does not invalidate the supreme mystical value of the underlying conception of sacrifice. The conception of satisfaction has never really been easy to reconcile with the thought of the supreme love of

[1] P. 72.

[2] Oxenham, *op. cit.* p. 285.

God, a thought upon which the Church of Rome has always laid stress. But in sacrifice is seen the love of the Son eternally responding to the Father's love, eternally making possible, through His union with man, the response of the love of the creature to the love of his Creator. In faith that is formed by love man meets the love of God.

And such a conception of sacrifice need lead to no belittling of the dreadful fact of sin. It was because of sin that sacrifice took the form of the Cross, and our union with Christ was wrought by Him through the Passion that our sin caused. It is therefore in its very essence a union with Him "into His death," that death which "condemned sin in the flesh."

In this development of the Satisfaction theory Abelard has indeed come to his own, though his conception too has developed almost beyond recognition. It is very striking that the bare Godward aspect of Atonement, as presented in Anselm, has been expanded, almost unconsciously, upon the manward side, until, in its emphasis upon the divine love and the response of human love, it almost touches the Moral theory. Two theories could not start from more diverse points of view. Yet in its later and more complete forms the Moral theory also depends upon the principle that the death of Christ can appeal to us because we are one with Him through the power of His love. Both theories ultimately find their force in mysticism. The one starts from reason and the language of the Bible. The other comes straight from the heart of man, touched by the Cross. But under expressions often singularly diverse, the meaning is one.[1]

[1] For recent statements of the Roman standpoint reference should be made to C. Van Cambrugghe, *Tractatus de Verbo Incarnato*, C. Pesch, *Compendium Theologiae Dogmaticae*, vol. iii., J. Pohle, *Dogmatic Theology*, vol. v., *Soteriology* (trans. A. Preuss).

CHAPTER IX

THE REFORMERS AND THE PENAL THEORY

THAT the work of the Reformers[1] profoundly affected the doctrine of the Atonement is one of the outstanding facts of the history of theological thought. Before the Reformation only a few hints of a Penal theory can be found. After the Reformation it becomes common ground for the great majority of Protestant writers. It is, therefore, of the first importance for a right appreciation of that theory to realize that the Reformers had at the outset no direct intention of remodelling the doctrine of Atonement, though such a remodelling was a natural result of some of the principles which underlay their work. The whole problem of sin and grace was set in a new light by Luther and his companions, who saw as central aspects of St. Paul's teaching hitherto almost universally ignored, and so radical a change in point of view could not but affect profoundly the appreciation of the Fact in which that problem finds its solution.

It cannot be too much emphasized that it was upon a practical issue that the Reformation controversy began. The abuses of the indulgence market had thrown into strong relief the dangers involved in the doctrine of merits, as ordinarily preached in the Middle Ages. Luther's whole soul, filled, as the souls of St. Paul and of Augustine had been filled, with the overmastering sense of the supremacy of the loving grace of God,

[1] Upon this whole subject Ritschl's work is indispensable. It is very complete, and unsurpassed for acuteness of insight.

recoiled in utter horror from either practice or precept which might seem to set anything human upon a plane with the sole sufficiency of Christ. This religious self-estimate was indeed no new thing. We have already seen it exemplified in Bernard, and Francis, and Wessel. But, as Ritschl points out, there is an important variation. "Luther constantly looks at the comparative imperfection of the works of believers, while his mediaeval antecedents directed their attention chiefly to the relative perfection of such works wrought in the believer by grace, although bidding men disregard their meritorious value."[1] It was in direct contrast to sin, and the horror of sin, that Luther, like Augustine, viewed the grace of God, and it was salvation from sin, and not good works wrought in righteousness, that filled his mind.

Thus it is natural to find that Luther and the other Reformers held a view of sin far deeper and more intense than that of the Middle Ages. It was no longer sufficient to regard sin, after the manner of Anselm, as disobedience, a dishonour done to God, an act which deprives God of His due, and Luther went back to the strong positive view of sin as a corruption, bringing death, the view which had been held by Athanasius and Augustine. He recoiled utterly from the mediaeval view that the Fall merely deprived man of the special gifts[2] of holiness and immortality bestowed upon Adam by God. It was no mere *privatio* but a *pravatio* too, a corruption of man's very nature, bringing with it an inordinate desire to sin. For all his early zeal Luther felt that his "monkish baptism" had not left him clean, able to do good works pleasing to God. He still fell, even before the very least temptation. He was without strength, without certainty, and desperately inclined to sin. And this seemed to him to be of the very essence of the condition of fallen man. It was in faith, trust in God, that original righteousness had centred, and in the Fall that faith had been lost. For all time man

[1] Ritschl, *op. cit.* p. 137.

[2] *Dona gratuita.*

stood trembling and guilty before the wrath of the Judge, with nothing to offer in lieu of punishment.

The one great necessity, therefore, in order that man may be put right with God, is the restoration of that faith which man has lost. Faith, and faith only, can justify. Thus the Augsburg Confession says:

> Men cannot be justified before God by their own powers, merits, or works, but are justified freely for Christ's sake through faith, when they believe that they are received into favour, and their sin forgiven for Christ's sake, who by His death has made satisfaction for our sins. This faith God imputes for righteousness before Him.[1]

The justification here mentioned is regarded by all the Reformers, with the sole exception of Osiander, in a purely forensic sense. Thus Melanchthon says:

> To justify, in accordance with forensic usage, here signifies to acquit the accused and to pronounce him righteous, but on account of the righteousness of another, namely of Christ, which righteousness of another is communicated to us by faith.[2]

This technical and Pauline sense of release from the verdict of guilty is that constantly given to the term "justification" by the Reformers, in direct and conscious opposition to the mediaeval view. The infused righteousness included under justification by the Council of Trent is very definitely distinguished from justification. Sanctification, though it shows itself in the Christian life as the fruit of justification, is quite separate from it. Justification in itself is solely the act of God, having no relation to our own righteousness, but solely to the righteousness of Christ imputed to us, as it were, by a legal transfer.

[1] Homines non possunt justificari coram Deo propriis viribus, meritis, aut operibus, sed gratis justificantur propter Christum per fidem cum credunt se in gratiam recipi, et peccata remitti propter Christum, qui sua morte pro nostris peccatis satisfecit. Hanc fidem imputat Deus pro justitia coram ipso (Art. IV.).

[2] Justificare hoc loco forensi consuetudine significat reum absolvere et pronuntiare justum, sed propter alienam justitiam, videlicet Christi, quae aliena justitia communicatur nobis per fidem (*Apol. Conf. Aug.* p. 125, *ap.* Hagenbach, *op. cit.* iii. 112).

The faith which justifies is, therefore, simply the assurance that this transfer is valid, the certitude that the promises of God have been fulfilled, and that we are adopted in Christ as sons of God. It is no longer the "faith formed by love" of the Roman theologians, for the very idea of such a faith carries with it the idea of an "infused righteousness," thus involving the danger of the confusion of justification and sanctification. Faith for the Reformers wears a much more intellectual aspect, though it has a true ethical value in its implication of a complete self-resignation of the soul. Thus the Second Helvetic Confession says:

> Human faith is not an opinion or a human persuasion, but a most firm assurance and an evident and constant assent of the soul, and, finally, a most right comprehension of God's truth.[1]

So also the Heidelberg Catechism says that true faith

> . . . is not only a certain knowledge whereby I hold for truth all that God has revealed to us in His word, but also a heartfelt confidence, which the Holy Ghost works by the Gospel within me, that not only to others, but to me also, remission of sins, everlasting righteousness, and blessedness, are freely given by God, of pure grace, only for the sake of Christ's merits (Q. 21).

This language is characteristic of the general Protestant standpoint, going back to Luther. It is in fact, as the emphasis upon the Divine grace shows, an attempt to force the language of theory to conform to that of the practical religious consciousness, an attempt right and indeed necessary in itself, and yet dangerous in so far as it changed the meaning of current terms too far from that which they bore in the ordinary usage of the day.

For Luther the thought of God's grace dominated all else. It is upon grace and grace only that justifying faith depends. Man cannot of himself establish such

[1] Fides humana non est opinio ac humana persuasio, sed firmissima fiducia et evidens et constans animi assensus, denique rectissima comprehensio veritatis Dei (c. 16).

faith, for his will is enslaved to sin. And so Luther, like Augustine before him, was led to reject all belief in man's free will to do right. Apart from God's grace all is sin. Man has not even power to respond to God's call to freedom. His every act, apart from grace, is a sin. This theme Luther worked out at length in his powerful treatise, *On the Will Enslaved*,[1] a reply to a defence of the ordinary Roman view by Erasmus. One or two quotations will serve to set in a clearer light the presuppositions from which the Reformation started, and especially the emphasis upon grace and the strong sense of the corruption of the human will.

> If by my own zeal I obtain God's grace, what need is there to receive Christ's grace instead of my own grace? Or what do I lack, since I am to have God's grace?[2]
>
> Briefly Paul decides concerning him that worketh and him that worketh not, nor has he left any mean between these two. He denies that righteousness is imputed to him that worketh; but to him that worketh not he asserts that righteousness is imputed, let him but believe. Here is no way for free will to slip out or escape by its own effort or zeal. For either it is accounted of him that worketh, or of him that worketh not. If of him that worketh, here learnest thou that no righteousness is accounted to him; if of him that worketh not, who yet believeth in God, to him is it accounted righteousness. . . . If therefore righteousness is not accounted to him that worketh, it is clear that his works are nought but sins, evil and impious in the sight of God.[3]
>
> Therefore is there need of grace, therefore is the aid of grace bestowed, because free will could of itself do nothing and . . .

[1] *De Servo Arbitrio*, *Werke*, vol. xviii. (Weimar, 1908).

[2] Si meo studio gratiam Dei obtineo, quid opus est Christi gratia pro mea gratia accipienda? Aut quid mihi deest ubi gratiam Dei habuero? (*ib.* p. 777).

[3] Breviter Paulus componit operantem et non operantem nec reliquit medium inter hos duos; operanti reputari justitiam negat, non operanti vero asserit reputari justitiam, modo credat. Non est quo hic liberum arbitrium evadat aut elabatur cum suo conatu aut studio. Aut enim cum operante aut cum non operante numerabitur. Si cum operante, audis hic ei non reputari ullam justitiam. Si cum non operante, qui credit tamen Deo, reputatur ei justitia. . . . Si autem non reputatur justitia operanti, manifestum fit, ejus opera nihil nisi peccata, mala et impia esse coram Deo (*ib.* p. 772).

could not even will the good. In the commending, therefore, of grace, and the declaring of the aid of grace, the impotence of free will is declared also.[1]

The same view appears, though perhaps less violently put, in the Augsburg Confession.

As to free will they hold that man's will hath some liberty to work a civil righteousness, and to choose such things as reason can reach unto; but that it hath no power to work the righteousness of God, or a spiritual righteousness, without the Spirit of God; because the natural man receiveth not the things of the Spirit of God.[2]

The Calvinists were strongly of the same opinion.

Man that is not yet regenerate hath no free will unto good, nor any strength to perform the good.[3]

While Calvin himself says that

. . . man's mind is so utterly alienated from God, that it can conceive, desire, and effect nothing but what is impious, perverted, foul, impure, and flagitious; the heart is so steeped in the poison of sin that it can breathe forth nothing but fetid corruption.[4]

Such language was natural until the reaction against the mediaeval doctrine of merits had spent its force. But it is noteworthy that even Melanchthon, the master theologian of the Lutheran Church, recoiled from it in

[1] Ideo gratia opus est, ideo auxilium gratiae confertur, quod liberum arbitrium per sese nihil possit et . . . non possit velle bonum. Commendata itaque gratia et praedicato auxilio gratiae simul impotentia liberi arbitrii praedicatur (*ib.* p. 755).

[2] De libero arbitrio docent, quod humana voluntas habeat aliquam libertatem ad efficiendam civilem justitiam et diligendas res rationi subjectas. Sed non habet vim sine Spiritu Sancto efficiendae justitiae Dei seu justitiae spiritualis, quia animalis homo non percipit ea quae sunt Spiritus Dei (c. 18).

[3] Nullum est ad bonum homini arbitrium liberum, nondum renato, vires nullae ad perficiendum bonum (*Conf. Helv.* i. Art. 9).

[4] Mentem hominis sic alienatam prorsus a Dei justitia ut nihil non impium, contortum, foedum, inpurum, flagitiosum concipiat, concupiscat, moliatur: cor peccati veneno ita penitus delibutum ut nihil quam corruptum foetorem efflare queat (*Institutio*, ii. 5. 19).

his later years,[1] returning to a doctrine much more like that of the Council of Trent, to the effect that the human will was at least free to respond to, and to co-operate with, God's grace. This position gave rise to the "Synergistic" dispute among the Reformers.

With this dispute we need not now concern ourselves. Despite certain variations in the language used by different writers the central fact remains that Protestant theology as a whole continued to lay an emphasis upon the sinfulness and helplessness of man which was utterly foreign to the thought of contemporary Roman divines, and which, indeed, had little precedent save in Augustine himself. And this new emphasis naturally brought the doctrine of the Atonement into a new prominence. From henceforth it occupies a more central position than it had ever held for the mediaeval theologians. The overmastering realization of man's utter helplessness naturally turned men's thoughts to the great Fact whereby that helplessness is made good.

But the age when the doctrine of the Atonement thus became a pivot of theological thinking was also an age when new canons of thought were rapidly developing. It was an age of change and progress. And nowhere is this change more patent than in the conceptions of political theory, conceptions which have always exercised a profound influence upon the formulation of doctrines of the Atonement. Political theory had made great strides since the days of Anselm. The feudalistic principle had to a great extent worked itself out, and the conception of abstract law was reasserting itself beside that of the personal dignity of individuals, which was indeed coming to be viewed rather as a sovereign right vested in individual representatives of the abstract law. And thus law came to be regarded as having a certain absolute intrinsic validity, claiming

[1] In the later editions of his *Loci Communes*. The Augsburg Confession owes to Melanchthon its very moderate tone. Luther's own Smalcaldic Articles (1537) are much more definite in standpoint.

punishment from the offender not on personal grounds, or on grounds of expediency, but simply on grounds of justice. We have already seen that hints of the application of this principle to the Atonement may be found in various pre-Reformation writers, and Ritschl suggests the possibility that Luther may have been influenced by Gerson, though he points out that the idea seems to spring up independently in Zwingli also.[1]

The truth probably is that the transformation was quite an unconscious one, due to the new thoughts which were moulding the age. The Reformers were certainly not aware that they were departing from the Anselmic position, and they make free use of Anselmic language. They were in fact more Thomist than Rome herself. But it was only natural that the new intellectual atmosphere should affect their formulations of doctrine, and while the phrases of the Satisfaction theory were still often used, especially at first, in reality the whole conception of the nature of Christ's work was changed.

With this slight sketch of the main ideas which underlay the Reformation we may pass on to the specific contribution of the Reformers to the study of the Cross—the Penal theory.

Luther himself is mainly important in that he supplied the principles upon which the other Reformers built, reversing the Scotist and even Pelagian tendencies of the later Middle Ages. His own treatment of the Atonement is not worked out in detail. Its most complete statement occurs in his comment on the words, "Christ redeemed us from the curse of the Law, having become a curse for us" (Gal. 3 13),[2] and it is marked rather by the force of Luther's mystical and passionate rhetoric than by accuracy of thought. Yet the elements of the characteristic Reformation doctrine are all present.

It is from the point of view of legal justice that the

[1] Ritschl, *op. cit.* p. 198.

[2] The following quotations, except where otherwise stated, are from this passage in the *Commentary on Galatians* (1535).

transaction of the Atonement is stated. The death of Christ is the legal penalty for sin, and there is no trace of the old alternative, "either punishment or satisfaction." The law demands punishment and that punishment must be inflicted and endured.

And so that general law of Moses took Him, innocent though He was in His own person, because it found Him among sinners and robbers. . . . When, therefore, the law found Him among robbers, it condemned and slew Him as a robber.[1]

Sin having been laid upon Him the law cometh and saith: Let every sinner die. So, if Thou wilt, O Christ, be surety, be guilty and bear the penalty, bear also the sin and the curse.[2]

When the merciful Father saw that we were oppressed by the law, and were held under the curse, and that nothing could free us from it, He sent His Son into the world, and cast upon Him all the sins of all men, and said to Him: Be Thou Peter that denier, Paul that persecutor, blasphemer, and violent, David that adulterer, that sinner who ate the apple in Paradise, that robber upon the cross, in a word be Thou the person of all men, who hast wrought the sins of all men; consider Thou therefore how Thou mayest pay and mayest make satisfaction for them. Then cometh the law and saith: I find that sinner taking upon Him the sin of all men and I see no sin beside, save in Him, therefore let Him die upon the Cross. And so it attacks Him and slays Him. This being done the whole world is purged of all sin and expiation made; therefore also is it free from death and from all ills.[3]

---

[1] Itaque lex illa generalis Mosi comprehendit eum, quamvis pro sua persona innocentem, quia invenit eum inter peccatores et latrones . . . Cum ergo lex eum inter latrones invenit, ut latronem condemnavit et occidit.

[2] Peccato ei imposito venit lex et dicit: Omnis peccator moriatur. Itaque si vis, Christe, spondere, reus esse et poenam ferre, feras etiam peccatum et maledictionem.

[3] Cum videret misericors Pater per legem nos opprimi et sub maledicto teneri nec ulla re nos posse ab eo liberari, quod miserit in mundum filium suum in quem omnia omnium peccata conjecit, et dixit ad eum: Tu sis Petrus ille negator, Paulus ille persecutor, blasphemus, et violentus, David ille adulter, peccator ille qui comedit pomum in Paradiso, latro ille in cruce, In summa, tu sis omnium hominum persona qui feceris omnium hominum peccata, tu ergo cogita, ut solvas et pro eis satisfacias. Ibi Lex venit et dicit: Invenio illum peccatorem suscipientem omnium hominum peccata in se · t nullum praeterea peccatum video nisi in illo, Ergo moriatur in cruce. Atque ita invadit eum et occidit. Hoc facto totus mundus purgatus et expiatus est ab omnibus peccatis, Ergo etiam liberatus a morte et omnibus malis.

But it would not be just that Christ should suffer unless He were a sinner Himself. He must not merely be among men, but one with men, identified with them in their sin. Luther does not shrink from the very strongest language in reaffirming St. Paul's almost forgotten phrase "Him who knew no sin He made to be sin on our behalf."

And this saw all the Prophets, that Christ was to be of all men the greatest robber, murderer, adulterer, thief, profaner, blasphemer, etc., than whom none greater was ever in the world, for now He bears not His own person, now He is not the Son of God, born of a virgin, but is a sinner, who has and bears the sin of Paul, who was a blasphemer, a persecutor, and violent, of Peter who denied Christ; of David who was an adulterer, a murderer and who made the Gentiles blaspheme the name of the Lord, in a word, who has and bears in His own body all the sins of all men—not in that He committed them, but in that He took upon His own body the things committed by us, to make satisfaction for them with His own blood.[1]

To explain the way in which this bearing of the punishment of sin is made available for man Luther falls back upon the barest possible conception of substitution. The sin and its penalty cannot be both on Christ and on us too. Therefore we are free.

If the sins of the whole world are upon that one man, Jesus Christ, then are they not upon the world. But if they are not upon Him, they are still upon the world. Further, if Christ Himself was made guilty of all the sins which we all have committed, then are we absolved from all sins, yet not through ourselves, our own works or merits, but through Him.[2]

---

[1] Et hoc viderunt omnes Prophetae quod Christus futurus esset omnium maximus latro, homicida, adulter, fur, sacrilegus, blasphemus etc., quo nullus major unquam in mundo fuerit, Quia jam non gerit personam suam, jam non est natus de virgine Dei filius, sed peccator, qui habet et portat peccatum Pauli qui fuit blasphemus, persecutor et violentus; Petri qui negavit Christum; Davidis qui fuit adulter, homicida et blasphemare fecit Gentes nomen Domini; in summa, qui habet et portat omnia omnium peccata in corpore suo. Non quod ipse commiserit ea, sed quod ea a nobis commissa susceperit in corpus suum, pro illis sanguine proprio satisfacturus.

[2] Si peccata totius mundi sunt in illo uno homine Jesu Christo, Ergo non sunt in mundo. Si autem non sunt in ipso, sunt adhuc in mundo. Item, si Christus ipse factus est reus omnium peccatorum quae nos omnes commisimus, Ergo nos absoluti sumus ab omnibus peccatis, sed non per nos, nostra opera aut merita, sed per ipsum.

The justice to which Luther appeals is blind indeed. His theory, at least as here stated, is based upon a verbal literalism which takes two wrongs and would fain fashion of them a right. The difficulties which faced Gregory of Nazianzum so long before return in all their force. Is the punishment of the innocent any pleasure to God, or any satisfaction of outraged justice? And indeed, such language as the above seems to admit no manward theory of Atonement at all. It is utterly objective and external. It leaves no place for faith, though faith lies at the very centre of Luther's thought, or for the love and grace of God whereby that faith is implanted in the hearts of the elect. In reality Luther's fullest thought comes strikingly close to the higher types of Moral theory. It is in looking upon Christ that we see God, in viewing His death for us that we come to realize God's love, whereby faith, *i.e.* the assurance of forgiveness, is awakened in our hearts. But all this is viewed by Luther in the most objective manner possible. His whole mind is turned to God, and away from man, and his theory of Atonement remains Godward throughout.

This tendency of his thought is shown in the mystical account which he gives of the conflict with sin, wrought out in Christ Himself.

> The sin of the whole world therefore runs upon righteousness with the utmost force and fury. What happens? Righteousness is eternal, immortal, unconquered. Sin too is a most mighty and cruel tyrant, lording it and reigning in the circle of the earth, taking all men captive and bringing them into his service. . . . He, I say, runs upon Christ, and wills to devour Him, as all others. But he sees not that He is the person of unconquered and eternal righteousness. . . . So in Christ sin universal is conquered, slain, and buried, and righteousness victorious and regnant abides for ever.[1]

---

[1] Peccatum ergo totius mundi irruit maximo impetu et furore in justitiam. Quid fit? Justitia est aeterna, immortalis, et invicta. Peccatum est quoque potentissimus ac crudelissimus tyrannus, dominans et regnans in toto orbe terrarum, captivans et redigens omnes homines in servitutem sui. . . . Is, inquam, incurrit in Christum et vult eum, ut alios omnes, devorare. Sed non videt

Not only is sin conquered, but death also:

> So death, who is the almighty queen of the whole world, slaying kings, princes, and, in short, all men, clashes in full force with life, to conquer and whelm her, and, of a truth, she does what she essays. But because life was immortal, the conquered came forth conqueror, conquering and slaying death. . . . And so through Christ death is conquered and destroyed in all the world, so that now it is but a painted death, which having lost its sting can no more hurt them that believe in Christ, who is made the Death of death.[1]

An echo is heard in these passages of the old language of a warfare with the devil, though, as in John of Damascus, the actual mention of the devil is avoided, sin and death being substituted. In commenting on Gal. 4 5 Luther uses similar language of the law:

> This is in truth a wondrous conflict, in which the law thus clashes, the creature with its Creator, and against all right exercises upon the Son of God all its tyranny, which it exercised upon us, the children of wrath. Therefore because the law sinned so horribly and impiously against its God, it is called to judgement and is accused. . . . Then the law, which before had condemned and slain all men, when it had no power to defend or to purge itself, is in its turn so condemned and slain that it loses its right, not only against Christ, whom so unjustly it outrages and kills, but also against all who believe in Him.[2]

---

eum esse personam invictae et aeternae justitiae. . . . Sic in Christo vincitur, occiditur, et sepelitur universum Peccatum et manet victrix et regnatrix Justitia in aeternum.

[1] Sic Mors quae est omnipotens imperatrix totius mundi, necans reges, principes, et simpliciter omnes homines, congreditur toto impetu cum Vita victura et absorptura eam, et certe quod conatur efficit. Sed quia Vita erat immortalis, victa evasit victrix, vincens et occidens Mortem. . . . Itaque per Christum Mors victa et abolita est in toto mundo, ut jam non sit nisi picta mors quae amisso aculeo amplius non possit nocere credentibus in Christum, qui factus est Mors Mortis.

[2] Hoc profecto mirabile duellum est, ubi Lex Creatura cum Creatore sic congreditur et praeter omne jus omnem tyrannidem suam in filio Dei exercet, quam in nobis filiis irae exercuit. Quia ergo lex tam horribiliter et impie peccavit in Deum suum, vocatur in jus et accusatur. . . . Hic Lex, quae damnaverat et occiderat prius omnes homines, cum non habeat quo se defendat aut purget, vicissim ita damnatur et occiditur, ut amittat jus suum, non solum in Christo (in quem tam injuste saeviit et occidit), sed etiam in omnibus qui credunt in eum.

In estimating the real value of such language as this two points must be kept constantly in mind. In the first place Luther is filled with the sense of the great love of God. God is not to him a cruel Judge, pressing for the full penalty of the law, but a loving and merciful Father, who gave His Son for us. In this, says Ritschl, he "surpassed all previous theology when he brought love into prominence as the character which exhaustively expresses the Christian idea of God; and in this fundamental conception of God he recognizes also the ultimate determining motive for the redemption and reconciliation of the sinner that were wrought by Christ." "His true opinion is essentially that God's love as the ultimate motive of the sinner's redemption is the superior determination of His will, while penal justice, or wrath . . . is considered as the subordinate motive of His action in carrying out the work of redemption." Luther's strong insight carries him beyond his theory. He is not consistent with himself. The full substitutionary view leaves little room for God's love, but when, with Melanchthon, consistency comes, we are immeasurably the losers.

The second point is Luther's constant insistence that the Atonement must be appropriated by faith, and herein lies his one contribution to a true manward theory.

> We ought to gaze upon this image and grasp it with sure faith. He who does this has this innocence and victory of Christ, however great a sinner he be. But it cannot be grasped by the good will of love, but by reason illuminated by faith. Therefore by faith alone are we justified, because faith alone grasps this victory of Christ.[1]

This faith, though it comes wholly from God, by the inspiration of His Holy Spirit, a point upon which

[1] Hanc imaginem oportet nos intueri et firma fide apprehendere. Qui hoc facit, habet hanc innocentiam et victoriam Christi, quantumvis magnus sit peccator. Sed ea non potest apprehendi voluntate dilectionis, sed ratione illuminata fide. Ergo sola fide justificamur, quia sola fides apprehendit hanc victoriam Christi.

Luther constantly insists, is yet a personal thing. It is a real act of the heart of man. It is the sinner himself realising his need and turning to God for its supply. The sinner, as Luther puts it,[1] must grasp the meaning of the pronoun " our " and must be found among those that say " our sins," that so he may learn to trust not himself but Christ only. Man's reason prefers to bring to Christ a sham sinner, with no real sense of sin. Faith arises when this sham is put away and the personal conviction of sin is real and deep, and so in faith man begins once more to give to God that honour and glory that is His.

Luther is a mystic, in the best sense of the word, rather than a theologian. His presentment of the great truth of Atonement is neither systematic nor consistent. Yet he is a creative thinker of the highest order and is unsurpassed in his clear discernment of the personal relation to Christ which men must possess if they are to make the Atonement their own, of that justice of God which is also His love, and of the confidence of faith made possible even for sinners by God's grace. And he realises most profoundly the universal significance of that mysterious conflict wrought within the very holiness of Christ Himself, through His identification with sinful man. Yet, though he gives us that which is better than theory, he does not give us a theory. For that we must turn to the other theologians of his day, and especially to Melanchthon and to the formulae which bear the impress of his learning and care, and which have remained as the very foundation stones of the Lutheran Church. It is here that we first find in a developed form the Penal theory of Atonement.

The general Penal Theory can be very simply stated: Justice demands the punishment of sin. Therefore the attitude of a just God towards the sinner can only be one of wrath. But if the punishment is endured to the uttermost by One who adequately represents the

[1] See his comment on Gal. 1 4.

sinner, justice is satisfied and God's mercy towards the sinner can have free play. The thought is wholly Godward, and that from the assertion of which the early fathers shrank is now boldly proclaimed. By the death of Christ God's attitude towards man is actually changed. Wrath is transformed to love. Mercy is the result of Calvary, or, at least, is freed by the Cross from the necessity of enforcing the stern obligations of justice.

This is the conception which underlies the short and simple statement of the Augsburg Confession, which speaks of Christ as having

> . . . truly suffered, been crucified, dead, and buried, that He might reconcile the Father to us, and might be a Victim not only for original guilt but also for all actual sins of men.[1]

The words are slight enough, and could hardly be stressed in themselves. Yet it is very significant, in view of Melanchthon's own theology, that the careful usage of St. Paul, who always speaks of man as reconciled to God, and never of God as reconciled to man, is here abandoned. And with it passes every trace of a manward view of Atonement. All that remains is the thought of an angry God, who demands and receives the penalty that indignant justice claims. And thus the sacrificial metaphor, which is retained by the Protestant theologians, receives here and elsewhere a new emphasis. Sacrifice is no longer so much a supreme honour done to God, the highest of all acts of worship, but before all things an expiatory offering, a shedding of blood that wrath may be turned aside.

In Melanchthon's own writings this thought is quite explicit. For him the central fact of all is the justice

[1] Vere passus, crucifixus, mortuus, et sepultus, ut reconciliaret nobis Patrem, et hostia esset, non tantum pro culpa originis, sed etiam pro omnibus actualibus peccatis hominum (*Conf. Aug.* 3). This language is followed verbally in the XXXIX Articles of the Church of England.

of God calling for vengeance upon the sinner, and only to be turned to grace by the sacrifice of Christ.

> God's wondrous plan is set forth, that though He is just and is horribly angry at sin, yet at last He will be willing that His most just wrath should be placated, because His Son is made a suppliant for us and has drawn down the wrath upon Him, and is made an expiation and a victim for us.[1]

This conception might have been expanded, as it had been by Luther, with the emphasis upon the love and grace of God whereby so wonderful a means of Redemption was found, and in Melanchthon's expansion of the Augsburg Confession for the Saxon Churches this aspect finds a place.

> But the Son of God, our Lord Jesus Christ, who is the image of the eternal Father, was made a mediator, propitiator, redeemer, justifier, and saviour. By the obedience and merit of Him alone the wrath of God is placated. . . . In this Victim are seen the justice of God, and His wrath against sin, and His immense mercy towards us, and the love in the Son towards all mankind. Such is the severity of His justice that reconciliation would not be made unless the penalty were utterly paid. Such is the greatness of His wrath that the eternal Father would not be placated save by the entreaty and death of the Son. Such is His mercy, that the Son was given for us. Such love was in the Son towards us that He drew down this true and great wrath upon Himself.[2]

---

[1] Exponitur mirandum Dei consilium, quod cum sit justus et horribiliter irascatur peccato, ita demum placari justissimam iram voluerit, quia filius est factus supplex pro nobis et in sese iram derivavit et pro nobis piaculum et victima factus est (*Declamatio*, C.R. xi. p. 779, *ap.* Ritschl, *op. cit.* p. 202).

[2] Sed filius Dei, dominus noster Jesus Christus, qui est imago aeterni Patris, constitutus est mediator, propitiator, redemtor, justificator, et salvator. Hujus unius obedientia et merito placatur ira Dei . . . Conspiciuntur in hac victima, justitia Dei, et ira adversus peccatum, et immensa misericordia erga nos, et amor in filio erga genus humanum. Tanta est justitiae severitas ut non sit facta reconciliatio, nisi poena persolveretur. Tanta est irae magnitudo, ut aeternus Pater non sit placatus nisi deprecatione et morte filii. Tanta misericordia ut filius pro nobis datus sit. Tantus amor in filio erga nos ut hanc veram et ingentem iram in se derivaverit (*Conf. Eccl. Sax.*, 1550, in Melanchthon's *Corpus Doctrinae Christianae*, Leipzig, 1560, from which volume this and the following references are taken).

But for Melanchthon the love of God is never so prominent as His wrath against sin.

For the heart, truly feeling that God is angry, cannot love God, unless He is shown to be placated. While He terrifies us and seems to be casting us into eternal death, human nature cannot raise itself up to love Him that is angry, that judges and punishes.[1]

Again and again he returns to this thought of God's wrath, and it is this that determines the form which the Anselmic argument takes in his hand. Like Anselm he ascribes the Atonement to the demand of justice for satisfaction, but justice for him is simply avenging justice, and satisfaction is no longer an alternative for punishment, but the punishment itself. Indeed, though Melanchthon sometimes speaks, in conventional language, of the satisfaction offered by Christ, he prefers to keep the term satisfaction for human attempts to appease God's anger in penance, and to dwell rather upon Christ as enduring the penalty of our sins. The old conception of God's honour as demanding satisfaction has quite passed away. God being just demands the penalty due to justice, and since man has sinned it is fitting[2] that one of human race should bear man's punishment. The thought proceeds quite on Anselmic lines. Sin is infinitely wicked. Therefore He who bears the punishment must also be God, and indeed only a God-man could bear the infinite suffering due for infinite sin. Melanchthon has summed up his position in a phrase:

Christ's benefits are these: to bear guilt and eternal death that is, to placate the great wrath of God;[3]

---

[1] Non enim potest cor vere sentiens Deum irasci, diligere Deum, nisi ostendatur placatus. Donec terret et videtur nos abjicere in aeternam mortem, non potest se erigere natura humana, ut diligat iratum, judicantem, et punientem (*Apol. Conf. Aug.* p. 71).

[2] Congruebat ordini justitiae.

[3] Christi beneficia haec sunt, tollere culpam et mortem aeternam, id est placare ingentem iram Dei (*Loci Praecipui Theologici*, p. 603).

and " eternal death " is defined as being

> . . . to feel God's horrible and unutterable wrath abiding.[1]

That such a conception is in any way unworthy of God does not seem to occur to Melanchthon. Nor, indeed, does he make any serious attempt to overcome the flagrant injustice of this substitution of one victim for another, the innocent for the guilty. We miss both Luther's stress on the love of God and Luther's strong conviction of the identification of Christ with sinful man. It is difficult to avoid the feeling that the treatment of Christ by the Father has become ethically repulsive.

Before leaving Melanchthon it should be noted that he constantly uses sacrificial language of the death of Christ, the one true Victim for sin. The phrase used in the Augsburg Confession is quite typical and it is abundantly clear that for Melanchthon the objective, expiatory, aspect of sacrifice is dominant, based upon Old Testament conceptions.

> But in truth there was but one propitiatory sacrifice in the world, namely the passion or death of Christ.[2]
>
> That we may know the death of Christ, and not the ceremonies of the law to be truly a satisfaction or expiation for our sins.[3]

And he defines a propitiatory sacrifice as

> . . . a work which merits for others remission of guilt and of eternal punishment, or a work reconciling God, and placating God's wrath on behalf of others, and making satisfaction for guilt and for eternal punishment.[4]

And while he admits the conception of a sacrifice of thanksgiving it is especially that of a propitiatory

[1] Sentire horrendam et inenarrabilem iram Dei manentem (*ibid.*).

[2] Sed revera unicum tantum in mundo fuit propitiatorium sacrificium, videlicet passio seu mors Christi (*ib. De Sacrificio*, p. 572).

[3] Ut sciamus mortem Christi vere esse satisfactionem pro peccatis nostris, seu expiationem, non caerimonias legis (*ibid.*).

[4] Opus quod meretur aliis remissionem culpae et poenae aeternae, seu opus reconcilians Deum, et placans iram Dei pro aliis, et satisfactorium pro culpa et poena aeterna (*ib.* p. 571).

sacrifice which he applies to Christ, as the remainder of his theory would lead us to expect.

This retention of sacrificial language in Protestant theology is interesting. It receives a very different interpretation from that given to it by the divines of the Counter-Reformation, and the connexion with Eucharistic doctrine ceases completely. Yet it forms a certain common Catholic basis for doctrinal statement, the value of which for mutual understanding has been very great, and may perhaps become greater still.

In passing to Calvin, the other great protagonist of the Reformation, we pass to a theologian in the fullest sense of the word, a theologian who is even more precise in his statements than Melanchthon, and who has left in his *Institutio* a clear and reasoned account of his belief. His view of the Atonement [1] is thus more easily defined than that held by Luther, with whom, however, he is in essential agreement. Like the other Reformers he follows the Anselmic method, modified by the aspect of justice as avenging, demanding punishment for sin in its own right. Yet he is not, as were some of his followers, unmindful of the love of God, and his general position is very similar to that of Augustine in its failure to reconcile this Divine love with the necessity for the form which Atonement actually took.

In his view of sin and justification Calvin practically agrees with Luther and nothing need be added to what has already been said. It should be noted, however, and the difference is characteristic of the two men, that Calvin's definition of faith is stated rather more in terms of knowledge. Faith for him is

> . . . a sure and certain knowledge of the Divine good will towards us, which, having been founded upon the truth of a gracious promise in Christ is both revealed to our minds and sealed in our hearts by the Holy Spirit.[2]

---

[1] Stated in *Institutio*, ii. 12-17, esp. c. 16.

[2] Divinae erga nos benevolentiae firmam certamque cognitionem quae gratuitae in Christo promissionis veritate fundata, per Spiritum sanctum et revelatur mentibus nostris et cordibus obsignatur (*Inst.* iii. 2. 7).

This rather lacks the personal note so prominent in Luther, though for Calvin, too, faith is ultimately assurance. But the source of this assurance lies for Calvin less in a personal relation to Christ than in the certainty of the Divine election, a thought to which Luther does not give clear expression, though it is implicit in his writings. Nothing could be more emphatic than Calvin's repeated assertions of the dependence of all things, good and bad alike, upon the choice of God. Sometimes his statements do not go beyond those in which Luther assigns all good things to the free grace of God.

> A will inclined to good is not to be found save in the elect. And the cause of election is to be sought beyond man, whence it comes about that a right will is not in man of himself, but flows from that same good pleasure in which we were elected before the creation of the world. . . . Since the beginning of good willing and acting is of faith we must see whence faith itself is. But since all Scripture cries that it is God's gracious gift, it follows that it is of pure grace when we begin to will the good, who are in all our soul naturally inclined to evil.[1]

Thus justifying faith, with all that depends upon it, rests solely upon God's election. Apart from election man can do nothing. But sometimes Calvin's stern thought of predestination goes further still, and he does not hesitate to assert that some are foredoomed to eternal death—a logical conclusion from the idea of election, but one from which almost all theologians have shrunk.

> No one who wishes to be thought pious dare directly deny that predestination, whereby God adopts some into the hope

[1] Neque enim voluntas reperietur ad bonum propensa nisi in electis. Atque electionis causa extra homines quaerenda est, unde conficitur, rectam voluntatem non esse homini a se ipso, sed ex eodem beneplacito, quo ante mundi creationem electi sumus, fluere. . . . Quum bene volendi et agendi principium sit ex fide, videndum est unde sit ipsa fides. Quum vero gratuitum esse Dei donum clamet tota Scriptura, sequitur ex mera gratia esse ubi velle bonum incipimus, qui ad malum toto animo sumus naturaliter propensi (ii. 3. 8).

of life, adjudges others to eternal death. . . . By predestination we mean God's eternal decree, by which He has determined with Himself what He wills to become of each separate man. For all are not created in like condition, but for some eternal life, for others eternal condemnation, is preordained.[1]

The hardness of such language as this does not, however, prevent Calvin from emphasizing the love of God. The Divine decree which determines our election, and therewith the whole method of redemption, is for him a great display of love.

If a question is asked as to the necessity (of the method of redemption), it was not simple or absolute necessity, but it flowed from a heavenly decree, on which the salvation of men depended. But the most clement Father determined what was best for us.[2]

Calvin thus adopts the ordinary mediaeval position as to the necessity of the Atonement, and he goes on, quite in the Anselmic manner, to show that only One who is both God and man could accomplish what was needed. Even without sin man would have been too lowly to come to God without a Mediator. Sin made the need far more great. Therefore it was necessary for the Son of God to come and to dwell with us in holy brotherhood, Himself both human and Divine, that we may have good hope that God is among us.

Trusting in this pledge we believe that we are sons of God, because God's natural Son took to Himself a body of our body, flesh of our flesh, bones of our bones, that He might be one and

---

[1] Praedestinationem, qua Deus alios in spem vitae adoptat, alios adjudicat aeternae morti, nemo, qui velit pius censeri, simpliciter negare audet. . . . Praedestinationem vocamus aeternum Dei decretum, quo apud se constitutum habuit, quid de unoquoque homine fieri vellet. Non enim pari conditione creantur omnes : sed aliis vita aeterna, aliis damnatio aeterna, praeordinatur (iii. 21. 5).

[2] De necessitate si quaeritur, non simplex quidem . . . vel absoluta fuit : sed manavit ex coelesti decreto, unde pendebat hominum salus. Caeterum quod nobis optimum erat statuit clementissimus Pater (ii. 12. 1).

the same with us. He did not grudge to take what was properly ours, that what was properly His might pertain to us, and that so he might, together with us, be Son of God and Son of Man.[1]

God most clement, therefore, made our Redeemer in the person of the Only-begotten, when He willed that we should be redeemed.[2]

Calvin here touches a very lofty thought indeed, though he does not pursue it very far. His language suggests the mysticism of the Greek fathers, who saw the secret of redemption in the union of all mankind with God in Christ. But for Calvin this conception of mystical union is not present in any clear form. He does not pass beyond the idea that the ultimate goal of Redemption is union with God.

So, however far we wander from God, Christ comes between and leads us little by little to firm union with God.[3]

Despite such suggestions as these the act by which this union is to be brought about remains for him utterly objective and substitutionary. Christ took flesh that He might work Redemption for us, rather than in us.

But that which I have just set forth is above all to be held, that the common nature is the pledge of our fellowship with the Son of God; that clothed in our flesh He conquered death with sin; that the victory of the triumph might be ours; that He offered in sacrifice the flesh which He took from us, that by expiation wrought He might destroy our guilt and might appease the Father's just anger.[4]

---

[1] Hac ergo arrha freti nos esse filios Dei confidimus, quia naturalis Dei filius sibi corpus de corpore nostro, carnem ex carne nostra, ossa ex ossibus aptavit, ut idem nobiscum esset: quod nobis proprium erat, suscipere gravatus non est, ut vicissim ad nos pertineret quod proprium ipse habebat: atque ita in commune ipse nobiscum et Filius Dei esset et filius hominis (ii. 12. 2).

[2] Sese ergo clementissimus Deus in persona unigeniti Redemptorem nostrum fecit, dum nos redemptos voluit (*ibid.*).

[3] Ita quantisper a Deo peregrinamur, Christus intercedit medius, qui nos paulatim ad solidam cum Deo conjunctionem perducat (ii. 15. 5). Cf. also ii. 16. 3, quoted below.

[4] Sed illud quod nuper exposui praecipue tenendum est, communem naturam pignus esse nostrae cum Filio Dei societatis: carne nostra vestitum debellasse mortem cum peccato, ut nostra esset victoria et triumphus noster: carnem, quam a nobis accepit, obtulisse in sacrificium, ut facta expiatione reatum nostrum delcret, et placaret justam Patris iram (ii. 12. 3).

God's anger must be met before union with God, or sanctification, is possible.

And how can this be the work of God's own love? In what way is His love related to His wrath? The difficulty which had faced Augustine reappears with redoubled force now that the justice of God is regarded primarily as avenging wrath against sin. And Calvin sees and states the difficulty.

> Before proceeding further we must see, in passing, how it is consistent that God, who prevents us in His pity, was hostile until He was reconciled to us by Christ. For how could He have given us in His only-begotten Son a singular pledge of His love, unless He had already beforehand embraced us in gratuitous favour.[1]

His answer is at first sight curious, and even casuistical.

> Phrases of this kind are accommodated to our understanding, that we may comprehend the better how wretched and calamitous is our state apart from Christ. For unless it were said in clear words that God's anger and sentence, and eternal death, lay upon us we should the less recognize how wretched we were without God's pity, and should hold at less price the boon of liberation.[2]

Fear of God's wrath and horror of eternal death are the only sufficient appeal to man's heart, and therefore it is that apart from Christ God is seen as "in some way hostile" to us, having armed His hand for our destruction.[3]

[1] Verum antequam longius progredimur in transcursu videndum est quomodo conveniat Deum, qui nos misericordia sua praevenit, fuisse inimicum, donec per Christum nobis reconciliatus est. Nam quomodo in Filio unigenito singulare amoris sui pignus nobis dedisset, nisi jam ante fuisset gratuito favore complexus? (ii. 16. 2).

[2] Hujus generis loquutiones ad sensum nostrum sunt accommodatae, ut melius intelligamus quam misera sit et calamitosa extra Christum nostra conditio. Nisi enim claris verbis diceretur iram ac vindictam Dei mortemque aeternam nobis incubuisse, minus agnosceremus quam miseri essemus sine Dei misericordia, et beneficium liberationis minoris aestimaremus (ii. 16. 2).

[3] *Ibid.*

But Calvin goes on to say that this accommodation to our understanding is not a veiling of the truth. The language about God's wrath corresponds very really to that which is the essential character of His being.

For God, who is the highest justice, cannot love that iniquity which He beholds in us all. Therefore we all have in us that which deserves God's hate. First according to our corrupt nature, and secondly in respect of our wicked life, we are all truly offensive to God, guilty in His sight, and born to the damnation of hell. But since the Lord wills not to lose in us what is His own, still He finds somewhat which in His kindness He may love. For though we are sinners by our vice, we yet remain His creatures; although we have taken death to ourselves, He yet had fashioned us for life. So by bare and free love for us He is stirred to receive us back into grace. But since there is a perpetual and irreconcilable discord between justice and iniquity, He cannot, so long as we remain sinners, receive us wholly; and so, in order that all matter of enmity having been removed He may reconcile us further to Himself, by setting forth the expiation in Christ's death, He abolishes whatever is of evil in us, that we who before were unclean and impure may appear just and holy in His sight. First by His love God the Father prevents and anticipates our reconciliation in Christ. In short, because He first loves us, He afterwards reconciles us to Himself. But since in us, until Christ rescues us by His death, there remains iniquity which merits the wrath of God, and is cursed and condemned before Him, we have no full and firm union with God until Christ joins us to Him. And so if we would find God appeased and propitious towards us, we ought to fix our eyes and minds on Christ alone, that through Him alone we may in very deed gain that our sins may not be imputed to us, the imputation of which draws down with it the wrath of God.[1]

---

[1] Deus enim, qui summa justitia est, iniquitatem, quam in omnibus nobis conspicit, amare non potest. Habemus ergo omnes in nobis quod Dei odio dignum sit. Proinde secundum corruptae nostrae naturae, et deinde accedentis pravae vitae respectum, in offensione Dei revera sumus omnes in ejus conspectu rei, et ad gehennae damnationem nati. Verum quia Dominus quod suum est in nobis perdere non vult, adhuc aliquid invenit quod pro sua benignitate amet. Utcunque enim peccatores vitio nostro simus, manemus tamen ejus creaturae; utcunque mortem nobis asciverimus, ipse tamen nos ad vitam condiderat. Sic mera et gratuita nostri dilectione excitatur

This passage is perhaps Calvin's most characteristic exposition of his theory and its principal elements are all present. The overruling love of God, which is, indeed, in some way one with His justice or righteousness, is firmly maintained. But Calvin has grasped quite clearly the great truth of which Augustine had caught a glimpse, that a righteous love cannot love iniquity. God does not hate us, but sin in us; and so long as sin is in us His wrath must needs fall upon the sin, and upon us so far as we are identified with the sin. And so arises the great contradiction. We are so utterly identified with sin that God's love has no place for us. We can only look up and see the wrath of the Judge. How then can wrath give place and love find a way?

It can only be by the full satisfaction of the claims of avenging justice. Justice must not give way to iniquity. No mere remission by a word will suffice. And so Christ the Mediator must take upon Him, as our brother and our substitute, the pains and penalties of sin even to the uttermost. So alone can justice triumph. As Calvin says again:

> This is our absolution, that the guilt, which held us liable to punishment, was transferred to the head of the Son of God. For we must hold above all to this compensation, that we may

---

ad nos in gratiam recipiendos. Atqui si perpetuum et irreconciliabile dissidium est inter justitiam et iniquitatem, quamdiu peccatores manemus, suscipere nos totos non potest. Itaque ut sublata omnis simultatis materia nos sibi prorsus reconciliet, proposita in morte Christi expiatione, quicquid in nobis mali est abolet, ut justi in ejus conspectu et sancti appareamus, qui antea immundi eramus ac impuri. Proinde sua dilectione praevenit ac antevertit Deus Pater nostram in Christo reconciliationem. Imo quia prius diligit, postea nos sibi reconciliat. Sed quia in nobis, donec sua morte succurrit Christus, manet iniquitas quae Dei indignationem meretur, et est coram eo maledicta ac damnata: non ante plenam habemus firmamque cum Deo conjunctionem, quam ubi Christus nos conjungit. Adeoque si Deum nobis pacatum ac propitium volumus polliceri, in Christum solum oculos mentesque defigere convenit: ut revera per ipsum solum consequimur, ne imputentur nobis peccata, quorum imputatio iram Dei secum trahit (ii. 16. 3).

not be frightened and anxious all our life, as though there still remained upon us that just vengeance of God which the Son of God has transferred to Himself.[1]

This transference is regarded quite objectively, though hardly with the literalism which appears in Luther. Christ suffers as our substitute, and as a result we are not only free, but are even accounted righteous and holy. This indeed is the very meaning of the justification which is made ours.

> He will be justified by faith, who, shut out from the righteousness of works, apprehends by faith the righteousness of Christ, clothed in which he appears in God's sight not as a sinner, but as just. And so by justification we simply mean that acceptance in which God holds us received into grace as just.[2]

The only righteousness which is ours in God's sight is an imputed righteousness, made ours, apparently, by a mere legal fiction.

The whole position is rendered difficult by this forensic bias, which makes Calvin's language quite inadequate to his thought. It still remains, when all is said, an attempt to make one wrong good by means of another wrong. And, further, Calvin's discussion depends upon the equation of sin with guilt, an equation which is not even consistent with his own conception of sin as an inherent corruption. Even if it could be shown by his argument that guilt and its penalty could be laid on Christ and so put away, it would still be unexplained how the corruption of the soul might be healed. When Calvin says, in the passage quoted above, that God, through Christ, "abolishes whatever

[1] Haec nostra absolutio est, quod in caput Filii Dei translatus est reatus, qui nos tenebat poenae obnoxios. Nam haec compensatio imprimis tenenda est, ne trepidemus atque anxii simus tota vita, acsi nobis instaret justa Dei ultio, quam in se transtulit Dei Filius (ii. 16. 5).

[2] Justificabitur ille fide, qui operum justitia exclusus, Christi justitiam per fidem apprehendit, qua vestitus in Dei conspectu non ut peccator sed tanquam justus apparet. Ita nos justificationem simpliciter interpretamur acceptionem, qua nos Deus in gratiam receptos pro justis habet (iii. 11. 2).

of evil is in us," the words stand rather as an independent statement of a great truth than as an integral part of the argument. Calvin's very manward view of sin cries out for a statement of the Atonement upon the manward side. But it is just in this respect that his thought is incomplete.

There are indeed some attempts to make good the gaps in the discussion. Calvin sees the apparent injustices of his view and has something to say upon both. With regard to the endurance of penalty by Christ he is careful to point out that God's wrath must not be conceived as resting upon Christ, but only its effects. God treats Him as though He were angry.

> But we do not suggest that God was ever hostile to Him or angry with Him. For how could He be angry with the beloved Son, in whom His soul was pleased? Or how could Christ placate by His intercession for others a Father who was hostile to Himself? But we say this, that He bore the weight of the Divine severity, in that, being stricken and afflicted by God's hand, He experienced all the signs of an angry and a punishing God.[1]

This does not carry us much further. If pressed it could only mean that Christ did not bear God's wrath in the sense in which we should have borne it. But this is to deprive the Atonement, even upon Calvin's own argument, of all significance.

With regard to the manward side, too, he has some suggestions to offer. We have already noted that he regards the effect of the Atonement as being the abolition of evil in man, and, ultimately, the union of man with God. But when he comes to work this thought out the external, substitutional, character of the transaction

[1] Neque tamen innuimus Deum fuisse unquam illi vel adversarium vel iratum. Quomodo enim dilecto Filio, in quo animus ejus acquievit, irasceretur? Aut quomodo Christus Patrem aliis sua intercessione placaret, quem infensum haberet ipse sibi? Sed hoc nos dicimus, divinae severitatis gravitatem eum sustinuisse: quoniam manu Dei percussus et afflictus omnia irati et punientis Dei signa expertus est (ii. 16. 11).

which he presupposes is at once apparent. He is again hampered by his forensic language.

> Now when it is asked how, in abolishing sin, Christ endured the dispute between us and God, and acquired righteousness, which makes Him favourable and benevolent towards us, it can be answered in general that He procured this for us by the whole course of His obedience. . . . So in His Baptism He asserted that He was fulfilling a part of righteousness, because He was obediently doing the Father's command. In short, from the time when He put on the person of a slave, He began for our redemption to pay the price of freedom. Yet Scripture, where it defines the mode of salvation more accurately, ascribes this as it were in a peculiar and special manner to Christ's death.[1]
>
> Hence is that imputation of righteousness without works, of which Paul speaks; because, that is to say, the righteousness which was found in Christ alone, being accepted, was transferred to us.[2]

Thus Christ's whole life of obedience is emphasized as doubly significant. It not only justifies us by removing our guilt, but it also sanctifies in God's sight by the imputation to us of His righteousness. The argument is very like that of Anselm.[3] The merits, or fruits, of Christ's life of holiness could add nothing to His blessedness. Therefore they are imputed to us, His brethren, and God accepts us, clothed with His obedience and righteousness. The idea here suggested was to become very important in later Protestant theology. But

[1] Jam ubi quaeritur quomodo abolitis peccatis dissidium Christus inter nos et Deum sustulerit, et justitiam acquisierit, quae eum nobis faventem ac benevolum redderet: generaliter responderi potest, toto obedientiae suae cursu hoc nobis praestitisse. . . . Ita in ipso quoque baptismo asseruit impleri justitiae partem, quod obedienter Patris mandatum perageret. Denique ex quo induit personam servi, coepit ad nos redimendos pretium liberationis solvere. Scriptura tamen, quo certius definiat modum salutis, hoc morte Christi quasi peculiare ac proprium ascribit (ii. 16. 5). The last sentence is noteworthy as showing that Calvin, in laying stress upon the life of Christ, still sees in the Cross the central fact of the Atonement.

[2] Hinc illa justitiae imputatio sine operibus, de qua Paulus disserit; quia scilicet accepta nobis fertur, quae in solo Christo reperta fuit justitia (ii. 17. 5).

[3] ii. 17. 6; cf. *Cur Deus Homo?* ii. 19.

Calvin does not work out at all definitely the distinction between the active and the passive obedience of Christ, and Ritschl regards the whole section which deals with the subject as a mere appendix, of no vital importance in his thought.[1]

Calvin hardly raises the question as to whether such a transference or imputation of guilt and of righteousness is either theoretically possible or ethically proper. The references already given show that he emphasized the solidarity of Christ with mankind, very much in the manner of St. Paul, and he develops this at some length in connexion with the place of Christ as Head of the Church. This is the thought which underlies his analysis of the functions of Christ as Prophet, King, and High Priest, though it is not very clearly stated, nor are its mystical implications at all fully grasped.[2] They are further developed, however, in the sections where Calvin opposes Osiander's view, arguing for a real *unio mystica* of the believer with Christ.

> This conjunction therefore of Head and members, the dwelling of Christ in our hearts, in a word, the mystical union, are accounted by us of the highest value; so that Christ being made ours makes us partakers of the gifts wherewith He is endowed. We do not therefore behold Him without us from afar, so that His righteousness may be imputed to us; but because we have put Him on and are implanted in His body, and He, in short, has deigned to make us one with Himself, therefore do we boast that we have fellowship in righteousness with Him.[3]

---

[1] See Ritschl, *op. cit.* pp. 207-209, where this is argued in detail. The chapter in question (ii. 17) was added in the 1559 edition of the *Institutio*, when Calvin had been in correspondence with Laelius Socinus, who had attacked the whole conception of the efficacy of the merits of Christ.

[2] ii. 15. The development of the idea of sacrifice closely resembles that found in Melanchthon.

[3] Conjunctio igitur illa capitis et membrorum, habitatio Christi in cordibus nostris, mystica denique unio a nobis in summo gradu statuitur: ut Christus noster factus donorum, quibus praeditus est, nos faciat consortes. Non ergo eum extra nos procul speculamur, ut nobis imputetur ejus justitia: sed quia ipsum induimus et insiti sumus in ejus corpus, unum denique nos secum efficere dignatus est, ideo justitiae societatem nobis cum eo esse gloriamur (iii. 11. 10). He also in this context speaks of the *unio mystica* as a *spiritualis conjunctio*.

Here the thought certainly appears to be definitely mystical, and so to overcome the crudeness of the substitutionary theory as elsewhere stated. Ritschl however, decides that "Calvin's *unio mystica* indicates the individual's membership in the Church as the condition under which he becomes conscious within himself of justification through Christ's obedience."[1] Ritschl is no friend of mystics, and his judgement is perhaps biassed. Yet it is impossible to feel that the mystical element in Calvin's thought is either clear or strong, and it is his substitutionary penal theory that has had the widest influence among his followers.

The remaining great leader of the Reformation, Zwingli, is unimportant for the history of the doctrine of Atonement. Like both Luther and Calvin, he attempts to find a place for the Divine love, but the prior claim is that of God's justice, which must find satisfaction in Christ before mercy can accept His redeeming works. For him, too, the application of the Atonement to our individual needs is conditioned by faith, regarded as an assurance of justification through the objective reconciliation accomplished by Christ. The conception of satisfaction is perhaps more emphasized by Zwingli than by his contemporaries, but his underlying thought is the same.[2]

The almost unconscious transition from the Anselmic conception to the Penal theory is in itself a remarkable fact, and it is still more remarkable that when the change came there, was such unanimity among the Reformers in their presentation of the new ideas, despite their great divergence amongst themselves in other respects. This fact is in itself sufficient to show that the

[1] *Op. cit.* p. 233.

[2] Ritschl (*op. cit.* pp. 203 ff.) has sufficiently answered the attempt (made by Sigwart and Zeller) to show that Zwingli holds a much more manward view of Atonement than the other Reformers, making the essence of Atonement lie in the exhibition of God's justice, and in its effect in stimulating man to zeal for the good. This view rests upon a single passage, quoted by Ritschl, which, as he points out, "is mmediately surrounded by distinct statements of an opposite sort."

Penal theory was no accidental outgrowth, the chance product of a moment or of a man. Its roots were deep in the soil of its age. It sprang from conceptions of polity and justice, and from a religious attitude towards God, which had had a long and gradual development, and which were now firmly established. In more writers than one during the later Middle Ages we saw traces of their influence, and it only needed the liberating power of the Reformation to break through the restraints imposed by tradition and to set the Penal theory free. How adequate that theory was is shown by its immediate and continued success. For three hundred years, despite Roman and Socinian protests, it dominated the Protestant Churches and, in Jansenism, it even won a foothold within the Roman citadel itself. And if we find it hard to sympathize with its sternness and severity, and believe that we have won to a truer conception of the justice of God, we should remember that it was against sin that it was stern, and against those that would make light of sin. To-day we are building our theories anew. It will be ill building if we so emphasize God's love that we leave sin out of account.

CHAPTER X

THE DEVELOPMENT OF THE PENAL THEORY

THE theology of the schoolmen found no place in the Protestant Churches, but their methods and instincts remained. The beginnings of the impulse which developed in later Lutheranism a scholasticism quite as technical and quite as arid as that of the Middle Ages at its worst, appeared at an early date, and the doctrines of the Reformers, the Penal theory with the rest, were soon subjected to the most detailed scrutiny. As far as the Penal theory was concerned this scrutiny resulted in little change in the main principles enunciated by Luther and Calvin. There was, however, a considerable advance in formal accuracy, developing the implications of Luther's forensic language. The cost of this advance was the loss, to a very great extent, of the emphasis upon the Divine love, which, however inconsistently, both Luther and Calvin had endeavoured to retain. Its one definite result, a result in no way commensurate with the loss, was the doctrine of the Active and Passive obedience of Christ.

It is at once clear that this distinction of an active and a passive side in the work of Christ is no new one. Again and again in the early fathers the obedience of Christ's life is closely associated with the sufferings of His death in the accomplishment of redemption. The one is roughly equivalent to His merit, the other to the satisfaction wrought by Him.[1] But merit and satis-

[1] The parallel is only loose. Anselm, for example, regards the obedience of Christ's life as something already due. Only His death,

faction were not clearly distinguished by the schoolmen, nor, indeed, upon their general theology of Atonement was a distinction either necessary or practicable. The whole position was changed so soon as the Reformers introduced the penal view of satisfaction, regarding it simply as the vicarious endurance of the suffering inflicted by avenging justice. This left but little place for the obedience of Christ, whether in His life or in His death. If justice is wholly penal, suffering alone is the fulfilment of its demands. That the Victim should even be willing is not logically necessary. This would seem to be the implication of the language of Luther and especially of Melanchthon. But as a matter of fact the importance of the obedience of Christ never wholly passes out of sight, though in one or two writers, notably Melanchthon and Zwingli, it is almost completely obscured by the emphasis upon penal suffering as the source of justification. Both Luther and Calvin are too clear-sighted to leave Christ's active obedience wholly out of account. Luther emphasizes this obedience especially as obedience to the law, regarding Christ's vicarious acceptance of the curse as the supreme instance of that obedience. Christ obeyed the law willingly, whereas we, as sinners, must do so under constraint. But this willing obedience is only regarded as a source of our justification in so far as it involves endurance of suffering. As active doing it is rather an example to them that are justified, who, by the Spirit of Christ, can from henceforth fulfil the moral law. It is no longer a mere code of precepts, binding from without, but the free life of the Spirit within. The conception here is ethical or mystical, and has little relation to the

---

as not due, had supererogatory worth. Thus merit and satisfaction are practically identified, though the former looks rather to the voluntary obedience of Christ's death, the latter to the suffering. The later schoolmen find a more distinct place for merit, which is associated with the whole of Christ's incarnate life, culminating in the obedience of His death.

later formal doctrine. A nearer approach to this is made by Calvin, who, as we have seen, advanced more and more definitely towards the conception of an imputation to the elect of the righteousness of Christ.[1] The elect stand before God clothed with His obedience. But Calvin does not, any more than Luther, attempt to work out the formal connexion of this active obedience of Christ with our justification. He contents himself with the thought that not only upon the Cross but throughout His life Christ paid through penal suffering the price of our redemption,[2] and this idea dominates his whole conception of the active obedience. Thus while his language might readily be cited as in accordance with the later Protestant view, his real position is more akin to that of Aquinas and the mediaeval Church.

Luther and Calvin made it impossible for those who followed them to ignore the positive side of Christ's obedience, but they did not establish it in their doctrinal scheme. This task of formal statement was begun, curiously enough, by one who, though in intention an interpreter of Luther, was in many respects not a true Protestant at all.

Osiander is an interesting figure among the early Reformers. Nominally a Lutheran, and actually Lutheran in many of his ideas, he yet retains more than one of the older beliefs. He even agrees in some respects with Scotus, whose position was utterly repugnant to the Reformers as a whole. This is shown especially in his view of the Incarnation,[3] which he regards not as due to man's sin, but as an eternal idea in the mind of God. This idea was the image of God in which Adam was created, and the means whereby God appeared to the patriarchs, and was finally realized in Jesus Christ. Adam's original condition was one of intercourse with

[1] See p. 218 and note. [2] See the passage quoted on p. 218.
[3] See his *An filius Dei fuerit incarnandus, si peccatum non introivisset in mundum, item, de imagine Dei quid sit* (1550).

God through this idea, the eternal Word, who dwelt in him by grace. From this state he fell, and to that state man is restored through the mediation of Christ.

Thus at the very outset Osiander's theory takes a manward turn, and his theory of justification is an attempt to do justice to this conception of the Divine indwelling as the result of the Atonement.[1] Luther's view seems to him inconsistent. If justification is the external forensic fact, once and for all accomplished, that Luther describes, how can it be that faith is necessary before man can appropriate it ? If the Atonement is accomplished and complete, what action or change on the part of man can possibly be demanded for its fulfilment ? Faced by this problem Osiander goes back quite explicitly to the Roman view of justification, as a making righteous and not a mere imputation of righteousness. God justifies believers by imparting to them the eternal Word, or "inner Word," as he calls it, thereby making them righteous.

In order to relate this conception to the Penal theory Osiander is compelled to make a distinction between redemption and justification, redemption being that reconciliation of God with man accomplished once for all by Christ's vicarious endurance of penal suffering, and justification being the subsequent influence of Christ upon the lives of those who accept Him by faith. Redemption is as completely historical as in the case of a man who is free because his ancestor was bought out of slavery. Justification takes place here and now, through faith.

> After the treasure of redemption is offered to us in the external Word, we apprehend it by faith unto our justification, knowing that we certainly have the same in the inner Word, which abides in our heart.[2]

---

[1] See his *Disputatio de Justificatione* (1550), and his *De Unico Mediatore Jesu Christo et Justificatione fidei Confessio* (1551).

[2] Posteaquam thesaurus redemtionis . . . in externo verbo nobis offertur, apprehendimus eum fide ad justificationem nostri, scientes quod eundem in verbo interno, quod in corde nostro manet, certo habeamus (*Confessio*, ch. 4).

Osiander's view of redemption is precisely the ordinary Penal theory, and his conception of justification is a real attempt to make good its deficiency upon the manward side. Unfortunately Osiander himself is not consistent. Sometimes he dwells upon a real imparting to man of the righteousness of Christ.

> Christ fills us with His righteousness . . . so that, since Christ is ours and is in us, God Himself and all the angels see in us unmixed righteousness. . . . And although some sin may still dwell in our flesh and cling tightly to it, yet it is but as an impure drop in all the purest sea. And God wills not to observe it, for the righteousness of Christ which is in us.[1]

But sometimes his thought changes and he identifies the righteousness of Christ not with His human nature but with His deity. It is not so much His human obedience as His divine holiness that He brings into our lives. And this holiness, Osiander says, is imputed to us.

> I answer readily and clearly that He is our righteousness according to His divine, and not His human nature, although we cannot find, attain, or apprehend this divine righteousness outside His human nature. But when He dwells in us by faith He brings with Him into us His righteousness, which is His divine nature, which is then also imputed to us as though it were our own; nay, further it is also bestowed upon us, and flows from His human nature, as from the Head, even into us, as His members, and moves us to show our members as weapons of the righteousness of God.[2]

---

[1] Christus implet nos justitia sua . . . ita ut Deus ipse et omnes angeli, cum Christus noster et in nobis sit, meram justitiam in nobis videant. . . . Et quamvis peccatum adhuc in carne nostra habitet et tenaciter adhaereat, tamen perinde est sicut stilla immunda respectu totius purissimi maris. Et propter justitiam Christi, quae in nobis est, Deus illud non vult observare (*ib.* Q. 3).

[2] Diserte et clare respondeo, quod secundum divinam suam naturam sit nostra justitia, et non secundum humanam naturam, quamvis hanc divinam justitiam extra ejus humanam naturam non possumus invenire, consequi, aut apprehendere; verum cum ipse per fidem in nobis habitat, tum affert suam justitiam, quae est ejus divina natura, secum in nos, quae deinde nobis etiam imputatur ac si esset nostra propria, immo et donatur nobis manatque ex ipsius humana natura, tanquam ex capite, etiam in nos, tanquam ipsius membra, et movet nos, ut exhibeamus membra nostra arma justitiae Dei (*ib.* M. 3).

God imputes to us His essential righteousness, simply because it is in us, irrespective of the fact that we are not perfectly obedient as we ought to be.[1]

In so far as Osiander here goes back to the forensic conception of imputation he is untrue to his own thought. He has not the mystical insight or the courage of the early Greek fathers who dared to speak of the deification of the believer in Christ.[2] He is, indeed, too thoroughly imbued with the religious distrust of self characteristic of the Reformation to feel at ease in stressing the righteousness of the individual, even though that righteousness rested solely upon the righteousness of Christ. The doctrine of imputed righteousness came naturally to his lips, as meeting the sinner's need. It was of sin and not of good works wrought in Christ that the Reformation was so vividly conscious, and for the sinner in his sin imparted righteousness has as yet no meaning. Sanctification may come, but for present comfort the thought of imputed righteousness alone can avail.

It is this fact of the religious consciousness which explains Osiander's failure to carry the Reformers with him in his efforts to give a coherent account of justification. The attempts made by Flacius and Strigel[3]

[1] From the *Widerlegung der ungegründeten undienstlichen Antwort Philipp Melanchthon's* (1552).

[2] It is this hesitancy that lays Osiander open to Calvin's charge that his conception of the relation of the believer to Christ is not a true union but a *crassa mixtura* (*Inst.* iii. 11. 10).

[3] Ritschl, *op. cit.* pp. 218 ff. Strigel (in *Censurae der fürstlich-sächsischen Theologen*, 1552) urges that redemption and justification were together wrought by Christ for the world as a whole, and are applied, through faith, to each individual believer. Flacius (*Verlegung des Bekenntnisses Osiandri*, 1552) points to the real identity of the two ideas. This is, indeed, obvious enough, so long as justification is interpreted in a purely forensic sense. But the defenders of Lutheranism were too concerned with the defence of this position to do justice to the further truth of sanctification, to conserve which was Osiander's real purpose. Melanchthon (*Antwort auf das Buch Herrn A. Osiander's*, 1552) dwells, very rightly, upon the working of the Holy Spirit as immediately accompanying the sentence of justification. But this thought, if pressed, would have modified profoundly the whole Reformation

to construct an alternative scheme are of no great importance. Both they and Melanchthon defended the forensic view of justification ultimately on the sole ground of the sinner's need of an assurance that is not merely subjective, even going so far as to admit that the justice of God in thus imputing righteousness to man in his sin is quite other than human justice. In argument neither side can be acquitted of inconsistency, but Osiander was certainly less in touch than his opponents with the practical religious feeling of his day.

If, however, Osiander failed to carry his main point, he exercised a determining influence upon Protestant theology in his development of the conception of the active and passive obedience of Christ. It was natural that one who so emphasized the new regenerate life in man should look to Christ's life of obedience to God's will as a fact of central importance, and more than once he refers to this active obedience as in itself a part of the objective fact of Atonement, which, may, therefore, be imputed to man to make good the imperfections due to sin.

> Since sin is remitted and yet still inheres in us it behoves Him to bestow upon us His obedience, wherein He fulfilled the law, and to offer it for us, lest it should be imputed to us that we cannot yet fulfil the law, but still sin and offend daily.[1]

> Thou must not rely in this life upon thy obedience nor upon thy purity, but upon the obedience and purity of My Son, who has perfectly fulfilled the law for thee ; for His righteousness is not imputed to thee by Me because it works in thee any works, be they great or small, but only because it is in thee by faith.[2]

---

theology. Melanchthon does not allow it to interfere with the objective and prior character of justification as the sole assurance of the sinner. The difference between Osiander and his opponents as to justification is largely one of verbal usage, but it is significant of a real and wide divergence of religious standpoint.

[1] Cum peccatum sit remissum et tamen adhuc in nobis haereat, debet ipse obedientiam suam, qua legem implevit, nobis donare, ac pro nobis pendere, ne nobis imputetur, quod legem nondum possumus adimplere, sed adhuc quotidie peccamus et offendimus (*Confessio*, P. 2).

[2] *Widerlegung*.

Thus Osiander comes to assign a special part to Christ's active obedience in the external work of redemption, imputed to us through faith. By Christ's suffering the penalty of sin was completely paid. By His fulfilment of the law the imperfection of our righteousness is covered and can no more be imputed to those who believe. This forensic distinction is of little importance for Osiander's own thought, which is essentially a protest against forensic methods of thinking, but it was soon adopted more or less definitely by his Lutheran opponents, who gave vicarious obedience no less than vicarious suffering a place in the satisfaction offered by Christ.

The passage of this distinction into doctrine is marked by the Formula of Concord (1577).

By His most absolute obedience, even unto death, which He offered to the Father, Christ merited for us beforehand remission of all sins and eternal life.[1]

For since Christ is not only man but God and man in one undivided Person, He was not subject to the law, just as He was not liable to suffering and death (by reason of His Person), because He was Lord of the law. On that account His obedience (not that only which He rendered to the Father in the whole of His suffering and death, but also that by which for our sake He willingly subjected Himself to the law and fulfilled it) is imputed to us for righteousness; so that God on account of that whole obedience which Christ, by doing and suffering, in His life and death, offered on our account to His heavenly Father, forgives our sins, accounts us good and righteous, and bestows upon us eternal salvation.[2]

---

[1] Christus obedientia sua, quam Patri ad mortem usque absolutissimam praestitit, nobis peccatorum omnium remissionem et vitam aeternam promeruit (*Form. Conc. Art. III. Epitome*, p. 584).

[2] Cum enim Christus non tantum homo, verum Deus et homo sit in una persona indivisa, tam non fuit legi subjectus, quam non fuit passioni et morti (ratione suae personae) obnoxius, quia Dominus legis erat. Eam ob causam ipsius obedientia (non ea tantum, qua Patri paruit in tota sua passione et morte, verum etiam qua nostra causa sponte sese legi subjecit, eamque obedientia illa sua implevit) nobis ad justitiam imputatur, ita ut Deus propter totam obedientam, quam Christus agendo et patiendo in vita et morte sua nostra causa Patri suo coelesti praestitit, peccata nobis remittat, pro bonis et justis nos reputet, et salute aeterna donet (*ib. Solida Declaratio*, p. 684).

The form which the doctrine here takes is noteworthy. The two parts of Christ's obedience are quite clearly distinguished and yet emphasis is laid upon the unity of that obedience. The active and passive obedience of Christ together accomplish our justification, which justification is one only and not two, whether regarded as the non-imputation to man of his sin, or as the imputation to him of the righteousness of Christ. Thus the position of the Formula of Concord is in essence identical with that already attained by Luther and Calvin, despite the dependence of its language upon Osiander. At the same time the conclusion that the active obedience of Christ was actually a part of the satisfaction offered by Him to the Father is not inconsistent with the language used.

This conclusion is a definite reversion from the Lutheran position in the direction of the Catholic doctrine of the merits of Christ, and soon became current in Lutheran circles. The Lutheran pastor of Ansbach, Georg Karg (*c.* 1570), protested against it without success, and, indeed, himself withdrew his opposition. But it was mainly by the Calvinists that the doctrine was developed, until in the seventeenth century it was a widespread though never a universal opinion, both in the Lutheran and in the Reformed Church, that satisfaction was made to the justice of God both by Christ's fulfilment of the Law and by His suffering and death.

The general position at the beginning of this century may be briefly summarized: The central emphasis was laid, as in the earliest days of the Reformation, upon the penal suffering of Christ, whereby satisfaction was made to the justice of God. Thus Christ's passive obedience, in which He submitted to the penalty imposed upon sin, is the key to Atonement. The Protestant divines tended to go beyond even the strong language of Luther and Calvin in describing the suffering of Christ. Calvin's reminder that God must not be supposed to have been angry with His beloved Son was often forgotten, and it was explicitly stated that Christ endured the Divine wrath. And this endurance was not confined to the Passion, but extended to all the incarnate experience of Christ. Thus the Heidelberg Catechism asserts that He bore the Divine wrath throughout the whole period of His earthly life.[1] Further, the conception was made to include the idea that Christ underwent the pains of hell, and even eternal death, though this "new, unheard-of heresy" as Bellarmine called it,[2] did not pass without protest. But this payment of the penalty through the passive obedience does not in itself make man fit for God's favour and fellowship. Therefore Christ's active obedience, that willing, complete, conformity to the law which He showed, is also imputed to us as our righteousness. His obedience in both its aspects is vicarious. So far the theory is coherent enough. But with this conception of the active obedience as imputed to man is conjoined, and often confused, the very different conception that the active obedience is something directly offered to God, thus constituting a part of the meritorious ground of Atonement. The thought is not really consistent with the strict Penal theory, and simply depends upon the human and true instinct that willing obedience is of more real worth than unwilling obedience.

A further and separate development may also be noticed here. Calvin's doctrine of predestination and reprobation had been definitely developed by his followers to its logical conclusion that the effects of Christ's satisfaction extended only to the elect. Thus the conception of particular redemption was held to involve the limitation of the effects of the Atonement.[3] The inference that Christ died not for all but only

[1] Q. 37. [2] *Ap.* Hagenbach, *op. cit.* iii. p. 212.

[3] Especially in the controversy of Zanchius with the Lutheran Marbach, at Strassburg.

for those chosen beforehand by Divine decree was disputed by the Lutherans. The Formula of Concord, for example, attempts to meet the difficulty by distinguishing predestination and foreknowledge.

> This foreknowledge of God pertains both to good and to bad, but meanwhile is not the cause of evil or of sin, impelling man to wrong-doing. . . . But God's foreknowledge disposes evil and has fixed its bounds, how far it should go and how long it should last, and so directs it that though bad in itself it yet makes way for the salvation of God's elect. . . . Now predestination or God's eternal election pertains only to the good and beloved children of God, and this is the cause of their salvation.[1]

Thus, in opposition to the Calvinists with their doctrine of unconditional election and limited redemption, the Formula holds conditional election and unlimited grace.

> Now Christ calls all sinners to Him and promises them relief, and sincerely wishes that all men should come to Him.[2]

> That which is written, "Many indeed are called but few chosen," must not be understood as though God did not will all to be saved, but as a cause of condemnation to the wicked, because either they do not hear God's word at all, but obstinately despise it . . . or else they count the word which they have heard as of little weight and cast it away. For their doom, therefore, neither God, nor His election, but their wickedness is to blame.[3]

---

[1] Haec praescientia Dei simul ad bonos et malos pertinet, sed interim non est causa mali, neque est causa peccati, quae hominem ad scelus impellat. . . . Sed praescientia Dei disponit malum, et metas illi constituit, quousque progredi et quamdiu durare debeat, idque eo dirigit, ut, licet per se malum sit, nihilominus electis Dei ad salutem cedat. . . . Praedestinatio vero seu aeterna Dei electio tantum ad bonos et dilectos filios Dei pertinet, et haec est causa ipsorum salutis (pp. 617 f.).

[2] Christus vero omnes peccatores ad se vocat et promittit illis levationem, et serio vult ut omnes homines ad se veniant (*ibid.*).

[3] Quod vero scriptum est, multos quidem vocatos, paucos vero electos esse, non ita accipiendum est, quasi Deus nolit ut omnes salventur, sed damnationis impiorum causa est, quod verbum Dei aut prorsus non audiant, sed contumaciter contemnant . . . aut certe quod verbum auditum flocci pendant atque abjiciant. Quod igitur pereunt, neque Deus, neque ipsius electio, sed malitia eorum in culpa est (*ib.* p. 619).

These doctrinal developments are well illustrated by the writings of the Lutheran Gerhard,[1] and especially by his reply to Piscator,[2] who had protested against the doctrine of the active obedience on the general ground that Christ owed obedience for Himself (so Anselm), and that therefore His obedience cannot affect us. Only the passive obedience, which was not due since He had not sinned, can have redemptive value. In maintaining this position Piscator was not alone, and Gerhard cites a number of divines who agreed with him. Ritschl[3] argues that this shows the continuance of Melanchthon's influence within the Reformed Church, though the scope of this influence was limited. "The divergence of John Piscator upon this point, although he found supporters in the Reformed party, is to be regarded merely as an episode which rather helped than hindered the essential oneness of the Lutheran and Reformed theologians upon this point."

Gerhard sums up Piscator's view as being

> . . . that Christ merited justification for us solely by the passive obedience or obedience of death, to the exclusion of His active obedience or obedience of life.[4]

He then goes on to develop Piscator's argument, quoting from him a careful distinction between the two obediences.

> By obedience of life I mean that which He paid to law, by His holy life in accordance therewith. I call obedience of death that which He paid to the Father's special command concerning suffering and dying for the elect. . . . These two obediences, so to speak, are to be accurately distinguished and in no way to be confused, for they are very different. For Christ was bound to obedience by the law of nature . . . so far as concerned the

---

[1] *Loci Theologici* (1610–1625). This learned work is full of references to the other divines of the period, and is quite invaluable historically.

[2] *Theses Theologicae* (1618). [3] *Op. cit.* p. 248.

[4] Christum exclusa activa sive vitae obedientia, sola passiva sive mortis obedientia justificationem nobis meruisse (*Loc. Theol.* xli., *De justificatione per fidem*, ch. 57).

moral law and the bond made by God with the descendants of Abraham and Israel. But to obedience of death He was bound by no law, but by a law of a different kind, viz. of voluntary undertaking.[1]

Only the latter obedience, "obedience of death," can, according to Piscator, have any redemptive value. The death of Christ would have been unnecessary, had He made satisfaction by His life. There is no need that the imperfection of believers should be covered by Christ's perfection, for the fault of imperfection is put away, with all other sin, by the death of Christ.

Against this Gerhard argues that such a separation between the active and passive obedience is quite untenable.

It is plainly impossible to separate the active obedience from the passive in this meritorious work, for in Christ's very death concurred that voluntary obedience and most ardent love, of which the former looks to the heavenly Father, the latter to us men.[2]

This last phrase shows how strongly the need for a more manward view of Atonement than the Penal theory in itself could provide was making itself felt, and this comes out again in Gerhard's summary of his argument:

Thus then we argue: If Christ the Mediator in the office of redemption not only died for us but also (1) did the heavenly Father's will; (2) fulfilled the law; (3) was made under the law; (4) that through His obedience we might be constituted righteous;

---

[1] Obedientiam vitae nomino quam praestitit legi sancte secundum illam vivendo. Obedientiam mortis voco quam praestitit speciali mandato Patris de patiendo et moriendo pro electis. . . . Hae duae, ut ita loquar, obedientiae accurate sunt discernendae et nequaquam confundendae nam plurimum differunt. Quippe ad obedientiam obligatus fuit Christus jure naturae . . . quantum ad legem moralem necnon jure foederis a Deo facti cum posteris Abrahami et Israëlis. Ad obedientiam vero mortis nullo jure fuit obligatus, sed jure diverso, nempe voluntariae sponsionis (*ib.* ch. 58).

[2] Quid quod plane ἀδύνατον est, activam obedientiam a passiva in hoc merito separare, quia in ipsa Christi morte concurrit voluntaria illa obedienta et ardentissima dilectio, quarum prior Patrem coelestem, posterior nos homines respicit (*ib.* ch. 55). It is noteworthy that in this passage the ideas of merit and of satisfaction have become quite synonymous (see below, p. 239).

(5) and that the justification of law might be fulfilled upon us; (6) since He Himself is the end of the law unto righteousness for all believers; (7) and further was made righteousness to us by God; (8) in whom we are made righteous; the consequence is, that our righteousness before God is not only the passive but also the active obedience.[1]

Thus it follows that both active and passive obedience are wholly present together in Christ's life and death. Piscator's distinction does not hold. It was under the moral law, *i.e.* as active obedience, that Christ undertook to be the Mediator and to undergo penal suffering.[2] Gerhard combines the two aspects of the active obedience. In its Godward reference it is a valuable part of the satisfaction offered by Christ. In its manward reference it is no mere empty imputation of holiness, identical in meaning with the non-imputation, or remission, of sins, but a real cause of a real change of condition. This latter point, however, must not be too much stressed. Gerhard's position is not that of the Roman theologians. He is not thinking so much of an infused righteousness, though this is the logical outcome of his thought, as of the legal condition of righteousness, from the point of view of the Judge. The whole argument is significant, as showing the real difficulty of doing justice to the manward aspect of Atonement so long as the forensic, substitutionary, language of the Penal theory is retained.

Gerhard's conception of the passive obedience is characteristic of the Lutheran Church. He emphasizes Christ's penal suffering in the most extreme manner.

[1] Sic igitur argumentamur: Si Christus mediator in officio redemtionis non solum pro nobis mortuus est, sed etiam (1) voluntatem Patris coelestis fecit; (2) legem implevit; (3) factus sub lege; (4) ut per obedientiam ejus constitueremur justi; (5) et justificatio legis in nobis impleretur; (6) cum ipse sit finis legis ad justitiam omni credenti; (7) ac proinde factus nobis a Deo justitia; (8) in quo efficimur justi; consequens est, non solum passivam sed etiam activam obedientiam Christi esse nostram coram Deo justitiam (*ib.* c. 60).

[2] *Ib.* c. 61.

> How could He have truly taken our sins upon Himself and have offered a perfect satisfaction, if He had not felt the wrath of God conjoined by an individual bond with sin? How could He have redeemed us from the curse of the law, having been made a curse for us, if He had not felt the judgement of an angry God.[1]

He goes so far as to assert that this suffering involved the very pains of hell, but will not take the further step, and declare, with the extreme Calvinists, that Christ endured " eternal death."

> Although He did not undergo eternal death (which was impossible, since He was, as to Himself, God's most innocent and most beloved Son; nor could He, on this hypothesis, have been our Redeemer) yet He truly felt the pains of hell and the judgement of God angered by our sins.[2]

The difference upon this point between the Lutherans and the Calvinists turns merely upon the meaning of the phrase, and corresponds to no real divergence of thought. But it is strange that the Calvinists especially should so far have forgotten their master's teaching on the unbroken love of the Father for the Son, to which, indeed, Gerhard's own thought is more akin.

Gerhard may be quoted further as illustrating the Lutheran position as to particular redemption. He devotes a section of his treatise to the demonstration, against the Calvinists, of the universal scope of the merits of Christ.

[1] Quomodo enim peccata nostra vere in se suscepisset ac perfectam satisfactionem praestitisset, nisi iram Dei individuo nexu cum peccatis conjunctam vere sensisset? Quomodo a maledicto legis nos redemisset, factus pro nobis maledictum, nisi judicium Dei irati persensisset? (*Loc.* xvii. 2. c. 54). Gerhard is careful to say, however, against Calvin, that it was not in the descent into hell but in the Passion, and especially in Gethsemane, that Christ suffered this " truly infernal anguish."

[2] Quamvis vero mortem aeternam non subierit (quod fuit ἀδύνατον cum fuerit sui ratione innocentissimus et dilectissimus Dei filius; neque hac ratione potuisset esse redemtor noster), tamen vere sensit dolores inferni et judicium Dei irascentis peccatis nostris (*Loc.* xli. c. 44).

Those for whom Christ poured out His precious blood beforehand upon the altar of the Cross, are not rejected of God by any absolute decree; for these two things are directly opposed to one another, as is clear. But now Christ has poured out His precious blood beforehand absolutely for all men upon the altar of the Cross. Therefore no one of them is rejected of God by any absolute decree.[1]

Because Christ calls all men to Him, because He orders us to preach repentance and remission of sins to all men in His name, because He orders the Gospel to be announced to every creature, therefore also Christ died for all and merited for all beforehand those benefits which are offered to men in the Gospel.[2]

Upon the two main points at issue the controversy had different results. Piscator and his friends failed to check the influence of the doctrine of the active obedience in the Reformed Church, and in 1675 it was definitely approved in the *Formula Consensus Helvetica*:

Also the Spirit of God plainly asserts that Christ by His most holy life made satisfaction for us to the law and to the Divine justice, and assigns that price at which we were purchased unto God not only to His sufferings, but to His whole life of conformity with the law.[3]

But upon the question of particular redemption the position of the Reformed Church remained unchanged, and it was in special opposition to the theory of the universality of grace that the *Formula Consensus* was

[1] Pro quibus Christus pretiosum sanguinem in ara crucis profudit, illi non sunt aliquo decreto a Deo rejecti; haec enim immediate sibi invicem repugnant, ut patet. Jam vero Christus pro omnibus omnino hominibus pretiosum suum sanguinem in ara crucis profudit. Ergo nemo eorum absoluto aliquo decreto a Deo rejectus (*Loc.* vii. 6 *de universalitate meriti Christi* c. 106).

[2] Quia Christus vocat ad se omnes, quia jubet in nomine suo poenitentiam et remissionem peccatorum omnibus praedicare, quia jubet evangelium annuntiari omni creaturae, ideo etiam Christus pro omnibus mortuus est, et beneficia illa, quae in evangelio hominibus offeruntur, omnibus est promeritus (*ib.* c. 122).

[3] Spiritus quoque Dei rotundo ore asserit Christum sanctissima sua vita legi et justitiae divinae pro nobis satisfecisse, et pretium illud, quo emti sumus Deo, non in passionibus duntaxat, sed tota ejus vita legi conformata collocat (*Art.* 15).

composed, in full agreement with the earlier Calvinistic formulae.

> Before the foundations of the world were laid God wrought in Christ the purpose of the ages (Eph. 3. 11), in which by the mere good pleasure of His will, without any prevision of merit, of works, or of faith, He chose, to the praise of His glorious grace, a fixed and definite number of those who lay in that same mass of corruption and in community of blood, and who were therefore corrupt in sin, to be led in due time to salvation through Christ their sponsor and sole mediator.[1]

For the full illustration of the development of these doctrines, and especially of the doctrine of the active obedience of Christ, reference must be made to larger treatises.[2] For our present purpose it will suffice to select two representative divines of the latter part of the seventeenth century, Quenstedt from among the Lutherans, and Francis Turretin, the greatest exponent of later Calvinistic orthodoxy.

Quenstedt[3] is important, not as showing any development in the Lutheran position, but because of the clear relief into which he throws its underlying ideas. The general tendency of Protestant theology had been to merge the active and passive obedience of Christ together in their causal relation to satisfaction, even while carefully separating them for purposes of theory.

[1] Deus ante jacta mundi fundamenta in Christo fecit propositum seculorum (Eph. 3 11), in quo ex mero voluntatis suae beneplacito, sine ulla meriti, operum, vel fidei praevisione, ad laudem gloriosae gratiae suae, elegit certum ac definitum in eadem corruptionis massa et communi sanguine jacentium adeoque peccato corruptorum numerum in tempore per Christum sponsorem et mediatorem unicum ad salutem perducendum (*Art.* 4). Among the earlier statements the Heidelberg Catechism is an exception, asserting (Q. 37) that Christ "sustained in body and soul the wrath of God against the sins of all mankind." The explaining of this away occasioned some difficulty to later Calvinists.

[2] The fullest collection of facts is given by Thomasius, *Dogmatis de Obedientia Activa Historia* (1846). Ritschl's account is, however, detailed enough for all practical purposes (*op. cit.* ch. vi.). See also Baur's *Die christliche Lehre von der Versöhnung.*

[3] *Theologia Didacto-polemica* (1685).

They are two, yet each is wholly present in the offering made by Christ to God. Thus it is natural to find that little distinction is made between the terms "merit" and "satisfaction." They are used, for example, quite indifferently by Gerhard in speaking of that work of Christ in which both the active and the passive obedience concur.[1] One or two writers,[2] however, show a certain consciousness that the idea of merit has naturally a special association with the active obedience and the idea of satisfaction with the passive obedience, even while they continue to assert the unity of this dual obedience as the ground of justification. Quenstedt is the first writer to state this in clear and set terms:

> The satisfaction and the merit of Christ are not of equal force, for (1) the former compensates the injury done to God, expiates iniquity, pays the debt, and frees from eternal punishments; the latter has restored us into the condition of Divine favour; acquires for sinners the free reward or grace of remission of sins, justification and eternal life; (2) the former has itself as a cause, the latter as an effect. For merit sprang from satisfaction. Christ made satisfaction for our sins and for the penalties due thereto, and so merited beforehand for us God's grace, remission of sins and eternal life; (3) satisfaction was made to the triune God, and to His justice, not to us, though it was made for us. But it was not for the Trinity but for us that Christ merited and acquired by His merits anything; (4) the acts of exinanition, as the fulfilling of the law, the passion, the death, are at once satisfying and meritorious, but the acts of exaltation, as the resurrection, the ascension into heaven, the session at the right hand of God, are acts not satisfying, but solely meritorious, and in this respect He merited beforehand for us resurrection to life, and unlocked heaven; (5) satisfaction arises of that which is due, but merit is a work plainly not due and free, and answered by a corresponding reward.[3]

---

[1] See above, p. 234 and note.

[2] Ritschl (*op. cit.* p. 261) quotes Amesius as the first writer to state the distinction, though he does not work it out fully.

[3] Satisfactio et meritum Christi non sunt *ἰσοδυναμοῦντα*. Nam (1) illa compensat injuriam Deo illatam, iniquitatem expiat, debitum solvit, et a poenis aeternis liberat,—hoc restituit nos in statum benevolentiae divinae, mercedem gratuitam seu gratiam remissionis peccatorum, justificationem, et vitam aeternam peccatoribus acquirit; (2) illa se habet ut causa, hoc ut effectus. Ex satisfactione enim

It would be possible to criticize this careful distinction in detail,[1] but it is of more importance to notice the real, though unconscious, breakdown of the Penal theory which it implies. For the Penal theory depends wholly upon the thought of an endurance of penalty whereby the demands of God's avenging justice are met. It had been sufficiently difficult to reconcile with this the position of the Formula of Concord, that the one obedience of Christ had an active as well as a passive side. But the difficulty is vastly increased when these two aspects are thus separated. It cannot be to God's avenging justice that an act that is meritorious, and not satisfying, has reference. The real implication of this developed conception of Christ's obedience is that the retributive aspect of justice is not in itself adequate to the justice of God. There must be in Him other attributes to which the active, meritorious, obedience bears a more direct relation.

Yet the Lutheran theologians, and even Quenstedt himself, show no signs of abandoning the penal view. Quenstedt goes on to argue that the satisfaction offered by Christ was the complete and sufficient payment of all man's debt, imputed to Him by God's judgement. God demanded from Him all that was due, remitting nothing from His right in the exaction of penalty. Socinian attempts to renew the Scotist theory of

---

meritum ortum est. Satisfecit Christus pro peccatis nostris et pro poenis illis debitis et ita promeruit nobis gratiam Dei, remissionem peccatorum, et vitam aeternam; (3) satisfactio facta est Deo unitrino ejusque justitiae, non nobis, licet pro nobis facta sit. At non ipsi Trinitati, sed nobis Christus aliquid meruit et merito suo acquisivit; (4) actus exinanitionis, ut legis impletio, passio, mors sunt simul satisfactorii et meritorii; actus vero exaltationis, ut resurrectio, ascensio in caelum, sessio ad dexteram Dei non satisfactorii actus sunt, sed solum meritorii, eo ipso resurrectionem ad vitam nobis promeruit et coelum reseravit; (5) satisfactio ex debito oritur, sed meritum opus plane indebitum ac liberum est, cui ex adverso respondet merces (P. iii. cap. 3 membr. 2 sec. 1. thes. 26. *ap.* Ritschl, *op. cit.* p. 261).

[1] See Ritschl, *loc. cit.*

acceptatio are uncompromisingly rejected. That which God's rigorous justice demanded, that Christ sustained, even to the enduring of the very pains of hell, though not in hell, or eternally. The one relaxation, which reveals God's mercy combined with His justice, is His acceptance of the Son of God Himself as our representative and substitute. But this, Quenstedt says, in no way detracts from the satisfaction.

Why not? This is just the flaw of the Penal theory, and it is fatal.

Three years before the appearance of Quenstedt's treatise, Francis Turretin published his monumental statement of Calvinistic belief,[1] a belief matured and carefully tested in every detail by a century of debate not only with the Lutherans and the theologians of the Counter-Reformation, but also with the acute rationalists of the Socinian school.[2] His position, in its main outlines, may be regarded as typical of the Reformed Church. It is very clearly set forth in the section of his *Institutes* which deals with the Office of Christ the Mediator.[3]

Turretin begins his discussion of satisfaction with a definition.

> The satisfaction which is here discussed is not regarded in a broad sense . . . but strictly as the payment of a debt, by which that is paid which another owes and by which satisfaction is made to the creditor claiming a debt or the judge claiming punishment.[4]

It is noteworthy that this definition seems almost to confuse the conceptions of civil and criminal justice, the law of equity and the law of retribution. The distinction, upon which the whole theory of satisfaction had originally depended,[5] but which had been largely

[1] *Institutio Theologiae Elenchticae* (Geneva, 1682).

[2] See below, pp. 282 ff.

[3] Pars ii. Locus xiv. *De Officio Christi Mediatoris.*

[4] Satisfactio de qua hic quaeritur non sumitur late . . . sed stricte pro solutione debiti, qua solvitur quod alius debet et qua satisfit creditori vel judici debitum vel poenam repetenti (*ib.* Q. 10).

[5] See pp. 121 f.

obscured in the Penal Theory, was brought into prominence again by the Socinian debate.[1] Turretin himself is clearly aware of it, as is shown when he goes on to point out the threefold character of sin—as a debt, as hostility to God, and as a crime. The satisfaction offered for sin must therefore be threefold too :

> And hence, secondly, can be perceived the nature of the satisfaction which ought to be offered for sin, viz. that in which these three characteristics concur, in that it is the payment of the debt, the placating of the Divine wrath, through our reconciliation with Him, and the expiation of guilt through the complete suffering of the penalty.[2]

But Turretin makes no use of this piece of analysis. The penal aspect of God's justice is uppermost in his mind, and he lays it down that though God may be regarded as a creditor, as lord, or as judge and ruler, it is in this last capacity that He demands satisfaction.

The next question to be discussed is the way in which it is possible for this penal satisfaction to be made by a substitute, so that mercy may temper the severity of the judge.

> But here again the actual punishment, which the judge demands, must be distinguished accurately from the mode and circumstances of punishment, for these two things are not upon the same footing. . . . For though a sinful person fully deserves punishment and may justly be punished, yet it is not so necessary and indispensable but that for certain definite and weighty causes a transference of punishment to a substitute may be made. And in this sense it is said by theologians that impersonally punishment must of necessity be inflicted upon all sin, but not immediately personally upon every sinner ; since by His singular grace God can exempt some from it, a surety being substituted in their stead. But that it may be conceived that God can accomplish this, He must be viewed, not as an inferior and subordinate judge, set up under the law, who would be unable

---

[1] Especially by Crell, see p. 298.

[2] Atque hinc secundo natura satisfactionis quae pro peccato praestari debuit percipi potest, nimirum in qua tres istae σχέσεις simul concurrant, quae sit et debiti solutio, et irae divinae, per nostri cum eo reconciliationem, placatio, et reatus per poenae perpessionem expiatio (*ibid.*).

to dispense from the rigour of the law by transferring the punishment to another, but as a judge supreme and free from liability, who, even as He wills to satisfy His own justice by the punishment of sin, so in accordance with His supreme wisdom and pity, was able to relax the strict justice of the law by exempting sinners from the punishment due, and by transferring it to a sponsor.[1]

Thus Turretin finds a place for the mercy of God. Had the offence only involved a civil obligation, or debt, it would have been completely put away by payment of the debt, whether by the offender himself or by another. With a crime, an offence against absolute justice, it is different. Only by the mercy of the judge can any substitute be accepted for punishment inflicted immediately upon the person of the offender.

And even so justice demands that certain conditions should be fulfilled, in order that vicarious punishment may have the character of satisfaction :

Again as the satisfaction which is demanded by God's justice it makes two special demands, (1) that it should be paid by the same nature which had sinned, and (2) that it should be of value and even of infinite price to take away sin's infinite demerit : In Christ were the two natures necessary to the payment of satisfaction, the human to suffer, the Divine to add value and infinite price to the sufferings.[2]

---

[1] Verum hic rursus poena ipsa, quam judex exigit, distinguenda est accurate a poenae modo et circumstantiis, nec enim eadem est utriusque ratio . . . Licet enim persona peccans omnino mereatur poenam et juste puniri possit, non est tamen ita necessarium et indispensabile, quin certis quibusdam gravibus de causis possit translatio fieri poenae in vadem. Et hoc sensu dicitur a theologis poenam omni peccato impersonaliter infligendam esse necessario, sed non statim personaliter in omni peccatori ; siquidem Deus singulari gratia nonnullos potest eximere ab ea, substituto in eorum locum vade. Hoc vero ut concipiatur exequi posse Deum, spectandus est, non ut judex inferior et subalternus sub lege constitutus, qui de legis rigore dispensare non posset poenam in alium transferendo. Sed ut judex summus et *ἀπεύθυνος*, qui ut justitiae suae vult satisfieri per peccati poenam ; ita pro summa sua sapientia et misericordia, potuit de *ἀκριβοδικαίῳ* legis relaxare eximendo peccatores a poena debita, et transferendo eam in Sponsorem (*ibid.*).

[2] Rursus ut satisfactio, quae a justitia Dei exigebatur, duo praecipue postulabat, (1) ut ab eadem natura quae peccaverat persol-

These requirements are precisely those laid down by Anselm, and Turretin's whole argument is entirely Anselmic in character, particularly in its assertion, on Thomist lines, of the infinite worth of the suffering endured for infinite sin. He proceeds to illustrate his meaning from history, quoting such examples of self-sacrifice as Damon and Pythias, and Q. Curtius. These, however, were imperfect, as also were the old sacrifices, though the latter make a nearer approach to the ideal. Only in Christ are all the requirements fulfilled.

But that that substitution may be wrought lawfully and without any mark of injustice, various conditions are required in the sponsor, all of which meet perfectly in Christ. (1) Communion of nature, that sin may be punished in that nature which was guilty, Heb. 2 14. (2) Consent of will, that he may take that burden upon himself freely and voluntarily, compelled by none, Heb. 10 9. . . . (3) Power and lordship over his own members, that in his own right he may be one who can determine concerning himself, John 10 18. . . . (4) Ability to bear all the penalties due to us, and of bearing them away both from himself and from us; otherwise, if he could be held by death, he would be able to free no one therefrom. That this ability was in Christ, the God-man, none can doubt. (5) Sanctity and purity unspotted, that being stained by no sin, he might have no need to offer for himself, but only for us, Heb. 7 25, 26, 27.

Under these conditions it was not unjust that Christ the righteous should be substituted for us the unrighteous. For here no injury is done to any. Not to Christ Himself, both because He willingly took this penalty upon Himself, and because He had power to determine concerning Himself, and ability to raise Himself from the dead. Not to God the Judge, because He willed and commanded this, or to His natural right which is safeguarded by the punishment of the sponsor. Not to the republic of the world through the death of the innocent by which it was deprived of its best citizen; for Christ having been freed from death, lives for ever; nor by the life of the guilty, surviving to the hurt of the republic, for they are converted through Christ,

---

veretur, (2) ut valoris tamen et pretii infiniti esse ad demeritum infinitum peccati tollendum: In Christo duae naturae necessariae fuerunt ad satisfactionem persolvendam, humana, quae pateretur, divina, quae valorem et pretium passionibus adderet infinitum (*ibid.*). In this passage and in that next quoted Turretin is replying directly to the criticisms of Socinus.

and are made new creatures. Not to the Divine law, which is guarded beforehand in its most perfect fulfilment accomplished by Christ, and by our twofold union with Christ, natural and forensic or mystical, through which, even as He was made one with us and we with Him, so He was able to take our sin and evil things upon Himself, and to pour out upon us His righteousness and good things.[1]

This passage is noteworthy, not merely as an excellent example of the scholastic method of the age, but also as showing the uneasy self-consciousness of the later Penal theory. It is no longer a joyful assertion of that wondrous substitution whereby man no longer trembles before avenging justice. The theory is already upon the defensive, not only against the criticism of its opponents, but against the human instincts of its own supporters. The attempt to describe the Atonement in terms of retributive justice seemed after all only to reveal a radical injustice within God's very being.

[1] Sed ut substitutio ista legitime et absque ulla injustitiae nota fieri possit, variae conditiones in sponsore requiruntur, quae omnes in Christum perfecte competunt. (1) Communio naturae, ut peccatum puniatur in ea natura quae rea erat, Heb. 2 14. (2) Consensus voluntatis, ut sponte et ultro nemine cogente onus illud in se recipiat, Heb. 10 9 . . . (3) Potestas et dominium membrorum suorum, ut sit sui juris qui de seipso statuere possit, John 10 18 . . . (4) Potentia poenas omnes nobis debitas ferendi, et auferendi tam a se quam a nobis, alias, si detineri potuisset a morte, neminem ab ea liberare potuisset. Quod in Christo θεανθρώπῳ fuisse nemo dubitare potest. (5) Sanctitas et puritas immaculata, ut nullo peccato inquinatus, opus non haberet offerre pro seipso, sed pro nobis tantum, Heb. 7 25, 26, 27.

His positis conditionibus injustum non fuit Christum justum pro nobis injustis substitui. Hic enim nulla facta est cuiquam injuria. Non ipsi Christo, tum quia volens hanc poenam in se recepit, tum quia potestatem habuit de se statuendi, et potentiam sese a mortuis excitandi. Non Deo judici, quia hoc voluit et jussit; vel juri ipsius naturali, cui cautum est poena sponsoris. Non Reipub. mundi per mortem innocentis qua optimo cive privata sit; Christus enim a morte liberatus in aeternum vivit; nec per vitam reorum, qui perniciem Reipub. sint superstites, quia per Christum convertuntur, et novae fiunt creaturae. Non legi divinae, cui prospectum est perfectissima impletione ejus a Christo facta, et duplici unione nostra cum Christo, naturali et forensi seu mystica, per quam ut unum factus est nobiscum et nos cum ipso, ita potuit peccatum et mala nostra in se recipere, et justitiam ac bona sua in nos derivare (*ibid.*).

And Turretin's defence, wise and true as it is, does not really meet the attack. It is a lawyer's defence to the end, based upon a legal substitution described in legal language, and the language fails to touch reality. When all is said the "just judge" remains alternately over-cruel and over-lenient, demanding penalty where it is not due, and remitting penalty where it should be enforced. The only explanation which can avail is that of a real unity of Christ with the sinner, as with God. But Luther's strong mysticism has passed away. Turretin can equate "forensic" and "mystical," and the latter word has only its bare mediaeval implication of unity in a corporation, with certain fixed conditions of membership.[1] It implies no mystical theory of Atonement in the modern sense.

Having thus laid down the conditions under which vicarious satisfaction is possible, Turretin passes on, again on Anselmic lines, to prove it necessary. He does not merely argue, as Calvin himself had done, for a hypothetical necessity, dependent on God's arbitrary decree, but for a real necessity based in the very nature of morality. He gives six reasons :

---

[1] This development in the meaning of the words "mystery," "mystical," is a matter of some importance, having had considerable influence upon theological usage. Their early implication is revelation rather than concealment, and St. Paul uses μυστήριον to connote, not a secret, but a revelation of God's purpose to the Church. This purpose would of course remain a secret to those outside — hence the common use of the word. In mediaeval England an apprentice would be admitted to the "craft or mystery" of a guild, *i.e.* to its corporate inheritance of trade knowledge. The mystery of Masonry, which is only mysterious to those who are not Freemasons, is a survival of this idea. In this sense the Church of England Baptismal Office uses the phrase, "Sanctify this water to the mystical washing away of sins," and the Prayer Book speaks of the Sacraments as "holy mysteries," not because there is anything mysterious about them, but because they are, as it were, the title-deeds of the corporate life of the Church, a legal "instrument" of membership (Article XXVII.). To say this, of course, does not deny the mystical interpretation of the Church and the Sacraments in another sense. For a good parallel to Turretin's usage cf. the phrase of Grotius, "Conjunctio . . . mystica, ut inter regem et populum" (*Def. Fid. Cath.* c. 4).

(*a*) God's avenging justice.

But since that justice is nothing other than a constant will to punish, and that will cannot be without effect in God, whose majesty is supreme and power infinite, it demands of necessity the infliction of punishment, either upon the sinner himself, or upon a surety substituted in his place.[1]

(*b*) The nature of sin, which of itself demands punishment, since moral and physical evil are naturally and properly connected.

If He smites the sinner He gives him his due and that which he has fully deserved by his fault.[2]

(*c*) The sanction of the law; (*d*) the New Testament witness; (*e*) the greatness of God's love, which the Scriptures commend to us; and (*f*) the augmenting of our hatred of sin and love to God. The first two of these reasons, clearly dominant in Turretin's mind, give the Penal theory in all its darkness, a darkness which the concluding hint of a Moral theory does little to relieve. A God whose constant will is to punish, whose natural right must be "safeguarded by the punishment of the sponsor," whose supremacy over the hearts of men is one primarily of terror, has no real supremacy at all. Love, even finite human love, is greater than He.

Passing on to the problem of the active and passive obedience of Christ, Turretin gives it as the accepted belief of the Protestant churches that each has a place in the work of Atonement.

But it is a general opinion, and accepted in our churches, that the satisfaction of Christ, which is imputed to us for righteousness before God, embraces not only Christ's suffering which He bore whether in life or in death; but also the obedience of the whole

---

[1] Primo, Justitia Dei vindicatrix . . . Cum autem justitia ista nihil aliud sit quam voluntas constans puniendi, et voluntas ista non possit irrita esse in Deo, cujus summa est majestas, et infinita potentia, necessario poenae inflictionem exigit, vel in peccatore ipso, vel in vade illius loco substituto (*ibid.*).

[2] Si plectit peccatorem reddit illi quod debet et quod vitio suo commeritus est (*ibid.*).

life, or the righteous and holy actions whereby He perfectly fulfilled the commands of the law in our stead; that of these two parts might arise the whole and perfect price of our redemption.[1]

Like the other divines of the period he extends the penal suffering of Christ to His whole life.

We presuppose (1) that the satisfying sufferings of Christ must be extended to all those which were laid upon Christ, not only on the Cross, but in the garden, nay throughout His whole life.[2]

But this penal suffering is not complete in itself; still less can any single act, whether of obedience or of suffering, be regarded as in itself constituting full merit or satisfaction.

Whence no one action or suffering can be said to be fully meritorious or satisfying, because the concurrence of perfect obedience is required thereto; hence, though various stages and acts can be observed in Christ's obedience, which He began with His very birth, continued in His whole life, and consummated in His death, it is yet one, so far as concerns the accomplishment of the work of salvation and the verdict of justification springing therefrom.[3]

The position here defended is almost exactly that which we have seen in Gerhard, in its emphasis upon the active obedience as inseparable from the passive obedience at

[1] Sed communis et in ecclesiis nostris recepta sententia est, Satisfactionem Christi, quae ad justitiam coram Deo nobis imputatur, complecti, non modo passiones Christi, quas sive in morte sive in vita pertulit; sed et totius vitae obedientiam, seu justas et sanctas actiones, quibus legis mandata perfecte loco nostro implevit; ut ex his duabus partibus integrum et perfectum redemptionis nostrae pretium exurgat (ii. loc. xiv. Q. 13).

[2] Supponimus (1) Passiones Christi satisfactorias extendendas esse ad eas omnes, quae Christo impositae fuerunt, non modo in Cruce, sed et in horto, imo per totam vitam (*ibid.*).

[3] Unde una sola actio vel passio non potest dici plene meritoria vel satisfactoria, quia ad eam requiritur concursus perfectae obedientiae: Hinc licet varii gradus et actus possint observari in obedientia Christi, quam cum ipsa nativitate inchoavit, tota vita continuavit, et in morte consummavit; unica tamen est quoad ἀποτέλεσμα operis salutis, et quoad δικαίωμα inde efflorescens (*ibid.*).

any point. Turretin does not, like Quenstedt, make the distinction between satisfaction and merit so great as to assign separate meritorious value to certain parts of the work of Christ. It is noticeable, too, that he follows Gerhard in assigning importance to the active obedience not only as the source of the imputation of Christ's righteousness, but also as necessary to the accomplishment of the work of salvation proper.

Yet he is quite aware of the distinction in idea between satisfaction and merit, between the functions of the two obediences.

> We assume, thirdly, that that obedience of Christ has a twofold force, satisfying and meritorious, the former by which we are freed from the punishments which we incur through sin, the latter by which through the loss of sin a right to life and to eternal salvation is acquired for us. For as sin brought upon us two evils, loss of life, and liability to death; so redemption should have brought to us the two opposite goods, liberation from death, and the right to life, an exit from hell, and an entrance into heaven.[1]

But even while he emphasizes this distinction, and points out, very rightly, the great difference between the negative remission of sin and the positive "right to life," he is careful to guard against unscriptural division of the obedience of Christ into parts.

> But though those two benefits, flowing from the obedience of Christ, are joined in the covenant of grace by an indissoluble bond, so that no man can obtain remission of sins who does not gain the right to life, they are not on that account to be confounded, as though they were one and the same, but to be distinguished; because it is one thing to free from death,

---

[1] Tertio supponimus istam obedientiam Christi duplicem vim habere, satisfactoriam et meritoriam, illam qua liberemur a poenis, in quas per peccatum incurrimus, istam qua acquiratur nobis jus ad vitam et salutem aeternam per peccatum amissum. Ut enim peccatum duo mala in nos accersivit, vitae jacturam et mortis reatum; ita redemptio dua bona opposita debuit afferre, liberationem a morte, et jus ad vitam, exitum ex inferno, et introitum in caelum (*ibid.*).

another to introduce to life, one thing to lead out from hell, another to bring into heaven, one thing to free from penalty, another to bestow a reward.[1]

But though we hold that these two benefits must be distinguished; yet we do not think that it should be anxiously enquired by what acts He made satisfaction, or won merit, as some do who ascribe satisfaction to His sufferings, but merit to His actions alone, so that He freed us from death through the former, but acquired for us the right to life through the latter; for Scripture seems nowhere to distinguish the obedience of Christ into parts, but sets it forth as one, whereby Christ presented all those things which the law could demand from us.[2]

The distinction is thus rather a matter of theological analysis than of any division in the functions of Christ. The passive obedience has itself an active character, and the active obedience a passive character.

Since the passive obedience proceeded from supreme love for us, which is the complement of the law, it cannot be denied merit. . . . He won merit, therefore, in making satisfaction, and in winning merit He made satisfaction.[3]

The same thought is given in a more analytical form:

Though each obedience of Christ, of life and of death, was perfect in its own kind, yet neither alone could suffice for satisfaction, which required both the observance of commands, and

---

[1] Licet vero duo ista beneficia ex Christi obedientia manantia, indivulso nexu sint copulata in foedere gratiae, ut nemo remissionem peccatorum possit obtinere, qui jus ad vitam non consequatur; non propterea confundenda sunt, quasi unum et idem essent; sed distinguenda; quia aliud est a morte liberare, aliud in vitam introducere, aliud ex inferis educere, aliud in caelum evehere, liberare a poena, et praemium donare (*ibid.*).

[2] Licet vero duo ista beneficia distinguenda esse censeamus; non putamus tamen anxie quaerendum quibus actibus satisfecerit, vel meritus sit, ut faciant nonnulli, qui satisfactionem passionibus, meritum vero solis actionibus tribuunt, ut per illas nos liberavit a morte, per istas vero nobis acquisiverit jus ad vitam; quia Scriptura nusquam obedientiam Christi ita videtur distinguere in partes, sed illam tanquam unicam proponit, qua Christus omnia illa praestiterit, quae a nobis potuit lex requirere (*ibid.*).

[3] Cum obedientia passiva processerit ex summa in nos charitate, quae est legis complementum, non potest meritum illi denegari. . . . Meruit ergo satisfaciendo, et merendo satisfecit (*ibid.*).

the full endurance of punishments, whereby liberation from death and right to life are acquired for us.[1]

In this very cautious defence of the doctrine of the active and passive obedience we see again, as in Quenstedt, the breakdown of the rigorous Penal theory. The forensic Protestant view of justification had originally depended for its force upon the exact equation of the vicarious sufferings of Christ with the penalty of human sin. This left out of account His willing obedience, and human sanctification. It was only natural to connect the two, but the process strained the forensic language of orthodoxy to the uttermost. The result was a gradual softening of the rigid outlines of the Penal theory. And with the coming of a more human theology the strict doctrine of the *obedientia activa,* as a separate part of the scheme, became unnecessary, and has gradually fallen out of sight. In later Calvinism little is heard of it.

Before leaving Turretin we may notice that his writings show no sign of any relaxing of the rigid doctrine of predestination, characteristic of Calvinism. He holds quite definitely to unconditional election, and the doctrine of perseverance, and argues strongly and at length against any attempt to hold the universal efficacy of the Atonement:

From the fact of the remission which they obtain who believe and repent, it follows indeed unquestionably that Christ died for them, and it would also follow, if the rest of mankind believed and repented, that Christ had died for them too, but he is wrong who would thence infer that Christ died for all, if they believe, for he would be arguing faultily from the conditioned to the absolute.[2]

---

[1] Licet obedientia utraque Christi, tam vitae quam mortis, fuerit perfecta in suo genere, neutra tamen sufficere potuit sola ad satisfactionem, quae requirebat et observationem mandatorum, et poenarum perpessionem, qua liberatio a morte et jus ad vitam nobis acquireretur (*ibid.*).

[2] Ex remissione vero, quam obtinent qui credunt et resipiscunt, sequitur quidem certo Christum pro illis mortuum esse, et sequeretur etiam Christum mortuum fuisse pro caeteris, si crederent et resipiscerent, sed perperam quis inde colligeret Christum mortuum esse pro omnibus si credant, quia argumentum duceret vitiose a conditionato ad absolutum (ii. loc. xiv. Q. 14).

Thus the Lutheran position that Christ won redemption for all, but that this redemption remains potential unless it is accepted by faith, is uncompromisingly rejected. Only if all were elect, Turretin holds, would it be possible to say that Christ died for all.

This logical, if unscriptural, corollary of the stern doctrine of predestination has remained characteristic of strict Calvinism, wherever its influence has extended. It became a characteristic tenet of the earlier English Protestantism, even within the Church of England, and found there some of its most thorough-going exponents.[1] Yet within the Calvinistic fold itself other and powerful forces were coming into play, even before the time of Turretin. The strong solvent criticism of Socinianism had influenced many thinkers, and new lines of defence were already being attempted. The Arminian school, though condemned by the Protestant churches as heretical, soon left its mark upon their theology, especially through the Rectoral theory of Grotius, which, however unconsciously, has been adopted in greater or less degree by the majority of the more recent Calvinistic writers.

[1] For the Calvinism of Owen and Edwards, see next chapter, pp. 272 ff.

CHAPTER XI

THE ENGLISH REFORMATION

THE Reformation in England had a peculiar character of its own. Drastic as was the political breach with Rome caused by the action of Henry VIII., neither Henry himself nor the Church of England was prepared for any very extreme doctrinal change. It is true that doctrinal change was inevitably involved, as on the Continent, by the practical issues themselves, the rejection of Papal authority and of the abuses of mediaeval sacramentalism. But the whole spirit of Church and Nation alike was conservative. There was no desire whatever for a new teaching. Henry was proud to the end of his days of his defence of orthodoxy against Luther. Cranmer's appeal, like that of Jewel [1] a few years later, was to primitive Catholicity rather than to the glad conviction of justification by faith which had dominated Luther's thought. And it is significant that while he was in close touch with Melanchthon, whose influence may be clearly traced in the English formularies, he was bound by a close tie, through his wife, to Osiander, the most Catholic of the Continental Reformers.

It is thus natural that there should not have been any very rapid development in England of the full Penal theory. Cranmer's own language is far less definite than that of Luther or Calvin, even while it rests upon

[1] Bishop of Salisbury, 1560, *Apologia Ecclesiae Anglicanae* (1562) and *Defence of the Apology, against Hardinge* (1566).

the same general presupposition that the satisfaction of justice must involve the satisfaction of God's avenging wrath against sin.

> And that all men may the better understand this sacrifice of Christ, which He made for the great benefit of all men, it is necessary to know the distinction and diversity of sacrifices.
>
> One kind of sacrifice there is, which is called a propitiatory or merciful sacrifice, that is to say, such a sacrifice as pacifieth God's wrath and indignation, and obtaineth mercy and forgiveness for all our sins, and is the ransom for the redemption from everlasting damnation.
>
> And although in the old testament there were certain sacrifices called by that name, yet in very deed there is but one such sacrifice, whereby our sins be pardoned, and God's mercy and favour obtained, which is the death of the Son of God our Lord Jesus Christ: nor never was any other sacrifice propitiatory at any time, nor never shall be.
>
> This is the honour and glory of this our High Priest, wherein He admitteth neither partner nor successor. For by His own oblation He satisfied His Father for all men's sins, and reconciled mankind unto His grace and favour.
>
> Another kind of sacrifice there is which doth not reconcile us to God, but is made of them that be reconciled by Christ, to testify our duties unto God, and to show ourselves thankful unto Him. And therefore they be called sacrifices of laud, praise, and thanksgiving.
>
> The first kind of sacrifice Christ offered to God for us; the second kind we ourselves offer to God by Christ.[1]

> He was so perfect a priest, that by one oblation He purged an infinite heap of sins, leaving an easy and a ready remedy for all sinners, that His one sacrifice should suffice for many years unto all men that would not show themselves unworthy. . . . And as He, dying once, was offered for all, so as much as pertained to Him He took all men's sins unto Himself.[2]

If the seed of the Penal theory is here, it has certainly not attained to any full development. The general conception of Atonement implied is not far from that of Aquinas. Here also it rests upon one sacrifice, infinite in satisfying worth, offered for infinite sin. The emphasis upon the sacrificial metaphor is quite in accord with the language of the later Roman writers

[1] *On the Lord's Supper* (Parker Soc. ed. p. 346). [2] *Ibid.*

and of the Council of Trent, though Cranmer is concerned to separate completely the sacrifice of praise and thanksgiving, offered in the Eucharist, from the propitiatory sacrifice, offered upon the Cross. This constituted, and has continued in the theology of the Church of England to constitute, a very definite difference from Rome, and this difference is brought out in the reply made to Cranmer by Gardiner, Bishop of Winchester.

> The daily offering is propitiatory also, but not in that degree of propitiation, as for redemption, regeneration, or remission of deadly sin, which was once purchased, and by force thereof is in the sacraments ministered; but for the increase of God's favour, the mitigation of God's displeasure, provoked by our infirmities, the subduing of temptations, and the perfection of virtue in us. All good works, good thoughts, and good meditations may be called sacrifices, and the same be called sacrifices propitiatory also, for so much as in their degree God accepteth and taketh them through the effect and strength of the very sacrifice of Christ's death, which is the reconciliation between God and man, ministered and dispensed particularly as God hath appointed, in such measure as He knoweth.[1]

All this Cranmer dismisses as "papistical inventions."

> All is nothing else but to defend your propitiatory sacrifice of the priests in their masses, whereby they may remit sin, and redeem souls out of purgatory.[2]

Yet Cranmer's own position is very far from the Lutheran and Calvinistic denial of all value to human good works. He does not press to any impossible lengths his belief in the sole sufficiency of the

> . . . full, perfect, and sufficient, sacrifice, oblation, and satisfaction for the sins of the whole world.[3]

His position does not in the least resemble the bare theory of substitution preached by Luther, nor has the forensic sense of justification, which was accepted by the English Reformers, distorted his outlook. It is

[1] Quoted by Cranmer (*ib.* p. 360). [2] *Ib.* p. 361.

[3] From the Consecration Prayer of the First Prayer Book (1549), retained in the subsequent Prayer Books.

only to deny the propitiatory value of good works that he is concerned, not their possibility. In substance, if not in form, he adheres to the doctrine of "infused righteousness."

For the sacrifice made upon the Cross doth both give us life, and also increase and continue the same; and the priest's oblation doth neither of both. For our redemption and eternal salvation standeth not only in giving us life, but in continuing the same for ever.[1]

Thus the importance of the manward aspect of Atonement finds recognition at the very outset in English theology, though it was soon to be overshadowed by the incoming of the dominant influence of Calvinism.

On the subject of justification the considered opinion of the English Reformers is given in the Homily of Salvation, which was drawn up by Cranmer and to which formal sanction was given in the Forty-Two Articles of 1552.

Justification by only faith in Jesus Christ, in that sense as it is declared in the Homily of Justification, is a most certain and wholesome doctrine for Christian men.[2]

The Homily gives full expression to the moderate position taken up by Cranmer and his friends.

This justification or righteousness, which we so receive of God's mercy and Christ's merits, embraced by faith, is taken, allowed, and accepted for our perfect and full justification. . . . God sent His Son into the world to fulfil the law for us, and by shedding of His most precious Blood, to make a sacrifice and satisfaction, or (as it may be called) amends to His Father for our sins, to assuage His wrath and indignation conceived against us for the same. . . . And they, which in act or deed, do sin after baptism, when they turn again to God unfeignedly, they are likewise washed by this sacrifice from their sins, in such sort that there remaineth not any spot of sin that shall be imputed to their damnation. This is that justification of righteousness, which St. Paul speaketh of, when he saith, No man is justified by the works of the law, but freely, by faith in Jesus Christ. . . .

---

[1] *Op. cit.* p. 364.

[2] Article XI.; cf. Article XI. of the XXXIX Articles.

The Apostle toucheth specially three things which must go together in our justification. Upon God's part, His great mercy and grace: upon Christ's part, justice, that is, the satisfaction of God's justice: . . . upon our part, true and lively faith in the merits of Jesus Christ, which yet is not ours, but God's working in us. . . . And yet that faith doth not shut out repentance, hope, love, dread, and the fear of God, to be joined with faith, in every man that is justified, but it shutteth them out from the office of justifying . . . it excludeth them, so that we may not do them to this intent, to be made just by doing of them.[1]

The true understanding of the doctrine, we be justified freely by faith without works, or that we be justified by faith in Christ only, is not, that this our own act to believe in Christ, or this our faith in Christ, which is within us, doth justify us, and deserve our justification unto us (for that were to count ourselves to be justified by some act or virtue which is within ourselves); but the true understanding and meaning thereof is, that although we hear God's word and believe it; although we have faith, hope, charity, repentance, dread and fear of God within us, and do never so many good works thereunto; yet we must renounce the merit of all said virtues, of faith, hope, charity, and all other virtues and good deeds, which we either have done, or shall do, or can do, as things that be far too weak and insufficient and imperfect, to deserve remission of our sins and our justification; and therefore we must trust only in God's mercy, and that sacrifice which our High Priest and Saviour Jesus Christ, the Son of God, once offered for us upon the cross, to obtain thereby God's grace and remission, as well of our original sin in baptism, as of all actual sin committed by us after our baptism, if we truly repent and turn unfeignedly to Him again.[2]

The Homily thus affirms very definitely the same religious self-estimate which is characteristic of the Continental Reformers. Our own works can never in themselves deserve anything at the hands of God. As in Luther and Calvin everything is assigned to God's mercy and nothing to man. But there is no sign of the hard development of thought which dwelt upon God's wrath almost to the exclusion of His love. Nor is faith utterly separated from works, they are rather its necessary fruit and complement.

[1] *Homily of Salvation*, Part I. [2] *Ib.* Part II.

> Although good works cannot deserve to make us righteous before God, yet do they so cleave unto faith, that neither can faith be found without them, nor good works be anywhere without faith.[1]

If the Calvinistic attitude to works were to be found anywhere among the writers of the reign of Edward VI. it would be in Bishop Hooper, the first of the Puritans, as he has been called. Hooper had been in touch with Calvinism on the Continent, before coming to England, and his language contains many echoes of Calvinistic orthodoxy.

> I believe also that while He was upon the said Cross, dying and giving up His spirit unto God His Father, He descended into hell, that is to say, He did verily taste and feel the great distress and heaviness of death, and likewise the pains and torments of hell, that is to say, the great wrath and severe judgment of God upon Him.[2]
>
> I believe that all this was done, not for Himself, which never committed sin, in whose mouth was never found deceit nor lie; but for the love of us poor and miserable sinners, whose place He occupied upon the Cross, as a pledge, or one that represented the person of all sinners that ever were, be now, or shall be unto the world's end. And because they, through their sins, have deserved to feel and taste of the extreme pains of death, to be forsaken of God and of all creatures, to feel the wrath and severe judgement of God upon them; Christ, which was their pledge, satisfying for them upon the Cross, hath felt and endured all the same, and that altogether to make us free, to deliver us from all these pains, from the wrath and judgement of God, from condemnation and eternal death.[3]

Here the Penal theory is coming to its own, yet Hooper can still go on to say:

> I believe also that good works are not superfluous, vain, and unprofitable, but necessary to salvation. I call good works, not those which are done after the fantasy or commandment of men, but only those that God by His word hath commanded: the which ought to be done, not to deserve or merit anything thereby at God's hand, or by the same to escape eternal condemnation; but only because God hath commanded them.[4]

---

[1] *Edward VI.'s Catechism.* See also *Noel's Catechism.*

[2] *A Brief and Clear Confession of the Christian Faith* (1550), Art. 24.

[3] *Ib.* Art. 25; cf. Arts. 88-90.

[4] *Ib.* Art. 91.

In such language as this the highest spirit of mediaeval piety survives, freed from the faulty development of the doctrine of merits, yet too human, and too conscious of God's goodness and of the real value of the humble response of the human heart, to hold utterly worthless in the eyes of God that which is wrought in His Spirit and informed by His love.

Such is the background of thought against which the Thirty-Nine Articles of the Church of England must be viewed.[1] While these depend very largely, both in form and in substance, upon the Augsburg Confession and the Confession of Würtemberg,[2] they adopt a very guarded attitude with regard to the more specifically Lutheran doctrines, while the accusation of Calvinism, commonly levelled against them, has no foundation at all.

The well-known definition of original sin, while accepting Luther's view of it as a corruption, and not merely the loss of certain special gifts, yet adopts a mediating position. Complete depravity is not asserted.

> Original sin . . . is the fault and corruption of the nature of every man, that naturally is engendered of the offspring of Adam; whereby man is very far gone from original righteousness, and is of his own nature inclined to evil, so that the flesh lusteth always contrary to the spirit; and therefore, in every person born into this world, it deserveth God's wrath and damnation. And this infection of nature doth remain, yea in them that are regenerated.[3]

---

[1] Issued 1563; authorized by Parliament 1571. The Latin and English versions are of equal authority.

[2] Drawn up by Brenz in 1552 as a conciliatory statement of Protestantism for discussion at the Council of Trent, to accompany Melanchthon's *Confessio Saxonica*, composed for the same purpose in 1551.

[3] Peccatum originis . . . est vitium et depravatio naturae cujuslibet hominis et Adamo naturaliter propagati, qua fit ut ab originali justitia quam longissime distet, ad malum sua natura propendeat, et caro semper adversus spiritum concupiscat. Unde in unoquoque nascentium iram Dei atque damnationem meretur. Manet etiam in renatis haec naturae depravatio (Art. IX.).

In such language a loop-hole, however slight, is left for the assertion of the place of good works in the Christian life, even while their complete dependence upon the grace of God is clearly recognized. The view adopted resembles the synergistic position of Melanchthon.

We have no power to do good works pleasant and acceptable to God, without the grace of God by Christ preventing us, that we may have a good will, and working with us, when we have that good will.[1]

The intimate connexion of good works and faith is re-asserted.

Albeit that Good Works, which are the fruits of Faith, and follow after Justification, cannot put away our sins, and endure the severity of God's Judgement; yet are they pleasing and acceptable to God in Christ, and do spring out necessarily of a true and lively faith; insomuch that by them a lively Faith may be as evidently known as a tree discerned by the fruit.[2]

This recognition of the value of good works is more outspoken than in the two Lutheran confessions. Yet the Thirty-Nine Articles adopt without qualification the Lutheran view of justification.

We are accounted righteous before God, only for the merit of our Lord and Saviour Jesus Christ by faith, and not for our own works or deservings.[3]

---

[1] Absque gratia Dei, quae per Christum est, nos praeveniente ut velimus, et cooperante dum volumus, ad pietatis opera facienda, quae Deo grata sint et accepta, nihil valemus (Art. X.).

[2] Bona opera, quae sunt fructus fidei et justificatos sequuntur, quanquam peccata nostra expiare et divini judicii severitatem ferre non possunt, Deo tamen grata sunt et accepta in Christo, atque ex vera et viva fide necessario profluunt, ut plane ex illis aeque fides viva cognosci possit atque arbor ex fructu judicari (Art. XII.). Cf. Art. VII. of the Würtemberg Confession.

[3] Tantum propter meritum Domini ac Servatoris nostri Jesu Christi per fidem, non opera et merita nostra, justi reputamur (Art. XI.). The Article goes on to refer to the "Homily of Justification," *i.e.* the Homily of Salvation, quoted above.

As to the actual objective work of Atonement upon which this justifying faith rests, the Augsburg Confession is quoted verbatim.

> Who truly suffered, was crucified, dead, and buried, to reconcile His Father to us, and to be a sacrifice, not only for original guilt, but also for all actual sins of men.[1]

This is little more than a hint of the Penal theory, yet it is noteworthy that the Lutheran inversion of St. Paul's language is retained, stress being thrown thereby upon the external and Godward character of Atonement. But there is no suggestion of the development of this thought, along the line suggested by Melanchthon, as implying a change in God's attitude from wrath to love.

Upon the question of the extent of the Atonement the Lutheran view is adopted, as against Calvin. Predestination is definitely asserted, but only in the form of predestination to life, or election. No attempt is made to solve the logical problem involved by this assertion, but the doctrine of reprobation is rejected and the universal character of the Divine promise maintained.

> Furthermore we must receive God's promises in such wise, as they be generally set forth to us in Holy Scripture.[2]

No formal doctrine of conditional election, however, is framed. Like Luther himself, the English divines prepared to leave the subject involved in mystery.

This very moderate position continued to be characteristic of Anglican theology, except where this came

[1] Qui vere passus est, crucifixus, mortuus et sepultus, ut Patrem nobis reconciliaret, essetque hostia non tantum pro culpa originis, verum etiam pro omnibus actualibus hominum peccatis (Art. II.). Cf. *Conf. Aug.* iii.

[2] Deinde promissiones divinas sic amplecti oportet, ut nobis in sacris litteris generaliter propositae sunt (Art. XVII.). By "generally" the meaning "universally" is certainly intended. Cf. the similar usage in the Prayer Book Catechism (1604) where the Sacraments are said to be "generally necessary to salvation."

under direct Calvinistic influence. A typical statement may be quoted from Hooker.[1]

> Satisfaction is a work which justice requireth to be done for contentment of persons injuried: neither is it in the eye of justice a sufficient satisfaction, unless it fully equal the injury for which we satisfy. Seeing then that sin against God eternal and infinite must needs be an infinite wrong; justice in regard thereof doth necessarily exact an infinite recompense, or else inflict upon the offender infinite punishment. Now because God was thus to be satisfied, and man not able to make satisfaction in such sort, His unspeakable love and inclination to save mankind from eternal death ordained in our behalf a Mediator, to do that which had been for any other impossible. Wherefore all sin is remitted in the only faith of Christ's passion, and no man without belief thereof justified. Faith alone maketh Christ's satisfaction ours; howbeit that faith alone which after sin maketh us by conversion His.[2]

Hooker openly rests his account upon the ancient fathers, and the above passage might almost be a quotation from Aquinas, in its emphasis upon the quantitative equivalence of the satisfaction necessary, upon the infinite demerit of sin, upon the alternative of an infinite recompense or an infinite punishment, upon God's love, whereby a way of redemption was found. Only in the latter sentences does the Reformation view of justification by faith make its influence felt, and Hooker goes on to expound this in a manner but little dissimilar to the better statements of the Roman divines, attributing satisfactory force, though only in a secondary sense, to human "repentance and the works thereof," which

> . . . draw that pity of God towards us, wherein He is for Christ's sake contented upon our submission to pardon our rebellion against Him; and when that little which His law appointeth is faithfully executed, it pleaseth Him in tender compassion and mercy to require no more.[3]
>
> It is therefore true, that our Lord Jesus Christ by one most precious and propitiatory sacrifice, which was His body, a gift

---

[1] 1554–1600. [2] *Ecclesiastical Polity*, vi. 5. 2. [3] vi. 5. 2.

of infinite worth, offered for the sins of the whole world, hath thereby once reconciled us to God, purchased His general free pardon, and turned away Divine indignation from mankind. But we are not from that cause to think any office of penitence either needless or fruitless on our own behalf, for then would not God require any such duties at our hands. Christ doth remain everlastingly a gracious intercessor, even for every particular penitent. Let this assure us, that God, how highly soever displeased and incensed with our sins, is notwithstanding for His sake by our tears pacified, taking that for satisfaction which is due [done ?] by us, because Christ hath by His satisfaction made it acceptable.[1]

For with these duties by us performed, and presented unto God in heaven by Jesus Christ, whose blood is a continual sacrifice of propitiation for us, we content, please, and satisfy God.[2]

Nevertheless Hooker decisively adopts the Protestant conception of justification, and maintains the principle of the imputation rather than the infusion of righteousness.

Being justified, all our iniquities are covered; God beholdeth us in the righteousness which is imputed, and not in the sins which we have committed.[3]

Justification washeth away sin; sin removed, we are clothed with the righteousness which is of God; the righteousness of God maketh us most holy.[4]

Thus sanctification follows justification, but is in no way to be confused with it. In adopting this view Hooker is a true Protestant, and he strongly opposes the Roman doctrine of merits and its practical abuses.[5] But in his general conception of Atonement he shows the survival in English theology of traditional language and thought, but little infected by the ideas of Calvinism.

The opinion represented by Hooker has never lacked exponents in the Church of England. As in the Church of Rome the Satisfaction theory has remained, for

[1] *Ecclesiastical Polity*, vi. 5. 3.

[2] vi. 5. 4.

[3] *Sermon* vi. 23. In the *Discourse on Justification* he argues definitely against the Roman doctrine.

[4] *Ib.* 27.

[5] E.g. *Sermon* vi. 21.

writers of this school, unchanged in general outline, but with a tendency to emphasize the Scotist view of the Incarnation, with its associated conception of sacrifice, together with the Thomist view of the worth of the satisfaction offered by Christ. Frequently this position is combined in greater or less degree with suggestions drawn from other schools of thought. The Church of England has been a very clearing-house for theories of Atonement. Almost every current view has received free expression among her divines, from the Moral theory to the extremest Calvinism, and this free play of ideas has tended to affect the language even of those who hold to the conservative tradition.

Waterland [1] is a notable example of this conservative type of Anglican, taking up a very similar position to Hooker. He dwells in a very Scotist manner upon the sacrificial aspect of Atonement.

> I begin with our Lord's sacrifice, that great sacrifice which was from all eternity forelaid in the high counsels of Heaven; which was intimated to mankind as soon as there was need for it. . . . Divine wisdom appointed it and called for it: from whence we may certainly infer that reasons of justice, or (which comes to the same) the unerring rules of Divine government, required it. God would not, or in reason could not, be appeased without it: but with it He might, and He has declared that He would.[2]

Here there is just a hint of penal language, and Waterland elsewhere uses the phraseology of the doctrine of the active and passive obedience.

> In truth of notion and precise accuracy of expression, it was His obedience, active and passive, which was properly the sacrifice, the acceptable offering to God.[3]

This language also appears in his classical discussion of the nature of justification. Here he explicitly defends the forensic usage of the term.

[1] 1643–1740.
[2] *Sermon* xxxi.: *Christ's Sacrifice of Himself Explained.*
[3] *Ibid.*

The word justification in this view, and in the active sense, will signify God's pronouncing a person just, and His accepting Him as such; while in the passive sense, it will signify man's being so declared, and thereupon accepted into new privileges, and his enjoying the benefits thereof.[1]

Thus he includes under justification both remission of sins and the right to life eternal, founded upon promise, and denies that it includes sanctification, though he points out the close connexion between the two. As to the causes of justification

. . . God the Father is here to be considered as principal . . .; the Divine philanthropy is of prime consideration in the whole thing. In the next place God the Son is here to be considered as the procuring and meritorious cause of man's justification, both by His active and passive obedience. . . . In the third place, God the Holy Ghost is here to be considered as the immediate, efficient cause.[2]

As the instruments of justification he assigns baptism and faith. Obedience, or good works, he calls a condition or qualification, but not an instrument. Faith is both a condition and an instrument. Waterland lays considerable stress upon these conditions of grace, strongly deprecating the tendency of the Reformed Church to under-estimate good works, even while he agrees that they have no part in the strict work of justification.

How precisely this work of justification was wrought in its Godward aspect, Waterland prefers not to define, save that he insists upon Christ's sacrifice as an offering to God as Lawgiver.

God the Father, without dispute, was Lawgiver in chief; and to Him our blessed Lord paid the price of our redemption, the sacrifice of Himself. If it be asked what need there was of any sacrifice to a person so benign, and so mercifully disposed to pardon all repenting sinners; I say, if this were asked, it might be sufficient to reply that we know the fact: God did require a sacrifice, and such a sacrifice; and He knows what

---

[1] *A Summary View of the Doctrine of Justification*, i. [2] *Ib.* iv.

need there was for it. However, without pretending to fathom the Divine counsels, or to understand all the reasons of State by which an all-wise Governor proceeds, we may presume to observe that two special articles, the glory of God and the felicity of man, have been admirably served by this mysterious dispensation. It is for the glory of God that He is seen not to connive at offences, nor to be too indulgent towards sin, while He requires a valuable satisfaction for offences committed. . . . On the other hand, man's eternal felicity appears to be best secured by the same means, because hereby provision is made to keep him the more humble and modest to all eternity.[1]

In this passage Waterland shows the influence of Grotius and the Arminians.[2] More important is his refusal to dogmatize upon so mysterious a subject, an attitude which has been very common in Anglican theology, but which, if consistently maintained, really involves the surrender of all hope of any intelligent apprehension of the truths of the faith.

Of this attitude of intellectual humility Bishop Butler has been the chief exponent. His positive statements are few and cautious.

He interposed in such a manner, as was necessary and effectual to prevent that execution of justice upon sinners, which God had appointed should otherwise have been executed upon them.[3]

Christ offered Himself a propitiatory sacrifice and made atonement for the sins of the world. . . . And this sacrifice was in the highest degree, and with the most extensive influence, of that efficacy for obtaining pardon of sin, which the heathens may be supposed to have thought their sacrifices to have been, and which the Jewish sacrifices really were in some degree and with regard to some persons.[4]

But Butler's heart is in his warnings against presumptuous dogmatizing.

How, and in what particular way, it had this efficacy, there are not wanting persons who have endeavoured to explain; but I do not find that the Scripture has explained it. . . . And if

---

[1] *Sermon* xxxi. [2] See below, pp. 290 ff.

[3] *The Analogy of Religion Natural and Revealed to the Constitution and Course of Nature* (1736), Pt. ii. 5. 5. [4] ii. 5. 6.

the Scripture has, as surely it has, left somewhat in it unrevealed, all conjectures about it must be, if not evidently absurd, yet at least uncertain. Nor has any one reason to complain for want of further information, unless he can show his claim to it.

Some have endeavoured to explain the efficacy of what Christ has done and suffered for us, beyond what the Scripture has authorised; others, probably because they could not explain it, have been for taking it away, and confining His office, as Redeemer of the world, to His instruction, example, and government of the church: whereas the doctrine of the gospel appears to be, not only that He taught the efficacy of repentance, but rendered it of the efficacy which it is, by what He did and suffered for us: that He obtained for us the benefit of having our repentance accepted unto eternal life: not only that He revealed to sinners that they were in a capacity of salvation, and how they might obtain it; but, moreover, that He put them into this capacity of salvation by what He did and suffered for them.[1]

There survives here an echo of the doctrine of the active and passive obedience, but, for the rest, Butler is content to assert the objective efficacy of Christ's death, as against Deistic rationalists, without enquiry into its method.[2]

In modern times the school of Hooker and Waterland has received a considerable impetus, especially through the stress laid upon traditional methods of thought by the leaders of the Oxford Movement. Nor has recent Roman theology been without its influence. A single example must here suffice, from Bishop Forbes, whose treatment of the idea of sacrifice is not unlike that of the later Roman theologians quoted in an earlier chapter.

[1] *Ibid.*

[2] Scott Lidgett (*op. cit.* pp. 488 ff.) has an interesting note, "On the recent Tendency to regard the Nature of the Atonement as Incomprehensible." As modern exponents of Butler's standpoint he cites Coleridge, Magee, Church, Balfour, and especially Dr. Horton, arguing very cogently that, even if a full theory is unattainable, the task of theological construction must yet be attempted. "It is not an inexplicable fact, but a fact which conveys truth, that can affect the spiritual life of men." "Spiritual power can only come from inherent reason, and where reason is inherent there must be no despair of discovering and setting it forth."

The idea of sacrifice is a necessary result of the relation between the Creator and His creature. The creature owes everything to his Maker, and therefore the self-devotion of his whole being is that Maker's due. This is the primary idea of sacrifice. It is the incommunicable privilege of God alone, and therefore is the highest form of worship. Yet this sacrifice is imperfect, if only because the creature hath nothing purely his own wherewith to propitiate his God. But beyond this there is a new idea introduced when we come to deal with sin. . . . A debt has been incurred which must be paid to the Honour of God; a stain has been imprinted which must be cleansed; an offence has been given that must be removed; a guilt incurred which must be atoned. Therefore into man's creaturely relations with His Maker there comes in the element of reparation.

Man's sacrifice is, therefore, now doubly imperfect, and therefore a full and perfect sacrifice, oblation, and satisfaction can only be found in one who is more than mere man. The life and death of one not only innocent, but the fountain and source of innocency, is required to the realisation of this idea. Such a condition is only to be found in the God-man, and, therefore, from the beginning, He was the Lamb slain, in purpose, from the foundation of the world. . . . His very human acts, because done by a Divine Person, savour of the attributes of Divinity, and thus there is no limit to the efficacy of His eternal sacrifice, which being thus superabundant and fulfilling all the ends of such sacrifice, is in itself: (1) the highest possible worship, praise, and adoration to God the Holy Trinity; (2) the only, the fullest, and most complete propitiation for sin; (3) the most grateful and acceptable *Eucharistia* or thank-offering which humanity in its head and members can render to its God; and (4) lastly, the most efficacious impetration of all blessings, mercies, and graces which humanity can require.[1]

This is not unlike the position of Hooker and Waterland, with whom, however, Bishop Forbes breaks decisively when he comes to speak of justification. On this he frankly adopts the Roman view, rejecting as "grave error" Luther's insistence on the forensic interpretation and on the worthlessness of good works. Of justification he says:

---

[1] *An Explanation of the Thirty-Nine Articles* (1867), Art. II. This work, as the "Postscript" shows, was written expressly against "the Calvinistic school in the Church."

> Actively, it is a certain admirable and supernatural act whereby God makes the unjust just. Passively it is a certain supernatural change by which a man from being unjust becomes just.[1]

And further

> He not only merited our justification,—whereby we are restored to the grace of God, our sins are remitted, our spirits renewed, and our adoption and heirship bestowed upon us—but He merited (1) that the sacraments should have a power of justifying, and that the good works which are necessary to the justification of adults should be sufficient for the purpose; and (2) that adults should have grace sufficient for such work.[2]

That the whole exposition is a reversion to the Roman point of view is unquestionable. It is upon the language of the Counter-Reformation, and not upon that of the Protestant Reformers that it depends. Yet it is possible to see in such doctrinal statements the climax of a tradition which goes back to the earliest days of the English Reformation, and which has always resisted the encroachments of a logical but unloving Calvinism.

But despite the presence of this tradition, to which the Thirty-nine Articles themselves bore testimony, Calvinism grew apace in the Church of England. During the reign of Elizabeth it became characteristic of the Puritan movement, and also dominated the thought of some of its leading opponents. Even Archbishop Whitgift, the merciless antagonist of Cartwright, came under its influence, and endeavoured, by issuing the Lambeth Articles of 1595, to supply the Calvinistic colouring which the Thirty-nine Articles lacked. Even though Dr. Whitaker's original draft was somewhat modified, these remain a very uncompromising statement of unconditional election and particular redemption:

> 1. God has from eternity predestined some unto life and rejected some unto death.

---

[1] On Art. XI. The whole of the section should be studied, and compared with the statements of the Council of Trent.

[2] *Ibid.*

2. The moving cause of predestination to life is not prevision of faith or of perseverance, or of good works, or of anything in the persons predestined, but only the will of God who is well pleased.

3. The number of the predestined is definite and fixed, and can be neither increased nor diminished.

4. Those who are not predestined to salvation will necessarily be condemned for their sins.

5. True, lively, and justifying faith, and the spirit of God who justifies, are not extinguished, do not fail, do not vanish, in the elect, either finally or totally.

. . . .

8. No man can come to Christ except it be given to him and except the Father draw him. And all are not drawn by the Father that they should come to the Son.

9. It is not placed in any man's will or power to be saved.[1]

The Lambeth Articles never had any definite authority, and though the Puritans urged at Hampton Court that they should be added to the Thirty-nine Articles, they failed to carry their point. From this time, and throughout the seventeenth century, the Church of England came more and more under Arminian influence. Calvinism and Puritanism tended to fall into opposition, associated with the desire for a Presbyterian system of Church government. And thus it is natural to find that the Puritan divines are the chief

[1] 1. Deus, ab aeterno, praedestinavit quosdam ad vitam, quosdam reprobavit ad mortem.

2. Causa movens praedestinationis ad vitam, non est praevisio fidei aut perseverantiae, aut bonorum operum aut ullius rei quae insit in personis praedestinatis, sed sola voluntas beneplaciti Dei.

3. Praedestinatorum definitus et certus est numerus, qui nec augeri nec minui potest.

4. Qui non sunt praedestinati ad salutem necessario propter peccata sua damnabuntur.

5. Vera, viva, et justificans Fides, et Spiritus Dei justificantis non extinguitur, non excidit, non evanescit, in electis, aut finaliter aut totaliter.

. . . .

8. Nemo potest venire ad Christum nisi datum ei fuerit, et nisi Pater eum traxerit. Et omnes homines non trahuntur a Patre, ut veniant ad Filium.

9. Non est positum in arbitrio aut potestate uniuscujusque hominis salvari.

exponents of the Penal theory, and that this was adopted, though not in its extremest form, in the Westminster Confession, the monument of Presbyterian supremacy in England from 1643 to 1648, and also in the Larger and Shorter Catechisms.

Here Calvin's view of the utter corruption of man is fully maintained.

> The sinfulness of that estate whereinto men fell, consisted in the guilt of Adam's first sin, the want of that righteousness wherein he was created, and the corruption of his nature, whereby he is utterly indisposed, disabled, and made opposite unto all that is spiritually good, and wholly inclined unto all evil, and that continually.[1]

The satisfaction made by Christ is described in moderate language, which suggests the doctrine of active and passive obedience.

> The Lord Jesus, by His perfect obedience and sacrifice of Himself, which He through the eternal Spirit once offered unto God, hath fully satisfied the justice of His Father and purchased, not only reconciliation, but an everlasting inheritance in the kingdom of heaven for all those whom the Father hath given unto Him.[2]

As to the method by which the Atonement is made available for man, the forensic theory of imputation is adopted. There is no suggestion of any infusion of righteousness, or that justifying faith must be informed by love. Even faith itself is not to be counted for righteousness, since God accounts man righteous

> . . . not by imputing faith itself, the act of believing, etc., as their righteousness, but by imputing the obedience and satisfaction of Christ.[3]

More fully:

> Although Christ, by His obedience and death, did make a proper, real, and full satisfaction to God's justice in the behalf of them that are justified; yet inasmuch as God accepteth the satisfaction from a surety which He might have demanded of them, and did provide this surety, His only Son, imputing His

---

[1] *Larger Catechism*, Q. 25. [2] *Confession*, c. viii.
[3] *Ib.* c. xi.

righteousness to them, and requiring nothing of them for their justification but faith, which also is His gift, their justification is to them of free grace.[1]

The definition given in the Shorter Catechism states this simply and tersely:

> Justification is an act of God's free grace, wherein He pardoneth all our sins, and accepteth us as righteous in His sight, only for the righteousness of Christ imputed to us and received by faith alone.

On the subject of election the general Calvinistic position is held, but is stated as moderately as possible. The doctrine of predestination is pressed to its logical result, but the doctrine of reprobation, though held, is not named, and it is emphasized as little as possible.

> Elect infants, dying in infancy, are regenerated and saved by Christ through the Spirit, who worketh when and where and how He pleaseth. So also are all other elect persons who are incapable of being outwardly called by the ministry of the word. Others not elected, although they may be called by the ministry of the word, and may have some common operations of the Spirit, yet they never truly come unto Christ, and therefore cannot be saved.[2]

Election is expressly said to have no relation to any future merit or worth. It rests simply upon the free and unchangeable purpose of God, ordained from all eternity by the most wise and holy counsel of His own will.[3]

The Westminster Confession has remained to a very great extent the standard of English Calvinism down to the present day, a fact which gives an added importance to the moderation of its language and tone. This moderation is not a characteristic of all the writers of the period. In such writers, for example, as Dr. John Owen,[4] the implications of the Calvinistic doctrine of election are drawn out with the most uncompromising rigour. The strongest possible view is taken of the

[1] *Larger Catechism*, Q. 71. [2] *Confession*, c. 10; cf. ch. 3. [3] *Ib.* c. 3.

[4] *Salus Electorum Sanguis Jesu* (1648). For a full discussion of the Calvinism of Owen and President Edwards cf. M'Leod Campbell, *The Nature of The Atonement*, ch. iii.

effects of the Fall. Man is utterly depraved, absolutely helpless. Of himself he can do nothing, and only the free pre-determining grace of God can avail for his redemption. The elect are predestined to salvation, and God's grace cannot fail to work out that salvation in them. The rest of mankind is equally predestined to eternal damnation, and for them there is no hope. Thus the characteristic doctrine of theologians of this school is that of limited Atonement. Christ died only for the elect. Owen writes at length, and with great rhetorical effect, to show the inconsistencies of the "universalists." The stern, Puritan, presuppositions of his thought may be illustrated by two sentences, of a type frequent in his writings:

> Christ died for all, and only, those, in and towards whom all these things recounted are effected: which whether they are all and every one, I leave to all and every one to judge that hath any knowledge of these things.[1]

> That innumerable souls shall to eternity undergo the punishment due to their own sins, I hope needs with Christians no proving: Now how can the justice of God require satisfaction of them for their sins, if it were before satisfied for them in Christ.[2]

Owen has no difficulty in citing New Testament evidence in confirmation of this attitude, and he goes on to derive its consequences upon strictly logical lines.

> I may add this dilemma to our Universalists: God imposed His wrath due unto, and Christ underwent the pains of hell for, either all the sins of all men, or all the sins of some men, or some sins of all men. If the last, some sins of all men, then have all men some sins to answer for, and so shall no man be saved. . . . If the second, that is it which we affirm, that Christ in their stead and room, suffered for all the sins of all the elect in the world. If the first, why then are not all freed from the punishment of all their sins? You will say, because of their unbelief; but this unbelief, is it a sin or not? If not, why should they be punished for it? If it be, then Christ underwent the punishment due to it, or not. If so, then why must that hinder them more than their other sins for which He died; if He did not then did He not die for all their sins. Let them choose which part they will.[3]

[1] *Salus Electorum*, ii. 3. [2] *Ib.* iii. 3. [3] i. 3; cf. iii. 3.

It is hard to see what answer can be given, upon the general principles which guided the Reformation. We have already seen that the difficulty here stated holds against Luther. The solution of strict Calvinism has clearly the advantage in logic, however repulsive it may be to natural human instinct.

It follows that the sufferings of Christ were those due to and for the sins of the elect, and are in no sense to be equated to all the sins of all the worlds.

> It was a full valuable compensation made to the justice of God for all the sins of all those for whom He made satisfaction, by undergoing that same punishment which, by reason of the obligation that was upon them, they themselves were bound to undergo: when I say the same, I mean, essentially the same, in weight and pressure, though not in all accidents of duration and the like.[1]

Though the underlying thought is clearly upon the lines of the Penal theory, this is not developed by Owen with any fulness, and his thought corresponds in this respect with that of the later Reformed Church. The results of Christ's work are stated in language which, while emphasizing the Godward aspect of Atonement in the customary forensic manner, yet makes allowance for the manward aspect also. Its effects, he says, are:

> First, Reconciliation with God, by removing and slaying the enmity that was between Him and us. . . . Secondly, Justification, by taking away the guilt of sin, procuring remission and pardon of them, redeeming us from their power, with the curse and wrath due unto us for them. . . . Thirdly, Sanctification, by the purging away of the uncleanness and pollution of our sins, renewing in us the image of God, and supplying us with the graces of the spirit of holiness. . . . Fourthly, Adoption, with that evangelical liberty and all those glorious privileges which appertain to the sons of God.[2]

This account of sanctification suggests something far more living and real than a mere imputation of righteousness. A real change is wrought, not only in man's relation to God, but in man himself. And in the

[1] *Salus Electorum*, iii. 7.

[2] *Ib.* i. 1.

statement of the Godward aspect it should be noted that Owen, like the Westminster Confession, avoids the direct assertion of any change wrought in God Himself.

But as to the way in which this work wrought by Christ is made available for the elect Owen has little to say. He falls back upon the barest substitutionary language.

> If He fulfilled not justice, I must; if He underwent not wrath, I must to eternity.[1]

This is just Luther's literalism over again, without the impassioned mysticism which had given it life and power. The stress upon Christ's unity with the sinner is wanting, save in the barest sense of legal representation. No serious defence is attempted of the justice which can allow the substitution of one victim for another, the vicarious punishment of the innocent. And the thought of the love of God has been swallowed up in the grand but cold conception of His eternal purpose, working through election, whereby all things are immutably fore-ordained to His glory displayed in righteous judgement upon some, in free grace to others. From such a view of God man has instinctively recoiled.

Owen represents the extremest form of English Calvinism, as developed in opposition to Arminian influence. In Presbyterian and other circles this type of Calvinism has continued to modern times, but there has been an increasing tendency to moderation of statement, especially in recent years. In particular the doctrine of limited Atonement, as a corollary from that of election, has to a great extent fallen out of sight, rejected by the common feeling of humanity.

Reference must be made to one other exponent of the extreme Calvinist position, Jonathan Edwards the elder, the greatest of American theologians,[2] who also developed his system in direct opposition to Arminian influences. Here the doctrine of predestination receives

[1] *Ib.* iii. 9. [2] 1703–1758.

its most complete philosophical statement. The most rigorous view possible is taken of the absolute subjection and impotence of the human will.[1] Edwards even adopts the supra-lapsarian position that the fall of Adam was itself predestined, a point upon which Calvin himself had wavered. As to the extent of the Atonement Edwards takes up a similar position to Owen. In the guilt of the original apostasy, by which the species first rebelled against God, all mankind is directly involved. Only to the elect does the grace of the Atonement, wrought by God's love, apply. Therefore it was only for the elect that Christ died.

Edwards adopts the ordinary substitutionary theory of penal suffering, but is more conscious than Owen of its difficulty and tries to safeguard it from some of the more obvious objections.

> Christ suffered the wrath of God for men's sins in such a way as He was capable of, being an infinitely holy person, who knew that God was not angry with Him personally, but infinitely loved Him. The wicked in hell will suffer the wrath of God, as they will have the sense, and knowledge, and sight of God's infinite displeasure towards, and hatred of, them. But this was impossible in Jesus Christ. Christ could bear the wrath of God in no other but these two ways: (1) in having a great and clear sight of the infinite wrath of God against the sins of men and the punishment they deserved . . . (2) Another way . . . was to endure the effects of that wrath.[2]

So again

> God dealt with Him as if He had been exceedingly angry with Him, and as though He had been the object of His dreadful wrath. This made all the sufferings of Christ the more terrible to Him, because they were from the hand of His Father, whom He infinitely loved, and of whose infinite love He had had eternal experience. Besides, it was an effect of God's wrath that He forsook Christ. This caused Christ to cry out, My God, My God, why hast Thou forsaken Me! This was infinitely terrible. Christ's knowledge of the glory of the Father, and

[1] *Freedom of the Will*, 1754; *Original Sin*, 1758.

[2] *Concerning the Necessity and Reasonableness of the Christian Doctrine of Satisfaction for Sin*, xxxi.

His love to the Father, and the sense and experience He had had of the worth of the Father's love to Him, made the withholding the pleasant ideas and manifestations of His Father's love as terrible to Him as the sense and knowledge of His hatred is to the damned, that they have no knowledge of God's excellency, no love to Him, nor any experience of the infinite sweetness of His love.[1]

These passages well illustrate both the very definite penal view adopted by Edwards, and the great difficulty which he finds in reconciling it with God's treatment of His beloved Son. It may well be asked whether the explanations given do not really destroy the whole force of the Penal theory. They really amount to an admission that the sufferings of Christ, though similar to those due to sinners, were not really the same, since the relation of Christ to God is unique and such as is impossible to man. But if this is so it is no longer true that the demands of avenging justice are paid in full, and we seem driven back to the Scotist idea that God has freely accepted a satisfaction, valuable, it is true, but not strictly equivalent to the offence.

The difficulty is partly due to the failure to grasp the personal relation of Christ and the sinner. Edwards dwells with considerable power upon the participation in misery and suffering due to love and sympathy.

Christ's great love and pity to the elect was one source of His suffering. A strong exercise of love excites a lively idea of the object loved. And a strong exercise of pity excites a lively idea of the misery under which He pities them. Christ's love, then, brought His elect infinitely near to Him in that grand act of suffering wherein He especially stood for them, and was substituted in their stead; and His love and pity fixed the idea of them in His mind as if He had been really they, and fixed their calamity in His mind as though it really was His. A very strong and lively love and pity towards the miserable tends to make their case ours; as in other respects so in this in particular, as it doth in our idea place us in their stead, under their misery, with a most lively feeling sense of that misery, as it were feeling it for them actually suffering it in their stead by strong sympathy.[2]

---

[1] *Ib.* xxxv.

[2] *Ib.* xxxii.

The idea of sympathy has been fruitful in later writers, but it is impossible to feel that Edwards has grasped its full force. He does not derive from it any conception of any real union of Christ with sinful man. Such an implication of the doctrine of the Incarnation does not seem to occur to him. The old Greek mystical view, derived from St. Paul, of a union in which our sins become Christ's, and His sufferings become ours, is far from his thought. The *unio mystica* to which he looks is simply a legal union, and is no real union at all, even though based on love, but only a substitution. In his posthumous *History of Redemption*[1] he states this clearly.

> The love of Christ to the elect is so great that God the Father looks upon it proper and suitable to account Christ and the elect as one; and accordingly to account what Christ does and suffers, as if they did and suffered it. That love of Christ which is so great as to render Him willing to put Himself in the stead of the elect, and to bear the misery that they deserved, does, in the Father's account, so unite Christ and the elect, that they may be looked upon as legally one.[2]

This emphasis upon the love of God and of Christ helps to explain the singular fact that this austere philosopher of predestination and of a limited Atonement is at the same time the enthusiastic evangelist and the successful missionary. It would hardly be true to say that the language of his preaching is inconsistent with his theology, but it sometimes sounds a very different note. The following passage, while strictly following the Penal theory, ignores the doctrine of election, and becomes almost Abelardian in its assertion of the love of God, revealed through the Cross.

> The justice of God is exceedingly glorified in this work. God is so strictly and immutably just, that He would not spare His beloved Son when He took upon Him the guilt of men's sins, and was substituted in the room of sinners. He would not abate Him the least mite of that debt which justice demanded.

---

[1] Edited by Hopkins and published in 1773.

[2] *The Wisdom of God displayed in the Way of Salvation*, sect. vi.

. . . The holiness of God is also exceedingly glorious in this work. Never did God so manifest His hatred of sin as in the death and sufferings of His only begotten Son. Hereby He showed Himself unappeasable to sin, and that it was impossible for Him to be at peace with it. . . . And lastly, God has exceedingly glorified His mercy and love in this work. . . . now God hath shown that He can find it in His heart to love sinners, who deserve His infinite hatred.[1]

The appeal of such a passage is unquestionable, but it is not due to the theology which Edwards adopts. Like so many of his predecessors he is most convincing when he is least consistent.

With Edwards the development of the Penal theory proper comes to a close. After his time a series of new tendencies come into play, and with these a new chapter must deal. No writer has given to that theory clearer or nobler expression; yet in no writer can its faults be seen more readily. Like Calvin and Augustine, Edwards tries to be both a prophet of God's wrath and a preacher of His love, and he fails, as they had done, to reconcile the two rôles. Despite all his care the conception of absolute penal justice remains repugnant to man's moral sense. And this repugnance is increased beyond measure by the insistence upon the doctrine of limited Atonement. Can the God who arbitrarily chooses out some for salvation, and, equally arbitrarily, condemns others to eternal torment, be in any true sense a God of love? The whole idea of limited Atonement, however inevitable by the rules of strict logic, seems untrue not only to the New Testament, but also to the needs of a world seeking for help. It may indeed be true that some will to all eternity reject the good gift of God. But this at least is equally true, that wheresoever there is need of Christ, need that is felt in the hearts of men, there is plentiful redemption, made and completed, waiting but for man to put forth his hand.

Further, this doctrine is in reality utterly inconsistent with the other great Protestant doctrine of justification

[1] *Ib.* sect. ii.

by faith. For the extreme Calvinist, in his logical moments, faith can have no meaning save bare assurance, itself the gift of God to His elect. It is no essential character of the heart of man, but something as utterly external as the vicarious suffering of Christ Himself. There is a great truth in this conception, but there is a great falsehood also. That cannot be wholly true which cannot be preached to the sinner in his sin. The gospel is meant to be preached, and unless it is preached, its power is gone. But who can preach to the sinner the doctrine of assurance? Where is the use of proclaiming that which is unintelligible to all, save to those who do not need the message? Only a universal gospel can have any appeal. If justification by faith is indeed to be "very full of comfort,"[1] faith must be something more than a barren certainty of election, and the gospel must be something more than the proclamation of an arbitrary Divine decree, to which man can but bow silently, and against which all his chafing is in vain.

[1] XXXIX. Articles, Art. XI.

CHAPTER XII

THE SOCINIANS AND THE REPLY OF GROTIUS

HITHERTO we have considered the development of Lutheran and Calvinistic theology without reference to the other tendencies of thought which found their opportunity at the Reformation. Of these by far the most important was Socinianism, which takes its name from Laelius and Faustus Socinus,[1] the latter of whom exercised a wide influence in his day, especially in Poland, the first home of Unitarianism. Despite many differences of outlook it is to Faustus Socinus that modern Unitarianism owes its impulse, and the unsparing rationalism which he and his successors initiated has been of the greatest service to orthodoxy, revealing in more than one case the inadequacy of its customary language to the facts enshrined therein. It was in direct reference to Socinian criticism that the later Calvinistic systems, of which some account has already

[1] Hagenbach (*op. cit.* iii. 213) gives, as predecessors of Socinus, Sebastian Frank and Thamer, and especially Occhino (*Dialogues*, Basle, 1463) who tried "to transform the objective satisfaction theory of the Church into an act of subjective reflection, whereby man comes to see that God is disposed to forgive him when he is penitent." For Socinus' view of the Atonement the most important source is his *De Jesu Christo Servatore*, which is a very full criticism of the orthodox Penal view. His *Christianae Religionis Institutio* gives a less prolix statement of the main points. A much clearer account is that of the *Racovian Catechism*, first published a year after Socinus' death in 1604. This underwent repeated revisions, without any important change of substance, down to the Amsterdam edition of 1680. The quotations in the text are from Rees' translation (London, 1818) of this edition.

been given, were framed, and the Arminian reaction from Calvinism owed Socinus a very considerable debt.

Unlike Luther and Calvin, Socinus was primarily a doctrinal reformer. His theology does not spring directly from an overmastering religious experience or from a strong sense of ecclesiastical abuses, but from the desire to submit doctrine to the bar of human reason, a desire laudable enough in itself, but not without its dangers if it makes everyday human experience the sole test of rationality. It is thus natural to find in Socinus the first direct critic of the whole Anselmic theory of satisfaction, not only in the form which it had assumed in the later mediaeval writers, but also in the penal restatement which it received from the Reformers. He has the latter especially in view in his great treatise, *Of Jesus Christ the Saviour*.

The two primary thoughts from which Socinus starts are not new. He adopts, in the first place, the Anselmic view of sin as disobedience, whereby injury is done to the honour of God. He does not conceive it as in any sense a corruption of the human will, an ineradicable depravity, extending to all mankind, but thinks rather of the offence than of the soul of the offender. In this respect his position is far less true to spiritual fact than that of Luther and Calvin.

In the second place he insists continually upon the absolute freedom of God. So, indeed, had all the early fathers, who, as we have seen, acknowledged that God might have saved man by a word, had He so wished.[1] But Socinus takes this to mean that God's will is wholly arbitrary, bound not even by its own law. He sees no opposition between God's justice and His mercy. Both are expressions of His free will. That same will which establishes justice, may also make any exception which it pleases to its rules. God can be just when He wills, merciful when He wills. The law which demands satisfaction for injured honour, punishment for sin,

[1] See p. 54.

does not bind Him. He may, if He will, remit satisfaction altogether.

> Since it has been shown by me that justice of that kind does not truly reside in God, or properly be called a quality of God, so far, that is, as it is opposed to mercy, but is only an effect of His will, nothing can result from it. . . . For God, especially as He is Himself Lord of all, can of His own right remit as much as He will.[1]

He points, with considerable effect, to the analogy of human forgiveness :

> If any man can by right freely pardon injuries inflicted upon himself, and avenge them in the smallest degree when the highest degree is possible ; not only may he rightly do this, but is for that very reason extolled to the skies. Shall we dare to deprive God of that right and power, and not shrink from making ourselves guilty of sacrilege unspeakable.[2]

In such passages the whole principle of the criticism levelled by Socinus against the Satisfaction theory is clearly seen. He has realised neither the seriousness of the offence of man, nor the utter holiness of God, holiness which can make no truce with sin. But he has grasped the other truth, of which the Reformers tended to lose sight, that those ideals which are highest in man are after all the least unlikely to aid us in conceiving the ways of God. And there are in man things higher than the strict exaction of civil satisfaction or penal justice.

Upon this basis Socinus draws out the inconsistencies

[1] Cum a me ostensum fuerit, ejusmodi justitiam vere in Deo non residere, neque proprie Dei qualitatem dici posse, quatenus scilicet misericordiae opponitur, sed tantummodo effectum voluntatis ejus : nihil ex ea fluere potuit. . . . Potest enim Deus, praesertim cum ipse omnium sit dominus, de suo jure, quantum velit, dimittere (*De Jesu Christo Servatore*, i. 1).

[2] Quod si quilibet homo jure potest injurias sibi illatas libere condonare, et quamvis maxime possit, eas tamen minime ulcisci ; non solum id facere jure potest, sed etiam ob eam ipsam causam laudibus ad caelum tollitur : An eo jure et potestate Deum privare audebimus, nosque infandi sacrilegii reos constituere non exhorrescemus ? (*ib.* iii. 1).

of the Satisfaction theory, making his points with great skill and acuteness. His arguments may be divided into four.

1. Satisfaction and pardon are incompatible. It is meaningless to say that God forgives sins upon receipt of satisfaction. For where satisfaction has been made there is no need of forgiveness. If our sins still need forgiveness no satisfaction can have been made.

For sin is not remitted or freely pardoned which is either punished or not remitted unpunished without satisfaction made.[1]

To a free forgiveness nothing is more opposite than such a satisfaction as they contend for, and the payment of an equivalent price. For where a creditor is satisfied, either by the debtor himself, or by another person on the debtor's behalf, it cannot with truth be said of him that he freely forgives the debt.[2]

2. The whole substitutionary theory is incompatible with any true justice. Anselm's postulate that he who makes satisfaction must be identical with the offender, or of the same race,[3] introduces an alternative which justice cannot allow. Each individual must bear the punishment of his own sin.

In no other way can satisfaction for sins be made to Divine justice, than by each sinner paying the penalty of his own sins.[4]

To impose this penalty upon the innocent would be unjust.

For what is that justice, and what too that mercy, which punishes the innocent, and absolves the guilty.[5]

Punishment so inflicted would cease to be punishment, and would become mere torture. It is of no avail to argue that Christ could bear this punishment as Head

[1] Neque enim remittitur liberaliterve condonatur peccatum quod vel punitur, vel non sine satisfactione impunitum dimittitur (*Christ. Rel. Inst.* i. p. 665, in *Bibliotheca Fratrum Polonorum*).

[2] *Rac. Cat.* v. 8. [3] *Cur Deus Homo?* ii. 8.

[4] Nulla alia ratione divinae justitiae satisfieri pro peccatis potest, quam si is, qui peccavit, poenas det peccatorum suorum (*Christ. Rel. Inst.* i. 665). [5] *Rac. Cat.* v. 8.

of the Church. Catholic mysticism is utterly foreign to Socinus, and he rightly sees that the forensic *unio mystica* of the Protestant theologians gives no true union. And his own reduced Christology made this argument even less applicable. If, as he urged, Christ only became Head of the Church by His resurrection, it is clearly impossible to argue that His death was representative in character, for when He died He had not yet been exalted to His representative position. For the same reason Socinus denies that Christ's active obedience can be imputed to us. As man He owed such obedience for Himself. It cannot avail for others, save by way of example.

3. In any case Christ's suffering does not meet the demands of satisfaction. For every sinner deserves eternal death, and Christ did not suffer eternal death at all. And, further, His suffering of temporal death was only undergone once, in respect of His humanity. It would, therefore, at the most, only be a substitute for the death of one sinner, not for many. Nor does the introduction of the idea of Christ's divinity give a higher value to the passion, since even if the divinity in Him could suffer at all, it could only suffer upon the finite scale of humanity, in finite moments of suffering.

It would follow that Christ, if He has satisfied God for our sins, has submitted to eternal death; since it appears that the penalty which men had incurred by their offences was eternal death; not to say that one death, though it were eternal in duration—much less one so short—could not of itself be equal to innumerable eternal deaths. For if you say that the death of Christ, because He was a God infinite in nature, was equal to the infinite deaths of the infinite race of men—besides that I have already refuted this opinion concerning the nature of Christ—it would follow that God's infinite nature itself suffered death. But as death cannot in any way belong to the infinity of the divine nature, so neither, literally speaking (as must necessarily be done here where we are treating of a real compensation and payment), can the infinity of the divine nature any way belong to death. In the next place it would follow that there was no necessity that Christ should endure such sufferings, and so dreadful a death; and that God—be it spoken without offence—was unjust, who, when He might well have been contented with one drop (as they say) of the blood of Christ, would have Him so severely tormented.[1]

4. A satisfaction so made, and accepted by God simply in its own rights, is a simple licence for antinomianism.[2] If salvation is so utterly apart from man, why should not man do what he pleases, sure that God's grace cannot fail.

Socinus could hardly have pushed his case further. As a negative criticism it is complete and convincing, if once his premisses are granted. He is able to use the very methods of orthodoxy to show the inherent contradictions of its position and the unworthy view which it gives of the being of God. But this show of logical superiority is only apparent. It is easy to be consistent by ignoring hard facts, and, as we have seen, Socinus is far inferior to his opponents in his grasp of the vital fact of sin. He does not deny it, as some of his successors have done, but it has clearly little meaning for him, and his theology does no justice to its supreme power over the unregenerate heart of man. And, in consequence, he has no adequate appreciation of the doctrine of justification by faith, with all its glad power of conviction of release from sin. Whatever errors have been made by the Reformers in their statement of this doctrine, and in the view of Atonement which is corollary to it, they have at least grappled with things as they are, and have not contented themselves with a statement of things as they might have been.

The inferiority of the position of Socinus appears when he himself advances to positive statement. A single sentence will serve to illustrate the character of his thought

And so Christ is the Mediator of God and men, not because He establishes peace between God and men, but because He

[1] *Rac. Cat.* v. 8.

[2] *Ibid.*

was sent by God to men that He might set forth to them the will of God Himself, and might establish an agreement with them in His name.[1]

It is plain that what is here implied is no mere criticism or restatement of current doctrine. It is the abandonment of the whole idea of Atonement. Where there is no need to establish peace there is no enmity and no estrangement. Socinus, as we have said, has but a superficial view of sin. Serious as it is to disobey God, such disobedience has no radical effects upon human nature. Fallen man is free to rise again, if he will. He is free, just as God is free. And if he exercises his freedom in repentance and the effort to amend, God on His part has freely chosen to forgive. There is no need for satisfaction or Atonement.

The primary function of Christ, according to Socinus, was prophetic. As a prophet He taught men the promises of God and also gave them an example of a perfect life.

Christ takes away sins because by heavenly and most ample promises He attracts and is strong to move all men to penitence, whereby sins are destroyed. . . . He takes away sins because by the example of His most innocent life, He very readily draws all, who have not lost hope, to leave their sins and zealously to embrace righteousness and holiness.[2]

This is the Moral theory of Atonement in its very baldest form, and suffers from the constant defect of that theory, that it gives no adequate explanation either of the fact of the Cross or of its central power in Christian

[1] Itaque non quod pacem inter Deum et homines Christus componat, sed quod a Deo ad homines missus fuerit, ut ipsius Dei voluntatem illis exponat, ejusque nomine cum illis foedus pangat, idcirco Dei et hominum mediator est Christus (*Christ. Rel. Inst.* i. 666).

[2] Tollit peccata Christus, quia ad poenitentiam agendam, qua peccata delentur, coelestibus iisque amplissimis promissis omnes allicit et movere potens est . . . Tollit . . . peccata, quia vitae suae innocentissimae exemplo omnes, qui deploratae spei non fuerint, ad justitiae et sanctitatis studium, peccatis relictis, amplectendum, facillime adducit (*Prael. Theol.* p. 591, *ap.* Hagenbach, *op. cit.* iii. 215; cf. *Christ. Rel. Inst.* i. 667).

experience. For Socinus the Cross is mainly important as the completion of the exemplary life of Christ, without which it would have been incapable of stirring man's zeal.

> How could Christ by His example have stirred and induced believers in Him constantly to preserve that singular probity and innocence, without which they cannot be saved, had He not Himself first tasted that bloody death which is its ready consequence.[1]

The thought here is wholly subjective, but Socinus has the beginnings of a more objective theory in his assertion that the Cross is also a ratification of God's promise of pardon, carrying with it the assurance of free forgiveness.

> And in this manner He confirmed the Divine promises that He might in a way bind God Himself to bestow them upon us and that His blood might cry unceasingly to the Father, that He may be willing to remember His promises, which Christ Himself announced to us in His name, and to confirm which He did not refuse to shed His own blood.[2]

Socinus really combines two thoughts. In the first place, like the primitive Church, he sees the Cross the fulfilment of prophecy, necessary for our assurance. The second thought is far higher, and, indeed, is not remotely akin to the mystical conception of the eternal sacrifice, as found in the mediaeval Roman theologians. Socinus believes strongly in the High Priestly function of Christ, who offered Himself to the Father, a Lamb without spot. But he does not follow the orthodox tradition in associating this heavenly oblation with the

[1] Quomodo vero suo exemplo potuisset Christus movere atque inducere suos fideles ad singularem illam probitatem et innocentiam perpetuo retinendam, sine qua servari nequeunt, nisi ipse prior cruentam mortem, quae illam facile comitatur, gustasset (*Christ. Rel. Inst.* i. 667).

[2] Et adeo hac ratione divina promissa confirmavit ut Deum ipsum quodammodo ad ea nobis praestanda devinxerit, et sanguis ejus assidue ad patrem clamet, ut promissorum suorum, quae ipse Christus nobis illius nomine annunciavit, pro quibus confirmandis suum ipsius sanguinem fundere non recusavit, meminisse velit (*De Jesu Christo Serv.* i. 3).

Cross. For him the Resurrection is the central fact of all, the turning-point of the history of salvation. By the Resurrection Christ was exalted to His Divine estate at the right hand of God, so becoming the High Priest who offered sacrifice for sin. And hence Socinus argues that Christ's death upon the Cross was not sacrificial in character, since Christ died as man only, and the real importance of that death was that it opened the way to the Resurrection, wherein God manifested His love and power by exalting Christ to His own right hand, there to offer the sacrifice for sin. Here the Racovian Catechism speaks slightly more vaguely, saying of Christ's priestly office that the Cross was only

> . . . a certain commencement of it: for the sacrifice was then offered when Christ entered into heaven.[1]

Finally, Socinus emphasizes the present Divine power in which Christ bestows freedom from sin, in proportion as men fulfil the impulse to imitate Him, together with assurance of immortality by the bestowal of the Holy Spirit. But it is with Christ's compassion rather than with His sacrifice that these gifts are associated.

The positive aspects of the theology of Socinus are of less importance historically than the negative criticism of which he was a master. His immediate following was comparatively small. Men for the most part realized that orthodoxy, whether Catholic or Protestant, did more justice to the spiritual experience of man than this apparently easy rationalism. But as a negative solvent the influence of Socinianism was enormous. The Protestant divines especially girded up their loins to meet the charges which he developed with such power against the Penal theory. And the Penal theory was not easy to defend. Its undoubted strength in some directions was counterbalanced by glaring defects in others. It was hard in its view of God and almost inhuman in its view of man. And mysticism alone

[1] *Rac. Cat.* v. 8.

could have saved its substitutionary theory from the charge that its basis was a twofold injustice. Calvinism, however, did not give way, though the long-drawn explanations of such writers as Turretin[1] show the difficulty with which it maintained its position. So long, indeed, as the two positions were directly opposed, there was no question as to the superiority of the Reformed theology. Men were too sure of the truth of the doctrines of election and of justification by faith lightly to surrender any part of the doctrinal system founded thereupon.

The change which has profoundly modified modern Calvinism came in a different way. We have already seen that an underlying factor of the Reformation theology was the development of the conception of abstract justice, demanding punishment for sin in its own right. This is the very corner-stone of the Penal theory proper, and it is against this that Socinus is really protesting, though the issue hardly came into clear light at the time. But this view of justice, though widely current then, and by no means extinct now, was already undergoing modification. The idea of the State as resting not upon the arbitrary supremacy of an individual ruler, but upon the need for settled, orderly government, was slowly being developed, and with this development went that of the idea of constitutional justice, justice, that is, which rests not upon any intrinsic force of its own, but upon the demands of "law and order."

It was to a great political lawyer that it occurred to apply this conception of justice to the defence of the orthodox theology of the Atonement. Hugo Grotius[2] took up the cudgels against Socinus on behalf of Calvinism. His intention appears clearly enough both

[1] See especially the passages quoted on pp. 242 ff., which are intended to meet the arguments of Socinus. Ably as they are stated it cannot be felt that they are entirely satisfactory.

[2] 1583–1645. *Defensio Fidei Catholicae de Satisfactione Christi adversus Faustum Socinum senensem* (1617). On the juristic ideas which underlie the work of Grotius see Franks, *op. cit.* ii. pp. 66 ff.

in the title of his treatise, *A Defence of the Catholic Faith as to the Satisfaction made by Christ*, and again in the statement with which he opens his case:

> The Catholic opinion, then, stands thus: God, being moved by His own goodness to do us signal benefit, but met by the obstacle of sins which deserved punishment, determined that Christ, being willing of His own love towards men, should by bearing the severest tortures and a bloody and ignominious death pay the penalty for our sins, so that without injury to the display of the Divine justice we might be liberated, upon the intervention of a true faith, from the penalty of eternal death.[1]

This is the language of the Penal theory, with but one slight change. If it stood alone we should certainly assume that Grotius intends to equate the sufferings of Christ, upon which he lays such emphasis, with the punishment due to human sin. But the inserted clause, "without injury to the display of the Divine justice," is symptomatic of a wide gulf of thought between Grotius and his Calvinistic friends. When Grotius proceeds to expand his theory, this conception of the display of God's justice receives a stress which profoundly modifies his whole position.

> The end of the matter which is being discussed, as to the intention of God and of Christ, is twofold: the display of the Divine justice; and, so far as we are concerned, the remission of sins, that is, our release from punishment. For if you take the exaction of penalty impersonally, its end is the display of the Divine justice; but if personally, that is, why Christ is punished, its end is that we may gain release from punishment.[2]

---

[1] Catholica ergo sententia sic habet: Deus motus sua bonitate ut nobis insigniter benefaceret, sed obstantibus peccatis quae poenam merebantur, constituit ut Christus volens ex sua erga homines charitate, cruciatus gravissimos et mortem cruentam atque ignominiosam ferendo poenam penderet pro peccatis nostris, ut salva Divinae justitiae demonstratione, nos, intercedente vera fide, a poena mortis aeternae liberaremur (*Def. Fid. Cath.* c. 1).

[2] Finis rei de qua agitur secundum Dei et Christi intentionem . . . duplex est: justitiae nimirum Divinae demonstratio; et peccatorum remissio quoad nos, hoc est impunitas nostra. Nam si sumas poenae exactionem impersonaliter, finis ejus est Divinae justitiae demonstratio: si vero personaliter, hoc est, cur Christus sit punitus, finis est, ut nos impunitatem consequeremur (*ib.* 1).

The penal aspect of Atonement is thus given the second place. Its primary purpose is not the satisfaction, but the assertion, of the justice of God.

In reality Grotius is stating an altogether new theory of Atonement, the theory which has come to be known as the Governmental or Rectoral theory. Despite the original purpose to which it was put, its affinity with Calvinism is of the slightest. It depends upon a changed conception of God and of His justice, and in several points it agrees with the Socinianism against which it was devised.

Grotius gives up completely both the conception of God as a judge administering absolute, inviolable justice, which had lain at the base of the Penal theory, and the conception of God as creditor, the offended party claiming compensation for injury wrought, upon which the Anselmic theory had rested. He regards punishment as the special function of the State.

> To punish is an act not competent to the offended party as such.[1]
>
> For all punishment has as its purpose the common good; viz. the preservation of order and the giving of an example.[2]

And thus God, in His administration of punishment, is not to be regarded as absolute Lord, or as an offended party, but rather as the Head of a State or of a family,

> . . . for to inflict punishment, or to release from punishment one whom you can punish, which Scripture calls justification, belongs only to the Ruler, as being such primarily and in himself; as in the family to the father, in the state to the king, in the universe to God.[3]

Thus God is not bound to secure either the full demands

[1] Punire non est actus competens parti offensae qua tali (*ib.* 2).

[2] Poena enim omnis propositum habet bonum commune; ordinis nimirum conservationem et exemplum (*ib.* 2).

[3] Nam poenas infligere, aut a poenis aliquem liberare quem punire possis, quod justificare vocat Scriptura, non est nisi Rectoris qua talis primo et per se: ut, puta, in familia patris, in republica regis, in universo Dei (*ib.* 2).

of absolute, ideal justice, or the full compensation for injury wrought, but only the ends of His own good government. The importance and urgency of dealing with sin is that it is an offence against public order, and it is to the restoration of public order that punishment must be adapted. And such administration of punishment is distinct in kind.

> The ruler's right to punish is neither the right of absolute dominion nor the right of debt.[1]

Grotius follows Socinus in asserting God's supreme freedom. As Ruler of the universe He may secure the ends of His government in whatever way He will. It is true that there is a law imposing death as the punishment of sin, yet the incidence of this law is entirely subject to the free will of God.

> All positive laws may be relaxed, in the absolute sense. . . . For a law is nothing internal to God, nor is it God's very will, but a certain effect of that will. But that the effects of the Divine will are mutable is most certain.[2]

It is entirely a matter of good government. If God sees reason for so doing the law may be relaxed, and in this case

> . . . He had a most weighty reason for relaxing the law, when mankind had fallen into sin ; for if all sinners had been handed over to eternal death two most beautiful things would in the nature of the case have perished, on the part of men religious devotion to God, and on the part of God the testifying of His special beneficence to men.[3]

---

[1] Jus puniendi in rectore non est aut jus absoluti dominii aut jus crediti (*ib.* 2).

[2] Leges autem positivae omnes absolute sunt relaxabiles . . . Nam lex non est aliquid internum in Deo, aut ipsa Dei voluntas, sed voluntatis quidam effectus. At voluntatis Divinae effectus mutabiles esse certissimum est (*ib.* 3).

[3] Causam enim habuit gravissimam, lapso in peccatum genere humano, legem relaxandi ; quia si omnes peccatores morti aeternae mancipandi fuissent, periissent funditus ex rerum natura duae res pulcherrimae, ex parte hominum religio in Deum, et ex parte Dei praecipuae in homines beneficentiae testatio (*ib.* 3).

God might, indeed, simply have remitted sin, but that would have caused no fear in wrong-doers. Punishment was therefore necessary, for a deterrent purpose, and it rested with God to impose it.

The problem of government thus created was solved by the vicarious punishment of Christ. Grotius adopts whole-heartedly the substitutionary aspect of the Penal theory. It sufficed, for administrative purposes, that Christ should suffer instead of the guilty, and it was open to God, as supreme Ruler, to impose this suffering upon Him, the one proviso being made that He who so suffers must be connected with the offender, and must be Himself of sufficient dignity.

> There is therefore no wrong in this, that God, who has supreme power as to all things not unjust in themselves, and who is liable to no law, willed to use the torments and death of Christ for the setting up of a weighty example against the immense faults of us all.[1]

This tempts the immediate question: Is not such a treatment of the innocent a thing "unjust in itself"? Grotius is very ready with examples to show that it is not. He quotes parallels and precedents freely from the Old Testament and from pagan history. The Tyrian sacrifices to Moloch, the Roman decimation of the legions, are pressed into service. He argues that though punishment necessarily follows crime, it need not of necessity light upon the offender himself. God can repeal the positive law, "Every man shall be put to death for his own sin," [2] as easily as He made it. Of all which special pleading, making injustice on the part of man a precedent for injustice on the part of God, it can only be said that here the lawyer has got the better of

[1] Nihil ergo iniquitatis in eo est quod Deus, cujus est summa potestas ad omnia per se non injusta, nulla ipse legi obnoxius, cruciatibus et morte Christi uti voluit ad statuendum exemplum grave adversus culpas immensas nostrum omnium (*ib.* 4).

[2] Dt. 24 16, a verse which Socinus had quoted against the substitutionary theory.

the Christian. The one positive suggestion of value which Grotius adopts is that of the willingness of Christ to suffer, a fact in which writers of every age have seen the hope of a solution, though few, and certainly not Grotius himself, have been able to give that solution any clear doctrinal expression. For Grotius the whole transaction remains forensic.

> But where another pays on the debtor's behalf, and where something other is paid than that which is due, here a twofold act of will is required for the release. For both he who pays must wish the debtor to be released—otherwise release does not take place, as we have shown above—and also the creditor or ruler must be willing to admit the payment of one thing for another.[1]

It is noteworthy, as Crell subsequently pointed out, that Grotius has to re-introduce conceptions drawn from the civil law of debt in order to make his point. Upon his own theory the question of the justice to Christ Himself of God's action finds no answer. He is interested, indeed, less in this question than in that of the justice of God's action in relation to the sinners whose penalty is thus remitted.

It is by satisfaction that the demands of God's justice are met. So far Grotius agrees with the Catholic view. But since the justice at stake is administrative justice merely, a relaxation of the strict demands of absolute justice is possible, so long as the supreme object of good government is attained. Indeed, as we have seen in the passage quoted above, some relaxation is necessary, if God's government is not to defeat its own purpose. Grotius grants the point made by Socinus that the satisfaction made by Christ could not be the complete equivalent for sin. It was a relaxation in respect both of the person who paid the debt and of that

[1] At ubi alius solvit pro debitore et ubi aliud solvitur quam quod debebatur, hic ad liberationem duplex actus voluntatis requiritur. Nam et qui solvit hoc velle debet ut debitor liberetur, alioqui non contingit liberatio, ut supra ostendimus, et alterius rei pro altera solutionem debet creditor aut rector velle admittere (*ib.* 6).

which was paid. It sufficed, however, for the ends of God's government, though not to meet the demands of abstract justice.

This view sounds, at first hearing, like the Scotist Acceptilation theory, with which, indeed, it has much in common. It has the appearance of making God's arbitrary pleasure the sole source of the sufficiency of the satisfaction offered by Christ. But this opinion, which was that of Socinus himself, Grotius decisively rejects, applying to it the term *acceptilatio*.[1] And, indeed, his own position is essentially different, in that it does not really make God's action purely arbitrary. The satisfaction accepted is subject to the demands of government. God does not accept less than is necessary to secure His rectoral purpose.

It is as to this rectoral purpose of satisfaction that Grotius deviates most from orthodoxy. He draws very near indeed to the barest type of Moral theory. It was necessary to government that God should display both His severity and His mercy. Punishment fell upon Christ, therefore, simply to vindicate God's hatred of sin by an outstanding example, so that the exercise of His clemency towards individual sinners might be counterbalanced by a deterrent exhibition of His wrath.

> But because amongst all the properties of God love of mankind came first, therefore though God was moved to punish the sins of all men with a fitting and lawful punishment, *i.e.* eternal death, and could justly do so, He yet wished to spare those who believe in Christ; moreover since they were to be spared by setting either some example or none against sins so numerous and so great, He most wisely chose that way whereby the greater number of His properties were shown together, viz. His clemency and His severity, or hatred of sin, and His care to preserve the law.[2]

---

[1] *Ib.* 3.

[2] Quia vero inter omnes Dei proprietates antestat amor humani generis, ideo Deus cum juste posset et moveretur ad punienda peccata omnium hominum digna et legitima poena, hoc est morte aeterna, his qui in Christum credunt parcere voluit: parcendum autem cum esset, aut

Thus the purpose of Christ's suffering becomes rather prospective than retrospective, rather subjective than objective. Yet it would not be true to set Grotius beside Abelard, and to say that his view of Atonement is wholly manward. The Cross is for him an objective fact, an offering made to God by Christ, whereby God was once and for all enabled to deal with man by the way of mercy. But this is made possible because God, as supreme Ruler, knows that this display of His wrath will for ever suffice to deter man from sin. It takes effect psychologically, through an appeal especially to the emotion of fear, just as Abelard saw in the Cross the appeal to the emotion of love.

Grotius is rather hard put to it to show that vicarious punishment would actually have this deterrent effect. Here again his parallels from the Old Testament and from classical writers are more numerous than convincing. Some doctrine of a real union between Christ and the believer is necessary if the argument is to have any force. But Grotius is at least as lacking in mysticism as any of his contemporaries.[1]

To the specific Socinian objection that satisfaction and remission are mutually exclusive Grotius is enabled by his theory to give a reply. He does so by making a distinction between satisfaction and the payment of a debt (*solutio*).[2] A full payment of a debt does, indeed, preclude pardon, which has no further place. When the debt is paid there is nothing to forgive. But a satisfaction accepted as sufficient for purposes of government does not exclude God's clemency, which remits the full penalty that might justly be exacted. It is because God's government springs from His loving

aliquod exemplum aut nullum adversus tot et tanta peccata statuendo, sapientissime eam viam elegit, qua plures simul ipsius proprietates manifestarentur, nimirum et clementia et severitas, sive peccati odium, legisque servandae cura (*ib.* 5).

[1] See p. 246 and note.

[2] *Def. Fid. Cath.* c. 6: omnis satisfactio (hoc est solutio recusabilis) ideo admittatur ut remissioni sit locus.

purpose for man that satisfaction is accepted by Him. There is therefore a true remission, resting upon love, of that penalty which strict justice might have enforced.

This attempt by Grotius to find a new defence of orthodoxy against the Socinians was not allowed to pass unchallenged. John Crell, whose own doctrine is precisely that of Socinus and the Racovian Catechism, published a detailed answer to Grotius, point by point.[1] And it must be admitted that he has the best of the debate. He finds it easy to show that Grotius has failed to justify the punishment of an innocent person. Evil so imposed would not be regarded as punishment at all, but simply as affliction. The examples given by Grotius fail, because those punished always have at least some share in the guilt. And, as Crell points out very clearly, Grotius has confused the principles of private and public law. He has asserted that God applies rectoral and not civil justice, and yet the principle that "both he who pays and that which is paid may be other than that which is in the bond"[2] is a principle of civil law only. That the ruler has any right to make such a transference of punishment from the guilty to the innocent, or that the transference so made would have any deterrent effect, Grotius has failed to show.

It is pleasant to read the courteous letter in which Grotius acknowledged the receipt of Crell's treatise, but the advantage clearly lay with the Socinian, and subsequent theology, outside the ranks of Calvinistic orthodoxy, shows a fusion of Grotian and Socinian ideas.

This fusion may be seen clearly in the writings of the Arminian divines, Curcellaeus[3] and Limborch,[4] the former

[1] *Responsio ad librum Hug. Grotii quem de satisfactione Christi adv. Faustum Socinum senensem scripsit*, 1623.

[2] Non solum solvit alius sed etiam aliud quam quod est in obligatione (*Resp. in* c. 2, quoted by Ritschl).

[3] 1586–1659. His *Institutio Religionis Christianae*, from which the following quotations are taken, was published by Limborch in 1675. Ritschl connects Curcellaeus with Crell through Episcopius.

[4] 1633–1712. *Theologia Christiana*, 1686. See esp. iii. 16-22.

of whom was a contemporary of Grotius and Crell, and shows the influence of both writers in a very marked degree.

The conception of God in these writers is quite Socinian in type. They lay great stress upon His freedom. He is under no necessity to exact penal justice. He can, if He will, renounce even His own rights. Thus He Himself, and no rectoral necessity, determines what satisfaction will suffice, or whether, in the exercise of His natural benevolence towards humanity, He will remit satisfaction altogether.

> It must be said then that the death of Christ was only equivalent to so many penalties because God of His grace chose to hold and accept it as such; which is no small concession from the rigour of that plenary satisfaction which some urge.[1]

This is, quite explicitly, the Scotist doctrine of *Acceptatio*.

An immediate result of this view of God is the repetition by Curcellaeus and Limborch of the Socinian arguments as to the purpose of Christ's death, which they regard as a proof of love, an example of character, and the necessary precursor of the Resurrection. In any case, they urge, it could not be the equivalent for the punishment due to sin, since Christ only died one human death, and did not undergo eternal death at all.

> Christ did not suffer eternal death, which was the punishment due for sin. For He hung but a few hours upon the Cross, and rose on the third day from the dead, a time which bears no relation to eternity. Indeed even if He had endured eternal death, it does not seem that He could have made satisfaction for all the sins of the whole world. For it would only have been one death, which would not have been equivalent to all the deaths which all men deserved, each for his own sin.[2]

---

[1] Dicendum itaque Christi mortem alio modo non fuisse aequivalentem tot poenis, nisi quia Deus ex gratia eam voluit pro tali habere et acceptare; quod est non parum recedere a rigiditate plenariae satisfactionis quam nonnulli urgent (*Inst.* v. 19. 16).

[2] Christus non est passus mortem aeternam, quae erat poena peccato debita. Nam paucis tantum horis in cruce pependit, et tertia die

Yet with such arguments as these are mingled others quite clearly derived from Grotius. The first part of the following passage states the Rectoral theory quite plainly:

> For though God might have remitted all our sins by a single nod, yet, that He might show how greatly He hated sin, and might deter us from it the more effectively for the future, He would not do without the intervention of that sacrifice whereby Christ offered to Him His slain body.[1]

This adoption of the Rectoral theory is characteristic of the Arminian theology, but, as is suggested by the latter part of the passage, a new element enters in. Curcellaeus, and still more fully Limborch, emphasize the idea of sacrifice, in contrast to that of satisfaction through the endurance of punishment. The former explains the meaning of sacrifice thus:

> He did not therefore, as men often think, make satisfaction by suffering all the punishments which we had deserved for our sins. For, firstly, that does not pertain to the nature of a sacrifice, and has nothing in common with it. For sacrifices are not payments of debts, as is evident from those of the law. The beasts which were slain for sinners did not pay the penalties which they had deserved, nor was their blood a sufficient ransom for the souls of men. But they were simply offerings by which men sought to turn God to compassion, and to obtain from Him remission of sins.[2]

---

resurrexit ex mortuis; quod nullam cum aeternitate proportionem habet. Imo etiamsi mortem aeternam pertulisset, non videtur satisfacere potuisse pro omnibus totius mundi peccatis. Haec enim fuisset tantum una mors, quae omnibus mortibus, quas singuli pro suis peccatis meruerant, non aequivaluisset (*Inst.* v. 19. 16).

[1] Nam etiamsi Deus potuisset solo nutu peccata omnia nobis remittere; tamen ut ostenderet quantopere peccatum odisset, et nos efficacius ab eo in posterum deterreret, noluit id facere nisi interveniente sacrificio illo quo Christus ipsi corpus suum mactatum obtulit (*Inst.* v. 19. 14).

[2] Non ergo, ut vulgo putant, satisfecit patiendo omnes poenas quas peccatis nostris merueramus. Nam *primo*, istud ad sacrificii rationem non pertinet, et cum ea nihil commune habet. Sacrificia enim non sunt solutiones debitorum, ut potest apparere ex illis legalibus. Pecudes quae mactabantur pro peccatoribus, non luebant poenas quas erant commeriti, nec sanguis illarum erat λύτρον sufficiens pro anima hominum. Sed erant tantum oblationes quibus studebant flectere Deum ad misericordiam, et obtinere ab eo remissionem admissorum (*Inst.* v. 19. 15).

The sacrifice of Christ is thus for these writers the source of the reconciliation between God and man, the sole ground of all justification. But such a view is quite foreign to the thought of Socinus, and constitutes a profound modification of the Rectoral theory. It has, indeed, close affinities with the development of Roman Catholic thought upon the Atonement during this period, in which, as we have seen, the original Satisfaction theory, while never repudiated, came more and more to be expounded in terms of sacrifice. Yet Catholic orthodoxy could never have spoken so crudely of "turning God to compassion," as though God's love were in some way not prior but due to the Atonement. Such language shows rather the influence of Socinianism, with its emphasis upon the freedom and mutability of the will of God.

The Socinian type of Arminianism which thus found currency in Holland remained, naturally enough, in the strongest opposition to Calvinism. In England, to which Arminian ideas quickly spread, opposition was also marked, but the breach between the two types of thought was not so great as on the Continent. The Rectoral theory is found with fewer Socinian elements, and in alliance with the developed Satisfaction theory. It was, indeed, not many years before Calvinism itself began to come under the spell of Grotius.

The theology of the Anglican Arminians [1] presents no very novel or striking features. It was strongly dominated by the thought of Grotius, and the Rectoral theory appears with little variation. At a later date, when Arminianism became dominant in the Wesleyan movement, the Wesleyan theologians adopted the Rectoral theory entire. It does not appear, in any definite form, in the writings of John Wesley himself, who was content rather with the moderate forms of the Satisfaction theory current in the Anglicanism of the

[1] *E.g.* Tillotson (1630–94), Whitby (1638–1726), Samuel Clarke (1675–1728).

day. But it is stated in unmistakable terms by the clearest thinker among his followers, Richard Watson.[1] A characteristic passage from his *Theological Institutes* is quoted by Scott Lidgett:

> With respect to God's right to be obeyed, nothing can be more obvious than that the perfect rectitude of His nature forbids Him to give up that right, or to relax it at all. No king can morally give up his right to be obeyed in the full degree which may be enjoined by the laws of his kingdom. No parent can give up the right to obedience, in things lawful, from his children, and be blameless. In either case, if this be done voluntarily, it argues an indifference to that principle of rectitude on which such duties depend, and therefore a moral imperfection. This cannot be attributed to God, and therefore He never can yield up His right to be obeyed; which is both agreeable to abstract rectitude, and is, moreover, for the benefit of the creature himself, as the contrary would be necessarily injurious to him. But may He not give up His right to punish, when disobedience has actually taken place? Only, it is manifest, where He would not appear by this to give up His claim to obedience, which would be a winking at offence; and where He has not absolutely bound Himself to punish. But neither of these can occur here. It is only by punitive acts that the Supreme Governor makes it certain that He stands upon His right to be obeyed, and that He will not relax it.[2]

Nothing could be more "Rectoral" than this last sentence. Yet in this very passage it is noteworthy that Watson declares God's action to be not only "agreeable to abstract rectitude," but also "for the benefit of the creature himself." This constitutes quite a new emphasis, and enables Watson to assign to God not merely the character of an upholder of law and order, but also the holiness and righteousness of One who cares for His subjects. A new ideal of government seems to be making its influence felt, softening down some of the harsher outlines of the Grotian scheme.

As has been said, it was not very long before the Rectoral theory began to affect Calvinism. The writings of the English Arminian divines had a great

[1] 1781–1833. [2] *Theol. Inst.* ii. 19. p. 13.

influence, not only in England, but also in America, where they helped to bring about the rise of the "Edwardean school." This school took its inspiration from the work of Jonathan Edwards himself, as we have seen, one of the most rigid of Calvinists, though even in his writings some traces of Grotius' language appear. His immediate followers, and notably Samuel Hopkins,[1] the editor of his posthumous works, modified his standpoint considerably, surrendering in particular the doctrine of limited Atonement, while his son, Jonathan Edwards Junr.,[2] accepted, and even elaborated, the Rectoral theory in its entirety.

The Edwardean theologians are noteworthy for their careful analysis of the idea of justice, a most necessary task, as the controversy between Grotius and Crell had shown. They distinguished three types: commutative justice, controlling property transactions; distributive justice, regulating the punishment of crime; and general, public, or rectoral justice, determining the action of the ruler of the State. Grotius himself had been quite aware of these distinctions,[3] but was not consistent in applying them. The Edwardean writers are more logical in this respect. Neither commutative nor distributive justice, but only rectoral justice, is satisfied by the Cross.

For a general outline of the Edwardean position we cannot do better than follow the example of Professor Stevens,[4] who quotes the summary given by Professor Park:

"(1) Our Lord suffered pains which were substituted for the penalty of the law, and may be called punishment in the more general sense of that word, but were not,

[1] 1721–1803. For a summary of the general principles of "Hopkinsianism" see Hagenbach, *op. cit.* iii. 296.

[2] 1745–1801. On the Edwardean school, cf. Professor E. A. Park's Introductory Essay in *The Atonement, Discourses and Treatises by Edwards, Smalley, Maxcy, Emmons, Griffin, Burge, and Weeks.*

[3] The three types are roughly his *jus crediti*, *jus absoluti dominii*, and *jus rectoris*.

[4] *The Christian Doctrine of Salvation*, p. 202.

strictly and literally, the penalty which the law had threatened. (2) The sufferings of our Lord satisfied the general justice of God, but did not satisfy his distributive justice. (3) The humiliation, pains, and death, of our Redeemer were equivalent in meaning to the punishment threatened in the moral law, and thus they satisfied him who is determined to maintain the honor of this law, but they did not satisfy the demands of this law itself for our punishment. (4) The active obedience, viewed as the holiness, of Christ, was honorable to the law, but was not a work of supererogation, performed by our substitute, and then transferred and imputed to us, so as to satisfy the requisitions of the law for our own active obedience. (5) The law and the distributive justice of God, although honored by the life and death of Christ, will yet eternally demand the punishment of every one who has sinned. (6) The atonement rendered it consistent and desirable for God to save all who exercise evangelical faith, yet it did not render it obligatory on him, in distributive justice, to save them. (7) The atonement was designed for the welfare of all men; to make the eternal salvation of all men possible; to remove all the obstacles which the honor of the law and of distributive justice presented against the salvation of the non-elect as well as the elect. (8) The atonement does not constitute the reason why some men are regenerated and others not, but this reason is found only in the sovereign, electing, will of God. 'Even so, Father, for so it seemed good in thy sight.' (9) The atonement is *useful* on men's account, and in order to furnish new motives to holiness, but it is *necessary* on God's account, and in order to *enable* him, as a consistent Ruler, to pardon *any*, even the smallest sin, and therefore to bestow on sinners any, even the smallest, favor."[1]

How far such a conception as this is removed from ordinary Calvinism is abundantly clear. Its two most characteristic tenets, the penal view of the sufferings of

[1] *Op. cit.* pp. x. xi.

Christ, and the doctrine of limited Atonement, are both explicitly repudiated. And the very literal interpretation which Calvinism placed upon the conception of the Atonement as vicarious is robbed of much of its crudeness by the assertion that Christ's sufferings were only such as the wisdom of God saw to be necessary in order that the honour of the law might be maintained. That such a theory should have grown up within the pale of Calvinism is a remarkable historical fact, and, at first sight, it is still more remarkable that Calvinism, vastly superior as it is to the Rectoral theory in logical coherence, should so readily have yielded to its influence. Later Calvinistic writers, both in England and America, almost all tend to give Rectoral explanations of the justice of the Atonement.[1]

Calvinism was, indeed, played out, so far at least as its theory of Atonement was concerned. Its conception of God, with all its grandeur and with all its worth as a stern corrective to sin, was hard and narrow. In the God of a limited Atonement it was almost impossible to recognize a God of love. And the difficulty was fundamental. Attempts to frame a purely Godward theory of Atonement have always found a stumbling-block in the sufferings of Christ. If the Atonement is really wrought for God alone, if man only shares in its fruits indirectly or even by accident, as appears to be the case in all forms of the Anselmic scheme, then must it not be said that God takes pleasure in the sufferings of the innocent? Which may not be.

The great merit of the Rectoral theory is that its conception of God as a benevolent Ruler of the Universe, interested in the establishment and maintenance of good government, is far truer than that of Anselm or of the exponents of the Penal theory. In Grotius himself,

[1] *E.g.* R. Wardlaw, *Discourses on the Nature and Extent of the Atonement of Christ* (1844); J. Pye Smith, *Four Discourses on the Sacrifice and Priesthood of Jesus Christ, and the Atonement and Redemption thence accruing* (1847).

indeed, the stress is wrong, inasmuch as he thinks rather of good government in the abstract than of the good of the governed. But it is obvious how easily his thought could be expanded in a manward direction, and, in fact, a very distinct manward interest may be seen in the Edwardean theologians. One of the purposes of the Atonement was to furnish man with new incentives to holiness. A barren imputation of the righteousness of Christ is not enough. The heart of man must itself be changed. God is not a Ruler who cares nothing for the character of His subjects. His government is such that they have every opportunity of rising to be worthy of their King and of Him who suffered to do honour to the law in their stead.

Some of the defects of this theory have been noted above in speaking of Grotius himself and of his critics, and they are glaring enough. But with all its faults the Rectoral theory was prophetic of the dawn of a better age, an age when men were not to be content with any thought of God less than the highest thought of all, the thought that " God is love," an age when men were to become distrustful of the application of political analogies to God's government of the world, and were to turn rather to that which He does within the heart of man himself, fashioning it through the Fact of the Cross to be His own Temple.

CHAPTER XIII

THE DOCTRINE OF THE ATONEMENT IN MODERN TIMES

WE have now completed the main part of our task, the characterization of the great historical theories of the Atonement which have from time to time dominated the thought of the Church. Ransom theories, Bargain theories, Satisfaction theories, Penal theories, Rectoral theories, all have had their day, and all have added their contribution to the thought of subsequent ages. Only one of the old theories, the Moral theory, with its emphasis upon the manward aspect of Atonement, remained to receive a fuller and more adequate expression in recent years. It, too, had a contribution to bring, a contribution which the Church has been slow to accept. The receiving of that contribution is the special mark of the present day.

No attempt will be made in this chapter to give a complete account of modern thought upon the doctrine of the Atonement. Writers upon the subject have never been so numerous, or so diverse in their conclusions. We do not as yet stand far enough away from them to estimate them at their true worth. One or two great treatises stand out as landmarks. Certain tendencies can be observed in different quarters. But the complete exposition of those tendencies must be left to the historian of the future. The historian of to-day can only set the present, as he sees it, against the background of the past, hoping thereby to read its meaning the more clearly, but conscious that the broad outlines of the picture may well be obscured by the very wealth of detail.[1]

To one tendency of modern theology allusion has already been made,[2] the tendency in Roman, and in some Anglican, writers to retain the Satisfaction theory with a strong emphasis upon the conception of sacrifice as the means whereby the love of the Son, responding to the love of the Father, makes possible, through His union with man, the reconciliation of man to God. Thus the Satisfaction theory has developed in its recognition of the manward aspect of Atonement, taking up into itself what was best in the Moral theory, to its own great enrichment.

In more definitely Protestant circles this same manward tendency of thought has been very marked. The older and more rigid theories of the typical scholastic theologians of the seventeenth and eighteenth centuries have found few exponents during the last hundred years. It would hardly be untrue to say that among reputable theologians the Penal theory is now extinct. In Germany, its original home, Philippi, who died in 1882, is declared by F. A. B. Nitzsch[3] to have been its last supporter. Modern Lutheran writers have all tended to a more manward interpretation, whether upon the lines of the Rectoral theory, as modified by the Arminians, or upon those of the Moral theory, which received a new impetus through the work of Schleiermacher, Rothe, and Ritschl.

In English theology the most prominent recent supporter of the Penal theory has been R. W. Dale, whose lectures on the Atonement[4] still exercise a very wide influence. But Dr. Dale's treatise is not consistent with itself. Its earlier chapters, it is true, dwell upon the Penal aspect of Atonement as that of the New

[1] The present writer cannot claim to have made himself a master of this very wide field. In what follows he has been indebted to several sources, but especially to the very full section in G. B. Stevens, *op. cit.* pp. 174-261. [2] See pp. 180 ff. [3] *Dogmatik*, p. 483.

[4] The Congregational Union Lecture for 1875.

Testament writers. But the later chapters, as we shall see shortly, contain elements of a very different character. Dr. Stevens, in his admirable review of recent writers upon the subject, quotes two Scotch theologians, G. Smeaton [1] and T. J. Crawford,[2] as the most recent exponents of the full Penal theory upon this side of the Atlantic. Both writers, however, are concerned primarily with Biblical theology, and they make little attempt to defend or to develop the theory which they find in all the language of the New Testament. For them the Penal theory is "a pure matter of revelation," [3] beyond the scope of human explanation, save in a very limited degree. Smeaton objects strongly to the growing tendency to emphasize the love of God, spiritual life, and moral redemption, as "a new phenomenon in theology," and defends the old forensic method of discussion. He has all Luther's literalism, with none of Luther's spiritual and ethical fire.

> Jesus was visited with penal suffering, because He appeared before God only in the guise of our accumulated sin; not therefore as a private individual, but as a representative, sinless in Himself, but sin-covered; loved as a Son, but condemned as the Sin-bearer, in virtue of that federal union between Him and His people which lay at the foundation of the whole. Thus God condemned sin in the flesh, and in consequence of this there is no condemnation to us.[4]

Crawford is even more precise in his terms. He defines justice as being "God's purpose to inflict penalty." [5] Punishment is the only way in which justice can find expression, and only by the infliction of punishment can satisfaction to justice be made. Upon such premisses, of course, only one theory is possible. The sufferings of Christ are definitely stated to have been

[1] *The Doctrine of Atonement as Taught by Christ Himself* (1868); *The Doctrine of Atonement as Taught by the Apostles* (1870).

[2] *The Doctrine of Holy Scripture respecting the Atonement* (1871).

[3] *Ib.* Pref. p. v. Smeaton uses almost precisely the same phrase.

[4] *The Doctrine of Atonement as Taught by the Apostles*, p. 177.

[5] *Op. cit.* p. 378.

penal in their character, the infliction upon an innocent Victim of the punishment pronounced upon sin by the law. Yet despite this very penal language Dr. Stevens is able to quote one or two passages in which the influence of the Rectoral theory is very strongly marked. Christ's sufferings, Crawford says,

> . . . were accepted by the Supreme Lawgiver and righteous Moral Governor of the universe as a ground on which He might show mercy to His sinful creatures consistently with the rectitude of His character and the authority of those laws which, as a just God, He is concerned to uphold.[1]

Both in his point of view and in his somewhat inconsistent way of applying it, Crawford closely resembles an American contemporary, Charles Hodge,[2] who defines punishment as suffering inflicted for the satisfaction of justice. This again ought to lead to the strict Penal theory, but Hodge at least makes an attempt to avoid its greatest inconsistency. He admits that the demand of the penal law is not merely for punishment in general but for punishment of the offender. In commercial law it is unimportant who pays the debt. In penal law the sinner himself must pay. This would seem to exclude the possibility of vicarious satisfaction, but Hodge goes on to argue that it is within the right of the sovereign power to make an arrangement whereby an innocent person may suffer the punishment of the guilty. It is open to God, therefore, through a Divine covenant, to lay upon Christ the vicarious punishment for the sin of man. And so, by the aid of a hint taken from the Rectoral theory, the Penal theory is reaffirmed in all its rigour. But for the fundamental assumption upon which his argument depends, the assumption that

[1] *Op. cit.* p. 176, cf. p. 185. Dr. Stevens seems to go too far when he suggests that this passage is tainted with the "heresy" of *acceptilatio*. The theory is exactly that of Grotius, and is distinguished from that of Scotus by the feature that God's acceptance of satisfaction is by no means arbitrary, but is determined by the needs of good government.

[2] *Ob.* 1878. His theory is given in his *Systematic Theology*.

such an "arrangement" lies within the right of the sovereign power, whether human or divine, Hodge offers neither analogy nor proof.

In even more recent years America can show two considerable attempts to reaffirm the strict Penal theory. The late Dr. Shedd,[1] in particular, followed very closely in the footsteps of Dr. Hodge. His definition of the scope and necessity of retributive justice is at least as rigorous as that of his predecessor.

> Retributive justice is necessary in its operation. The claim of the law upon the transgressor for punishment is absolute and indefeasible. The eternal Judge may or may not exercise mercy, but He must exercise justice.[2]

With regard to the punishment demanded by retributive justice Shedd reproduces the Satisfaction theory in its most objectionable form. It must be "mathematically" equivalent to the whole punishment due in the case of every sinner and of every sin.[3] And even in one sinner the guilt of sin is infinite. How then is it possible for the eternal Judge to exercise mercy at all? Shedd's answer, though different in form, is in essence much the same as that of Hodge. Justice, he says, lies in God's "essence," mercy in His "disposition."[4] Justice is an eternal, impersonal principle of God's very Being. Mercy, the Divine compassion, is His personal attitude towards the sinners. Thus God is capable, at one and the same time, of the opposite feelings of wrath and mercy. And both feelings find their satisfaction in vicarious punishment. It is God's supreme right to substitute one Victim for another if He pleases. He Himself determines the justice of such an exchange, since He Himself is the sole source of law. Justice is satisfied, since the whole penalty is exacted. Mercy is

[1] *Ob.* 1894. See his *Dogmatic Theology* and *Theological Essays*.

[2] *Dogmatic Theology*, ii. 436.

[3] *Ib.* ii. 444. Cf. Anselm's dreadful sentence: Patet quia secundum quantitatem exigit Deus satisfactionem (*Cur Deus Homo?* i. 21).

[4] *Theological Essays*, pp. 270 f.

satisfied, since the penalty is not exacted from the sinner.

Against such a theory all the old objections reappear in full force. Is law something superior to God, to which He must needs conform? Or is mercy a mere accident in His character? Can it be true that the personal element in His Being is inferior to the impersonal? And, if the whole penalty of sin is already paid, how is it that there are some not saved, some who still bear, at least in part, the penalty of their sins? *Deus non judicat bis in id ipsum.*

The last prominent representative of this American school has been A. H. Strong, whose *Systematic Theology* follows closely upon the lines laid down by Shedd. The distinction between the two opposing attributes of justice and mercy is retained and emphasized. God's complex nature is strangely capable of both these mighty emotions, hatred and love, at one and the same time. They meet and are reconciled in the Cross. The language tends to become mystical at this point, but the emphasis throughout is upon the rigorous demand of justice, or holiness, for satisfaction, upon penal lines. Justice is definitely said to be superior to love. The mystical side of Strong's thought seems, however, to have tended to dominate his theology. In a more recent treatise [1] he abandons the conception of substitution for that of identification. Christ is not only identically God, but also identically man. And thus in all sin we actually crucify Christ, who is our very life. Christ suffers, not by substitution, but because He is one with us. The thought is true and profound, mysticism in its most triumphant form, but it is the Penal theory no longer.

That the days of the Penal theory, in the more extreme form to which it was developed by the seventeenth-century scholastics, are over is a fact obvious to any student of doctrinal history. Whether the theory

[1] *Christ in Creation and Ethical Monism* (1899).

is capable of moderating its claims, and so of surviving in a guise that does not repel the moral sense of mankind, is one of the questions which is being wrought out in the present, and the answer cannot be said to have yet been given. The assertion that retribution is the primary function of justice is ardently combated, and as ardently defended. And by the result of the debate the Penal theory must stand or fall.

Many attempts have been made in recent years to state the theory in a form less liable to the objections hurled against it by its various critics from the time of Socinus onwards. The increasing influence of the dreaded Moral theory has lent courage to its supporters, even while, all unknown to themselves, it has often infected their own defensive arguments. And hardly one of these writers is wholly free from suggestions drawn from the Rectoral theory, with its apparently easy way of mediating between the two extremes.

As a typical modern statement of the Penal theory we may take Dr. Dale's Congregational Union Lecture,[1] to which reference has already been made. In this work the Penal theory appears on its defence against such contemporary exponents of the Moral theory as Jowett, whose work seemed to threaten not only orthodox theories of Atonement but even belief in the very fact itself. It is thus natural to find that the greater part of Dale's book consists in a vindication of the fact. Few pieces of modern theology are more impressive, or more valuable, than his analysis, in his first six chapters, of the evidence of the New Testament writers, showing that in each case the central point of the doctrine lies in remission of sins through the Death of Christ. " In this reference Dr. Dale had a work to do, and he has done it with effectiveness. . . . He has shown quite convincingly that no conception of the

[1] *The Atonement* (1875). The references below are to the twenty-fifth edition (1909). Moberly has a full and valuable appreciation and criticism of Dale in his *Atonement and Personality*, pp. 382-396.

work of Christ, or of the hope of Christians, is really compatible with the New Testament, which would sweep aside the fact, or minimize the transcendent significance, of the death on Calvary, regarded as the unique atoning sacrifice for the sins of mankind. He has shown quite convincingly that this atoning sacrifice is regarded, from one end of the New Testament to the other, as being the climax of the Incarnation, the central fact in the history of the world, the transformation of human possibility."[1] Dale's seventh chapter shows that this same objective fact, however interpreted, lies at the basis of all the history of theology. It has not been the invention of theologians, as rationalists such as Jowett were claiming.

> That the Death of Christ is the ground on which sin is remitted has been one of their chief difficulties. To explain it they have been driven to the most monstrous and incredible speculations. Had they been able to deny it, their work would have been infinitely simplified.[2]
>
> If it had been possible to expel the Idea from the faith of Christendom, the task of theology would have been made wonderfully easier. The history of the doctrine is a proof that the idea of an objective Atonement was not invented by theologians.[3]

Up to this point, apart from continual attacks upon the Moral theory, which is, for Dale, equivalent to the denial of the objective fact of the Atonement, he has not expanded his own theory, though the general penal character of this is often apparent.[4] In his eighth chapter Dale turns to the theoretical aspect, and it at once becomes clear that his presuppositions are those of the strict Penal theory. He writes with two types of theory in view, both of which seem to him to make any true remission of sins impossible :

(*a*) He cites at length a treatise by Dr. Young,[5] who

[1] Moberly, *Atonement and Personality* (6th ed.), p. 389.
[2] *The Atonement*, p. 329.
[3] *Ib.* p. 361.
[4] See esp. pp. 304 ff., in which Rom. 5 and 6 are discussed.
[5] *The Life and Light of Men.*

had argued that eternal law must inexorably and inevitably avenge all sin, and that God Himself cannot forgive it, but can only help us to struggle not to sin. Any breach of the eternal spiritual law at once brings its own punishment. There is no failure or mistake. The penalty must come down.' This draws out from Dale a statement more important than his reply to Young:

> I do not regard the Remission of sins as being absolutely identical with escape from the penalties. Sin is sometimes forgiven, although some of the penalties of sin are not recalled. But the Remission of sins must be understood to include the cancelling of at least the severest penalties with which unforgiven sin is justly visited; and the theory of Dr. Young, therefore, which asserts that the penalties of sin, "to the veriest jot and tittle," are uniformly and necessarily inflicted, involves the conclusion that the Remission of sins is impossible.[1]

The thought contained in this passage explains Dale's attitude towards

(*b*) The Moral theory, as advocated by Bushnell, and indeed in all its forms. Upon this Dale has no mercy. By it, he says, the true idea of Remission, though not suppressed, is relegated to a position of insignificance.[2] Bushnell had identified it with "the restoration of fallen character."[3] Dale declares this to be a confusion of thought.

> It is one thing to receive the Divine pardon, it is another to recover the Divine image. The first is the initial grace granted to the penitent sinner, the second is the glory of the perfected saint.[4]

Bushnell had even ventured to speak of Remission, in its strict sense, as "only a kind of formality,"[5] and Dale is righteously indignant.

[1] *Op. cit.* p. 380.
[2] *Ib.* p. 396.
[3] In *The Vicarious Sacrifice*, p. 245.
[4] *Op. cit.* p. 397.
[5] *The Vicarious Sacrifice*, p. 360. Dale has really misquoted Bushnell, who in this very passage deprecates as quite inadequate the view here attacked.

> Only "a kind of formality"! It is no wonder that the awful reality of the propitiation for the sins of the world is denied, when the Remission of sins is declared to be nothing more than this. For a mere "formality" it would not have been worth while for Christ to die.[1]

He passes on to speak most impressively of the stern reality of the wrath of God.

> He is . . . incapable of looking upon sin without displeasure; and sin unrepented of and unforsaken provokes not mere displeasure but wrath—wrath which will some day be revealed in all its terrible and fiery energy. From this wrath Christ came to save us. We are exposed to it no longer when we receive Remission of sins.[2]

And the wrath of God is not only against the sin but also against the sinner.

> But for the transcendent work of mercy consummated by Christ on Calvary, God would be not only hostile to sin, but hostile to those who take sides with sin. . . . For sin is a personal act; it has no existence apart from the sinner.[3]

What then is "the relation between the Death of Christ and this great act of the Divine mercy" whereby the wrath of God is put away? To this question Dale devotes his last two chapters. At the outset he dismisses such conceptions as those of Ransom, Sacrifice, Vicarious Death, as being illustrations, descriptions, rather than a real basis for a theory. With regard to the last he points out that in the sphere of government

> . . . such a substitution could not be admitted. It would be contrary to the principle of justice and in the highest degree injurious to the State.[4]

Yet Dale's own theory does not seem to avoid the difficulty. It is entirely penal in character. He goes on to argue that the idea of retribution is essential to all justice, and not least to that of God.

[1] *Op. cit.* p. 399. [2] *Ib.* p. 403. [3] *Ib.* p. 406. [4] *Ib.* p. 416.

> In all cases, punishment receives its moral significance from the fact that the infliction of it is the active assertion of the principle—either by a person or a law—that those who have violated a law deserve to suffer.[1]
>
> It is the fact that the criminal deserves to suffer which constitutes the ultimate foundation of criminal law, and apart from this the infliction of suffering is a monstrous tyranny and injustice.[2]

And the punishment inflicted by God

> . . . is the suffering which has been deserved by past sin. To make it anything else than this, is to destroy its essential character.[3]

All theories of punishment as primarily deterrent or reformatory in character Dale utterly rejects. Justice may have these characteristics, but they are secondary. The essential fact about punishment is that it is deserved.

How then is he to avoid the morally revolting consequences of the Penal theory, which he himself has seen, since clearly man himself cannot both suffer the punishment of his sin and be saved? He introduces what seems to be a form of the Rectoral theory.

> But if the punishment of sin is a Divine act—an act in which the identity between the Will of God and the eternal Law of Righteousness is asserted and expressed—it would appear that, if in any case the penalties of sin are remitted, some other Divine act of at least equal intensity, and in which the ill-desert of sin is expressed with at least equal energy, must take its place. . . . If God does not assert the principle that sin deserves punishment by punishing it, He must assert that principle in some other way. Some Divine act is required which shall have all the moral worth and significance of the act by which the penalties of sin would have been inflicted on the sinner.[4]
>
> It belonged to Him to assert, by His own act, that suffering is the just result of sin. He asserts it, not by inflicting suffering on the sinner, but by enduring suffering Himself.[5]

---

[1] *Ib.* p. 447. [2] *Ib.* p. 435. [3] *Ibid.*
[4] *Ib.* pp. 450, 451. [5] *Ib.* p. 452.

And thus that which Christ suffered was the actual penalty of sin

> . . . that the justice of the penalties of sin might be affirmed before the penalties were remitted.[1]

And why was not this unjust? Why does not the criticism of the Penal theory, which Dale quotes from Martineau, hold good against Dale's own argument? Because God does not inflict man's punishment upon another than Himself. Because Christ, Himself Very God, was not only the Victim but also the Judge. He was Himself the Moral Ruler of the world, and His submission to that which He might have inflicted has "all the moral worth and significance of the act by which the penalties of sin would have been inflicted on the sinner."

> Without further explanation, the conscience will grasp the assurance that since He has suffered, it must be possible for Him to grant Remission of sins.[2]

But how this can be so Dale fails to explain, and Moberly's reply seems fair enough:

> May I, if my child is shamefully wicked, "forgive" him, provided that as an adequate expression of "hostility," I cut off my own finger first.[3]

Dale himself feels that his case is imperfect, and in his last chapter makes some suggestions from a very different standpoint, not easy to reconcile with the penal presuppositions of the rest of his book. He realizes that some account must be given of the relation of Christ to the human race, which enables Him to stand as its Representative in suffering. One of the most emphasized truths in the New Testament is the truth that Christians are "in Christ." In attempting to describe the relationship which this phrase denotes, Dale lapses, in a not very lucid manner, into mysticism. And just so far as his language becomes mystical the substitutionary element seems to vanish out of his

[1] *Ibid.* [2] *Ib.* p. 454. [3] *Atonement and Personality*, p. 393.

theory, and his emphasis is placed upon the essential unity of our life with that of Christ.

He makes three points: in the first place

> The power and perfection of our moral and spiritual life are a perpetual revelation of the power and perfection of the life of Christ.[1]

Our great difficulty is to confess the rightness of the penalty inflicted for sin.

> He endured the penalties of sin, and so made an actual submission to the authority and righteousness of the principle which those penalties express. What we had no force to do, He has done; and through our union with Him, His submission renders our submission possible. . . . The act in which He submitted to the righteousness of the law by which we were condemned, is the very life and vigour of the moral act in which we, in our turn, make the same submission.[2]

Secondly, Christ's relation to the Father becomes ours, but that this may be so it must contain an expression of that relation into which we had entered through sin. Hence it was that He had to submit to that awful experience of desertion which wrung from Him the cry of desolation upon the Cross. He expressed the truth of our relation to God by His death.[3] And in His death was contained the possibility of the recovery of our original and ideal relationship with God, the loss of which had been the supreme penalty of transgression.

In the third place Dale points to the language in which St. Paul speaks of Christ's death as a real event in the life of each individual Christian. That we die with Him unto sin is a truth verified in many a life.

> The Death of Christ is the objective ground on which the sins of men are remitted, because it involved the actual destruction of sin in all those who through faith recover their union with Him.[4]

But this is mysticism outright, and the Penal theory is left far behind.

[1] *Op. cit.* p. 478. [2] *Ib.* p. 481. [3] *Ib.* p. 482. [4] *Ib.* pp. 489 f.

The eloquence and the spiritual insight of Dr. Dale's work, together with the impressive moral earnestness of his vindication of the fact of the Atonement as the sole remedy for the fact of sin, have made his book a classic. It has been dwelt upon at some length partly for that reason, and partly because it is an excellent example of the way in which modern statements of the Penal theory have departed from the strictness of the older orthodoxy. In using the language and ideas of the Post-Reformation in conjunction with presuppositions drawn from widely different sources, it is typical of much that has been written on conservative lines about the Atonement. Dale retains, quite definitely, the view that punishment, and so justice, rests upon retribution, and, rather less definitely, the conception of an equivalent payment.[1] And though he rejects any crude view of the imputation of sin to Christ, he retains much of the language of the theory of vicarious punishment. The modifications which he introduces are partly Governmental in character and partly mystical. But he ignores, or rather attacks, all ethical treatment of the subject, despite the ease with which the thought of his last chapter might have been developed in that direction. And, as Moberly points out, he makes no real use of Trinitarian doctrine. The relation of the work of the Holy Spirit to that of Christ receives no recognition in his argument. In his exposition of the Epistle to the Romans he stops short of the eighth chapter.[2]

A considerable number of modern writers resemble Dale in their retention of the language and the general conceptions of the Penal theory in combination with other views of various kinds. It is inevitable that this language should remain in vogue so long as punishment is regarded as essentially retributive in character, its

[1] The act by which Christ makes satisfaction must be "of at least equal intensity," a phrase of very dubious meaning.

[2] See Moberly, *op. cit.* p. 395.

deterrent and reformatory aspects being treated as dependent and derivatory. Despite such philosophers as T. H. Green,[1] and such theologians as R. C. Moberly,[2] and H. Rashdall,[3] and, in general, the supporters of the Moral theory, this view is still widely held and ably defended, by philosophers and theologians alike. One of the most recent writers upon the subject, Dr. R. Mackintosh, can still declare that to deny the retributive theory of punishment is "a poisonous moral heresy," "the collapse of the idea of justice."[4]

Among such exponents of a modified Penal theory we may cite Dr. Orr, who, in the eighth of his Kerr Lectures,[5] vigorously attacks M'Leod Campbell for giving up the conception of a "vicarious endurance of the penalties of transgression." Yet Orr's own language, though unmistakable in intention, is full of caveats and qualifications. Our Lord entered, he says, "so far as a sinless Being could, into the penal evils of our state." The Scriptures "appear to assert" that the sacrifice of Christ is directly related to the guilt of men. In the following passage Orr seems to show his sympathy with the tendency which has influenced the better forms of the Moral theory:

> If I might indicate in a word what I take to be the tendency of the modern treatment of the atonement, I would say that it consists in the endeavour to give a spiritual interpretation to the great fact which lies at the heart of our redemption—not necessarily to deny its judicial aspect, for that, I take it, will be found impossible—but to remove from it the hard, legal aspect

---

[1] In his *Prolegomena to Ethics*, and *Lectures on the Principles of Political Obligation*. Cf. also W. Temple, *The Faith and Modern Thought*, p. 140.

[2] *Atonement and Personality*, see p. 364 below.

[3] Especially in his Bampton Lectures for 1915, which unfortunately have not been published in time to be used in this book.

[4] *Christianity and Sin* (1913), p. 214.

[5] *The Christian View of God and the World*, esp. pp. 354 ff.

it is apt to assume when treated as a purely external fact, without regard to its inner spiritual content; and, further, to bring it into harmony with the spiritual laws and analogies which obtain in other spheres.[1]

Such language is valuable in that it recognizes the inadequacy of the Penal theory in itself, as failing to give an interpretation of the fact of Atonement which meets the spiritual needs of man. Few will be disposed to deny that the judicial metaphor, so prominent in the New Testament, has its own peculiar value, and that we could not set it aside without loss. But it is no complete account of God to say that He is Judge.

Even more definitely penal is the language used by Dr. Denney in his *Studies in Theology* and *The Death of Christ*. Like Dale his great object is to insist upon the complete objectivity of the Atonement, and he does this by adopting the word "substitution" with all that it implies.

His death is conceived as putting away sin, because in that death our condemnation came upon Him. That is the apostolic interpretation, the apostolic theory, of the atonement. That is the ultimate fact which gives significance to Christ's death, and makes it a sin-annulling death. It is a death in which the divine condemnation of sin comes upon Christ, and is exhausted there, so that there is thenceforth no more condemnation for those that are in Him.[2]

The "apostolic doctrine," Dr. Denney says,

. . . declares that God forgives our sins because Christ died for them; and it maintains unambiguously that in that death of Christ our condemnation came upon Him, that for us there might be no condemnation more. This is the truth which is covered and guarded by the word substitution.[3]

---

[1] *Op. cit.* p. 341 (cited by G. B. Stevens, *op. cit.* p. 192). With Dr. Orr's standpoint that of another Kerr Lecturer, Dr. Forrest, may be compared (*The Christ of History and of Experience*, Lect. vi.). Here again we have definite penal language: "He suffered as their representative the penalty of God's displeasure at human sin, and acknowledged it to be just." Christ actually experienced the Divine wrath. But Forrest denies the conception of equivalence. Christ did not die the death due to the sinner. And the conception of Christ's "voluntary identification of Himself with sinners" is emphasized.

[2] *Studies in Theology*, p. 108.

[3] *Ib.* p. 126.

This, he tells us, is "the barb on the hook." Moral and ethical considerations have no place until the external, objective propitiation for sins has been made. Justification and sanctification are wholly distinct. It is small wonder that he was charged with teaching a "forensic" or "legal" or "judicial" doctrine of man's relation to God, and yet in his later lectures, delivered in answer to criticisms of his *The Death of Christ* [1] he expresses astonishment at the charge.[2] These lectures maintain in general the position of the two earlier books, but the whole conception seems to have become broader and more vital. The Penal theory loses much of its rigour, while retaining that which has given it power in appealing to men, in such passages as the following:

> What would be the value of a forgiveness which did not recognise in its eternal truth and worth that universal law in which the relations of God and man are constituted? Without the recognition of that law—that moral order or constitution in which we have our life in relation to God and each other—righteousness and sin, atonement and forgiveness, would all alike be words without meaning.[3]

The conception of law here implied is still rather difficult to understand. As in Dale, the view seems to be suggested that there is a law in some way more absolute than God Himself—though doubtless both writers would have repudiated such an interpretation. But if that is not the meaning there is in such passages as these a distinct approximation to those expositions of the Moral theory which dwell indeed upon the law of God, but identify it with His love. Dr. Denney is hampered by his assertion that to speak of "personal relations" does not make for intelligibility,[4] and by his very definite repudiation of all mystical language. Yet he really admits all that is essential to a manward theory

[1] *The Atonement and the Modern Mind*, 1903. Issued in one vol. with *The Death of Christ* in 1911.

[2] *Ib.* p. 271.

[3] *Ib.* p. 273.

[4] *Ib.* p. 272. It might fairly be replied that only the language of personal relationship is ultimately intelligible at all.

of Atonement, conceived through the personal relationship of love:

> Nothing else in the world demonstrates how real is God's love to the sinful, and how real the sin of the world is to God. And the love which comes to us through such an expression, bearing sin in all its reality, yet loving us through and beyond it, is the only love which at once forgives and regenerates the soul.[1]

But this, again, is the Penal theory no more. The words might easily be a quotation from one of the more recent and more moderate statements upon the lines of the Moral theory.[2]

In such writers as the above the transition from the penal to a mystical or ethical theory is but beginning, and is, indeed, more or less unconscious. Others more consciously endeavour to mediate, usually upon lines ultimately leading back to Grotius. The most notable feature of this mediation appears in the characteristic modern insistence upon the conception of God as Father, the Head rather of a family than of a state. In the Fatherhood of God a clue to the problem of Atonement has more than once been sought.

The use of this analogy—for analogy, of course, it is—appears in writers of all schools. It is prominent in Dale's book, though only as an illustration. Denney, in one passage, admits that

> The relations of father and child are undoubtedly more adequate to the truth than those of judge and criminal; they are more adequate, but so far as our experience of them goes, they are not equal to it.[3]

---

1. *Ib.* p. 297.

2. The above account of Dr. Denney's position was written before the publication of his posthumous lectures, *The Christian Doctrine of Reconciliation* (1917). These lectures do not seem to demand a modification of the estimate given above. The penal, retributive standpoint remains, but there is an increased consciousness of the difficulties on the manward side. Denney still repudiates all mystical interpretations, and even seems to depreciate the work of the Holy Spirit, but his own emphasis on faith as the means whereby God's reconciling love is appropriated contains the essential elements of a true manward theory.

3. *Op. cit.* p. 272. Cf. also R. Mackintosh, *op. cit.* p. 206.

The doctrine of the Fatherhood of God became the most typical feature of the breach with Calvinism associated with the names of Erskine of Linlathen and M'Leod Campbell, as well as of the Broad Church movement led by F. D. Maurice and F. W. Robertson. In these writers, and still more in their successor, R. C. Moberly, it becomes the touchstone of doctrines of the Atonement, though applied in differing ways.

A direct attempt to mediate by the aid of this analogy is made by Dr. Scott Lidgett.[1]

> What is the relationship of God to mankind in virtue of which He demands and provides Atonement? Our unhesitating answer is, His Fatherhood; and this for three reasons. First, because this is the relationship which Christ Himself, "in the fulness of the times," has revealed as that in which God stands to men. Secondly, because this relationship is intrinsically the highest, containing and controlling all others. And, thirdly, because the revelation of the Holy Trinity, and of the constitution of the world in the Son of God, forces us to treat this relationship as the paramount one in the dealings of God with mankind. . . . The motive as love, the end as fellowship, the method as the education of the home, all these are set forth when we speak of the Fatherhood of God.[2]

It will at once be seen that the Fatherhood to which reference is made is something wider and grander than human fatherhood. Yet the mingled severity and love of human fatherhood, which are not two but one, are the nearest parallel which we possess for God's attitude towards His erring children. Human fatherhood is no mere benevolence. The Socinian claim that a father requires no satisfaction before forgiving does no justice to some of the deepest elements in his relationship to his child.

> The forgiveness of a child is his restoration to the fellowship of life and love. And the first condition of that restoration is that the sanctity of the parental and filial bond—of the law and of the spirit which are based upon that bond—should be so

[1] *The Spiritual Principle of the Atonement* (1897). Cf. esp. ch. v.

[2] *Ib.* pp. 226 f.

effectively honoured, as to enthrone them in the heart of the child, and for ever to prevent their being violated. The father, therefore, as the guardian of the family bond, of the law which is the condition of the life of the child, inflicts the punishment which vindicates them. He is wroth until the child comes to the true mind with regard to them. His anger has nothing of personal resentment about it. It is therefore all the intenser and more impressive. His demand has nothing of harsh exaction about it. It is in the interest of the child himself and is felt to be so by the child. It cannot be waived. The sense that the demand for righteousness is the demand of love is the most powerful influence upon the child, bringing him to make satisfaction. Only through such satisfaction can right relations be restored. And behind the special satisfaction to righteousness offered by submission to authority and by homage to law in and through punishment stands the satisfaction, in the larger sense, of the father in the well-being of his child, by his realisation of the filial spirit and of all which it includes. Atonement to fatherhood lies in restored, realised, and manifested sonship. That restored sonship is brought about and is proved only by homage to the violated law, in submission to the punishment which expresses the mind of the father and asserts the supremacy of the law.[1]

Such is the basis upon which Scott Lidgett works out a very modified form of the Governmental theory. He retains the view that justice is essentially penal, and follows Dale in his strong expression of the hostility of God towards sin. Yet he is not content with the ordinary view of God's justice as retributive.

Ordinary retributive justice is both an insufficient attribute for the explanation of the Atonement, which has to do with higher, broader, and deeper interests than those of justice, though, of course, those interests are not out of harmony with justice.[2]

He goes much further in the direction pointed out by Dale in his last two chapters. He emphasizes the idea of fatherhood not only as including real love, which gives strength and motive force to the exertion of a very real authority, but also as involving, in the case of God, a real mystical relationship with the Son, and through Him with all mankind.[3]

[1] *Ib.* pp. 269 f. [2] *Ib.* p. 287. [3] See esp. ch. vii.

And thus the theory of Atonement here given is far more manward in type than that of the writers hitherto considered. Scott Lidgett quotes from Denney the passage in which he says that "the divine condemnation of sin comes upon Christ and is exhausted there so that there is thenceforth no more condemnation for those that are in Him."[1] This, he says, is merely the negative side of the Atonement, and cannot be truly represented except in union with the positive side.

> Sin must be annulled if the condemnation and the consequences of sin are to be annulled. . . . The surrender of the life under, in, and through penal conditions, its acceptance by God, these are the vital elements in the matter. The perfect union with and surrender to the Father, the fulfilment of all righteousness—all this in, under, and through the penal consequences of sin—it is this positive, active, and spiritual sacrifice which annuls sin.[2]

Thus the essence of Atonement is in its spiritual significance. It is positive and active, and

> . . . must carry us into a reign higher than the consequences of sin and wrath, to make satisfaction to that spiritual order of love and righteousness which has been set at naught.[3]

The substitution theory, therefore, though not untrue in itself is totally inadequate. Nor indeed is it the penal suffering which fell upon Christ, but the perfect obedience rendered by Him, which makes satisfaction.

> Death, the witness of wrath against sin, is here doing the worst against Him who stands for guilty men. But His response is the perfect filial response, which makes satisfaction and completes reconciliation.[4]

And it is through our union with Him who rendered it that this filial obedience annuls sin in us.

It is perhaps hardly possible for the Penal theory to make more concessions than this to those "modern tendencies," as Denney calls them—though, indeed, they are as old as the New Testament itself—which have

[1] *Studies in Theology*, p. 108.
[2] *Op. cit.* p. 272. [3] *Ib.* p. 271. [4] *Ib.* p. 277.

pressed for a recognition of the truth that God's action in Atonement must not be something utterly external, but something wrought out in the very heart of man himself. Godward theories of Atonement of all kinds, Anselmic, Scotist, Calvinistic, have played a great and a necessary part in the history of theological thought. It can now never be argued that the Atonement is a mere easy accident in the Being of God. It meant, it means, for Him a most bitter "making cost." The satisfaction which He demands is indeed paid to the uttermost. But man is no mere passive recipient of the benefits of Christ's passion. The Atonement is for him, too, no accidental change wrought wholly from without. It is something vital and living. It involves a real response of the human heart to the offer of the love of God, a response which, however directly dependent upon the Holy Spirit, is yet the response of man himself and not of another. It is wholly of God, but it is of man too. We are left with an antinomy. Unless remission of sins is given the response is impossible. Until the response is given remission is meaningless. And both these propositions are true in the experience of man.

The Penal theory has emphasized, and rightly, the prior need for remission of sins. Yet we have seen how there has been a tendency, within the ranks of orthodoxy, to ethicize or to spiritualize the old rigorous language in which this remission was expressed. Towards this tendency has converged another, finding expression very often in unorthodox quarters, and always rather under suspicion, even in recent years, when many of its exponents have been recognized theologians of the Church. The characteristic feature of this tendency has been its interest in man and its desire to express religion in terms of man. It is thus not surprising to find that "manward" explanations of the doctrine of the Atonement have been associated historically with "Rationalism," or that Abelard, the greatest early exponent of this point of view, was also a rationalist, before his time. In more recent times the same combination is found among the Deists.[1] It has become customary to class such theories of Atonement together under the general heading of the "Moral theory," and it is small wonder that they have been looked upon as suspect in orthodox quarters, seeing that they often seemed to ignore, or even to deny, that Godward aspect which had for so long been regarded as central. The association with rationalism—an association by no means imaginary—naturally made the opposition more acute. And there still remains in many minds the feeling that any attempt to expound the Atonement on "moral" lines must necessarily be heretical. But it is no more necessarily heretical than an attempt to expound the Atonement on purely Godward lines. Inadequate the language of the Moral theory has often been. But those who defend it are seeking after a truth, and a truth which must not be ignored, if our view of God, supremely loving, and therefore supremely just and supremely merciful, is not to be partial and one-sided.

It was in Germany, through the influence of Schleiermacher,[2] that this movement towards a more ethical treatment of the doctrine of the Atonement first became powerful.

Schleiermacher equates redemption with liberation from sin. But he conceives this liberation in quite a new way. It is wrought in us not so much by the death of Christ, though that has for us a very real importance and meaning, as by the imparting to us Christ's own consciousness of fellowship with God, "God-consciousness,"[3] as he calls it. By sympathy

[1] *E.g.* in Matthew Tindal (*ob.* 1733).

[2] 1768–1834. Schleiermacher's views are discussed at length by Ritschl, *op. cit.* ch. ix. A good summary is given by Fisher, *History of Christian Doctrine*, pp. 502 ff. His greatest work, from the theological standpoint, is his *Der christliche Glaube* (1822). For the importance of this work for the development of modern theology see Franks, *op. cit.* ii. pp. 225 ff.

[3] *Gottesbewusstsein.*

Christ entered into union with us, and it is in this that His atoning work lies. It brings about forgiveness of sin, for, though sin remains in the Christian, it is no longer at the centre of his life, but something near the surface, nigh to vanishing away. And by thus entering into union with us Christ became implicated in the suffering due to our sin. But this suffering, though necessary to the manifesting of the Kingdom of God, and to the revelation of the Divine blessedness which could endure even upon the Cross, was not in itself the ground of Atonement. It was ideal humanity suffering the death unto sin. And into the fellowship of that humanity all may enter through faith, dying to sin, and thereby admitted to new life in the God-consciousness of Christ.

Since Christ, in order to take us up into the fellowship of His life, must enter into the fellowship of our life which is sinful, where sin is continually begetting suffering and evil, He suffered for the entire human race; for to the whole race He chose to ally Himself. As High Priest, moreover, His sympathy with human guilt and ill-desert, or His sympathetic apprehension of it, which was the motive of His redemptive work, reached its highest pitch when it inspired Him to undergo death at the hands of sinners. Here was His victory over sin; and, with it, over evil which sin brings in its train. Hence by the sufferings of Christ punishment may be said to be abolished, because in the communion of His blessed life, evil, which becomes a vanishing element, is no longer felt as a penalty. It is in His sufferings that we behold His holiness, and His blessedness also, which are seen to be invincible under the severest test. By entering into His sufferings, the conviction of His holiness and blessedness is brought home to us. The suffering of Christ is vicarious, in that His sympathetic apprehension of sin is complete, even as regards those who are not themselves distressed by the consciousness of sin; and in the sense that, being Himself sinless, He is not under obligation to suffer. His sympathetic compassion for men as sinners is strong enough to take in all; it exhibits itself fully in His freely giving Himself up to death; and it serves ever to complete and perfect our imperfect consciousness of sin.[1]

---

[1] Fisher quotes this with some other passages from *Der christliche Glaube*, ii. 1, § 51 ff.

This is a wonderful and a rich conception, containing within its scope not only the strong ethical feeling of Abelard but the more mystical intuitions of the early Greek fathers. And it is as wholly manward as the Satisfaction theory had been wholly Godward. Sin is not conceived as an offence against God, carrying with it guilt, and the impending wrath of God. It is rather a lower stage in the progress of human nature, from which it is raised by union with Christ. Only in such union does the sinner become conscious of sin and strive to put it away. And in that effort guilt has already vanished. The sufferings which in the order of nature sin would bring upon us cease to be penal in character. The inward calm of Christ's own filial relation to God becomes ours. In Him we live.

The effect of this half-ethical half-mystical treatment of the problem of Atonement was immediate and far-reaching. There was, of course, opposition from such orthodox writers as Steudel, but there were others who adopted Schleiermacher's ideas in whole or in part. Attention was especially directed to the failure of Schleiermacher to assign any special function to the sufferings of Christ, His passive obedience, in distinction to His active obedience. C. I. Nitzsch,[1] while directly following Schleiermacher's general treatment of the subject, endeavours to give a more real meaning to guilt and its remedy, separating expiation and reconciliation as things apart, each having its own function in the work of redemption. This distinction has lain at the very foundation of all Godward theories of Atonement from Anselm downwards. As we have seen, it has been defended as a central position by modern exponents of the Penal theory, such as Dale and Denney.

[1] (1787–1868) *System der christliche Lehre.* G. B. Stevens sums up his general position thus: "Christ unites Himself with us in suffering, and thus brings home to us both the evil of sin and the grace of God. In His sympathy He bears the penalty of the world's sin. But His work is wrought upon and in men; it is a work of enlightenment, of inspiration, and of moral re-creation." This is just Schleiermacher's own standpoint.

All have insisted that until guilt is put away no reconciliation is possible. The reassertion of this principle by Nitzsch was therefore definitely a reversion towards the older orthodoxy.

The same mediating tendency is to be seen in the turn given to Schleiermacher's position by R. Rothe.[1] Rothe felt that Schleiermacher had given no adequate explanation of the changed status of the individual sinner. The holiness of God cannot possibly forgive the sinner until he is freed from his sin, and yet he cannot be freed from his sin until he is actually forgiven. How was this dilemma solved? Rothe suggested that the function of the Atonement was to furnish God, as it were in advance, with a guarantee that sin will in the end be overcome. This guarantee is offered to God by Christ, who has fitted Himself for the task by His life of perfect obedience. He achieved perfect harmony with God's will, perfect sympathy with man, even in his sin. And therefore He suffered vicariously, suffering because by His self-identification with man He entered into man's own experience of evil and its consequences. It was the vicarious suffering of sympathy. And His sinless triumph over the suffering is the assurance of the destruction of sin, both to those who trust Him and also to God. Upon His guarantee God may rightly give, and man may rightly receive, remission of sins.[2]

The tendency shown in these writers to give some place at least to a Godward view of Atonement was destined to be cut short by the work of Albrecht Ritschl,[3] who may fairly be said to have dominated subsequent German thought, especially in what are known as

[1] (1799–1867). See his *Dogmatik*, ii. 36 ff. A useful summary in Fisher, *op. cit.* pp. 516 ff.

[2] So also F. A. B. Nitzsch, *Dogmatik*, pp. 490 ff.

[3] (1822–1889). The references below are from *Justification and Reconciliation*, a translation of the third volume of Ritschl's *Die christliche Lehre von der Rechtfertigung und Versöhnung.* Frequent reference has already been made to the first volume, which contains a history of the doctrine, and which has been translated separately.

Liberal Protestant circles. Ritschl states his general view of justification in the following manner:

> Justification, or the forgiveness of sins, as the religious expression of that operation of God upon men which is fundamental in Christianity, is the acceptance of sinners into that fellowship with God in which their salvation is to be realised and carried out into eternal life.
>
> Justification is conceivable as the removal of guilt and the consciousness of guilt, in so far as in the latter that contradiction to God which is realised in sin and expressed in guilt, works on as mistrust, and brings about moral separation from God.
>
> In so far as justification is viewed as effective, it must be conceived as reconciliation, of such a nature that while memory, indeed, preserves the pain felt at the sin which has been committed, yet at the same time the place of mistrust towards God is taken by the positive assent of the will towards God and His saving purpose.[1]

This thesis is the text of Ritschl's great treatise, great despite its many difficulties of style and thought. It is clear at the very outset that the position taken up is entirely ethical in type, and that the resulting theory of Atonement will be wholly manward. And, indeed, the reduced Christology [2] which Ritschl adopts renders any other theory impossible to him.

Ritschl at once breaks with the whole conception of the penal wrath of God. The anger of God has no meaning in the present. God already loves the sinner who is to be saved, whatever might be His attitude towards final persistence in sin.

> The authority of Holy Scripture gives us no right to relate the wrath of God to sinners as such, for *ex hypothesi* we conceive sinners to be known and chosen by God, as partakers in His Kingdom, and objects of His redemption from sin. If we assume that God foresees their final inclusion in His Kingdom, as theologians we have no alternative but to trace their redemption back to His love in an unbroken line. [3]

---

[1] P. 85. It is interesting to note, in view of what has been said above (see pp. 324 ff.), the remark that "Justification, or the reception of sinners into the relation of children of God, must be referred to God under the attribute of Father." But this hint of modified Governmentalism is not developed in Ritschl's thought.

[2] Chap. vi.

[3] P. 323.

If we must assume that they are sinners, then God loves even sinners in view of their ideal destiny, to realise which He chooses them. Why sin should make this relationship unthinkable it is impossible to see. For even though sin is active opposition to God's final end, yet persistence in such a course would make the love of God to sinners impossible only if in all cases sin were definitive and conscious opposition to His final end.[1]

Nor does Ritschl admit the value of the judicial metaphor.

The forensic interpretation of Christ's priestly work conflicts in every respect with the religious interest of the Christian.[2]

God's righteousness is not the righteousness of the judge, and is in no way opposed to His grace.

The righteousness of inexorable retribution, which would be expressed in the sentence *Fiat justitia, pereat mundus,* is not in itself a religious conception, nor is it the meaning of the righteousness which in the sources of the Old and New Testaments is ascribed to God. God's righteousness is His self-consistent and undeviating action in behalf of the salvation of the members of His community; in essence it is identical with His grace.[3]

A penal satisfaction to God is therefore wholly unnecessary, nor can it be possible that One who knew no guilt should regard His sufferings as in any sense penal.

For Christ had no sense of guilt in His sufferings, consequently He cannot have regarded them as punishment, nor even as punishment accepted in the place of the guilty, or in order to deter men from sin.[4]

Ritschl's whole conception of penal suffering is, indeed, wholly unlike that of his opponents. He does not regard guilt as necessarily involving penal evils of an external kind. The guilt is itself the punishment, or at least constitutes the penal character of those evils which the guilty conscience accepts as penal.

The sense of having forfeited one's right of Divine sonship, which forces one to regard an experience of external evils as a

---

[1] P. 320. [2] P. 473. [3] *Ibid.* [4] P. 479.

Divine penalty, is the feeling of guilt that separates from God. . . . Divine punishment must be constituted precisely by the consciousness of guilt, as being an index of the forfeiture of access to God or of Divine sonship.[1]

Sin and guilt are therefore identical with the interruption of fellowship with God, and it is to the restoring of that fellowship that Atonement is directed. Ritschl seems to have little of the evangelical sense of the urgency of sin.

In so far as men, regarded as sinners both in their individual capacity and as a whole, are objects of the redemption and reconciliation made possible by the love of God, sin is estimated by God, not as the final purpose of opposition to the known will of God, but as ignorance.[2]

How then did Christ bring about the Atonement? In the first place He Himself preserved unbroken the experience of the fellowship of God.

For since Christ was the first to possess complete and exhaustive knowledge of God, He is therefore also the first who was qualified in the true and final manner to exercise that fellowship with God which was the aim of every religion, and to experience in Himself in its fulness the reciprocal and saving influence of God.[3]

The whole object of His life was to bring men into this same fellowship with God.

Christ lives with the intention of transmitting to His disciples His own fellowship with God.[4]

And this is accomplished, not by any expiation or satisfaction offered to God, but by introducing men into the membership of the Church, the Kingdom of God, which is the community of those who share Christ's own consciousness of sonship.

When Christ reconciles sinners with God, He establishes peace for them Godwards, and does it in such a way that they enter His community. This is a very different thing from the literal exposition of that formula, namely, that Christ reconciled

---

[1] P. 365. [2] P. 384. [3] P. 475. [4] P. 476.

God with the sins of pre-Christian humanity, brought Him into a state of peace with their sins. For God did not enter into the relation of peace with pre-Christian humanity, but humanity, in the form of the community of Christ, attained to peace with God. Therefore Christ's expiation of the sins of humanity . . . can have no reference to God.[1]

The individual can experience the peculiar effect which proceeds from Christ only in connexion with the community founded by Him, and on the presupposition of its existence. . . . For religion is always social. Christ did not aim at any action upon men which would merely be a moral instruction of individuals.[2]

It is clear that we have here the Moral theory in one of its purest forms. The mysticism of Schleiermacher has been repudiated utterly,[3] though many traces of its influence remain. The whole conception of fellowship, the very corner-stone of the theory, is interpreted upon ethical, or social, lines. Ritschl regards Christ as the great Teacher, the Founder of a society wherein men may find the fellowship for which they have always sought. But the Divine Healer of guilty souls seems to have passed out of his view. He has little to say of Christ's death. That was encountered "as a consequence of faithfulness to His vocation."[4]

Therefore, these sufferings, which, by His enduring of them even to the death, He made morally His own, are manifestations of His loyalty to His vocation, and *for Christ Himself* come into account solely from this point of view.[5]

Thus the death of Christ is regarded as having exactly the same purpose as His life. It was one great manifestation of perfect holiness, perfect obedience, perfect fellowship with God. And by that manifestation sin was condemned. It could not stand in the presence of the light.

[1] P. 569. [2] P. 578.

[3] Ritschl's abhorrence of mysticism of the mediaeval type led him to reject all mysticism. He failed completely to see that the practical and doctrinal excesses of mystics did not render wholly untrue the fact of experience for which they stood.

[4] P. 479. [5] P. 448. The italics are Ritschl's own.

And still we are left with the great difficulty, the difficulty that must always face all purely ethical theories of Atonement—How is man enabled to receive this manifestation of Divine fellowship? The Example is there indeed, but how shall eyes blinded with sin perceive it, how shall those who are chained by sin—and the metaphor is no mere metaphor—rise up and follow? That Liberal Protestantism of to-day which takes its inspiration from Ritschl has yet to give us an answer.

We can do no more than mention the very similar movement of thought which has shown itself in recent French theology, largely under the influence of Vinet,[1] who is called by Stevens "the French Schleiermacher." It must suffice here to quote a single passage from Sabatier,[2] which may be set beside those from Ritschl already given. Sabatier's general thesis is that penitence is the only satisfaction which God requires. The whole object of Christ's life, culminating in His death, is to evoke this penitence. His death

> . . . is the most powerful appeal to repentance which humanity has ever heard, and also the most efficacious, the most fruitful in marvellous results. The cross is the expiation of sins only because it is the cause of the repentance to which remission is promised. The more I have reflected upon it, the more have I arrived at this firm conviction, that there is in the moral world, and before the God of the Gospel, no other expiation but repentance, that is to say, this inner drama of the conscience in which man dies to sin and rises again to the life of righteousness. There is nothing greater nor better, for repentance is the destruction of the sin and the salvation of the sinner; it is the accomplishment in us of the work of God.[3]

This more extreme type of Moral theory has exercised a very considerable influence in English theology, on both sides of the Atlantic. America has perhaps, upon

[1] (1797–1847). For a sketch of this movement, as illustrated in the writings of Bouvier (1826–1893) and Sabatier (1839–1901), see Stevens, *op. cit.* pp. 227-230.

[2] *La Doctrine de l'Expiation et son évolution historique.* See pp. 105 ff.

[3] *Ib.* Cited by Stevens, p. 229.

the whole, been less conservative than England in this respect, though the first and greatest American writer of this school, Horace Bushnell,[1] is, in form at least, far less removed from the spirit of orthodoxy than are the followers of Schleiermacher. Throughout his writings he uses the language of the Penal and Rectoral theories in a remarkable degree. The third section of his great book, *The Vicarious Sacrifice*, has for headings such phrases as "Legal Enforcements not Diminished," "God's Rectoral Honour effectively Maintained." And the very title of the book itself suggests the ordinary Calvinistic point of view. And yet Bushnell is in fact one of the most radical and most powerful critics of conventional Protestant theology. He completely rejects both the Penal and the Rectoral theory, and, while adopting much of their terminology, expounds it upon ethical lines.

His main principles are two in number:

1. Love, or sympathy, is vicarious in character, whether in man or in God. The sacrifice of Christ is the supreme instance of this, vicarious because it is love. It does not differ in kind but in degree from human suffering endured for love's sake.

> He suffered simply what was incidental to His love, and the works to which love prompted, just as any missionary suffers what belongs to the work of love he is in. It was a vicarious suffering in no way peculiar to Him, save in degree.[2]

Satisfaction and Penal theories alike fail, Bushnell says, because they fail to express the true principle of substitution, not regarding the Cross as simply due to love.

> Here then we have the true law of interpretation, when the vicarious relation of Christ to our sins comes into view. It does not mean that He takes them literally upon Him, as some of the old theologians and a very few moderns appear to believe; it does not mean that He took their ill desert upon Him by some

[1] *God in Christ* (1849), *The Vicarious Sacrifice* (1866), *Forgiveness and Law* (1874).

[2] *The Vicarious Sacrifice* (1st ed., London), p. 68.

mysterious act of imputation, or had their punishment transferred to His Person. A sickness might possibly be transferred but a sin cannot by any rational possibility. It does not mean that He literally came into the hell of our retributive evils under sin, and satisfied, by His own suffering, the violated justice of God; for that kind of penal suffering would satisfy nothing but the very worst injustice. No, but the bearing of our sins does mean, that Christ bore them on His feeling, became inserted into their bad lot by His sympathy as a friend, yielded up Himself and His life, even, to an effort of restoring mercy; in a word, that He bore our sins in just the same sense that He bore our sicknesses. Understand that love itself is an essentially vicarious principle, and the solution is no longer difficult.[1]

The true and simple account of His suffering is, that He had such a heart as would not suffer Him to be turned away from us, and that He suffered for us even as love must willingly suffer for its enemy. The beauty and power of His sacrifice is, that He suffers morally and because of His simple excellence, and not to fill a contrived place in a scheme of legal justification. He scarcely minds how much He suffers, or how, if only He can do love's work.[2]

2. But Bushnell does not break completely with the past and utterly disregard the demands of justice as resting upon supreme law. He retains, in fact, the essential feature of the Satisfaction theories, but prevents the conflict between God's justice and His mercy by separating Eternal Law from the Being of God. Eternal Law is prior and supreme, independent even of God, who first obeyed it, and before His government, which asserts and maintains it.

It is very obvious to any thoughtful person, that, in order of reason, whatever may be true as respects order in time, there was law before God's will, and before His instituting act; viz. that necessary, everlasting, ideal, law of RIGHT, which simply to think is to be for ever obliged by it. . . . And this allegiance to an idea, viz. *right*, was His righteousness—the sum of all His perfections, and the root and spring, in that manner, of all He governs for, or by instituted government maintains.[3]

But the rule of Eternal Law was broken by man's sin. Man, once fallen, could not himself recover the integrity of his allegiance. The Law itself was "trampled in dishonour."

[1] *Ib.* p. 11. [2] *Ib.* p. 69. [3] *Ib.* p. 187 f.

Is there anything that God will certainly undertake? His infinite righteousness contains the answer; for by that He is everlastingly fastened, in profoundest homage, to the law, and about as certainly to the well-being of all moral natures related, with Himself, to the law. He will therefore regard Himself as elected, by His own transcendent powers of will and working, to assume the charge of a Ruler, and will institute government; contriving by what assertions of authority, supported by what measures, He may reinforce the impersonal law and repair its broken sway. . . . Nor is it a matter very widely different, that He will undertake the redemption or restoration of the fallen race, or races; for He can hardly do for the law broken down all that He would, without recovering the disobedient to their full homage and allegiance. Besides, they are fellow-natures with Himself, and the righteous love He bears them will unite Him to their fallen state, in acts of tenderest sacrifice. And so the instituted government and the redeeming sacrifice will begin together, at the same date and point.[1]

By the application of these two principles Bushnell imposes a completely new meaning upon the old juridical metaphors. It is no longer a matter of the first importance that the penalties of the law should be paid in full, or satisfaction made to its injured honour. As a matter of fact, Bushnell declares, Christ paid very high honour to the law, but this was not His main task. It was no satisfaction that was needed, but a transformation of the hearts of men, bringing them back under the sway of that Eternal Law, the allegiance of which they had flouted.

By the previous exposition, Christ is shown to be a Saviour, not as being a ground of justification, but as being the Moral Power of God upon us, so a power of salvation. His work terminates, not in the release of penalties by due compensation, but in the transformation of character, and the rescue, in that manner, of guilty men from the retributive causations provoked by their sin. He does not prepare the remission of sins by a mere letting go, but He executes the remission, by taking away the sins, and dispensing the justification of life. This one word Life is the condensed import of all that He is, or undertakes to be.[2]

---

[1] *Ib.* pp. 195 f.

[2] *Op. cit.* p. 383. Cf. pp. 359 f., the passage misquoted and attacked by Dale. What Bushnell actually says is that a remission which is "only a kind of formality . . . carries practically no discharge at all," and that therefore some fuller and deeper conception is needed. See p. 315, and note.

And, most clearly of all:

> The general conclusion is, that all the Scripture symbols coincide, as nearly as may be, in the one ruling conception, that Christ is here in the world to be a power on character—to cleanse, to wash, to purify, to regenerate, new-create, make free, invest in the righteousness of God, the guilty souls of mankind. Beyond that nothing plainly is wanted, and therefore there is nothing to be found.[1]

It would not be true to say that Bushnell wholly ignores the Godward, juridical, aspects of Atonement, but he quite explicitly assigns to them a secondary position. The great primary truth is the change wrought in the heart of man, by what he terms the "moral power" of God.

> When He commands—"Let there be light"—and the new sprung day flashes athwart all orbs and skies, it is indeed a mighty and sublime power that He wields, but His great character in good, what He is, and loves to do, and is willing to suffer, as discovered in the incarnate mission of Jesus—how much vaster, and nobler, and more sovereign, is the power, new-creating all the fallen sentiments, affinities and choices of souls! It did not burst fiat-like on the world, six thousand years ago, and stop, but it flows out continuously, as a river of great sentiment, bathing men's feelings as a power of life, raising their conceptions of good and of God, and dissolving their bad will into conscious affinity with His. Doing this from age to age, it will finally transform, we can easily believe, the general apostasy and corruption of mankind.[2]

Forgiveness is thus executed by an inward change—though, indeed, it is not possible to feel that Bushnell gives us any clear suggestion as to how this change comes about. Such passages as the above suggest a merely sentimental or emotional view of Atonement. This, however, he tries to counterbalance by his conception of Eternal Law. No ground of forgiveness is needed, he says, but only that the forgiveness be executed in a way to save all the great interest of eternal authority and government.

[1] *Ib.* p. 412. [2] *Ib.* pp. 129 f.

This in itself sounds like the Rectoral theory, which, however, Bushnell is very far from maintaining. It is not upon any Godward aspect that he dwells, but upon the attitude of Christ, and of God Himself, to the Eternal Law.[1] Christ honours the law by His obedience, revealing God's own everlasting obedience, by His Incarnation, in which the Law is incarnate, and thereby brought home to men, by His sacrifice, offered as much for the sanctification of the Law as for our recovery. And thus Bushnell comes to the remarkable result that the Death of Christ has nothing directly to do with the Atonement. It was due simply to the fact that Christ would do nothing to interfere with God's instituted government, and the system of "retributive causes" upheld thereby. That was His payment of honour, His "compensation," to the Law.

> Nothing, in short, is so conspicuous, in the vicarious suffering and death of Christ, as the solemn deference He pays to God's instituted justice in the world, and even to the causes from which He comes to redeem.[2]

But this is still secondary. There is no doctrine of an infinitely sufficient satisfaction.[3] The re-establishment of the law in the hearts of men as a living power is the all-important work of Christ.

We have in Bushnell the curious phenomenon of a writer who holds to the retributive view of punishment and yet does not accept the Penal theory of Atonement. Retribution is seen in the action of the fixed laws of nature, by which sin works out its own punishment.

> To us the effects of sin are its curse, and the laws of retribution, set in deep and firm in the economy of nature itself, are God's appointed ministers of justice. In this manner we conceive that everything up to the stars—the whole realm of causes—is arranged to be, in some sense, the executive organ of God's moral retribution. Accordingly, the moment any sin breaks out,

---

[1] Cf. Dale, *op. cit.* ch. ix., which is undoubtedly influenced by Bushnell's conception.

[2] *Op. cit.* p. 328.

[3] Cf. p. 332.

all the causes set against it fall to being curses upon it. . . . Now this state of corporate evil is what the Scriptures call the curse; and it is directly into this that Christ is entered by His incarnation. In this taking of the flesh, he becomes a true member of the race, subject to all the corporate liabilities of His bad relationship. The world is now to Him what it is to us; save that the retributive causations reach Him only in a public way, and never as a sufferer on His own account.[1]

Thus it was that He came into the curse and bore it for us. Not that He endures so much of suffering as having it penally upon Him—He has no such thought—and yet He is in it, as being under all the corporate liabilities of the race. He had never undertaken to bear God's punishments for us, but had come down simply in love, to the great river of retributive causes where we were drowning, to pluck us out; and instead of asking the river to stop for Him, He bids it still flow on, descending directly into the elemental rage and tumult, to bring us away.[2]

Bushnell's later book, *Forgiveness and Law*, was intended to replace the middle chapters of *The Vicarious Sacrifice*, and to offer a more adequate exposition of the Godward aspect of Atonement. With this purpose he asserted "a real propitiation of God,"[3] a conception which his doctrine of Eternal Law had hitherto enabled him to avoid. Forgiveness, he says, involves for God both such a sympathy with the sinner as virtually takes his nature, and also a "making cost" to Himself in that nature by suffering, or expense, or painstaking sacrifice or labour.

The Vicarious Sacrifice has exercised a very wide influence in American theology, though Bushnell's followers have to a great extent discarded his legal and rectoral terminology. His ethical interpretation of the Atonement has survived its companion doctrine of Eternal Law, of which little has been heard in recent years. And thus the breach with the Penal theory has tended to grow wider. We may notice two typical writers.

W. Newton Clarke[4] sees in the Cross the revelation of God as the sin-bearer.

[1] *Ib.* pp. 324 f. [2] *Ib.* p. 327. [3] P. 12.
[4] *An Outline of Christian Theology* (1898).

The action of God in the work of Christ was self-expression with reference to sin—expression of God as hating sin, as Saviour to sinners, and as sin-bearer. The twofold object in making this expression was to win men and to satisfy God. In Christ this expression of God was made within humanity.[1]

It is because God loves men that sin must be a burden upon His heart, since it is ruining those whom He loves. He endures by sympathy.

It is the glory of God that He can bear : and upon God comes all the burden of endurance and endeavour that sin casts upon a Saviour. Upon Him it comes from all the sin of the world, and all the time. All that the pure One must feel in contact with evil He is made to endure, and upon Him is laid all the burden of endeavour against it that a Saviour-God can bear. . . . Sin burdens God.[2]

And this suffering is redemptive, and God would wish to substitute it for all other suffering.

Penal suffering comes uncalled, except by sin itself, according to God's own order, and is sure to follow sin. Love's suffering for the sake of salvation comes when some one is willing to bear it, as God is. If this gladly endured pain of saving love could render needless all penal suffering by bringing sinners out of sin, the thing dearest to God would be done.[3]

And the suffering of Christ was not penal, but just such suffering as God Himself endures, only limited by human nature. His life was a revelation of the way in which God endures that He may save.

In all this God was representing and expressing to men the fact of His own sin-bearing.[4]

And so God Himself is satisfied.

There is no question here, as we have seen elsewhere, of satisfying law, or primitive justice. But there is a question of satisfying God Himself, the same God who is ever bearing sin that He may save sinners. Such a God could not be satisfied without opening His heart to those whose sin He was bearing. God is eternally satisfied with the suffering of love for sinners and desires that it may take the place of all other suffering for sin. It would seem plainly essential to His complete satisfaction, in His relation to sin, that this fact should become known to men.[5]

---

[1] *Ib.* ed. 13 (1904), p. 339. [2] *Ib.* p. 343. [3] *Ib.* p. 344.
[4] *Ib.* p. 347. [5] *Ib.* p. 348.

And this expression of God's sin-bearing is what is meant by "propitiation."

God alone can set forth His righteousness in a full and satisfactory exhibition. This He may do, and if He does this it may be said that propitiation proceeds from Him. This is what in Christ has actually occurred. Through the life and death of Christ God has given expression, for His own satisfaction as well as for the sake of winning men, to the truth that by voluntary and perpetual sin-bearing He is doing all that His own demand requires for the saving of sinful men.[1]

The vicarious element in this life and death is that real vicarious element which comes from community of life, depth of sympathy, and intensity of love.[2]

And thus Christ's work was human in character,

. . . but the degree of it is beyond our reach, because of the divineness of His sympathy.[3]

The language is different. The conception of God is more personal and so more adequate. The rectoral metaphors are discarded. But the position is in all essentials similar to that of Bushnell.[4]

A very similar point of view is defended by G. B. Stevens, in the book so often quoted in the above pages.[5] He expresses his adherence to the Moral theory quite definitely.

The moral view of the work of Christ—the interpretation which construes it in terms of personal relationship and influence —is the truest and most satisfactory conception which we are able to form of His mission, life-work, and passion.

The term "righteousness" is explained as covering both God's mercy and His holiness. It is God's justice to Himself, His benevolence to man.

To define righteousness in the narrow sense of retributive justice, the impulse and necessity to punish, is radically unscriptural and involves a series of inferences and corollaries which are incongruous with the Christian concept of God.

---

[1] *Ib.* p. 349. [2] *Ib.* p. 353. [3] *Ibid.*

[4] For a more detailed statement of a very similar position cf. T. V. Tymms, *The Christian Idea of Atonement* (1904).

[5] *The Christian Doctrine of Salvation* (1905). The following quotations are taken from the summary, pp. 532-6.

And thus Christ's passion satisfies not merely one attribute of God but all His nature, His " total moral perfection."

His passion is the consummate revelation of the Divine love because it shows what love is willing to do, and what it is its very nature to do, in order to save. It reveals what sin is, since it shows how a sinful world treats perfect love. The passion of Christ thus exhibits the sinfulness of the world on the background of perfect holiness.

And how does this save man? This has always been the difficulty of the Moral theory. Stevens gives substantially the same answer as Ritschl.

Christ saves men by bringing them into fellowship with God, by enabling them to realise the life of sonship to God, which is their true design and destiny, and by founding and fostering by the Spirit of His life among and in men the Kingdom of the Godlike. . . . Christ saves men from sin by saving them to holiness. To represent the death of Christ as a device whose primary intention is to provide an escape from penalty, is to adopt too negative a conception of salvation and to lay the chief stress upon a subordinate aspect of it.

The death of Christ is thus not the ground of forgiveness, but rather its outcome and expression. It is the method of grace, whereby God's eternal willingness to save is revealed.

Christ atones for sin in the sense of judging, condemning, and abolishing it. He is substituted for men in the sense in which perfect love takes the place and bears the burdens of its objects. He gives the ransom which love always pays in its vicarious devotion. But this is no mere transactional procedure done outside of us. We must enter into its meaning and make it our very own. We must die with Christ in self-giving if we would rise and walk with Him in newness of life. His work avails for us by our appropriation of His Spirit and by the realisation of His law of life within us.

Thus God only appears as Judge to the sinner in his sin. Christ enables us to see Him as He really is. But how is this " enabling " wrought. Stevens' next section seems to show a trace of the impatience of one who has no very clear answer to an awkward question.

> Christ's whole aim was to induce men to desire and accept pardon. His death created no new fact in God. His mission was to incite mankind to faith in the infinite love of God. When men thus see Christ in love bearing the burdens of their sins in His profound sympathy and suffering, how can they help hating their sin? They must see that God will save at whatever cost of suffering.

And so Christ's work is a revelation of the truth of "eternal atonement."

> In the work of Christ we behold a transcript of the eternal passion of the heart of God on account of sin. Over against the sin which pierces the Saviour's heart we see the holy love which will not abandon us and let us be lost to itself.
>
> Salvation is no mere acquittal, a letting-go or remission; it is a recovery to God-likeness, to holiness, and all that Christ does to save us is an assertion and maintenance of the standard of holiness.

Yet Stevens insists that this is no mere provision for, but an actual work of, salvation. It is objective, not subjective, since it is

> . . . a real moral recovery of men from sin to goodness.

The final sentences are slightly more mystical in language, perhaps not intentionally, but convey the same idea.

> Christ saves us by taking us into the fellowship of His own life of perfect love and sacrifice and by introducing us into a sonship to God like His own. . . . Man can come to himself only as he comes to God in free obedience and love. This recovery of man alone can satisfy God. It is God's nature to seek and to save; for Him to do that is not to be doing something extraordinary, peculiar, and special; it is not an exceptional, but a natural, procedure. Hence atonement is a perpetual, eternal, work of God.

Of the intensely religious character of such a conception of Atonement there can be no doubt. Its great strength is in its stern refusal to believe anything less than the highest of God, to bind Him by any metaphor which would make his action appear partial and one-sided. So too it is of the highest value that emphasis should be laid on the truth that that which on the temporal plane was wrought by Christ once and for all must have an eternal meaning for God Himself. Otherwise, indeed, Christ did not reveal the Father. Yet it is difficult not to feel that there is still something incomplete in these forms of Moral theory. The old charge that they are too subjective is perhaps untrue. A revelation of love is quite as objective a fact as an endurance of vicarious penal suffering. But they do not seem to have attained to a full interpretation of the meaning of love, in its direct application to the souls of men. There is no clear conception of sin as a positive power of evil in the soul and no account of the way in which the soul is enabled to break away from this power, to enter the fellowship of the sons of God. We need the Moral theory, but he who is oppressed with the sense of guilt must be given something clearer and more definite before the burden will roll away to the foot of the Cross. He must know that God's action through Christ is no mere general display of love, but that it has a direct meaning for each individual sinner. The Penal and Rectoral conceptions, inadequate as they are, have at least this power of definite appeal. And no form of Moral theory will win general assent until it is able to do justice to the truths for which they have so long stood. The Gospel that is with power is not "Christ died for men," but "Christ died for me." And this Gospel means nothing unless it means that Christ's death has a real relation to my sins, and not merely to sin in general, that Christ's life is not something apart from me, but a reality in which I, freed from sin, may find my own true life.

In England a theological development has taken place very similar to that in America, and in close touch with it. A dominant factor, indeed, has been

Bushnell's *The Vicarious Sacrifice,* published in London as well as in the United States. But the classical English exposition of the Moral theory is that of J. M'Leod Campbell,[1] written ten years before the publication of Bushnell's treatise, and rendered the more influential through the persecution of its author, who in 1831 was excluded from the ministry of the Scottish Church for his denial of the Calvinistic doctrine of Limited Atonement.

As is natural, in view of the controversies of his earlier life, M'Leod Campbell writes with the older Protestant orthodoxy directly in view. The earlier part of his book contains admirable and sympathetic sketches of Luther and Calvin, of the stern form which their doctrine took in the hands of Owen and Edwards, and of its later rectoral modifications. From every form of Calvinism he himself recoils, seeing in all penal language a denial of the truth that the love of God must be prior to Atonement, and not its consequence.

> An atonement to make God gracious, to move Him to compassion, to turn His heart toward those from whom sin had alienated His love, it would, indeed, be difficult to believe in; for, if it were needed, it would be impossible. To awaken to the sense of the need of such an atonement would certainly be to awaken to utter and absolute despair. But the Scriptures do not speak of such an atonement; for they do not represent the love of God to man as the effect, and the atonement of Christ as the cause, but—just the contrary—they represent the love of God as the cause, and the atonement as the effect.[2]

> The first demand which the gospel makes upon us in relation to the atonement is, that we believe that *there is forgiveness with God.* Forgiveness—that is, love to an enemy surviving his enmity, and which, notwithstanding his enmity, can act towards him for his good; this we must be able to believe to be in God towards us, in order that we may be able to believe in the atonement. . . . If God provides the atonement then forgiveness must precede atonement; and the atonement must be the form of the manifestation of the forgiving love of God, not its cause.[3]

[1] *The Nature of the Atonement, and its Relation to Remission of Sins and Eternal Life* (1856). The references below are to the 3rd ed. (1869). For a good criticism see Moberly, *op. cit.* pp. 396 ff.

[2] *Op. cit.* p. 20.

[3] *Ib.* p. 18.

He therefore regards it as impossible that the sufferings of Christ can have been in any sense a punishment of sin. They were not something external, imposed upon Him.

If the sinfulness of sin, and the misery to which it exposed sinners, were painful to Christ because of His holiness and love, then must they have been painful in proportion to His holiness and love.[1]

It seems to me impossible to contemplate the agony of holiness and love in the realisation of the evil of sin and of the misery of sinners, as penal suffering. Let my reader endeavour to realise the thought: The *sufferer suffers* what He suffers *just through seeing sin and sinners with God's eyes, and feeling in reference to them with God's heart.* Is *such* suffering a *punishment?* Is God, in causing such a divine experience in humanity, inflicting a punishment? There can be but one answer.[2]

The sufferings of Christ are due to His perfect, Divine sympathy. They are

. . . the sorrows of holy love endured in realising our sin and misery.[3]

And thus on the manward side the Atonement consists in the manifestation, through Christ, of the attitude of God towards sin and sinner—His hatred of sin, His unfailing love for the sinner. Christ's sufferings

. . . are themselves the expression of the divine mind regarding our sins, and a manifestation by the Son of what our sins are to the Father's heart.[4]

It is manifest, if we consider it, that Christ's own long-suffering love was the revelation to those who should see the Father in the Son, of that forgiving love in God to which Christ's intercession for men would be addressed.[5]

But this exhibition of the Divine sympathy and love is by no means the whole of the mediatorial work of Christ. M'Leod Campbell is very far from ignoring the Godward aspect of Atonement.

We have to consider also His dealing with God on behalf of men.[6]

[1] *Ib.* p. 115. [2] *Ib.* p. 117. [3] *Ib.* p. 133.
[4] *Ibid.* [5] *Ib.* p. 135. [6] *Ib.* p. 134.

He believes that the various forms of the Satisfaction theory have erred not so much in their belief that the justice or holiness of God demands a satisfaction as in the kind of satisfaction which they had regarded as necessary to meet that demand. Christ does "deal with God" on man's behalf, but the God with whom He deals is not merely just but loving, and His love and His justice are one. M'Leod Campbell takes as his starting point a suggestion made by Jonathan Edwards, who had argued that

There must needs be, "either an equivalent punishment or an equivalent sorrow and repentance." [1]

Edwards himself had assumed that only the first alternative was possible.

But, upon the assumption of that identification of Himself with those whom He came to save, on the part of the Saviour, which is the foundation of Edwards' whole system, it may at the least be said, that the Mediator had the two alternatives open to His choice,—either to endure for sinners an equivalent punishment, or to experience in reference to their sin, and present to God on their behalf, an adequate sorrow and repentance. . . . But the latter equivalent, which also is surely the higher and more excellent, being a moral and spiritual satisfaction, was, as we have now seen, of necessity present in Christ's dealing with the Father on our behalf.[2]

Thus M'Leod Campbell regards the Atonement as the offering of a perfect penitence for human sin, the perfect acceptance of God's hatred of sin and wrath against sin as just.

That oneness of mind with the Father, which towards man took the form of condemnation of sin, would in the Son's dealing with the Father in the relation to our sins, take the form of a perfect confession of our sins. This confession, as to its own nature, must have been *a perfect Amen in humanity to the judgment of God on the sin of man.* Such an Amen was due in the truth of things. He who was the truth could not be in humanity and not utter it,—and it was necessarily a first step in dealing with the Father on our behalf.[3]

---

[1] *Ib.* p. 137 (citing *Satisfaction for Sin*, ch. ii. 1-3).
[2] *Ibid.*
[3] *Ib.* pp. 135 f.

And in this acceptance of God's sentence upon sin was involved the acceptance of death as the wages appointed in God's law for sin.

> As our Lord truly tasted death, so to Him alone had death its perfect meaning as the wages of sin, for in Him alone was there full entrance into the mind of God towards sin, and perfect unity with that mind. . . . The tasting of death in full realisation of what it is that God who gave life should recall it, holding it forfeited, was only possible to perfect holiness. . . . We can see the fitness of the presence of this element in Christ's cup of suffering, and that His perfect realisation of the relation of death to sin naturally connected itself with the confession of the righteousness of the divine condemnation on sin. . . . Had sin existed in men as mere spirits death could not have been the wages of sin, and any response to the divine mind concerning sin which would have been an atonement for their sin could only have had spiritual elements; but man being by the constitution of humanity capable of death, and death having come as the wages of sin, it was not simply sin that had to be dealt with, but an existing law with its penalty of death, and that death as already incurred. So it was not only the Divine mind that had to be responded to, but also that expression of the Divine mind which was contained in God's making death the wages of sin.[1]

It is clear that there is a very strong transactional element in M'Leod Campbell's thought. He is by no means an exponent of the Moral theory as efficient in itself to describe the work of redemption. Again and again he emphasizes the "dealing with God" undertaken by Christ upon man's behalf. And while he repudiates substitutionary language he does not altogether avoid the danger, to which the older Godward theories had been liable, of making it appear that the action of Christ was something apart from men. Such phrases as "dealing with God on behalf of men," "a perfect confession of our sins," suggest contrast rather than identity as the relation of Christ to humanity. The real underlying thought, as Moberly has pointed out,[2] is that in Christ humanity offers a perfect penitence to

[1] *Ib.* pp. 302 ff. [2] *Op. cit.* pp. 402 ff.

God, for its own sin. The "dealing with God" is not vicarious. It is wholly the work of Christ, yet by that very fact it is man's also. Neglect to emphasize this truth has made it appear that M'Leod Campbell regards Christ's work as consisting in a twofold exhibition, the exhibition by Christ of God's love to man and of man's penitence to God. But this provides no real mediation wherein love and penitence may meet. It makes no real use of the great fact of the Incarnation. God's love is not merely exhibited in Christ, but through His mystical union with humanity is made operative and powerful upon and in the heart of man himself. Man's penitence is not offered to God by Another, but in Christ man makes the offering Himself, in Christ man confesses the justice of the ways of God. And this is M'Leod Campbell's true thought. It is his meaning when he speaks of the "Amen in humanity," yet he never gives clear expression to the identity of that humanity in Christ and in all mankind, and in such passages as the following, despite the truth and grandeur of the conception of faith which they involve, there still seems to rise up some barrier between the being of man and that of Him who is the Life of man.

> Our faith is, in truth, the Amen of our individual spirits, to that deep, multiform, all-embracing, harmonious Amen of humanity, in the person of the Son of God, to the mind and heart of the Father in relation to man,—the divine wrath and the Divine mercy, which is the atonement.[1]

There is an effort in the direction of the Pauline mysticism, but the strong simplicity and directness of the Pauline "In Christ" is lacking here. And often there is no suggestion of this thought at all, and the impression conveyed is that left by the book upon Dr. Dale, viz. that Christ "simply made a confession of sin in our name." [2]

This weakness, rather of expression than of real

[1] *Ib.* p. 225. [2] *Op. cit.* p. 482.

thought, is shown in M'Leod Campbell's treatment of the Cry from the Cross, "My God, my God, why hast Thou forsaken Me?" He assumes that it cannot mean that Christ was actually forsaken, since He was then in the very act of offering to God a perfect penitence on man's behalf. And therefore he sees in it all the confidence of the later verses of Psalm 22, an expression not of despair but of glad assurance. But this is to separate Christ from that fallen humanity with which He is one, a humanity separate from God and in despair, by the fact of sin. M'Leod Campbell implies that Christ cannot have entered into this separation. But, if not, was He perfect Man?

A very similar protest against the current Calvinism was made by the theologians of the "Broad Church" school, who were much influenced by such writers as Erskine of Linlathen and M'Leod Campbell, and emphasized the importance of the conception of God as Father, who brings about the Atonement in love.

The protagonist of this school was F. D. Maurice,[1] who criticizes penal conceptions very strongly, from the standpoint of the Moral theory, though his own positive thought is not very clearly defined. He quotes with approval the position of an objector to ordinary evangelical theology.

> We prefer our carnal notion of justice to your spiritual one. We can forgive a fellow-creature a wrong done to us, without exacting an equivalent for it; we blame ourselves if we do not. . . . We do not feel that punishment is a satisfaction to our minds; we are ashamed of ourselves when we consider it is. We may suffer a criminal to be punished, but it is that we may do him good, or assert a principle. And if that is our object, we do not suffer an innocent person to prevent the guilty from enduring the consequences of his guilt by taking

[1] See especially his *Theological Essays* (1853), Essay VII. These essays are directed especially against Unitarians, but admit the value of much of the ethical side of Unitarianism.

them upon himself. Are these moral maxims in our case, or are the opposing maxims moral? If they are moral, should we, because God is much more righteous than we can imagine or understand, attribute to Him what we should consider a very low righteousness, or unrighteousness, in us.[1]

Accordingly he rejects unhesitatingly all views of Christ's suffering as punishment inflicted.

How, then, can we tolerate for an instant that notion of God which would represent Him as satisfied by the punishment of sin, not by the purity and graciousness of the Son.[2]

The suffering is rather the moral suffering of sympathy and antipathy combined, such antipathy to sin as was only possible in One who was Himself sinless, such sympathy as was possible in One who was perfect Man. In his twelfth sermon [3] Maurice dwells upon this point at length. He speaks of Christ, in contact with the Gadarene maniac, looking into his inmost being with the insight of perfect sympathy, experiencing the sense of loathing for all that was unclean there in a degree impossible to ordinary men.

Are you not sure that this could not have been, unless He had the most perfect and thorough sympathy with this man, whose nature was transformed into the likeness of a brute, whose spirit had acquired the image of a devil? Does the coexistence of this sympathy and this antipathy perplex you? Oh! ask yourself which you could bear to be away; which you could bear to be weaker than the other.[4]

And this pain and shame of Christ must extend to all the sin and deformity of all mankind. What less can St. Paul mean by his words " made to be sin "?

He knows no sin, *therefore* He identifies Himself with the sinner.[5]

---

[1] *Ib.* p. 139. [2] *Ib.* p. 147.
[3] Cited at length by Moberly, *op. cit.* pp. 384 ff.
[4] *Ibid.* [5] *Ibid.*

And even this is weaker than the Apostle's phrase.

It conveys no impression of the sense, the taste, the anguish of sin, which St. Paul would have us think of, as realized by the Son of God—a sense, a taste, an anguish, which are not only compatible with the *not* knowing sin, but would be impossible in any one who did know.[1]

It was in this sense of supreme sympathy, extending to that physical ill which is the fruit of sin, that Christ "endured the death which is the consequence of sin in all men." It was no vicarious penal suffering, but an endurance of infinite love, infinite sympathy.

What then was it that Christ offered to the Father? Such a Father could demand nothing else than the return of His own love.

All orthodox schools have said,[2] that a perfectly holy and loving Being can be satisfied only with a holiness and love corresponding to His own; that Christ satisfied the Father by presenting the image of His own holiness and love, that in His sacrifice and death, all that holiness and love came forth completely.[3]

Supposing the Father's will to be a will to all good, the Son of God, being one with Him, and Lord of man, to obey and fulfil in our flesh that will by entering into the lowest condition into which men had fallen through their sin;—Supposing this Man to be, for this reason, an object of continual complacency to His Father, and that complacency to be fully drawn out by the Death of the Cross; is not this, in the highest sense, Atonement? Is not the true, sinless root of Humanity revealed; is not God in Him reconciled to man.[4]

This is not language easy of interpretation, and indeed it is difficult to draw out any clear theory of Atonement from Maurice's writings. But it is obvious how similar his general standpoint is to that of contemporary German and English exponents of the Moral theory. Sympathy and fellowship are for him central conceptions, and he goes further than some other writers

[1] *Ibid.*

[2] A very unsafe generalization!

[3] *Theological Essays*, p. 146.

[4] *Ib.* p. 147.

of the same school in the direction of a belief in a real mystical union of the believer with Christ. And his account of Atonement is in the main manward and ethical in type. Its whole purpose is the moral transformation of the believer, but how this is effected Maurice has hardly shown. It cannot be said that he is successful in establishing the connexion between the transformation of human character and the Cross of Christ, or, indeed in giving the Cross any special place in the work of redemption, further than as a supreme and final revelation of that which all Christ's life revealed, the holy love of God.

Maurice, whether successful or not, was a thinker of a constructive type, and his theology has a distinct positive value. But the conception of Atonement which he sought to expound became, in the hands of some other writers of the period, a definite attack upon the objective character of the fact itself. As in Germany, the tendency to give an ethical account of Atonement has been combined with rationalistic attempts to explain away both its supernatural character and the strong language under which it is described in the New Testament. A good example of this attitude is the Essay in which B. Jowett [1] attacked the whole of the phraseology under which theologians had described the Atonement, regarding it as inseparably bound up with crude and immoral ideas of substitution and penal suffering. It is impossible, he declares, to use the language of satisfaction, atonement, sacrifice, at all, without denying the ethical quality of the work of Christ and of the character of God. He dwells upon the frequency with which the New Testament speaks of the believer as identified with Christ, and declares that this "language of identity or communion" is completely inconsistent with all sacrificial conceptions—an assertion sufficiently disproved by the frequency with which writers of every age have combined sacrificial and mystical ideas. His whole

[1] *Essays and Dissertations* (1894), pp. 317 ff.

attitude is negative and critical. The full phrases of Scripture are dismissed as popular rhetoric, providing no basis for scientific theory. Christ, he says, never suggested that satisfaction was necessary to forgiveness. The historical theories of Atonement are based mainly on rhetoric misunderstood and upon Jewish elements which Christianity did not succeed in extruding. They fail completely to show how these "fictions" and "immoralities," such as imputed righteousness and the penal suffering of the innocent, can possibly win men to a holy life.

Jowett assumes, as completely as Dale assumes it upon the other side, the complete incompatibility of the moral account of redemption with its objective, transactional, Godward aspect. The possibility that there may be truth in both does not seem to occur to him at all. And he is so occupied with his polemic that he hardly so much as states his own positive view of the value of the Cross. But such a passage as the following places him among the more extreme exponents of the Moral theory.

> The death of Christ is the fulfilment and consummation of His life, the greatest moral act ever done in the world, the highest manifestation of perfect love, the centre in which the rays of love converge and meet, the extremest abnegation or annihilation of self. It is the death of One who seals with His blood the witness of the truth which He came into the world to teach, which therefore confirms our faith in Him as well as animates our love. . . . It is a death in which all the separate gifts of heroes and martyrs are united in a Divine Excellence—of One who most perfectly foresaw all things that were coming upon Him—who felt all and shrank not—of One who, in the hour of death, set the example of praying for His enemies. It is a death which, more even than His life, is singular and mysterious, in which nevertheless we all are partakers—in which there was the thought and consciousness of mankind to the end of time, which has also the power of drawing to itself the thoughts of men to the end of time.[1]

However true such a thought as this may be, it is

[1] *Ib.* pp. 365 f. (cited by Stevens, *op. cit.* p. 233).

poor and inadequate taken by itself. It cannot but be felt that the whole trend of Jowett's essay is simply destructive. The blows which he deals at the older orthodoxy, if sometimes shrewd, are quite reckless. He does no justice to the solid basis upon which it rests, in the facts of human sin and Divine pardon and grace. Set side by side with Dale's impressive reply his essay seems little more than captious. "Whatever there may be about his thought that is of beauty or value; it is, in respect of its negations, its attempts to evaporate away the vital facts, and vital faith, of Christianity, a strange exhibition of ineffectiveness, if not of perversity."[1]

It is perhaps going too far to suggest, as Moberly does, that the day of such destructive criticism is past. But the tendency which appears in Jowett's essay in so unattractive a guise is one which is making a very real positive contribution to the thought of the age. It may be seen in writers of very various types. J. Caird, for example, in his Gifford Lectures,[2] takes up a position very like that of Maurice, and defends it from the standpoint of a philosopher. He emphasizes the principle that goodness must always suffer for sin, just because it is goodness. And therefore the presence of sin created in Christ

> . . . a repugnance, a moral recoil, a sorrow and shame, which the fallen and guilty could never feel for themselves.[3]

And this suffering constitutes a real Atonement, more real than that due to any outward infliction, as a "profound response" to the condemnation of God as just and righteous. And by faith we may partake in this Atonement, for unless Atonement has the meaning of a moral regeneration in the believer it is not possible to account for the fact that penitent and impenitent

[1] Moberly, *op. cit.* p. 388.
[2] *The Fundamental Ideas of Christianity* (1899).
[3] *Ib.* ii. 223.

do not share alike in its results. And faith is explained on personal, and even mystical, lines.

> Faith is the spiritual link that brings us into living union with Christ; so that not by any arbitrary supposition or legal fiction, but actually, in the fundamental principle of our moral life, we become one with Him.[1]

Only thus, he declares, can the doctrines of satisfaction and imputed righteousness be freed from the character of unreality and fiction.

When it takes such a form as this the Moral theory is drawing very close to the broader and more personal forms of the Satisfaction theory which have become current in Roman and Anglican circles in recent years. The Scotist thought of the Incarnation as central, rather than the Passion, has been worked out by such writers as Bishop Westcott upon mystical lines. The thought is exactly that which underlies Caird's philosophy. Man through the Incarnation is made one with God. The union which was before the Fall is restored. The satisfaction for sin is not denied, but it tends to remain in the background. The whole emphasis is upon the triumphant restoration of man to new life.

A few sentences from Bishop Westcott[2] will illustrate this conception:

> Christ, I repeat, was and is perfectly man: He was and is also representatively man. Seeing that He unites in Himself all that is truly manly and all that is truly womanly, undisguised by the accidental forms which belong to some one country or to some one period, every one can therefore find in Him for his own work union with the eternal. . . . For Him, consciously or unconsciously, all men were looking: to Him all history tended: in Him a higher life had its beginning and its pledge. . . . And for us the promise has had accomplishment. In

---

[1] *Ib.* ii. 226.

[2] From *The Historic Faith* (1883). In *The Victory of the Cross* (1888) Westcott worked out the conception, based on the Epistle to the Hebrews, that the sufferings of Christ had the power of purifying and perfecting the humanity with which He has become one in the Incarnation.

Him we are enabled to perceive that the broken unity of earth and heaven has been restored; in Him we are enabled to recognise that the earlier intercourse between the seen and the unseen worlds has been brought to an absolute fulfilment. Christ *the Son of man* has bestowed on the race the gifts which belonged to Him as *the Son of God*.

Thus Christ is representatively man; and it is by fellowship with His human nature, by taking it to ourselves as He offers it, by striving, as we may, to win that which in the end we shall receive freely from His love, that we all can obtain life.[1]

So we pass from the lesson of Christ's humanity to the lesson of Christ's sufferings. We believe that the Incarnation would have been necessary for the fulfilment of man's destiny even if he had perfectly followed the divine law. The Passion was necessary for the redemption of man fallen. This is a fact to be thought over. The presence of evil amongst us and in us, in its manifold forms of suffering and selfishness and loss and crime, is a reality which no ingenuity can hide or dissemble. Revelation did not cause this terrible affliction, but it shows that it does not belong to the essence of creation or to the essence of man. It shows therefore that it is remediable: that it can be removed from man without destroying his true nature, nay rather that his true nature is vindicated by its removal. . . . The confession of our belief in Christ's sufferings takes us into a new sphere. We embrace effectual forgiveness as the revelation of the Gospel. Christ took to Himself and bore to the grave the uttermost burden of sinful humanity, and, Himself sinless and victorious over death, offers to men fellowship in the fruits of His conquest. How His life and death avails with the Father for us is a question which we have no power to answer. It is enough for us to acknowledge the supreme triumph of divine love from first to last, one will of one God reconciling the world to Himself in Jesus Christ, His only Son, our Lord.[2]

Similar passages are scattered up and down Bishop Westcott's various works, and their influence has been very great. They have carried into many quarters the demand for a living, manward, doctrine of Atonement, a demand which few exponents of the doctrine to-day feel themselves able to ignore.

Archdeacon Wilson, in his Hulsean Lectures,[3] makes Westcott's position the basis of a thorough-going statement of a form of the Moral theory.

[1] *Ib.* (6th ed.) pp. 64 f. [2] *Ib.* pp. 66 f.
[3] *The Gospel of the Atonement* (1899).

The doctrine of redemption is embodied in the words "Who for us men and for our salvation came down from heaven." He came to make us what God intended us to be. That is all. If I may express in an aphorism which concentrates the leading truth but will mislead unless read in the light of the qualifications I have stated and implied, the Incarnation is itself the Atonement. The Life was manifested and we have seen it. Our fellowship is with the Father and with His Son, Jesus Christ. The reconciliation of the ancient dualism is found in the identification of the human and the divine Life in the person of Christ. This is the spiritual truth of which transactional theories were meant to be an embodiment, but have become an "immoral counterfeit." And here is a most hopeful sign of progress in modern theology. No one can fail to notice that the Incarnation is assuming in theological preaching and teaching the place which not long ago was taken by the Atonement. This is the great work of Bishop Westcott. And we must understand what this means and implies. It implies that to the doctrine of the Incarnation, not to any theory of vicarious and equivalent sacrifice, and not to any transaction between the Persons of the Blessed Trinity, we are looking for an explanation of the process how Jesus Christ saves us from our sins and redeems all mankind.

Let us say boldly that the Incarnation, that is, the life and death of the Christ—for the life and death were equally necessary—is the identification of the human and the divine Life. This identification is the Atonement. There is no other.[1]

The central conception here is that of the identity between God and man established by Christ. Archdeacon Wilson does not at all ignore the Cross, and devotes some space to an explanation of its central position. His view is not merely the old view that it is the final and supreme revelation of Divine love, though that is included. It is a revelation of the principle of self-sacrifice, "absolute, universal, and divine," as the one thing of power in the moral world.[2]

Christ's death is the supreme instance of that law. The power of Gethsemane and Calvary, in the light of such a law, needs no explanation. They open the heart as nothing else ever did. We know that whatever reservations we make for ourselves, whatever our own shrinking from utter self-sacrifice, Christ, living in perfect accordance with the laws of spiritual health and perfection, could not do other than die. Thus

---

[1] *Ib.* pp. 87 ff.

[2] *Ib.* p. 106.

without any thought of payment or expiation, with no vestige of separation of the Son from the Father, we see that the death on the Cross demonstrated that the human and divine know but one and the same law of life and being. Thus it is that the death of Christ, the shedding of His blood, has been, and ever will be, regarded by theologians, as well as by the simple believer, as the way of the Atonement.[1]

These lectures show the modern stress upon the Incarnation in quite an extreme form. The Cross and Atonement have been thrown far apart. The latter finds its efficacy in that mystical union between man and God of which the Incarnation was both the beginning and the power. The Cross is but a revelation, a supreme exhibition, of that common nature of self-sacrifice which, through Christ, is now both human and Divine. Such a view, true enough in itself, hardly does justice to the extreme reality and weight of sin, and the corresponding demand for a penitence which is something more than a formal renunciation of the past, the demand for such satisfaction as a holy and loving God must needs make.

The above examples of the types of theory usually classed together as the "Moral theory" will serve to show how wide an area of thought that term has been used to cover. The one clear point of contact between the various writers is in their insistence that the Atonement must mean something for man, not merely in its results, but in itself. There must be a real change of heart. Justification, however distinct it may be in strict logic from sanctification, cannot be severed from it in fact without becoming a valueless abstraction. Release from the sinful past is not the whole truth of salvation. There must be also an awakening of the soul, a quickening to new life.

This emphasis upon the manward aspect of Atonement, so characteristic of recent years, is making what is doubtless a permanent contribution to our under-

[1] *Ib.* pp. 108 f.

standing of the work of Christ. It would be too much to say that it has as yet quite adapted itself to meet the claims of the orthodox Godward theories, which also stand for an aspect of the truth which must not be ignored. We have already seen how modern restatements of the Penal and Satisfaction theories have tended more and more to incorporate Moral elements. And some of the forms of the Moral theory which have been quoted have at least attempted to meet the demand made by the fact of the justice and the holiness of God. Hitherto few of these efforts have met with any very great success, but it is at least becoming clear that in the theology of the future both types of theory will find their claims recognized, if not wholly satisfied.

Before closing this chapter we must dwell briefly upon the most notable attempt of recent years towards such a positive reconstruction, R. C. Moberly's *Atonement and Personality*.[1]

Viewed historically Moberly stands in the succession of the exponents of the Moral theory. The main formative influence upon his thought is that of M'Leod Campbell, while that which he especially opposes is the retributive theory as reasserted by Dale. Yet in more ways than one he marks the approximation of the two tendencies of thought upon the Atonement, that which emphasizes its objective transactional character and that to which it appeals chiefly as effecting an ethical transformation. He endorses Dale's vindication of the fact of the Cross as the central Fact of Christianity and the Christian life, and admits the failure of the usual statements of the Moral theory to do this fact justice. But the whole purpose of his book is to show that the Moral theory only fails in this way because its exponents fail to give full value to many of the terms which they use—such terms as punishment, penitence, forgiveness. It is for this reason that they lay themselves open to the criticism that their view of sin is

[1] 1901 ; the quotations are from the 1909 edition.

inadequate, and that their view of forgiveness assigns to God an act of mercy which is not really just.

Thus Moberly starts with a discussion of these three terms, and it is here that his connexion with M'Leod Campbell is most obvious. Punishment, he says, is not simply, or primarily, retributive in character. Dale's view of it as " pain and loss inflicted for the violation of a law," having as its object not discipline but suffering, is rejected. Punishment only has meaning as applied to conscious personalities, and even so it is nothing more than pain except in so far as the offender accepts it as his due. Punishment, therefore, attains its true character in proportion, not to the guilt but to the righteousness of the offender upon whom it is inflicted. It may, indeed, become "vengeance," if its moral purpose fails, but then it ceases to be punishment. It is only because earthly punishment is imperfect, and proceeds by general laws, that it has a retributive and equational appearance.

> Both these aspects, the retributive aspect and the equation aspect, of human justice belong indeed in fact to human justice; but belong to it not as it is justice, but as it is human; belong, that is, and can be seen directly to belong, to the necessary imperfectness of such corporate and social justice as is possible on earth.[1]

The State can only deal with men in the mass.

> The individual must be sacrificed to the community.[2]

Only Divine omniscience can deal with persons as persons, each individual for himself, and therefore only God can be exactly just.

Perfect punishment—God's punishment—would not only be exactly just but also wholly reformatory in principle, but to make it wholly reformatory in fact would demand perfect acceptance of it as punishment by the offender. In so far as it is not accepted it remains vengeance still.

[1] Pp. 8 f. [2] *Ibid.*

First that it is only so far as it is *not* transfigured into a personal self-identification with righteousness that punishment remains in the aspect of retribution; secondly, that it is just in proportion as it *is* a process of self-identity with righteousness, that there is atoning capacity in the bearing of punishment; but, thirdly, that precisely so far as it retains its character as inflicted retaliation, it has no atoning or restorative tendency whatever. . . . Either the suffering of punishment is more and more absolutely identified with penitential painfulness; or it has nothing atoning or restorative about it.[1]

Thus ideally perfect punishment demands perfect penitence, that is, perfect righteousness in the offender. This is the meaning of M'Leod Campbell's thought of a " perfect Amen in humanity " to God's sentence upon sinners. Penitence is the transformation of moral character in the self-identification of the sinner with righteousness in its loathing for sin.

But if the perfect identification of being with righteousness which perfect consummation of penitence would necessarily mean, is *ipso facto* impossible to one who has sinned, just because the sin is really his own: what is this but to say—hardly even in other words—that the personal identity with righteousness in condemnation and detestation of sin, which penitence in ideal perfection would mean and be,—is possible only to One who is personally Himself without sin? The consummation of penitential holiness—itself, by inherent character, the one conceivable atonement for sin—would be possible only to the absolutely sinless. . . . A true penitence is as much the inherent impossibility, as it is the inherent necessity, of every man that has sinned.[2]

How then does it come about that this moral transformation of penitence is a daily fact in the lives of countless Christians? Herein lies the mystery of the Atonement.

Forgiveness, again, loses its difficulty when made the correlative of such penitence. When it is the immediate complement of forgivableness, answering to the self-condemnation of the sinner, it can have no character of injustice. It will not then be any mere external im-

[1] Pp. 22 ff. [2] P. 43.

putation of righteousness to the unrighteous, or an empty remission of sin corresponding to no change of heart. Thus only the penitent, that is, only the righteous can be forgiven.

> Forgiveness *is* love, in its relation to a personality which having sinned, is learning, and to learn, what the sin-consciousness of penitence means.[1]

This is the true " Moral " view of forgiveness. It does not with some types of Moral theory make forgiveness a light and easy thing. It does not belittle the seriousness and gravity of sin. And while the truth remains that man has a duty of forgiveness to the sinner, it is also true that such forgiveness is impossible from the purely human side. Apart from the mystery of the Atonement there is no remission of sins which has any real meaning. To pardon the sinner is as unjust as to punish the innocent.

How then is Atonement possible, seeing that apart from Atonement is neither punishment, nor penitence, nor forgiveness. Moberly shows that the highest human analogy is in the relation of parent and child, where the grief of the parent has a real influence upon the child's sin. Yet even this breaks down, just because each is not the other. But the doctrine of the Incarnation meets just this difficulty. Christ is God and He is man, not merely generically, but identically. Conscious personality finds its expression even here on earth not in hard and fast separations, but in contact and relationship. Only in Christ has it its consummation.

> This mutual inherence, this spiritual indwelling, whereby humankind is summed anew, and included, in Christ.[2]

> If Christ's Humanity were not the Humanity of Deity, it could not stand in the wide, including, consummating relation, in which it stands in fact, to the humanity of all other men. But as it is, the very essence of the Christian religion is the indwelling of the Spirit of Christ.[3]

[1] P. 62. [2] P. 90. [3] *Ibid.*

And thus in Christ alone is there the possibility of perfect penitence, which shall really be that of all humanity. St. Paul's phrase, "Him He made to be sin," must be given its full meaning, in contrast and in connexion with the other conception, "God sending His own Son in the likeness of sinful flesh, and as an offering for sin, condemned sin in the flesh."[1] In Christ perfect holiness, experiencing the full fact of sin, realized perfect contrition.

He the eternal Righteousness in judging sin, judged it not in another, but judged it rather, as a penitent judges it, within Himself; He surrendered Himself for the judgment that He pronounced; He took, in His own Person, the whole responsibility and burthen of its penance; He stood, that is, in the place, not of a judge simply, nor of a mere victim, but of a voluntary penitent—wholly one with the righteousness of God in the sacrifice of Himself.[2]

Christ's death was a perfect offering of obedience, the perfect act of homage. But it was not His obedience that constituted the Atonement, the restoration of fallen humanity.

Human nature was not only disabled but guilty; and the disabilities were themselves a consequence, an aspect, of the guilt. In respect of this guilt of sin, consummated and inhering, human nature could only be purified by all that is involved in the impossible demand of a perfect penitence. Except it had also the character of perfect penitence atoning for the past, even the splendid perfectness of His present will-offering of obedience would be less than what was required for the re-identifying of human character with God.[3]

Besides the sacrifice of perfect obedience, He offered the sacrifice of perfect penitence. He voluntarily stood in the sinner's place, "in His own inner consciousness accepting the ideal consciousness of the contrite."

He did, in fact and in full, that which would in the sinner constitute perfect atonement, but which has for ever become impossible to the sinner, just in proportion as it is true that

---

[1] 2 Cor. 5 21; Rom. 8 3. [2] P. 110. [3] P. 117.

he has sinned. The perfect sacrifice of penitence in the sinless Christ is the true atoning sacrifice for sin. . . . The suffering involved in this is not, in Him, punishment, or the terror of punishment; but it is the full realising, in the personal consciousness, of the truth of sin and the disciplinary pain of the conquest of sin; it is that full self-identification of human nature, within range of sin's challenge and sin's scourge, with holiness as the Divine condemnation of sin, which was at once the necessity—and the impossibility—of human penitence.[1]

Moberly admits that this is in some sense a vicarious penitence. But this is due to us and our human imperfection and sin, in which we hold ourselves apart from Christ. It results from a false and, indeed, an inherently sinful ideal of personality, which strives to realize itself in distinction from others and not in identity with them. True personality, even in human relationships, involves "reflexive correspondence of other personalities," and thus even vicarious human penitence may sometimes, as in the case of the mother grieving for the sin of the child, pass over into the personality of the offender. In Christ this interrelation of personality becomes complete. He makes our guilt absolutely His own, with all the anguish that it entails for Him. He offers in love a real possibility of community of nature with Himself.

And thus the Cross is central—not as involving anything retributive, not as penal, save from the point of view of earthly justice—but as the voluntary and self-imposed destruction, through a perfect obedience, of everything that could be made an avenue for sin. It is the consummation of a life-long Passion, wrought through a perfect obedience; and without it that Passion would fail of completeness, and it is the Cry of Desolation from the Cross which marks both the completion of the Incarnation, in Christ's assumption of human guilt, and the completion of the offering of penitence which puts that guilt away.

[1] P. 130.

He did not—of course He did not—endure the vengeance of God. We do not deny this only because, in every instinct of our being, we feel that it would be—as indeed it would—too shocking and too blasphemous even for thought; but because we are able positively to recognise that, whilst it would, by implication, deny both the Divine character of the eternal Father, and the Divine Being of the Incarnate Son, it would also, not by implication only, but directly, contradict the entire conception of the atonement. The vengeance of God is not anyhow conceivable as a method—on the contrary it is the direct negation—of atonement. The vengeance of God is the final consummation of sin unrepented, unatoned, unforgiven, unforgivable. The Cross is not the symbol of unforgiveness! No, but with undimmed insight into sin, such insight as no spirit of man could bear, He offered Himself to consummate that reality of penitence by which alone real consciousness of sin (the universal property of humanity) could be righteously transformed and dissolved into—could grow into and become and be found to be, after all, more essentially and abidingly—a real identity with the absolute righteousness of God.

He did not—of course He did not—endure the damnation of sin. But in the bitter humiliation of a self-adopted consciousness of what sin—and therefore of what the damnation of sin—really is, He bowed His head to that which, as far as mortal experience can go, is so far, at least, the counterpart on earth of damnation that it is the extreme possibility of contradiction and destruction of self. He to whom, as the Life of life, all dying, all weakness, were an outrage to us inconceivable, bowed Himself to death—death in its outward form inflicted with all the contumely as of penal vengeance—death inwardly accepted as the necessary climax of an experience of spiritual desolation, which, but to the inherently holy, would have been not only material but spiritual death. In mortal agony of body, in strain inconceivable, through the body, on the mind and the will, in isolation of spirit (man's true consciousness towards sin)—*He died.*

The consummation of penitence carried with it the straining, to their breaking, of the vital faculties, the dissolution of the mortal instrument. But that dissolution was the consummation of penitence; and the consummation of penitence is the consummation of righteousness by inherent power, finally victorious through and over the utmost possibilities of sin.[1]

The remainder of the book is an attempt to show how this view does justice both to the objective and to

[1] Pp. 132 f.

the subjective aspects of Atonement. The truth is that these aspects are not really opposed, and it is only because of a false view of Personality that they have appeared to be opposed. The Atonement must, if it is true at all, be both objective and subjective. The two cannot be separated. If the personality of man is defined by limitation, by separation from God and from humanity, no theory of Atonement can avoid the charge of externality, that is, of ultimate injustice. Moberly insists that we must use all the riches which are at our disposal in the doctrine of the Holy Trinity. The real meaning for us of the fact of the Holy Spirit is just the overcoming of this separatist view of Personality. It is in the Holy Spirit that Christ the Incarnate is absolutely one with God and one with man. Man's claims to self-hood have no meaning and no fulfilment except in Christ. "I, yet not I but Christ" is the only formula of real, personal, existence.

Atonement and Personality is a difficult book to describe in any small compass. Moberly is struggling throughout to do justice to two points of view, to unite the two great tendencies of thought which have marked recent theology. While his own primary interest is manward, as his definition of Atonement shows, he stresses, as no exponent of the Moral theory has ever stressed, the tremendous meaning which Atonement has for God, how real and how bitter is the "making cost" of which Bushnell has spoken. And it is noteworthy that the way of union is through mysticism. Moberly's whole theory, with all its detail and elaboration, is simply an attempt to give mysticism a coherent expression. We have seen how, from the earliest times, mysticism has again and again been the connecting link in a chain of theological inconsistencies. Writer after writer has fallen back upon the phrases of St. Paul which told of the self-identification of the believer with Christ. It was this belief which made the Satisfaction theory comprehensible, the Penal theory endurable. It was this thought which underlay all conceptions of something wrought by a substitute for man. Failing this thought, we found everywhere confusion of ideas, or beliefs which the moral sense of man repudiated so soon as they were fully understood. And to this thought the Moral theory too has been tending. The only true manward theory is one which does not merely regard man as in some way rising to welcome the display of a nobler manhood, but which sees in Christ the re-union of man and God, the fulfilment of ideal humanity for and in each individual man who by faith puts on Christ.

It is only in recent years that interest has been taken in the philosophy of mysticism, and its connexion with the problem of personality has been seen. The investigation of this latter problem is one of the most important and most urgent tasks of to-day. To speak of God as Ruler, Judge, or even as Father, is but to use a partial and necessarily one-sided metaphor. But when we speak of Him as Personal we use a term within which is contained all the meaning which our human personality but faintly shadows forth. In the word "person" is contained that which we need to a true doctrine of Atonement. No theory can stand which makes God less than personal, in the fullest sense in which man can understand the term, and it is the attempt to apply to the Atonement this highest concept of which man is capable which makes Moberly's work so valuable. In the detail of his theory there may be much to modify. His critics, at any rate, have been many.[1] Yet few recent writings are at once so sane and so constructive, and, despite much misunderstanding, it is in such attempts that the hope of the future lies.

[1] See especially the invaluable review of his book by Dr. H. Rashdall (*Journal of Theological Studies*, iii. 178 ff.).

INDEX

The references to the passages in which the views of the various writers mentioned are more fully discussed are printed in heavy type.

Printed by R. & R. Clark, Limited, *Edinburgh*.